MAJORCA

MAJORCA

Culture and Life

Edited by Ute Edda Hammer,
Tonina Oliver and Frank Schauhoff

Photographed by Günter Beer,
Carlos Agustín and Belén Tánago

Contributions from Susanne Birnmeyer and Susanne van Cleve
Assisted by Raphel Pherrer

KÖNEMANN

Contents

264 Pla

486 Appendix

Majorca

Dream island
Majorca

A cosmos in itself, a mini-continent, a country and society cut off from the outside world by water, an island is always something special. It's thus not without reason that people sometimes say they wish they could escape to a desert island, with a hint of wistfulness or adventure in their voices, or try to decide which book, which photo, which absolutely essential item they'd take with them into their island exile. Islands are places of extradition and imprisonment. They limit freedom of movement yet also open up new horizons often broader than those visible from their shorelines. An island puts the dots on the i's in the ocean; in the case of Majorca, it forms an exclamation mark.

Previous double-page spread: Majorca is where the land meets the sea, with lush plains and bleak mountains.

Below: Winding streets and narrow flights of steps characterize the towns and villages of Majorca, as here in Palma.

Majorca! Just 1,405 square miles (3,640 km2) in size, it would fit into Sicily seven times over and is around five times as big as its little sister in name and size, Menorca. Around 68 miles (110 km) at its longest point from Sant Elm to the Cap de Formentor and 37 to 56 miles (60 to 90 km) wide, it lies like a clumsily formed trapezium in the Mediterranean, equidistant from Barcelona, Valencia, and Algiers at c. 124 miles (200 km) and equally close to Europe and Africa.

Approaching like the migratory birds who come here in spring and autumn or like the majority of the approximately ten million tourists a year – from the air – you will notice three things that are typical of Majorca. The first is the fantastic, clear light with that Mediterranean tinge of physical presence, as if the sky had woven a veil of silk, sheerer than sheer, and shrouded the island in it. The second is one not uncommon to islands: mountains. Majorca has two ranges which run parallel to one another from north to southwest and from east to southeast.

Third, there are the windmills. Hundreds of them encircle Sant Joan airport, as if there to create a portative upwind. They are in fact water mills which among other functions had the job of draining the airport site. Some let their sails droop sadly, some have been reduced to stumps, whereas others stand tall in their fresh coats of blue and white paint, proudly presenting their wheels to the wind. Windmills are a loyal companion in Majorca, found everywhere except in the mountains, and have become a true symbol of the island in the full sense of the word. For despite the mass tourism, these typical, functional farm buildings denote the true nature of the largest of the Balearic Islands: excluding its capital, Palma, Majorca is rural.

The palm of victory, La Ciutat, Palma

This makes the capital all the more surprising, especially as it's on an island. Palma is a marine metropolis. It greets the *mare nostrum* with its calling card, the Catedral La Seu, whose Majorcan Marès stone, a compact mixture of sand and chalk, gleams golden in the evening light. Since 1230, when construction was started in fulfillment of a pledge made during the Christian army's successful conquest of the island, its magnificent rose window and filigree spires and turrets have sent off a clear message to the outside world: here is La Ciutat, the town the Moors called Medina Mayurka, the big city, which is now in the hands of the Christians and endeavors not to be intimidated by anyone or anything.

The people of Majorca, both from Palma and *part forana*, the remaining part of the island, call their capital La Ciutat, regardless of the fact that since the 20th century it has officially been known as Palma de Majorca in memory of the name given to it by its Roman occupants in 122 BC: Palmeria, the palm of victory. Over 350,000 Majorcans live here, more than half of the island's 650,000 inhabitants. Palma isn't a would-be capital, it *is* one, with all the trimmings associated with capital cities: congested, four- to six-lane *avingudes* or avenues, problem parking, wide, tree-lined streets and inviting shopping precincts, spacious squares dotted with cafés and shady, winding streets in the old part of town (over 700 years old), which open out onto Majorca's urban architecture *par excellence*, onto inner courtyards and patios.

One of Spain's most beautiful medieval castles, the Castell de Bellver, towers above the town to the southwest, its spacious interior flooded with light caressing elegant pillars and sunny loggias. Beneath it on the Passeig maritím, yachts and motor boats rock gently at their moorings and cargo ships and ferries unload crates, containers and passengers, with typical Balearic fishing boats, the *llaüt*, weaving their way home between them at the end of the day.

A must for invaders

Palma is the only town in Majorca actually on the sea. In the *part forana* there are only small harbors, more often than not called "Port de" or port of the main town a few miles away from it inland. Almost 2,500 years of invasions from would-be conquistadors and pirates have taught the people of Majorca not to parade their wealth, or lack of it, along the coast.

During the island's history, all sections of the population and the various cultures in Majorca imported themselves. The first settlers to arrive here certainly didn't come as conquerors; the modern version of Majorca's early history suggests that they were driven here by hunger and poverty. It is thought that in the sixth millennium BC they came from the South of France to the island in simple boats, finding caves they could live in and a multitude of animals and plants

350,000 Majorcans, over half of the population, live in the capital of Palma.

as nourishment. Archeologist Joan Ramis from the neighboring island of Menorca gave this culture a name. He called it the Talayotic period after the striking, mysterious towers the first inhabitants built in or near their villages from 3000 BC onwards, the term coming from the Arabic word for tower, *atalaya*. Remains of two of these settlements still exist on the island, to the south near Capocorp Vell and in the northeast at Artà.

Historians assume that the settlers were left in peace until 300 BC, when news of the island's plentiful natural resources and sublime pastoral beauty had begun to spread around the Ancient Mediterranean. The Greeks called the archipelago *gimnesias* due to the islanders' tendency to go around almost naked like the athletes in the Greek *gymnasion*. From 300 BC the Phoenicians began erecting trading posts here, yet didn't settle. Both civilizations valued the Ancient Majorcans as mercenaries for their method of fighting which gave the group of islands the name still used today, *balearides* . The word comes from the Greek *ballein,* "to throw in a sling", the weapons the Majorcans were famous for using.

It was the impertinent piracy of the Majorcans which finally disturbed the *pax romana* to such an extent that in 123 BC the Romans were forced to take the island. Once Roman, Majorca was given its first streets, theaters, market places, temples and country villas. Romans tired of life in the city at the heart of the empire came here. The island also became home to those banished from the *imperium,* as Diodorus reports in the 1st century AD. Compared to other Roman provinces, Majorca was undoubtedly not the worst of places to be exiled to. The Romans were the first to make systematic use of the island's natural resources; vineyards, grain fields and olive groves were created, causing the economy to flourish. In Roman Pollentia, now Alcúdia, the avant-garde of the Roman fashion world wove and sewed togas which were so chic that they were eagerly snapped up by the style-conscious all across the empire.

When in the 5th century the Vandals invaded Majorca, lead by Gesoric, they demolished much of the Roman infrastructure within a very short space of time. Some towns, such as Manacor, were razed to the ground. The Vandals pillaged Majorca for almost a hundred years until the Byzantine emperor Justinian I annexed the island in 534. The Byzantine basilicas of Son Peretó and Sa Carrotxa near Manacor are, however, not the earliest records of Christianity on the island. The Cova de Sant Martí, a church in a cave near Alcúdia, documents the fact that there were Christians on the island as early as the 2nd century.

After a number of overtures the Arabs finally settled in Majorca in 902. If you look and savor your surroundings carefully, you will still find plenty of signs of their presence, even if from 1229 onwards the victorious Catalans did their best to extinguish all traces of the Moors' existence. What remains from the time when three cultures – Muslims, Jews, and a small Christian minority – coexisted on the island are the carefully thought-out agricultural irrigation systems, which made the best use of the island's precious water supply with terraces, channels and wells serviced by donkeys, and also extensive areas where apricots, grapes, figs and olives are cultivated. Another legacy is a partiality in Majorcan cooking for a pinch of cumin, for sultanas and almonds in spicy stews, distinguishing the taste of the East from that of the West.

The tide changed in Majorca in 1229. Those not willing to renounce Judaism or Islam could choose between exile – if they were lucky enough – and being burnt at the stake. The island became a country of big landowners, where before farmers had worked their land autonomously. Jaume I, the Conqueror, divided the land up between his followers and the church in an act of *repartiment* and recruited new settlers from Catalonia, Italy, Roussillon and the Provence. The new island melting pot produced a mode of speech which has survived the ravages of time, *Mallorquí,* a Catalan dialect spiked with elements of Old French and Old Italian.

Olive groves were planted in Majorca in Roman times.. Near Galilea, in the southwest, they cover the countryside with their silvery evergreen foliage.

What also remained almost until the dawn of the modern age was hereditary leasehold or feudalism which brought centuries of poverty and oppression to much of the population, despite the fact that the kingdom which introduced the system perished in the Battle of Llucmajor in 1349 when Majorca fell to Aragón and thus to the future kingdom of Spain.

A moment of perfection in the creation of the world

What was it that made Majorca irresistible to the Phoenicians and Romans, to the Vandals, Moors and Catalans? Perhaps the fact that it is a mini-continent, created in a moment of perfection, and an island of dreams. All kinds of shoreline imaginable are to be found here, from the giddy cliffs at the strands of the Serra de Tramuntana in the northwest to romantic rocky bays with tiny strips of sand on the east coast; from wide sandy beaches stretching out under the sky near Palma in the southwest and along the Bay of Alcúdia in the north to dunes in Migjorn, Majorca's Midi or deep south. In the hinterland the *garriga*, a Mediterranean bush of mastic trees, gorse, Aleppo pine and all kinds of fragrant herbs, alternates with arable land which has been farmed for centuries. With 300 days of sun per year, Majorca has a moderately subtropical climate which can produce fine days of 68°F (20°C) even in the winter. This phenomenon is known as *petit estivet*, the little summer, by inhabitants grateful for a change to the usual 44°F (7°C) winter daytime average. If the sun is particularly fierce between June and September, it can drive the mercury up to a sweltering midday average of 90°F (32°C).

March to May and September to December are Majorca's best times of year, spring and *primavera des'hivern*, the spring of winter. The first drops of rain to hit the summer-scorched ground in October produce a miraculous transformation from brown to green, bringing with it a new vitality and a gradual floral crescendo which climaxes in March, when the bare branches of almost seven million almond trees burst into pale pink blossom. This is followed by the sweet perfume of orange blooms which wafts heavily to the ground from the dark evergreen leaves, the fruit from the previous year's crop still clinging to the trees like forgotten Christmas baubles.

Only the Heavens can water Paradise

Such splendor is not something nature created in the twinkling of an eye, however. Majorca is undisputedly the result of a great moment in the creation of the earth, yet there are a few elements which are extremely scarce on the island, if they exist at all. Water is one of them. Not a single river supplies Majorca with the elixir of life, and the only springs not dependent on ground water, Font Santa and Font Sa Bassa near Campos, bubble not with drinking water but with sulfurous spa water, which at 101.7°F (38.7°C) is hot, has healing properties and is slightly radioactive. Drinking water in Majorca falls from the heavens and is stored by porous limestone in underground wells. In the north of the island, this can be as much as 60 inches (1,500 mm) per year. This also settles as snow on the highest peaks of the island, such as the Puig Major (4,734 ft/1,443 m) and Puig de Massanella (4,423 ft/1,348 m). Until refrigerators were invented, in winter the island's "white gold" was collected by *nevaters* or

Stone façades, flower pots, and decorative wrought iron characterize the villages and towns in Majorca.

"snowmen" and stored in *cases de neu*, snow houses, to be sold in summer when most needed. In the dry south, however, the yearly average is barely a third of that of the north and snow is only found in fairy tales, which traditionally start with the words: "Long before there was snow in Majorca..."

Under these conditions, it's thus all the more surprising that the island "allows" itself the luxury of a swamp, the S'Albufera, which lies in the northeast between Alcúdia and Can Picafort. Yet the 5,930 acres (2,400 hectares) which have been a nature reserve since 1985, providing over 200 different types of bird with a permanent or temporary home, constitute only a third of the area's original size. From the 17th century onwards, parts of the Albufera were drained in order to create land which could be cultivated for various purposes – attempts were even made to grow rice on a large scale and a paper factory set up business here – but also in an effort to combat malaria which brought death and disease to the Albufera.

The second section of marshland in the far south of the island is a very different kind of biotope, best suited to those with a predilection for salt. At Ses Salines the sea floods the land in spring and the sun bakes a crust in summer, enabling people to extract salt here as they have done since the days of the Romans.

The sound of sheep, cows, pigs, and donkeys in the land of wind and sun

It goes without saying that with such extremes at either end of the scale, the rest of the island is hardly a land of milk and honey. Majorca had to survive almost solely on what its agricultural activities yielded until the 1950s, when tourism became the main source of income within the space of a few years. Almost three quarters of the island are still used for farming, yet today only 11% of the inhabitants till the land, making up a mere 2.5% of the gross national product. 75% comes from the tourist industry and around 10% from the building and construction trade – a completely topsy-turvy world compared to 700 years ago.

Only a few decades ago, people's prosperity or poverty depended on whether it rained, whether the fisherman returned home safely with his catch, whether the cow calved, whether the donkey would endure last another year working the well and transporting heavy yokes and baskets with the harvest, whether the chickens laid eggs, whether the goats had enough milk and the sheep enough wool. These farm animals still fill the Majorcan air with their cries and provide traditional dishes with their ingredients from the hot plateaus of the Migjorn to the fertile heart of the island, the Pla and Raiguer, right up to the Serra de Llevant and the mountains of the Serra de Tramuntana.

Although Majorca is now divided into specific municipalities, the traditional partition of the land into districts or *comarques*, probably introduced by the Moors, still exists. The *comarques* are defined and named geographically, not politically. They get their names from

A country villa near Bunyola provides an unexpected tryst with *Modernismo*, Spanish Art Nouveau.

Above: Wayside crosses like this one, the Creu d'en rebassa in Sineu, are scattered across the entire island and act as places of brief reflection, boundary posts and symbols of protection.

the points of the compass and/or the direction of the wind, such as Ponent ("lying down") for the west, Llevant ("rising") for the east, Migjorn ("midi" or "south") for the south and Tramuntana ("over the mountains") to stand for the cold north wind. There are also names which denote topographical features, such as *Pla* for "plain". The only nomenclature which can no longer be slotted into one of these categories is that of the land bordering on the Tramuntana and the Pla, the Raiguer.

A network of stones and crosses

The *comarques* may vary greatly in their natural makeup, yet there are a few man-made features common to them all. Among these are the thousands of wayside crosses, which stand at the points where field tracks and country roads intersect. Whether made of wrought iron, chiseled in stone or carved in wood and decorated with pictorial tiles, they have both a geographical function, that of marking out district, field and farm boundaries, and a religious one; they symbolize hope that God will protect and bless the land and invite passers-by to pause a moment in reflection on their selves and the world.

Many of these wayside crosses are not found as solitary shrines punctuating the landscape but are instead flanked by *marges*, dry stone walls. Layers of stones expertly arranged without any adhesive substance holding them together lattice the island. These robust structures turn troublesome, undressed boulders into protective walls which shelter young crops and the harvest from the wind and any hungry trespassers. The most skillfully built of the *marges* line terraced fields with made-to-measure stone embankments and fashion domestic walls of a beauty as solid as it is elegant, thanks to the golden hue of the local Marès stone, which is used to decorate both palaces and simple farmhouses.

Solid walls of stone were for centuries the only protection the islanders had from marauding pirates. They enclosed towns such as Alcúdia and Santanyí, formed a ring of 85 watchtowers or *talayots* which from the 16th century on began appearing around the island, or deterred would-be assailants at mighty fortresses, such as in Artà and Capdepera.

Behind the cliffs: an island without sea

The deep-rooted belief of the Majorcans that nothing good can come from the sea (with the exception of fish and seaweed as a fertilizer) is not a surprising one, especially if we include the pirates as short-term island invaders. A handful of small harbors had to suffice as trading posts for inland goods and as a mooring place for the fleet of *llaüts*. *Estam sempre darrera sa roca,* roughly translatable as "we live behind the cliffs", is the motto of the island community.

Below: Where there's work to be done there are donkeys. These soft-muzzled beasts of burden have remained indispensable to Majorca to the present day.

The lack of value attached to the sea went as far as the inland farm or estate traditionally being left to the oldest son, with the younger siblings having to make do with the unprofitable land along the shore. The reversal of this process, with deepest irony, has been left to the most recent invasion of Majorca.

When in the 1960s tourism to the island began to take on giant proportions – in 1966 the magic number of one million visitors per annum was reached – suddenly a plot of land by the sea meant affluence guaranteed. The farmhouse home became a relict from the days of famine and disease, at most used as a place where people could (if they wanted to) spend their weekends recuperating from their new-found wealth. Within a few years Majorca's waterfront changed completely. What must previously have appeared to be a lonely coastline, practically devoid of buildings, mutated into a wall of concrete crammed with beds – the nearer the water, the better. Over a very short period, tourist investments turned what was Europe's poorest municipality, Calvià in the Ponent, into its richest, with the aid of coastal settlements such as Magaluf, Santa Ponça, and Peguera.

The invaders armed with Bermudas and beach sandals brought such quantities of cash to the island as would have made even the greediest of pirates swoon. Yet with this influx of capital came a

Above: Unspoiled coastline has become a rarity in Majorca. Yet those willing to look hard enough will still find the occasional idyllic lonely bay.

Opposite, bottom left: In front of Palma's cathedral stands one of the island's greatest personalities: the philosopher, poet, and missionary Ramón Llull.

tremendous change in values. Not only the old towns and villages but also the old way of life lost its worth overnight. Plastic and laminated wood replaced baskets woven from palm leaves and pine wood furniture; synthetic curtains ousted the hemp *roba de llengua,* with hamburgers and fries ordering the *frit mallorquí, sopes* and *pa moreno* to take a culinary back seat. It was only shortly before the dawn of the second millennium that a new national consciousness managed to salvage and revive traditional ways and styles. It took thousands of northern Europeans buying and restoring *finca* and town houses across the island before the Majorcans realized not just how valuable they were as financial assets, but also as their cultural heritage.

Coastline, caterpillars, and cement

Up to that time the Majorcans had given their guests exactly what they wanted, in a pragmatic, friendly yet reserved manner: German beer and English tea, highways and an airport which in summer has to cope with more flights than any other airport in Europe and whose departure lounge has signs in several languages warning passengers that they may have to reckon with a 20-minute walk to get to their gate. At a staggering number of almost 400,000, every fourth hotel and apartment bed in Spain is in Majorca. Golf courses were laid out, one after another, disregarding the environmental problems this would cause on an island where water is a rare commodity. The main concern was that visitors brought prosperity to the locals and otherwise left them in peace. It was only when water had to be ferried in from the mainland, when other sun, sea and sand destinations began offering better service and greater comfort at lower prices than Majorca, that the island was rudely awakened from its euphoria, which had begun to have more than a hint of hangover.

Quality tourism was the tourism experts new Holy Grail, and not the Majorcan trio of sandy coastline, droning Caterpillars and hideous concrete. The wrecking ball was let loose on some of the worst eyesores. Rural tourism began to attract a new type of customer; the promenades and beaches, hotels and apartment blocks in the clustered areas around S'Arenal, Calvià and Alcúdia were given a face lift and the only new hotels built were ones which replaced older constructions. More than six million came to the island in 1998; 50,000 non-Spaniards live here permanently and there is still no end to the island's population boom in sight.

Travelers prefer the beach

Some visitors spend a couple of days being driven up the Tramuntana by coach on the trail of one of the first to come here in self-imposed exile out of love for Majorca, Archduke Ludwig Salvator of Habsburg-Tuscany (1847–1915). He spent over half of his life in the mountains near Deià. Some take time for Valldemossa, going to the monastery to see where novelist George Sand and composer Frédéric Chopin spent a winter together. Or for Lluc Monastery, to admire the dark-skinned statue of the Virgin Mary and pray for a safe flight home. For Sa Calobra, to feel the frightening thrill of driving along the 7 miles (12 km) of Europe's most contorted road. Or perhaps for a musical boat trip on the vast underground lake in the caves at Porto Cristo and a shopping

Archeology and postmodernist leisure converge at this golf course near a Talayotic settlement.

spree in Inca and Manacor, so that they can show off new shoes and strings of pearls to the neighbors back home.

The majority, however, don't rent one of the 70,000 hired cars – or didn't to date in 1999 – and don't explore the heart of the island or the former capital of Sineu with its Wednesday cattle market. They fail to learn anything about church reformer Ramón Llull at the hilltop monastery in Randa, nor about the island's only saint, Catalina Tomàs. They remain ignorant of the fact that the town of Felanitx is said to be the birthplace of Christopher Columbus and also the native town of the most famous contemporary artist in Spain, Miquel Barceló. The ins and outs of wine-growing in Majorca near Binissalem are something else they fail to explore, as is the hermetic isolation of the village community in Pina.

People with completely diverse spheres of experience and faculties of perception thus coexist on one and the same island, an island the Romans called *Luminosa,* the luminous, and Catalan poet Santiago Rusiñol extolled as the island of peace, *la isla de la calma.* As an island of sun and flowers it has become synonymous with the unparalleled success of a mass tourist product. During the years when a concrete jungle disfigured the most beautiful beaches in the Mediterranean, the very same mass tourism and its clientele earned it the title "where the help goes on vacation ". With the second millennium looming large on the horizon, foreign investors and realtors, especially those from Germany, have come up with a new equivocal nickname, that of "Majorca, the glorified Germany", penned by a German news magazine. There is, however, one thing both those who worship Majorca and those who despise it can agree on; this island has never left anyone cold.

Majorcan cuisine
The enjoyment of food

The whole of Majorca knows the story about the Catalan writer, Josep Plà, who almost fell to his knees not out of infatuation for a village beauty in Porreres but from hunger in front of a restaurateur in Pollença. He wasn't actually asking for anything particularly special; all he wanted was *sopes,* vegetable stew with cabbage, which you would think wasn't too much to ask. Here, it was, the *patron* refused to serve anything as lowly as *sopes,* for at that time it was absolutely taboo to offer "poor man's food" in a good Majorcan restaurant. He did eventually come round, grumbling that he'd make an exception – today and today only! Thankfully, those days are gone; now you can find genuine Majorcan dishes on any self-respecting restaurant menu. Nobody has to get down on his or her knees for *sopes* any more.

Even if its name suggest otherwise, *sopes mallorquines* isn't a soup but a stew. Here, *sopes* refers to the thin dried slices of mixed-grain bread used to line the bowl before the cabbage stew is ladled onto them. Vegetable stew is one of the island's typical recipes. Another classic Majorcan dish is *tumbet.* Layers of fried squash, egg plant, red pepper, and potato are topped with tomato sauce and finished in the oven for 10 minutes. Like any other stew, *tumbet* tastes best when left to stand for a day so that the vegetables can really soak up the flavors.

Vegetarian delights of the Mediterranean kitchen from Majorca's fields and gardens; fruit and vegetable importers have little business here.

Multicultural cuisine

Almost all the people to invade, trade with or travel to Majorca have made a contribution to its cuisine. They either brought fruit, vegetables and spices with them or entire recipes which have gradually embellished and extended the assortment of dishes bubbling in the island's kitchens. The inhabitants were all too happy to try out new ingredients and ideas. Majorca's geography meant that they were dependent on produce grown on local plantations and the animals native to the island – and on making do with whatever grew here. They were thus grateful for any modicum of change which could be introduced.

Meat pies attractively arranged on a Majorcan tablecloth.

Maybe this is why variation is the norm in Majorcan cooking. For a long time, traditional recipes weren't written down but were something daughters "inherited" from their mothers. This explains the many discrepancies which still prevail in the methods of preparation of certain foods. It's usually possible to find small differences in or alterations to the same dish which vary from family to family and region to region. Many recipes are influenced by Arabia. It is thus perfectly common to combine apricots, almonds, pine nuts and sultanas with cinnamon, capers and aniseed, creating comestibles which tickle the taste buds.

Meat in Majorca is usually pork. The black pig, the *porc negre,* is a cross between the Celtic *Sus scorfa Ferns* and the Iberian *Sus scorfa mediterraneus.* In former times the annual *sa matança* feast was the event of the year out in the Majorcan countryside, with barely a morsel of the fattened, slaughtered pig left unused. As the Majorcans couldn't air-dry their ham because of the damp seaside climate, they hit upon the idea of drying sausages seasoned with paprika in their cellars, inventing the *sobrassada.* This is now also manufactured industrially, although it's often not quite clear what the ingredients are; only products which bear the label *Sobrassada de Mallorca de*

Fruit and vegetables grow here with very little assistance, yet conscientious farmers still make daily checks on their produce.

Cerdo Negro are guaranteed to contain the black Majorcan pig, powdered paprika, salt and other natural seasonings – and nothing more. The popular sausage with its harmless tinge of white mold is spread raw on bread and also eaten cooked. Some Majorcans swear that it only really tastes good if you smear honey on it.

Another favorite is delicious Majorcan lamb, cooked in a wood-burning oven with fresh herbs such as rosemary, thyme and garlic. There are also a number of recipes for rabbit and farm chicken, such as *conill amb ceba,* rabbit with onions, for example.

The range of desserts is inexhaustible. A sumptuous meal is usually followed by the famous Majorcan spiral pastry made with a yeast dough, the *ensaïmada,* or by almond gâteau with almond ice cream. The cake is baked without flour. It's wise not to ask how many eggs are beaten in instead of the flour as a binding agent; the same goes for the amount of sugar in the almond ice cream. Another refreshing close to a meal are the various types of *granissats,* crushed ice flavored with orange, lemon or other fruit juice, stored just under freezing point so that it forms a very thick liquid. Almost every menu also boasts *flam,* a caramelized pudding made with eggs which is extremely popular in both Spain and Portugal.

And there's more for the sweet tooth. The windows of Majorca's *pastisseries* and *xocolateries* are laden with homemade chocolate nougat, candied fruit, marrons glacés and marzipan sweetmeats. This love of concentrated sugar is something the Majorcans have inherited from their culinary mentors the Arabs, whereas the cocoa for chocolate is an import from the New World.

Coca, pizza *à la mallorquina,* can be sweet or savory.

Tramuntana

Un hiver à Majorque *(A Winter in Majorca),* which continues to be a bestseller in the island bookstores.

Thirty five years later, a homeless descendant of the Austrian royal family began buying up land near Deià regarded by the locals as nothing but scree and thus worthless, erecting a domicile which was the object of his almost manic affection over 41 years. Archduke Ludwig Salvator of Habsburg-Tuscany left many records of his love for generations to come; more than a dozen of the 60-odd books he wrote during his lifetime are dedicated to Majorca, among them the famous compendium entitled *Die Balearen* (The Balearics), a meticulous appraisal of Majorca and its island neighbors.

His estates, among them Son Marroig, S'Estaca, Son Moragues and Miramar, still exist, with Son Moragues in particular a unique product of his desperate yet jubilant love. One of the archduke's main concerns was that nature be preserved as God had created it; to

A symphony of sea, wind, and rocks
The Tramuntana

A few words of warning before we begin: the Tramuntana in the northwest of the island is treacherous terrain. Admittedly, attacks from pirates are now a thing of the past, as is the fear that you could fall prey to *bandolers,* the buccaneers of the hills, on the lonely mountain roads. Yet the two other dangers which characterize the area are still very much a force to be reckoned with.

The first covers everything affected by Newton's law of gravitation. Even if you don't fall yourself – down a precipitous rock face in the Torrent de Pareis, for example, from the top of a cliff into the sea or over a loose piece of turf into a rocky crevice – then something could fall on you: rocks, loose scree, branches torn off trees by the wind – or bird muck from an osprey flying overhead.

The power of love
The second hazard is of a more subtle nature yet has still taken its toll of victims. The majority have walked blindly into the trap and remained nameless in their fate, yet there are a few illustrious figures whose adoration has been imprinted on the memory of the island and of Europe. For the second peril which can befall you here is love; it ambushes its victims like the *bandolers* of old, crushing them in its embrace, never to let them go or forget.

In 1838 French writer George Sand was smitten during a winter spent in Majorca's beautiful town of Valldemossa, where she had fled with her companion, the Polish composer Frédéric Chopin, to the seclusion of the old monastery. While the consumptive Chopin battled with exhausting bouts of coughing in the damp, cold climate of Valldemossa, George Sand became enamored of the surrounding countryside, making a literary declaration of love in her memoirs,

The roads and paths through the mountainous Tramuntana are lined with interesting plants.

The Tramuntana is the region with the most water in Majorca. With up to 59 inches (1,500 mm) of precipitation a year, the hanging gardens drip with moisture.

Previous double-page spread: Looking south along the coast of the Tramuntana mountains.

The lush evergreen of the Tramuntana eloquently testifies to a plentiful supply of water in this area. It is composed of holm oak forest, olive groves and pine trees, stretching as far as the eye can see. With the exception of the olives, the plants are all native to the Tramuntana, whose flora and fauna man has gradually extended over the centuries to include those cultivars needed to guarantee his survival in this part of the country.

The magic formula for this agricultural architecture is made up of two methods which can still be admired today, particularly between Estellencs and Banyalbufar. Where nature has failed to create flat ground, man has leveled it, directing and diverting water using the force of gravity. Terraces have been dug for fruit, vegetables and grain, protected and supported by dry stone walls and expertly irrigated. The Arabs created a canal system here, collecting rain and meltwater and channeling it to each of the terraced fields in overflow basins and then into the village. Sluices and wells ensure that the

Even in the mountains the temperatures soar in summer. Yet water is rarely scarce here, thanks to the natural reservoirs which store the island's rainfall.

In spring thousands of almond trees burst into glorious blossom across Majorca.

this we owe one of the few unspoiled areas left on the island, the Son Moragues Park.

The archduke's love, and also that of British writers Robert Graves and D.H. Lawrence, was fired by a Mediterranean landscape which is unparalleled. There are indeed few islands which offer such immense variety. The Serra de Tramuntana overpowers the island, neither deceitfully nor unexpectedly, but openly and unreservedly, unable to act any differently. The mountain range is a symphony of the highest caliber. As an overture, a violin solo flies in across the Cap de Formentor, lingering a moment, surprised, before soaring on to the Puig Major in a new burst of energy. The highest elevation at 4,741 ft (1,445 m) beats out the rhythm on the timpani together with its nearby colleagues, leaving room for the gentle lament of the oboe while the sea watches its waves crash against the rocks.

A flute pipes cheerfully in answer through terraced gardens covered with olive trees, orange groves and almond plantations near Banyalbafur. And while a harp reflects on the beauty of Arabian parks such as Alfàbia and Raixa and the crackling of charcoal at a charcoal burner's, the triumphant sound of trumpets and trombones rises up above expanses of succulent green, above hillsides dotted with villages and above the wind which finds more places to hide here than anywhere else on the island.

Water in controlled abundance

Unlike the parched saltpans in the south of the island and the vast plains of the Pla, the Tramuntana is the wettest region in Majorca. The peaks of the Puig Major, Teix, Massanella, and Tomir are snow capped in the winter; in Bunyola rainfall can exceed 59 inches (1,500 mm) a year. At the end of the 19th century the hillside village of Esporles even erected a small-scale hydroelectric power station to drive the looms and spinning wheels at its first textiles factory.

The evening sun bathes the trees clinging to the precipitous coastline in a warm autumnal light.

water is still fairly distributed, for even in the Tramuntana the summers are hot and almost without rain.

Give and take in the mountains

However idyllic things may seem now, until the 20th century life here was anything but an existence in paradise where you could just help yourself to what you needed. Apart from water and acorns for the pigs, the mountains gave nothing of their own free will, taking much in return: freedom of movement; sheep, goats, pigs and mules who fell into crevices in the rocks; the lives of people who were killed by stray boulders or tumbled down cliffs and were pulverized on the rocks below by the waves. Survival here meant coping with solitude, getting on well with the people around you and immediately recognizing whether cloud, wind or rain spelled relief or disaster.

This gave rise to an occupation which could only have found a niche in these climes. Men worked as *nevaters* or "snowmen", collecting snow and ice from the tops of the mountains in winter and storing it in specially-erected buildings, the *cases desa neu*. In the summer this was transported down into the valleys where the frozen water was turned into gold. The trade persisted until the beginning of the 20th century, when the first ice works poached business from the snowmen of the hills.

The ice-makers shared their alpine terrain with the heating engineers, the charcoal burners who fashioned *sitges,* charcoal kilns, out of pine and holm oak, creating a fuel which transformed the cold farmhouse kitchen into a cozy home. Yet with the triumphant arrival of electricity the number of charcoal burners also began to dwindle, albeit not quite as drastically as that of the *nevaters.*

Soon after the *Reconquista,* the Reconquest of Majorca by the Christians, life in the mountains flourished. The victorious armies may have destroyed all buildings constructed by the Moors, but they left their agricultural legacy untouched. Bunyola continued to live off the plentiful yield of its olive trees and produced the finest oil in Majorca at its own press. Sóller, which lies in a "valley of gold" named after the pale liquid squeezed from its green fruits, concentrated on another line of merchandise which could just as easily have given the valley its epithet: oranges, which with their sweet perfume and brilliant fruit embedded in dark green foliage give the town its unique, Elysian appearance.

Pigs, sheep, goats and cows thrived on the lush, fragrant pastures of the mountains, with wild goats, hare and rabbits providing hunters with a means of earning a living. Huge estates were created by the *repartiment,* the division of the land by Jaume I among his followers, which rapidly brought riches to those who owned them. Nearly all of these manors still exist; many are still farmed and others have been turned into museums. The most famous is Sa Granja near Esporles, in itself a lesson in agricultural history with its stables and workshops, reception rooms and living quarters and, as a reminder of the days of the Spanish Inquisition, a torture chamber in the cellar.

Such prosperity soon attracted hoards of envious marauders and bandits to the island and for hundreds of years the coast of the Tramuntana was attacked by pirates and abused by smugglers. Hardly a village or town escaped the brutal raids by the rovers of the sea and many still commemorate their hard-fought victories over the freebooters today, such as Port de Pollença and Port Sóller. Here, too, watchtowers or *talàies* were built from the 16th century onwards, all within visible distance of each other, their round, defensive structures issuing a warning to the buccaneers and proclaiming the island would tolerate them no more. Some of these towers still stand; some, like the "Tower of Souls" at Banyalbufar, have been erected at such an impressive spot in the countryside that those who behold them feel giddy – either with the sheer beauty of it all or with vertigo.

"Snow chains must be used on the Tramuntana mountain roads" are words you will often hear in the winter months.

they were still fresh. The island government started looking for road engineers who considered mountains a challenge and not a handicap.

Antonio Paretti from Italy was just the man the island planners needed. His road from Port de Pollença to the Cap de Formentor and his *pièce de résistance,* the "Snake" to Sa Calobra, are a must for any visitor. Instead of simply dynamiting anything which happened to be in his way, Paretti studied the Tramuntana carefully and made an effort to understand its essence. Where a slope was too steep, he cleverly built a curve winding back up instead of blindly forging his way on down the mountain. Any rock he had to remove was "recycled" and used to fill in holes. The result are roads which curl down the mountainside like silk ribbons.

Now that Sóller, which until the 1990s could only be reached via a mountain pass, also has access to the outside world with its new tunnel, the Tramuntana seems to have revealed all of its secrets. Not quite. For barely half a mile from Paretti's snaking hairpin bends is the Torrent de Pareis, "Paradise Gorge", 2³/₄ miles (4.5 km) of river gorge which has etched its way into the limestone. Never mind the advance of modern means of transport; those wanting to pass through the ravine need lots of common sense, good trekking equipment, sure footing, pluck and plenty of time. They will be generously rewarded for their efforts with a stretch of country created by God's own hand, with a fanfare from the Tramuntana symphony which here, away from the roads and villages, can sing out its song loud and long.

Opposite: Sat under a roof of vines, among friends, festive meals can last for hours.

Following double-page spread: A deserted *finca* in the Serra de Tramuntana.

Below: Under an awning of green foliage and fruit like orange lanterns, chickens scratch for food in the shade.

In the Bay of Estellencs the water is so clear you can watch the fish swimming along the bottom of the ocean.

The arrival of the industrial age and the exiles

Yet even here in the Tramuntana the modern age dawned in Majorca. The 19th century saw the arrival of the first foreigners to the island who were not hoping to trade their wares or searching for a smugglers' cave where they could hide their contraband. The new arrivals came in search of peace and of a home, to get away from their world and to nurture their troubled souls. Towns such as Deià, Pollença, Valldemossa, and Sóller became multilingual places of refuge for a northern European society which even then began to feel the crush of the masses and to recognize that man was beginning to lose touch with nature.

The seclusion they were hoping for was soon hard to come by. The first industrialists appeared, bringing with them spinning and weaving mills. In 1912 the people of Sóller had a railway line to Palma built so that they could transport their oranges quickly and while

Tryst of the winds
The Cap de Formentor

The solid steps, walls, paths, and a light-house erected on the rock at the Cap de Formentor in 1862 were built to last, yet this doesn't stop vertigo sufferers from being absolutely terrified. When the visibility is good, the panorama from Majorca's land's end stretches as far as Menorca to the east and Cala Figuera to the west, with Alcúdia sunning itself on its sandy beach to the south. Yet the view from the crags down to the sea seething angrily 980 feet (300 m) below makes even the most hard-baked wonder just how robust their knees actually are. And as if that weren't enough, here at the northeast end of the island is also where the wild winds converge: *Tramuntana, Ponent, Migjorn, and Llevant,* the four big brothers, and their cousins *Grezal, Mestral, Llebetx,* and *Xalec.*

On an island like Majorca, which until well into the 20th century survived largely on fishing and farming, it was imperative that people knew the winds as well as the members of their own family. Which ones bring rain, for example, shrivel young crops and churn up the sea into a mass of dangerous waves? Which ones gently brush across your face, iron the washing, dry the cut corn for threshing and guide the fishermen safely home? Which are friend and which are foe? Which promise fresh air and which threaten catastrophe?

The cold *Tramuntana* from the west and north must first match its strength with the mountains it gave its name to, hurling enormous waves onto the cliffs before tearing into the Raiguer and Pla. It then cools blistering summer heat down to more pleasant temperatures. Its colleagues *Ponent* and *Llevant* can reach hurricane force in the winter, especially when they don't cut in from due east or west but curve into the island from the north where there are no obstacles to restrain them. The *Migjorn* from the south brings the sparkle and warmth of summer to tentative spring and autumn days and turns the summer into an open-air sauna.

The wind and sea have sculpted bizarre formations at the northernmost edge of Majorca.

Gentlemen detectives and island fishermen
The Port de Pollença

At the northern end of the Badia de Pollença, a promontory curls elegantly along Pollença harbor as if laying a protective arm around the little fishing town. Although the danger of attacks by pirates is long past, the harbor, the first inhabited stronghold from the northernmost tip of the island, can use a little protection. Behind it there is nothing but the storm-ravaged Cap de Formentor; below it, the slopes of the Tramuntana begin.

After Agatha Christie had spent a few weeks here in 1929, introducing the harbor of Pollença to world literature in her love story *Problem at Pollensa Bay* – not forgetting the magical beauty of its lighting – Britons expert at detecting good vacations began to

arrive for their summer breaks. Among them were famous names such as Winston Churchill and shipping multi-millionaire Aristotle Onassis. Some of the flair from the days when men were gentlemen remains and the seaside resort is vaguely reminiscent of the idyllic fishing villages found in Cornwall. Port de Pollença soon became affordable for the less well-endowed and after the Second World War was one of the first main tourist resorts on the island. English-speakers still dominate the fishing port in the summer months, on the surface at least; what they probably fail to realize is just how many of mainland Spain's celebrated public figures regularly gather here to discuss affairs with fellow politicians, negotiate deals with business associates or meet up with old friends.

Despite the often dubious blessings of tourism, Port de Pollença has managed to

Agatha Christie spent some time here, taking the Badia of Pollença as the setting for a love story.

retain much of its character. In the style of good old British understatement the town has kept its beach clean, furnished its town center with shops which are attractive but not showy and transformed its seafront into a paradise where people are invited to meander, to watch the world go by and to meditate Mediterranean-style. You can sit outside one of the cafés along the Passeig Anglada Camarasa for hours gazing at the fishermen mending their nets, or contemplate proud yacht owners scrubbing down their decks from the Club Nautico. Or maybe take a stroll along the mile-long Passeig Voramar under ancient trees, past grand, cozily old-fashioned villas, jetties and coves. At the end of the bay a small fortress built in 1634 guards the harbor, its ruins later converted into a lighthouse. As a backdrop to the long, wide sandy beach rises the Serrade Cavall Bernat, with the beach at Cala Sant Vicenç behind it glimmering a natural beige, gold and shades of aquamarine. On a clear day you can spare yourself the trip to the Cap de Formentor to wave in greeting to Majorca's little sister; you can see the town of Ciutadella and the Cap de Punta Nati on Menorca from the lighthouse.

Right: Yachts gently bob on the water, waiting for Aeolus to grant them a favorable wind.

Below: Foreign tourists began frequenting the Hotel Formentor in the 1920s.

Roasting spits versus scimitars
Moros i cristians

"Moros a terra" booms out from the loud-speakers in Sóller, Pollença, and Andratx – and then the fun starts. Men armed with wooden swords charge at their scimitar-wielding adversaries. Cloaks get tangled up with baggy pants, turbans fly through the air, and black mustaches flutter to the ground.

Moros i cristians, Moors versus Christians: corsairs dressed like extras in a pirate film and Majorcans in "typical national costume" as swashbuckling musketeers wrestle hard for the town. The costumes may not be recorded in any historical document but the outcome of the battle is; following the spirited scuffle, the Arab pirates are defeated and lead away as prisoners.

The desperate cry of "The Moors have landed!" heralds the beginning of a whole series of annual spectacles which see Majorcans along the coast enter into furious mock battle with one another. These festivals look back to the days when pirates made constant raids on the island between the 14th and 17th centuries, often assaulting their victims in the middle of the night. They usually took hostages whom they sold as slaves at North African markets or brought back to their families in return for a generous ransom. The Majorcans defended themselves bitterly; anyone in the village who could brandish a sword was expected to take the field. And not only a sword: roasting spits and frying pans were also used

Deep in thought, this young corsair watches Christians armed with pitchforks gradually get the better of their opponents.

Sometimes even the saints are in it up to their necks.

as weapons. Legend has it that the women were just as adept at handling weapons as the men, fighting with courage and pugnacity, and that they often helped win the bloody battles fought against their enemies.

On the evening of the festivities services are held at church, with the full details of the Christian conflicts and the names and rank of the Christian martyrs being read out year in, year out. The main attraction of the proceedings is then the staging of the various wars waged for Christianity.

The people in Pollença reenact the landing of Moorish pirates on 30 May 1550, the day when the Majorcan villagers overthrew troops headed by Dragut, a freebooter captain of the Turkish navy and comrade-in-arms of the pirate Barbarossa and Suleiman I the Magnificent, the sultan of Constantinople. The jamboree has been celebrated on the 2 August since the middle of the 19th century. The main protagonists, local men armed with clubs, spar in their nightshirts in deference to their ancestors, said to have been disturbed in their beds. Even half asleep, Majorca's intrepid warriors prove impossible to beat.

In the *Es Firó* in May, Sóller commemorates a dramatic raid from 1561, clashing with its "enemies" for an entire week as has been

the tradition since 1852. The story goes that on 11 May 1,700 pirates led by Ochalí, corsair and – as a sort of second job – Pasha of Tunis, attacked the town, hoping for easy pickings. They didn't reckon with the resolute curate of Santa Catalina, however, who, swinging his crucifix with all the ferocity he could muster, was able to protect his sanctum from the murderous heathens. At Ca'n Tamany, a house in the country, the Moors were even more surprised to find two women ruthlessly defending themselves with knives, axes and any other familiar kitchen implements they could find – successfully.

The attackers allegedly suffered a loss of 500 on this occasion which again documents just how many of them there were – and just how fearless the men and women defending their island proved themselves to be. The heroines of the above tale were subsequently known as the "Brave Women", the *Valentes dones de Ca'n Tamany,* and the town later erected a relief as a monument in memory of that day.

In Andratx, too, it was supposedly two women, this time sisters, who stood their ground against the pirates on 2 August 1578. As we can see, it was always members of the so-called "weaker sex" who warded off the Arabian aggressors with their extraordinary bravery. Skeptics claim, however, that the women, unveiled and draped in old linen, came down on the Arabs like wild spirits, causing their foe to run off as fast as their legs could carry them …

It's easy to lose sight of the "true enemy" in the chaos of battle.

No room at the inn
Pollença

Being destroyed was an occupational hazard for towns like Pollentia near the Majorcan coast. When attacked by Vandals in 440 AD, the town wasn't simply plundered; it was completely annihilated. It later had to be completely rebuilt, earning itself a new name (Alcúdia). The few people to survive the terror started a new settlement called Pollentia around 3 miles (5 km) inland from their obliterated home. Over the years, the town's name has been linguistically softened to Pollença.

New Pollentia was near a Roman road. Two thousand years on, the Pont Romà outside town, one of Majorca's two remaining Roman bridges, still pays homage to this fact. The two slightly different arches spanning the Torrent de Sant Jordi, the supporting pillars and the road across them are so well preserved

that you almost expect to see someone strolling towards you dressed in a toga.

Pirates, Templars, and Jesuits

Despite only having 12,000 inhabitants, Pollença is undoubtedly a town. It owes this and its overall appearance first and foremost to the Arabs, who laid the foundations for the winding, narrow streets, flights of steps and houses built in rough, undressed stone of warm yellow and pale red. Barely had the Arabs been driven out when the aggressive Knights Templar seized control of Pollença, founding the town's main church, Nostra Senyora dels Angels, in 1236. Just beside the church past Pollença's local landmark, the Font des Gall or cock fountain, the palace of the Templars still stands. The saint Vicenç Ferrer is said to have distributed food among the poor and preached at the fountain.

From here it's only a few paces to the church of Monti Sion, also founded by an

The Romans went to a lot of trouble to tame the Torrent de Sant Jordi. They even built a breakwater, thinking it indispensable.

order who fought for what they believed – not with swords but, more astutely, with words. Similar to the Knights Templar, who were eventually forced to disband, the Jesuits were banished from Spain for long periods. They founded the church in Pollença in 1697 and used it until the late 18th century. Thanks to the initiative of poet Miquel Costa i Llobrera, the building has survived as a town hall and school.

Most of the town dates back to the 16th century following its destruction in 1550, when corsairs sacked the city. Today, Pollença is a charming haven of peace and quiet with its reddish orange houses in stone, its delicate, wrought-iron windows and balconies and its shady squares.

Although it has plenty of impressive

town palaces, churches and sleepy back streets to offer, Pollença has failed to become a tourist trap. Maybe the people of Pollença had had enough of visitors after their experiences with the pirates. Whatever the reason, there are hardly any hotels in the town itself; the visitors who climb the famous Puig de Calvari, the Calvary hill, either to check whether there really are 365 steps leading straight up it or whether simply to enjoy the fantastic views of the valleys and the sea from the top, are forced to wend their way home when evening comes. Even at Easter it's no different, when the town is full to bursting with tourists. Easter is when the Pollensans celebrate the festival of *Davallament* on the Calvary steps. This is a passion play *à la mallorquina,* where actors depict the suffering of Christ in all its detail, with pomp, circumstance, poignancy, and extreme beauty.

The Glowing Virgin

On the 1,093 foot-high Puig de Santa Maria (333 m) opposite the Calvary hill, one night in the 14th century the grass began to glow. Three devout Christians watched in awe from Puig de Calvari. A nocturnal excursion to the Puig, lead by a local priest, found the obligatory figure of the Virgin Mary tucked away between the rocks, the Baby Jesus at her side clutching a bird in his hand. As is often the case with miracles, the holy relic in question proved extremely capricious. When the time came for it to be taken to the church in Pollença, it suddenly became so heavy that even eight strong young men couldn't move it. Those involved interpreted the message correctly and erected a chapel for the Virgin and her offspring where they stood. The three saintly souls who saw the light that night promptly founded a convent and a school at the new place of worship.

Another monastery, that of the Dominicans, has made Pollença famous far beyond the boundaries of Majorca. And not because of its architecture, which despite being a product of the early Baroque (1578) looks Romanesque. Its popularity is due to the concerts held here between June and September as part of the Pollença International Music Festival, usually in the courtyard of the Claustre del Convent Santo Domingo. One of the seats in the first row is frequently occupied by the festival's patron, Queen Sophía, who attends the concerts as often as she can. The queen of Spain is a great fan of music and an expert on the subject.

The Moors sought refuge from Christian conquerors lead by Jaume I at the Castell del Rei in 1230. Some 113 years later, Jaume III was forced to take cover in the castle high up above Pollença from advancing Aragonese troops.

A spectacular end to Lent
Easter

Those who make it to the top gaze out on a marvelous panorama of the Badia de Pollença, with the town spread out beneath them and the orchards, the *hortes,* stretching out across the plateau to the sea with the Port de Pollença and the Cap de Formentor. They also appreciate the effort which has to be put into the ascent. The path from Font del Gall, the cock fountain in the center of Pollença, has exactly 365 steps, one for each day of the year, which have to be climbed to reach the summit of the Puig del Calvari, the Calvary hill in Pollença. Once up there at 558 feet (170 m), however, you are rewarded by the view.

The hill used to belong to the mysterious Order of the Knights Templar, remembered in a street name in Pollença (Carrer Temple or Templar Street). In 1314 the hill was given to the Knights Hospitalers of St John of Jerusalem after the Templars were disbanded by a pope who thought them too secretive and, above all, too powerful. The way up is lined with cypress trees, which provide shade and a place to pause, and leads past buildings in roughly hewn stone, some of which accommodate shops and restaurants where thankfully you can fortify yourself for the rest of the climb.

There is one day in the year, however, when the view is of little interest to those who tackle the incline. Where tourists are pleased they have made it to the top, the faithful are somber. As the name suggests, the Puig de Calvari is where a yearly special ceremony is performed on the saddest day of the Easter period. On Good Friday the entire town, the young and old, those who live or have been born here, hurries to the Calvary hill to watch the *Davallament* procession. The festival chronicles the final stage of Christ's suffering with the Descent from the Cross. The Easter cortege heads for the chapel on top of the hill, then continues across it down to the 13th-century church of Nostra Senyora dels Angels in town, where the proceedings close with a ceremonial midnight mass.

In contrast to the north of Europe, religion in the south is much less "inward-looking" and less private, being more of a public affair where people exhibit their own form of religiosity for all to see. This is especially true of Spain, and particularly in the *Semana Santa,* Holy Week. Majorca is no exception. The most important religious holiday in the Christian year is primarily staged outdoors. Christ's triumph over death is celebrated in nearly every town and village on the island with processions and festivals.

The festivities begin on Palm Sunday but don't end on Easter Sunday as one might expect. The week after Easter the revelers are still in full swing. After all, people can once again freely indulge in the pleasures of the flesh (and especially the palate) now that Lent has passed, gathering plenty of strength to party on into the small hours. Over the

Shady cypress trees line the 365 steps that climb the Calvary hill in Pollença.

Re-enacting Christ's suffering in Pollença.

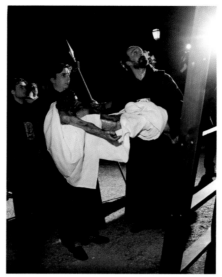

Dismayed, the faithful stand before the cross.

holiday period adults give each other meat pies or *panades*; the children look forward to their own elaborately decorated candy bars, their *mona de pascua*.

The Easter celebrations start with a Palm Sunday mass in the island's capital a week before Easter, where the Majorcans go to have the palm leaves they have purchased on the market blessed. On this last Sunday of fasting before Easter, the congregation of Sant Joan celebrates the *Festa del Pa i del Peix*, the festival of bread and fish. Following the cavalcade, small rolls made from unleavened bread are eaten in reference to when Jesus fed the five thousand.

From Maundy Thursday on there seems to be no end to the processions organized by the various Christian brotherhoods. All over the island, painted, golden figures of all sizes are carried through the towns and villages, elaborately decorated or dressed in robes; each scene from Christ's suffering is paraded before the crowds of people lining the streets. Incidentally, it's considered a great honor in Majorca to be part of one of the over 50 *confraríes*. There are two ways you can become one of the privileged few; either the sons inherit their membership from their fathers – sisterhoods are still extremely rare, even today – or they buy their way in, which can be a very expensive option.

Maundy Thursday in Palma sees the worship of the wounded figure of Christ on the cross from the old spital church. In the procession of Christ of the Holy Blood, the *Processó del Sant Crist de la Sang*, the penitents are clad in long robes with pointed hoods imitated by the Ku-Klux-Klan. When evening falls, they carry the heavy effigy of Christ through the streets of Palma, accompanied on their long march by the sound of drums. The spectacle lasts six hours and is the only procession in which all the *confraríes* on the island participate.

Good Friday is when the aforementioned *Davallament* takes place in Pollença; on the Tuesday after Easter a pilgrimage is made to the Crestaix chapel in Sa Pobla, the main purpose of this being the bread-blessing festival, the *pancaritat*. Once the group of followers has left the church and processed through town, copious amounts of *panades* brought along especially for the occasion are consumed. The highlight of the festival is the *tonades* competition, where a prize is awarded to the best performance of a work song. Naturally, the singers need to limber up their vocal chords before the contest starts, preferably with wine. In the midst of all the merriment, the hardships of Lent are soon forgotten …

The Mourning of Christ is a ceremonious affair.

Madonna of the minorities
Lluc Monastery

Shortly after the Reconquest, when Christians under King Jaume I recaptured Majorca from the Moors, an Arab couple lost their farm high up in the Tramuntana to the new lords of the manor. In order to survive, they rapidly converted to Christianity and also had their children baptized. One of them, a little boy called Lluc (Majorcan for Luke), was responsible for leading his father's sheep and goats into the mountains where they could find food. One day, Lluc noticed a strange light coming from the tangled bushes of the *massís*. Curious, he beat his way into the thicket and discovered a small figure of the Virgin Mary, half-submerged in the ground.

What surprised him most was the color of her skin; she was as dark as he was.

The Virgin Mary plays hide-and-seek

Excited, he took the figure to the priest in Escorca at the church of Sant Pere, the first records of which date back to 1247. The priest gave Lluc's priceless find a place of honor in his little church, yet the next day, once news of the statue had traveled to the nearest villages and people came to worship the Mother of God, the figure was gone.

The same afternoon, Lluc found her in exactly the same place she had been the day before. He again took her to the priest, who for a second time placed the black Virgin in her niche, only to find that the next day, to his utter astonishment, she had once more disappeared. This game of hide-and-seek went on until it dawned on the priest that the

Once discovered, the black figure of the Virgin Mary of Lluc found a picturesque home in a valley of the Tramuntana. The monastery is one of the most popular places of pilgrimage on the island.

statue was trying to tell him something. The Virgin Mary wanted to remain where she had first given the shepherd boy a sign. Soon afterwards a small chapel was built there.

This the romantic, poetic version. Those who have problems embracing the modern, rational explanation for the event – by going along with the prosaic notion that Lluc is Majorcan for "forest", of which incidentally there is still a lot left on the island, and is thus a figment of the pious imagination which has been given a suitable name – would do well to believe it. After all, this is what the population has long believed and indeed still does; the number of pilgrims

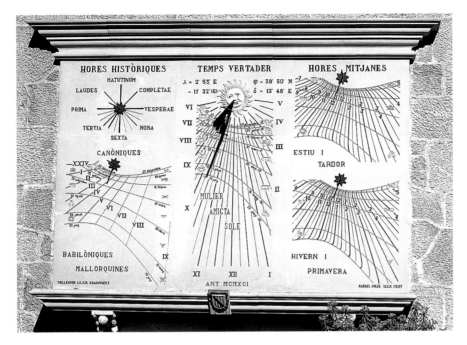

The sundial on the path up the Calvary hill shows the actual time in the center, how time was measured in the past on the left and the half-hours on the right.

who immediately began flooding to the site rose so dramatically that in 1260 foundations had to be laid for an Augustinian hermitage dedicated to Our Lady of Lluc. To this was later added a seminary, and today the monastery is inhabited and run by monks of the Sacred Heart.

Monk's cell or double room? monasterial hospitality majorcan-style

Considering how inhospitable the karst landscape of the Tramuntana can be, the black Virgin demonstrated extremely good taste when looking for somewhere to set up residence. The monastery is embedded in a gentle hollow in the mountains where tired souls can find respite among the highest peaks in Majorca. Three ancient routes of pilgrimage still used today lead here from Sóller, Pollença, and Inca, although many of the visitors prefer to struggle up the *serra* in their cars in search of peace – and somewhere to stay.

In keeping with the monastic tradition, the Lluc Monastery has rooms for guests in need of a place to rest and turns nobody away. Depending on how full it is there are simple monk's cells or extremely comfortable double rooms with a shower, and even apartments with a kitchenette, which seems rather superfluous when you savor the excellent fare the brethren serve in the monastery pub.

Lluc Monastery nestles contentedly in its dip in the hills, its impressive, rectangular complex protected from the outside world on almost all sides by pine trees. The road to the church runs past beautiful areas of green and carefully tended gardens, past the old stables and workshops which are now a souvenir shop and a small café. Commemorative plaques and stone crosses bequeathed by thankful pilgrims skirt the roadside, their finely chiseled ornamentation barely distinguishable beneath the weathered surfaces.

The Monestir de Lluc is not only the main pilgrimage center on the island; it can also claim to be the third most important example of *Modernisme,* Art Nouveau, in Majorca after the cathedral in Palma and the houses in Sóller. The master himself, Antoni Gaudí, and later his disciple, Joan Rubió, renovated the church interior and decorated the calvari, the Calvary hill at Lluc behind the monastery, with five sculptures dedicated to the Mysteries of the Rosary.

The façade of the monastery church itself is around 300 years later than the 13th-century church walls. The high altar inside is also Renaissance. In a chapel behind it, in an honorary niche better befitting its prize than the original small table, *Sa Moreneta,* the

Behind the Baroque façade lives *Sa Moreneta,* the "little black one", as the Majorcans affectionately call their favorite statue of the Virgin.

The elaborately ornate, frescoed dome is the only source of light in the pilgrimage church.

choir, whose title *Els Blavets* refers to its blue uniform, is as famous in Spain as the Vienna Boys' Choir in Austria and the Choir of Kings College, Cambridge in England. The boys serenade visitors to the church every morning, except during school vacations. For unlike young Lluc, these boys occasionally have time off.

black Virgin, has found a place for herself from which she no longer needs to flee.

Sa Moreneta has found a home

Here at least, in front of the most popular and most frequented figure of the Virgin Mary in Majorca, the worldly buzz of excited tourists is no longer audible, though a few feet away outside the portal of the church it's anything but peaceful. Here, where the only daylight is allowed in by a solitary window in the dome of the nave, bathing the area in a warm, diffuse semi-darkness conducive to piety, people automatically whisper or maintain a respectful silence.

At first, the "little black one", as the Majorcans affectionately call her, appears extremely static, in keeping with the period she probably originates from (pre-13th century). After studying her for a few moments, however, she seems so full of life with her delicate smile, her strong, elegant arm wrapped around the baby Jesus and the almost playful crown of stars around her head that you almost expect her to start speaking. Maybe because of this, or maybe because the color of her skin forms a strong

affinity with many minorities, so many people, both the deeply religious and the skeptical, feel content and protected here.

The monastery with the name of a Moorish child converted to Christianity is also a school of music and has around 60 boarders aged nine to fourteen. The school

Opposite: When the little boy Lluc, the son of Moorish converts, found the black Virgin in the forest near the monastery, the Virgin refused to remain anywhere else. Eventually a chapel was built at the place she was found, which later became a monastery.

The hallways of the monastery and the museum are full of votive pictures such as this one. Here, a fisherman who narrowly escaped drowning thanks the Virgin of Lluc for protecting him at sea.

So near and yet
so far: a few
yards before the
end of the gorge,
nature has a few
surprises in
store.

Dangerous Paradise
Torrent de Pareis

Now that even the remote seaside town of Sa Calobra has a road linking it to the outside world, a road which is a feature in itself and a must on any tourist itinerary, one could be permitted to doubt the words uttered time and again to the effect that there are still unspoiled areas of Majorca untouched by human hand, left as nature created them. OK, but where are they? As a matter of fact just around the corner from the most spectacular road in Majorca, leading to the same place. The second-largest ravine in the Mediterranean, the Torrent de Pareis, is barely half a mile east of the serpentine bends spiraling down to the Cala de Sa Calobra. Unlike a shimmering bay, a charming farmhouse or a meadow of almond trees in blossom signaling untold pleasures from the distance, the gorge does not hold promise of rapturous delight. The Torrent de Pareis is a red alert. Those who fail to take it seriously will be devoured.

St Peter at the Pearly Gates of Paradise Gorge

It's no coincidence that in one of the oldest and smallest churches on the island dating back to 1247, St Peter, the lord of skies and their trials and tribulations, keeps watch over the entrance to the "paradise gorge". Signs in several languages work hard to shatter the illusion that this is paradise, blaring out "Warning!" and "Danger!". Considering that there are fatal accidents every year, usually caused by irresponsible foolhardiness, these words of caution are to be taken seriously. The Torrent de Pareis is only a paradise in the sense that it remains one of the very few areas unspoiled by human hand. Those who have been here will understand why. Those who want to tackle it should know this: never go alone. Never go without climbing equipment. If you're new to canyoning, never go without a guide. Never go when the heavens seem unsettled; a heavy downpour can turn the Torrent into a deathtrap, even in the summer. And never, ever go in the winter, when the rain makes the rocks as slippery as an ice rink.

Almost 3 miles (4.5 km) separate Sant Pere from the shingle bay at Sa Calobra. The land drops almost 2,000 feet (600 m) down to the sea, incorporating steep drops of over 1,300 feet (400 m) in places. These clefts in the island's surface have been formed by rain over millions of years. The limestone walls of the gorge, sometimes almost white, often a pale gray, record how water has washed away and smoothed the rock, creating

After an almost 3-mile descent (4.5 km), the shingle beach at Sa Calobra awaits exhausted gorge hikers.

bizarre natural sculptures. One such example marks the start of the descent, just beyond the peaceful stretch of holm oak forest, where an arch cut out of stone spectacularly frames the entrance to the canyon.

Survival of the fittest

An hour further on down the ravine, the Torrent de Lluc and the Torrent de Sa Fosca join the Torrent de Pareis. The shrubs and bushes of the low mountain *macchia* have been replaced by the prickly *Ampelodesmus mauritanica,* a born survivor which forces its way into fissures in the rock where it can't be squashed by falling rocks. The Entreforc crevice is just wide enough for a climber to pass through – which he or she must to continue on through this stone Garden of Eden.

The Torrent de Sa Fosca soon becomes fairly impenetrable, but the distance which can be covered is sufficient to understand where it gets its name of the "gorge of darkness" from. The walls of rock gradually close in on one another until there is only a tiny

crack between them, 164 feet (50 m) up from the canyon floor. This quickly disappears too, completely cutting out the soft light of Majorca all the way to the foot of the Gorg Blau dam. Without a professional guide, the ravine is impassable.

Gliding through a dome of light

In the Torrent de Pareis, however, the sky is always visible, in places struggling through a mere crack in the rocks, at other times arching across the ravine like a dome of light high up above the valley floor. A rare feathered inhabitant of the gorge, the black vulture, nests and hunts here. He glides along the rock face, his wing span sometimes reaching 10 feet (3 m), on the lookout for food: a careless goat, perhaps, who doesn't know the gorge too well, a rabbit which has fallen down the cliff, a lost sheep. Unlike the osprey which also lives here, the black vulture doesn't hunt; his prey are carcasses. There are just 50 of these birds in Majorca and the scavenger has a difficult job when it

With the paradise gorge behind you, the rocks in the bay at Sa Calobra are a reminder of the difficult descent.

comes to securing his line of descendants; the females lay just one egg per year.

The air in the paradise gorge soon smells of the nearby sea, yet nature still has plenty of marvelous secrets to divulge. Suddenly, to the right, off the direct route to the beach, the Cova de Romagueral cave opens up like the nave of a cathedral, only accessible via the Sa Fonteta, a side valley of the Torrent. From this point, the vegetation finally recedes. Even the tough *Ampelodesmus mauritanica* has capitulated; the marks on the bare cliffs reveal just how high the water level can rise here. Even in summer, the small pools at the lower end of the ravine retain water, with fresh springs dribbling out of the rock, offering cool relief and refreshment.

The elusive ocean

As if to deprive its vanquishers of their final triumph, a few yards before the canyon ends

it blocks the way to the sea with several enormous boulders. At first there seems to be no way round them. Yet the mountaineering of the last four hours has trained eyes to look more carefully, making the challenge one which can be mastered.

Just beyond the rocks lies all the enchantment of the sea: the Morro de Sa Vaca, the "cow's mouth", a curious stone formation, and the half-moon Cala de Sa Calobra, with its beach of roaring shingle. With a little luck, the beach is not crammed to bursting point with tourists who have been driven here in large, upholstered vehicles, probably still a little giddy from the plunge down Paretti's hairpin bends. For compared to the routes winding through the paradise of rocks, even the most beautiful road in Majorca is still just a road. Signor Paretti was probably well aware of the fact.

Left: From darkness into the light. The blue hues of the sea are nature's enlightenment at the end of a rocky ordeal.

Below: Those who struggle through the gorge can look forward to the clear azure of the ocean.

Where there's a will, there's a way
The mountain pass to Sa Calobra

Until 1932, there weren't even 20 people living in the tiny hamlet of Sa Calobra at the end of the Torrent de Pareis. It was only possible to leave the village by sea or by hiking up through the Torrent to the mountains, a strenuous and dangerous undertaking. The next village of Escorca had no center, just a tiny church from the 13th century and a few scattered farmhouses. We could thus ask ourselves why the road was built at all. Surely not out of sheer kindness to the few souls of Sa Calobra, and surely not to make life easier for the coast's smugglers? To create jobs, perhaps? Or maybe simply to build the road to end all roads, using no machinery and relying on the skill of human labor, a case of *l'art pour l'art*?

Giddy from Sóller

The most famous of all of Majorca's roads begins its breath-taking ascent down to the sea just beyond the Embassament des Gorg Blau, the "blue pool" reservoir which is one of the island's major water storage points. Experienced drivers already feel giddy after leaving Sóller, trying to catch a last glimpse of the town from the dizzy heights of Mirador de ses Barques. The true hairpins only really start as you continue your journey past Majorca's mountain giants: the Puig Tossals, at the base of which is another reservoir, the Embassament de Cúber, holding water for the dry season, the Tossals Verds, the Puig Roig and the biggest of them all, the Puig Major. In front of you lies the refreshing bright green of the "blue pool", the Puig de Massanella reflected in it, balm for the eyes and the soul, a last point of rest before the madness starts.

North via twelve souths

It's only 2¹/₂ miles (4 km) north to Sa Calobra as the crow flies – and 7¹/₂ miles (12 km) along the road. Italian engineer Antonio Paretti's masterpiece makes twelve hairpin bends to the south to come out in the north. Is this right? It is. There were two things Paretti couldn't stand; the first was spoiling something as sublime and serene as mountains for the good of the majority of humankind, and the second were steep, sharp bends.

As it's not possible to drive along the road faster than about 12 mph (20 km/h), those who venture down it have plenty of time to study every single yard of Paretti's conservationist method of civil engineering in intricate detail – and to puzzle over his construction. From almost every point along the route it looks as though at least four asphalt ribbons curve their way down the mountainside; in your rear view mirror you can see sections of road you have yet to cross and in front of you winds the stretch you've just covered.

Inspired by a tie

This apparent confusion is how Paretti achieved the gentle descent he was aiming for, the pinnacle of his achievement being the section at Sa Moleta. Here, there seemed to be no alternative but to carve a bend into the mountain in order to make the next curve. While the engineer was knotting his tie one morning, so the story goes, he had a brilliant idea. As he couldn't continue down going forwards, why not try doubling back up the hill? He had the road run a ring around itself, erecting no supporting pillars but a bridge instead, under which the Nus de Sa Corbata, the "tie knot", completes its 360° curve.

In keeping with the sentiment of its creator, the road has made its way down the mountains without diminishing their size. Over a million cubic feet (31,000 m3) of mountain were removed by the laborers, only to be deposited further along the route to shore it up. The sole addition was tar, used as an adhesive.

A few yards further on from the Cúber reservoir, Paretti's "Snake" branches off down towards the sea.

Paretti's feat of civil engineering curls up from the serene Gorg Blau, the "blue pool".

The white gold of the mountains
Snowmen and their houses

*Quana les altes montanyes
Els cims blanquejen de neu,
També les planes blanquejen
amb la flor dels ametllers.*

The end of January and the beginning of February marks the period between winter and spring in Majorca. When the peaks of the mountains are white with snow, down in the valley the plains are covered in a pale carpet of almond blossom. Things then had to happen fast. There wasn't much time: two or three days, perhaps, in a harsh winter maybe a week, before the ice and snow disappeared and the meltwater in the *torrents* swept away everything it its path. There was a lot of hard work for the "snowmen" to do. When Tomàs Forteza wrote these words about Majorca in 1869, they still existed.

A *nevater,* a Majorcan snowman, has the arduous task of gathering snow and conserving it until it can be delivered to restaurants, butchers, fish shops and private

In winter, the *nevaters* collected snow from the highest peaks of the Tramuntana to sell as a refrigerant in the summer.

50

Majorca's mountains in snow, as depicted by Archduke Ludwig Salvator in his book on the Balearics.

households. Or rather had, for the last snowman stopped business in 1927.

The *nevaters* clambered up to the peaks of the highest mountains, the Puig Major, Massanella, Teix, and Tomir, to collect snow and ice and store it in their *cases desa neu,* snow houses. When temperatures started to rise in the spring, they began transporting their goods down from the mountains into the valleys. On the first, most difficult stage of the journey the snow was carried by pack-ass down to the next road, where it was loaded onto carts and wheeled to the consumer.

Until scientists had learned how electricity could be used to cool goods, the only source of refrigeration was nature. Until the

first ice works in Majorca came into operation it was down to the *nevaters* to collect snow and ice in the Tramuntana, to store it as long into the summer as possible and then carry it down to the valleys.

To this end they built *cases desa neu,* snow houses, in cool, shady places mostly pointing north. The buildings, which to our modern eyes seem quite strange, only protruded from the ground high enough for one window to be incorporated through which snow was shoveled inside. The main body of the construction, which was usually rectangular or oval, had to be dug into the cold, hard earth. To provide the best possible insulation, the snowmen covered the roofs with *carritx,* reeds bound together with rushes, or a combination of rushes and tiles called *canó i teulls,* and sometimes zinc. These natural refrigerators were of course not where the men lived and slept; they had their

houses in the nearest village.

According to historical documents, the practice of collecting and storing snow was common in Majorca from 1564 onwards or earlier. Some 42 *cases desa neu* are mentioned in ancient records, with over half of them supposedly located on Puig Major and the Monte de Massanella. There were also snow houses on the Teix, the Serra d'Alfàbia and the Tomir. Those fit on their feet wanting to trek up to the top of the Teix from Valldemossa pass one of these structures on their way to the summit.

The last snow house in Majorca ceased to run in 1927, when the first factory plants were already producing ice. The *nevaters* and their *cases desa neu* first became superfluous and were then forgotten. A few ruined walls in remote areas of the Tramuntana are all that's left now to remind visitors and Majorcans alike of a profession full of privation and hardship.

Paradise gardens
Alfàbia and Raixa

Pergolas smothered in dense green foliage, splashing fountains and tranquil pools in a subtropical world of plants at the old Arabian manor of Alfàbia enchant even those who normally have little time for the pleasures of horticulture. An avenue lined with plane trees runs as straight as an arrow to the ornate entrance portal. The Arabic inscription on the gatehouse thanks God for His creations, making a paradise garden such as this one possible: "Allah is the law. Allah is great. Grace comes from Allah. There is only one God. All riches lie in Allah."

Anyone who has visited a complex such as this can understand why the "desert religion" of Islam has chosen green as its color. Green is a rare commodity in the desert; caravan travelers spend much of their journey yearning for the next oasis and cool, fresh water. It's thus hardly surprising that the color has become synonymous with paradise. Like the Bible, the Koran describes the Garden of God as a place of peace and refreshment, a fertile land of plenty with shady trees and springs which never run dry. The creators of Moorish gardens – the most famous being those of the Alcázar in Seville and the Generalife in Alhambra in Granada – designed with this dream of paradise in mind, trying to make gardens which in their time were harmonious, peaceful and invigorating.

To their way of thinking, the green of paradise was also associated with green as the color of life. Their gardens were thus planted with an abundance of evergreens which were to bring the promise of the eternal spring of Eden to their country: palms, cypress trees, lavender, oleander, rosemary, box, ivy, laurel, acanthus, myrtle and thyme. Carefully placed flowering plants, such as wallflowers, carnations, roses, broom, irises, forget-me-nots, southernwood, lilies, cornflowers, violets and pansies, brought a splash of color and lively contrast to the green foliage; fruit trees, such as oranges and lemons, sweetened the air with their perfume. Steps, niches, low walls, trellises, benches and statues of animals split the garden up into sections, creating areas of intimacy and privacy for those who wished to be alone.

Another major component in the design of these often quite expansive paradise gardens was water and the various effects it

From the ancient Arabian estate of Raixa there are fantastic views out across olive groves to the Puig des Teix.

could be used to create. Fountains and cascades, small pools and wide reservoirs, water wheels and systems of canals not only irrigated the site but were also a popular design feature used to enhance the essence of the garden; fresh water cooled the air and caught the eye, opening up new perspectives with its reflections of the surrounding plants and trees.

This is true of Alfàbia. Date palms sway in the gentle breeze, their dense leaves conjuring up images of a desert oasis. Water plays an important role here, too: narrow channels, deep wells and tinkling fountains are not only here for decoration but also ensure that the many orange trees, cypresses, palms and sweet-smelling beds of flowers have enough moisture to survive in the dry climate. Ponds of water lilies which mirror the bamboo at their edges and a 72-arch arbor with fountains on both sides, dating from the 18th century, are special attractions. Arabian and European landscape gardening have combined to create a symphony in green.

Not far from Alfàbia is Raixa, also formerly an Arabian estate. In 1797 this was given to Cardinal Don Antoni Despuig i Dameto who came from one of the most important noble dynasties on the island, the counts of Montenegro. The cardinal, an aficionado of ancient art, had his gardens redesigned in a style befitting his hobby.

Landscaping at that time was dominated by the Italian technique. Like the cardinal count, whose enthusiasm for art bordered on obsession, many of the big landowners living in the capital of Palma selected Baroque and Neo-classical elements for the gardens at their *possessions,* their showpiece residences in the country. Strict geometrical forms overshadowed the beds laid out by Moorish gardeners, whose notion had been to keep the garden as natural as possible. Symmetry was the order of the day. Pompous flights of stone steps like the one which still dominates the garden at Raixa were constructed wherever there was room. Around them, flower beds, pergolas and gravel paths formed perfect circles, squares and rectangles. Fountains and ponds were placed meticulously to the left and right of the overall design, with pillars and statues added as a

The gardens at Alfàbia and Raixa read like a catalogue of the Mediterranean world of plants. Here, the cheerful blooms of yellow lilies delight the eye, …

… the heavy perfume of lilac trees in full bloom wafts down onto unsuspecting visitors, …

… while the Mediterranean dwarf fan palm provides cool shade under the trees.

The predilection for jungle green in combination with idyllic spots by the water at Alfàbia is the legacy of its first Arabian landscapers.

final mark of perfection. Despuig, whose favorite pursuit was archeology and who financed a number of excavations on the island, passionately indulged in the vogue for garden statues. Only a few can still be found here lining the famous steps; his successor, the count of Montenegro, sold most of them to Palma at the beginning of the 20th century.

The central stone staircase at Raixa with its 63 steps and dark green line of cypress trees is still a rewarding feature. The Majorcan writer Llorenç Villalonga found inspiration for one of his books in the stone steps and gardens here. His novel *Señor Bearn's Cabinet of Dolls,* which is often compared to Giuseppe Lampedusa's *Leopard,* traces the decline of the noble Bearn family at the end of the 19th century and stands for the lessening importance of the aristocracy in Majorca as a whole.

Regardless of the type of garden design you may personally prefer, a garden is inconceivable without water. The rectangular pond at Raixa, 330 feet (100 m) long, was for many years Majorca's largest reservoir. A bigger feature was made of the Baroque pool

in the 19th century, when a labyrinth of romantic, overhung paths leading to the pond was laid out.

With this, Raixa was once again in keeping with the fashions of the age. The romantic return to nature championed by

Below its low hill, the Renaissance façade of the stately manor house glows across the park.

the European garden architecture of the 19th century brought about changes in the parks and gardens of Majorca which still fascinate horticulturists from all over the world today. Man-made grottos, rockeries and waterfalls are hallmarks of the most lavish gardens where the wild, natural landscape has supplanted rationalist symmetry.

At Raixa, even Despuig demonstrated a partiality for the picturesque. He had a medieval window which had been removed from a destroyed monastery in Palma set into a ruin which was imaginative rather than authentic. In their quest for an "artistic naturalness", the gardens suddenly looked much as their Arabian predecessors had done. This and the successful blend of "elegant Italian proportion" and "English wilderness" make the garden at Raixa one of the most spectacular in Spain.

Only a handful of statues from the collection of amateur archeologist Despuig still adorn the 63 steps leading through the garden at Raixa.

The loggia at the manor house at Raixa looks out onto a Mediterranean paradise.

The "Vitamin C Express" from Palma to Sóller

Jogging along at a steady average speed you could almost keep up – for a short stretch at least. For the train from Palma to Sóller, known locally as "Red Lightning", takes an hour to cover just 16 miles (27 km). But what an hour! The train lazily chugs through the most beautiful part of the Tramuntana, past the olive groves at Bunyola and the romantic gardens at Alfàbia. The terrain is so steep in places that the only proof the train is actually moving is the countryside creeping past your window, as if in slow motion.

Red Lightning may not be Majorca's oldest railway, but it is without doubt the most leisurely and the most charming. And the one with the most misleading name; not only does it travel at nowhere near the speed of lightning, it isn't red either, but brown. When it first opened on 16 April 1912, decked with flowers and cheered into the brand new Art Nouveau station at Sóller, the train from Palma to Inca had been running for 37 years. This line is still open but, as the people of Sóller like to point out, it is only serviced by measly railcars. Red Lightning on the *Ferrocarril de Sóller* may also have an electric engine instead of the original steam, installed in 1929, but otherwise it is exactly as it was at

A much-polished plaque sparkles on the carriage door.

The "Vitamin C Express" has chugged along the 16 miles (27 km) to Palma from the Art Nouveau station at Sóller since 1912.

the beginning of the 20th century when the inhabitants of Sóller made their dream of a railway come true. It was paid for by the local community and ordered in England; the First Class carriages have leather seats, paneling in the finest mahogany and luggage racks made of leather straps which have proved indestructible over the years, while those traveling Second Class have faded wooden benches which are hard but honorably aged. As a special service there's even a separate compartment for locomotive-loving dogs.

The reason why Sóller of all places had the railway built was oranges, the town's number one export at that time. A delivery to Palma took ten hours on the roads and was dangerous, especially in winter, the main harvest period for oranges. Sóller needed a quicker means of transport which could carry as much of its produce as possible on one trip. The beginning of the 20th century had seen the discovery of vitamin C, with all its benefits to human health, and the demand for citrus fruit was enormous.

The people of Sóller thus clubbed together to raise the 3.5 million pesetas needed, which then was an incredible amount of money. Almost every family in town bought several of the 7,000 shares in the railway company for 500 pesetas apiece. They did it; in just three years, the line and train were finished and ready to run from Sóller station on the Plaça d'Espanya to the stop at Eusebi Estada in Palma. Or vice versa.

When in the mid-20th century the transportation of goods again took to the road,

Above: The mahogany paneling and leather seats have been in service since Red Lightning made its maiden voyage.

Right: Only the engine has changed, powered by electricity and not steam since 1929.

for a brief period it looked as if the "Vitamin C Express" would go out of business. This luckily wasn't the case; the quaint stretch of railway was discovered by tourists who found it a great attraction. While kids count the tunnels along the route, shouting "13!" at the end of the trip, adults can sit back and enjoy the fantastic scenery sliding past the window. And once a day, when the *Tren Turistic* extra service makes its only stop en route at a special platform, they can get out and snap away with their cameras for a whole ten minutes; the view from Mirador des Pujol d'En Banya is absolutely fantastic.

Valley of Gold
Sóller

How can you have a valley of gold on an island which apart from a modest quantity of brown coal has no mineral resources whatsoever? You can. The gold the Moors named *sulliar* after comes from the ground – after a fashion. We're not talking about the huge plantations of oranges here; the gold of the Moors was the dense liquid yielded by the many olive groves which encircled Sóller during Arab rule.

With its enormous *horta* or garden, the area around Sóller is still a golden valley – regardless of whether named so after its olives or its oranges. Some sources claim the name Sóller comes from the Arabian for shell, a pictorial and appropriate description for the town and its environs. Confined by four high mountains which isolate it from the rest of inland Majorca, Sóller huddles near the coast in a shallow valley basin.

The French in the Garden of Spain

Until well into the 20th century, Sóller and its economy were inextricably linked to the orange. At the close of the 18th century, French farmers, tradesmen, wine-growers and textile workers, who had fled here from a France in the throes of the Revolution, soon began organizing shipments of the fruit to their native country.

Back home, friends and relatives of the exiled French in Sóller opened the first stores selling citrus and tropical fruit from the exotic-sounding *Jardin d'Espagne,* garden of Spain. These shops built up an autonomous network of cooperatives which quickly expanded across the French border.

The good fortune which catapulted Sóller to riches and power was suddenly reversed in 1860. The orange plantations were decimated by pests, plunging Sóller into deep crisis after years of prosperity. Farmers who had just bought new land or started out in the orange business were hit the hardest, forcing them to leave Majorca

The church of Sant Bartomeu, with its delicate rose window, has watched over the hustle and bustle of the market place in Sóller since the 16th century.

In the early 19th century, French immigrants transformed Sóller's local orange trade into a flourishing international concern.

The Sóllerics not only know their stuff when it comes to oranges, they are also *au fait* with cakes and pastries, making *pastisseria* like this one impossible to pass without going in.

either for France or for Latin America, for Cuba, Puerto Rico and Venezuela.

The legacy of those who stayed and those who returned

This is why the fronts of the houses in Sóller are so different, each one disclosing the fate of its constructor. Those who remained during the crisis were rewarded with newfound wealth for their loyalty – due in part to the discovery of vitamin C and the growing demand for citrus fruit. They perfected their homes, built in the old Majorcan style, finishing exteriors with Marès stone, elegant entrance gates and courtyards and adding decorative portals, window frames and wrought-iron trellises and grilles.

Those returning home from the Caribbean also had to show that their new lives abroad had been successful. They erected Colonial urban palaces and indulged in the Neo-baroque and Neo-classical with pillars, temple gables, expensive house fronts in undressed stone and elaborate embellishments in wrought iron, many of which line the Gran Via, the main road running through Sóller.

Those who had emigrated to Europe were inspired by the fashions of the *fin de siècle,* Art Nouveau or *Modernismo* in Spanish. After Palma, Sóller is the most important town for Art Nouveau in Majorca. The façade of the parish church of Sant Bartomeu, for example, was designed by a pupil of Antoni Gaudí, Joan Rubió i Bellver, who was also responsible for the front of the *Banco Central Hispano* and the Villa Ca'n Prunera on the Carrer de Sa Lluna.

Besides the interesting effects the orange crisis had on the architecture of Sóller, there was a second positive aspect to the dilemma. A bankrupt manor house, the Camp d'En Prohorn on the edge of Sóller, was turned into the only botanical gardens on the island by a bank. Today, this is where the seeds of 1,700 autochthonous plants (only found in Majorca) are shock frozen. The gardens read like a text book on botany, with examples of the various shrubs and flowers which grow on the island on display, among them a large number of medicinal plants.

Handicap and gateway to the world: the harbor

Until the locals provided themselves with a comfortable, relatively fast way of getting across country with their railway in 1912, Sóller was completely cut off from the

Emigrants returned from abroad showed what they had achieved in the Caribbean by building elaborate urban palaces.

Left: Fornalutx often wins the prize for Spain's prettiest village.

Below: Beauty has never been of primary importance for the harbor of Port de Sóller; its main concern was protection and safety from pirates.

outside world in its remote valley basin. The harbor at Port de Sóller was thus its gateway to the world. The "orange sailboats", as the export ships which set sail for France were called, were heavily laden when they returned home to the protection of the almost circular bay. The *Sóllerics* used the ships to transport their shopping, having furniture, pots, carts and farm tools brought to them from France; considering the back-breaking haul through the mountains or the ten-hour journey by sea to Palma, this was the only viable alternative.

The harbor was also a major handicap, for where there was wealth, there were pirates. The attack in 1561, which laid the port to waste, finally compelled the inhabitants to fortify their harbor with mighty bulwarks. The fact that the Port de Sóller actually managed to defeat its opponents in 1561 against all odds is still the cause of much celebration. Like Port de Pollença, once a year Port de Sóller reenacts the battle for the town with its *Moros i Cristians* fête; the festivities last a whole week.

The two villages of Fornalutx and Biniaraix, just under three miles away in the mountains above Sóller, can also tell us a thing or two about raids by pirates, although today there are few reminders left of these violent times. Fornalutx regularly shines in competitions for the best-kept village in Spain, with its steep flights of steps, restored stone houses, balconies brimming with flowers and perfectly painted white door and window frames. Biniaraix plays host to the traditional meeting of artists in April, the *Trobada de Pintors des Barranc*.

A crack in the basin

The harbor's main purpose wasn't an aesthetic but a defensive one. Port de Sóller seems like a miniature copy of the Sóller valley in water form. The bay is an almost perfect circle. Flanked by fortifications and lighthouses at both ends, trading ships, fishing boats, yachts and naval vessels bob gently up and down on the ocean to the delight of the masses of camera-wielding tourists who come here each year.

For the seclusion of Sóller is now a thing of the past. In the mid-1990s a fast route to Sóller was finally supplied by a tunnel. Despite existing routes – and despite loud protest from local people and environmentalists – in 1995 the first holes were drilled into the mountainside. The project was marred by bribery and scandal, which in 1995 led to the then president of the Balearic government, Gabriel Canyellas, standing down. After more than eight hundred years of splendid isolation, the golden basin now has a crack in it.

With an impatient ringing of its bell, the tram from Sóller to Port de Sóller rattles along among the street cafés.

The fabulous fragrance of the south
Oranges

En los boschs naixen alsines,
En los plans arbres fruyters,
En la vall llargues rengleres,
D'olorosos tarongers ...

... are the words of the *Hymn of Praise to Majorca* written in 1869 by Tomas Forteza. He writes of the oak trees in the island's forests, of the fruit trees on the plains and mentions the long rows of fragrant orange trees in the valleys. He is referring to the *sulliar* of the Moors, the valley of gold near Sóller. The tram to Port de Sóller, the "Orange Express", passes so close to the orange trees in the Horta de Sóller that they're almost near enough to pick.

Everything revolves around the citrus here. It is even indirectly responsible for the Art Nouveau or *Modernisme* buildings in Sóller. When in 1860 the *horta* was plagued by disease and the orange plantations completely destroyed, many of the ruined villagers were forced to try and make a living elsewhere, emigrating to France, Belgium or Switzerland. Here they came across Art Nouveau – and liked it. When they returned to Sóller, affluent from their years in exile, they had Catalan architects design houses which were in keeping with the latest trend in Europe.

The Arabs had planted bitter oranges, *Citrus aurantium,* since the 11th century to decorate the courtyards of their palaces and their superbly designed gardens. The Sevilles were cultivated for their bewitching perfume, their *azahar,* and their legendary beauty. In 1523, the Duke of Bourbon was so

As if in the Garden of Eden, a solitary *finca* nestles among terraces of fragrant oranges.

enchanted by the dark green leaves and white blossoms of the *taronger,* the evergreen orange tree, that he immediately bought a tree grown by Eleanor of Castile and took it back with him to Fontainebleau to start the famous orangery there.

Bitter oranges were also used for medicinal purposes. The peel was chewed to sweeten the breath, their fragrance banished stale air from badly ventilated rooms and in the 17th century their juice was recommended as a tonic for "outbursts of seething rage".

The sweet orange, *Citrus sinesis,* comes from Southeast Asia, *sinesis* being a reference to the Latin word for China, Sina. The fruit with its sweet aroma was introduced to the Iberian Peninsula and Majorca by the Portuguese between 1520 and 1530. It has been cultivated in the sheltered valleys of Sóller, Andratx and Valldemossa since this date.

The island paved the way for the export of Spanish oranges towards the end of the 18th century, when the first "orange sailboats" sailed into port at Toulon and Marseille from Sóller, soon afterwards to travel on to harbors in the north of Europe. Demand for the fragrant product rose so steeply that in the 19th century long stretches of mainland coast from Tarragona to Alicante were planted with orange trees, whose yield soon trumped that of the Majorcan fruit farmers.

There are over 100 well-known varieties of the sweet orange found across the globe. In Majorca they are still cultivated using the system of mini-plantations set up in the 18th century. Some exporters have their own plantations, but most of the oranges are grown in relatively small areas, 80% of which are under two-and-a-half acres (one hectare). This system has demonstrated surprising flexibility in response to the growing demand for the fruit. Over the last 50 years, for example, many of the tiny plantations have managed to farm up to six different sorts of orange by grafting or to raise new cultivars.

The planting and harvesting of the golden citrus is carried out in much the same way as in the olden days. As soon as the orange groves bud in the spring, buyers from export companies travel to the land of the orange trees, inspect the coming crop and don't just order direct from the plantation but from the tree itself. The farmers and purchasers then discuss how the "reserved" fruit is to be tended until the harvest.

When in September the *taronges* are ripe, armies of pickers arrive from the exporter's. As soon as the dew has evaporated the harvesters begin filling their boxes and baskets. They have to work against the clock and the weather, for picking stops at the first sign of rain; the delicate fruit may on no account be packed when wet as it goes moldy.

The Majorcans have hundreds of recipes for oranges. They use them in salads, meat and fish dishes, ice cream, flans, mousse, marmalade and cakes. Or they simply pluck them from the laden trees, peel off the aromatic skin with practiced fingers and bite with relish into the juicy flesh.

An appetizing and flavorsome salad of oranges is the perfect accompaniment to any Spanish meal.

Radiant orbs of vitamin C are carefully packed in baskets during the harvest.

Ensalada de taronja

Orange salad

4 medium ripe oranges
2 sprigs of fresh mint
Salt, sugar, freshly ground white pepper
Olive oil
4 oz (100 g) small black olives (optional)

Cut the peeled oranges into slices and arrange on a platter. Season with salt, white pepper freshly ground from the mill and a pinch of fine white sugar.

Finely chop the fresh mint leaves and sprinkle over the orange slices. Drizzle generously with olive oil. The salad must be left to stand in the fridge for at least half an hour before serving.

Ensalada de taronja can be served as an unusual starter, a wonderfully light end to a Spanish dinner party or a refreshing snack between meals.

Global village
Deià

If you don't wish to spend the afterlife standing up, then don't die in Deià. Or, to be more precise, don't be buried here. Whether artist or aristocrat, those consigned to the grave at the cemetery in Deià rest in peace in the vertical position – due to lack of space. At least, this is the explanation locals give for the tiny headstones.

This hasn't stopped many people copying British writer Robert Graves and coming here not only for a quiet vacation but also for serenity in death. The high-lying graveyard is thus something of an attraction in itself. A tiny memorial plaque inscribed with the words "Robert Graves, Poeta" draws loyal admirers of the unconventional yet successful writer to Deià year after year. The world-famous author of *I, Claudius,* without whom Deià would not be what it is today, was buried at the cemetery at the foot of the Teix, the fifth-highest mountain on the island, in 1985. Bruno Neuhaus, a German painter, Baroness Gloria Victoria Ramirez, a relation of the Spanish royal family, and various other late celebrities accompany him here on his final journey. Upright.

Robert Graves, who became a permanent resident in the 1930s, wasn't the first famous foreigner to come to Deià. A travel guide reported a collection of strange and extravagant non-locals here as far back as in 1878. Almost all of these "outsiders", many of them now in their second or third generation like the Graves family, belonged to a community of freethinkers, young and old, who wanted to live out their very own philosophy of life in this remote village. Lured by the fame of the early artists' colony, they tried to settle here and in doing so found themselves exposed almost unintentionally to a very different kind of tourism, the kind long propagated by the Balearic island on its popular beaches.

From the beginning of the 20th century onwards the magnetism Majorca's fifth-smallest community held for authors, artists and musicians increased. Graves was followed by a number of creative Europeans and Americans – Anaïs Nin, Ava Gardner, Alec Guiness, Peter Ustinov, Gabriel García Márquez, Kingsley Amis, Alan Sillitoe and Anthony Burgess – who spent varying lengths of time in pursuit of peace, relaxa-

The first artists and writers arrived in Deià at the end of the 19th century, seeking to draw inspiration from the scenic solitude of the mountain village.

tion and inspiration in one of the most remote mountain villages on the island.

Village world

Peace and quiet in Deià is now a thing of the past, yet the village has remained secluded thanks to its precipitous seaside road which

boldly sidesteps the chasms carved into Majorca's west coast.

The name Deià comes from the Arabic *ad daia* which more or less stands for village. And this is exactly what Deià still is. The Moors planted fruit and vegetables in its terraced gardens. Following the *Reconquista* these were enlarged, with olives and citrus fruit being cultivated at heights of up to 2,000 feet (600 m). Fishing and sheep farming helped vary the villagers' diet. So that it was in a better position to defend itself against pirate attacks and the bitter north winds, the village grew with its back to the sea. This is how it stands today.

Wedged in between mountains, sea, and forest, Deià basks in the sun.

On a small hill, a mere 692 feet (211 m) high and simply called Es Puig, the mountain, stone houses the color of earth with brilliant green shutters look out over the sea

The contrast couldn't be greater; only a few hundred yards from Deià this sheep has the mountain all to itself.

Many here earn an extra crust from the fruit which grows on Deià's mountainsides.

and Deià's bay, one of the most inaccessible and most beautiful on the northwest coast. Up on top of the hill is the focal point of the village, the church of Sant Joan Baptista, with clusters of houses scattered around it. In the village, steep paths lead past buildings akin to small fortifications, built to protect those inside from marauding corsairs. Vines creep up the walls of old houses lovingly restored by their new owners, marigolds provide color with their pink and orange blossoms, palm and cypress trees sway in the wind. This little hamlet is heaven on earth – and its inhabitants know it. And want it to stay that way. The coaches crammed full of day-trippers crawling through Deià at a snail's pace can't stop for long, as the village has no parking lots for large vehicles. It doesn't want them; it wants everything to carry on as it always has done. And luckily –

for Deià, at least – it does. By remaining obstinate on matters concerning coach parks and planning permission, the people of Deià have achieved a lot for their beautiful home. It rests on the little hill at the foot of the Teix as unspoiled as it was when Robert Graves first set eyes on it in 1927.

Deià, the rich, and the beautiful
As shocked as the villagers of neighboring Valldemossa were by George Sand's lifestyle in 1838 and as quickly as they wanted to be rid of her – although they could charge her double for everything she bought – less than a hundred years later the people of Deià had learned to greatly appreciate what tourism had brought to their village: money. Many were delighted, selling most of their worldly possessions to the new arrivals. The consequences of this communal move to get rich

quick are still evident today; the local dialect in Deià is English mixed with a smattering of *Mallorquí* and is spoken all year round. Over a third of the inhabitants are from outside Spain.

The local consensus is that the numbers should stay at that. Unlike when Robert Graves was alive, it's now much harder for non-residents of Deià to find a home here. Unless you happen to be a Hollywood movie star and have a wife who originates from Majorca (and provided you have the necessary million or two), in which case you might be lucky enough to procure one of the very few desirable residences up for sale in the district of Deià. Like Michael Douglas. He was fortunate enough to buy the secluded villa of S'Estaca from the heirs of the Son Marroig estate, built by *Arxiduc* Ludwig Salvator in mock-Moorish style. The houses in the famous artists' colony are expensive and you can only build on plots of land which you can call your own and which must measure over 160,000 square feet (15,000 m2).

Lack of space is thus not only a problem for the deceased but also for the sun-loving living who have set their sights on romantic Deià as their holiday domicile. In the mountain village where the number of inhabitants totals a mere 600, concrete bunkers are an alien concept. The few hotel rooms and cottages rented out in the summer have gone to loyal regulars for years – writers, painters and actors from all over the world – who pay extortionate prices for them.

Some speak of the "ghetto of the rich", where the beautiful and affluent lend Deià the air of decadence it often adopts. Exclusive boutiques, half-hidden art galleries, not one but two luxury hotels and a number of excellent restaurants, where the crowned heads of Spain dine from time to time whilst on their traditional vacation in Majorca, "in" parties and other "musts" provide them with plenty of opportunities to show themselves off to the world.

Apart from an interesting museum of archeology, the village also holds a music festival, the *Festival de Deià,* in July and August. The events aren't advertised; they don't need to be, with a grapevine which functions better than any marketing campaign. The wooden pews in the church are full to bursting every night of the festival – often with people who have never been to a church service before in their lives.

The caves on the beach at Deià have been turned into boathouses.

Poet in Deià
Robert Graves

His grave is covered by a plain headstone simply marked "Poeta". It's hidden in a corner of the village cemetery, not that easy to find, right next to the church. Sometimes there are flowers on it. The sentiment of the inscription, modest yet discriminating, is that of a life led on a tightrope, like walking along the narrow ridge of the Sera del Norte, trying not to slip off and end up in limbo somewhere between emotion and kitsch, statement and sermon, dream and reality.

When Robert Graves died in 1985 at the age of 90, his fame as a man of letters had traveled all over the world. Born in Wimbledon in England in 1895, he studied philosophy and history at Oxford, as befitted the educated classes in England. An officer during the First World War, he came back from the trenches with a catalogue of traumatic experiences, seriously wounded and almost having been buried alive. He recovered and then embarked on his career as a writer, experimenting with verse and nature poetry until his breakthrough in 1929 with the satirical autobiography of his war years, *Goodbye to All That.*

At the time his novel was published, Graves had been living for three years with both his wife Nancy Nicholson, a feminist with whom he had four children, and the eccentric American writer Laura Riding. His friend Gertrude Stein managed to persuade him to put an end to the chaos and Laura helped him decide which of the two women he should keep. After her attempted suicide, the couple fled England and a pending court case for attempted murder to Majorca.

After only a few luxurious days in Palma's Gran Hotel, in 1929 Graves bought a house on the edge of Deià which he christened Can Alluny, "remote house". With printing equipment delivered from England, he and Laura began publishing works they had written at their own Seizin Press. The hand press still exists, run by Graves' youngest son Thomas in Deià.

Robert Graves moved to Majorca in 1929 where he lived until his death in 1985.

A simple gravestone marked "Poeta", poet, in the cemetery at Deià commemorates the famous writer from Wimbledon.

Graves' mistress Laura Riding was both his muse and his sharpest critic, hounding him from one crisis to another with her merciless remarks. Graves soon began to doubt whether he had chosen the right woman; Laura became more and more of a tyrant who barely had a kind word for either Graves or his work. In 1931 he voiced his self-doubt in a poem entitled *To whom else?,* where he recognizes that he has become a stranger to himself through his lover.

The relationship didn't survive the turmoil of the Spanish Civil War, during which the couple were forced to leave Spain. In 1939 Laura found another man in the United States, driving Graves to even deeper despair. His life only took a sudden turn for the better when he met and fell in love with Beryl Pritchard – and married her.

At the end of the Second World War he returned with his new wife to his steady amour of the 1930s, Deià, this time for good. His second marriage and second attempt to set up home on the island at last proved successful. Graves appeared to settle down and find inner peace.

A house in the country

In the 1950s Graves' writing career began to earn him international acclaim. He, Beryl and their four children were able to live comfortably off the royalties his publications brought in with increasing regularity. While the children were still at school, the family divided their time between Deià and Palma, where Graves had bought two apartments in a prefab block. So that the youngsters could have a normal education, during term-time he and his wife lived in one of the Palma apartments and the children in the other.

The historical topics Graves so often favors for his narratives and treatises are perhaps due to his being a descendant of the German historian Leopold von Ranke. His two most famous historical novels, *I, Claudius* and *Claudius the God,* were published in 1934. *King Jesus* followed in 1946 and *Homer's Daughter* nine years later. Detailed study of Greek history and mythology prompted him to write a novel entitled *The Golden Fleece* in 1944. His scholarly essays on Greek and Celtic mythology attest to his extensive knowledge of the subject. In 1960 his translations of Homer won an award. In 1968 he was given a gold medal in Mexico for his work as a whole and in the same year received the coveted Gold Medal for lyric poetry. He was made a member of the American Academy of Poets and was short-listed for the Nobel prize, even if he never received it.

Although he is best known for his novels, Graves saw them as a means to an end, as a way of earning a living, leaving him

Shaded by olive trees, Graves discusses the filming of *I, Claudius* with Alec Guiness.

free to indulge his passion for lyric poetry. Graves published over 20 volumes of verse and over 30 collections of poems, which he constantly reworked.

That he considered himself a poet and not a novelist is also evident in the fact that the topics of his novels usually bore little relation to his current situation, whereas his poems dealt with it in depth. The latter brought Graves academic repute; he lectured on poetry in Cambridge in 1951 and in Oxford from 1961 to 1966, besides giving numerous talks in America and Europe.

Talk of the idyllic life the Graves led in Majorca soon did the circuit of the literary world. Alec Guiness, Peter Ustinov, and Gabriel García Márquez rapidly packed their belongings and sped off to Graves' "remote house" near Deià. The miniature amphitheater dug into the hills below Graves' home provided the ideal stage for readings and discussion.

In 1955 the queen of Hollywood, Ava Gardner, arrived in Deià. Graves was completely captivated by the beautiful actress and dedicated a poem of love to her, *Can't Sleep,* and then a story entitled *A Toast to Ava Gardner,* which later also appeared in his book on Deià, *Majorca Observed.* In his stories Deià is called Binijiny, where the poet is such a composite part of the village

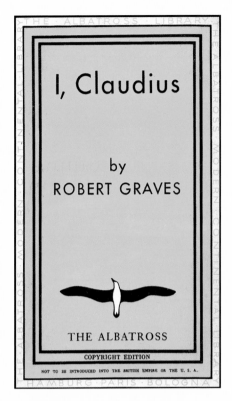

I, Claudius the novel was published in 1934, yet it was the film which brought Graves world acclaim.

that the locals respectfully refer to him as "Don Roberto".

Seeing Graves' home merely as a beacon for the jet set of film and literature would not be doing justice to his life's work. Graves spent his entire lifetime trying to bring some sort of equilibrium to his existence as a writer. His poetry is an attempt to balance narcissistic self-admiration with a cynical distance to the self, emotional candor with rational control, the archaic dominance of his urges and desires with modern intellectual logic or – to put it in the words of Nietzsche – Apollo with Dionysos.

Exclusive tourism
Valldemossa

The road from Palma climbs steeply, winding its way up into the mountains around Valldemossa. It spirals past dark green cypress and spindly carob trees. Beyond the last bend, which opens out onto a fertile valley, an ochre church steeple suddenly juts up into the sky. Stone houses jostle beneath it, their green shutters providing a splash of color which mirrors the foliage of the garden landscape around them. The ancient farming village on the mountain towers proudly above the orchards and olive groves which huddle in terraces below it.

This is what Valldemossa must have looked like when what was probably Majorca's most famous tourist couple first

Lovingly maintained, Valldemossa is like an open-air museum. Even its most famous visitors, George Sand and Frédéric Chopin, couldn't fail to be captivated by its beauty.

set eyes on it in November 1838. The road was maybe a little narrower then; where coachmen once argued over who had the right of way, there's now room for two buses packed with tourists to pass alongside one another. Despite the passage of time, the area is still tinged with romanticism.

Foreign visitors flock to the idyllic town of Valldemossa in droves – not to see the wonderful gardens and houses smothered in flowers but to try and recapture some of the romance which blossomed between French writer George Sand and Polish composer Frédéric Chopin all those years ago.

The Valldemossa of Sand and Chopin can still be found only in the lower reaches of the village, in whose narrow, steep streets inquisitive tourists seldom stray. Here, hundreds of pelargoniums shower carpets of red blossoms from the window sills. The air is filled with pleasant smells; a baker takes warm, yeast *ensaïmada* out of the oven, ready for his customers to eat with their breakfast or afternoon coffee.

The fantastic setting of its onion fields

and lemon groves has given the little town its name. During the Arab period the area was known as *Vall d'en Mussa,* the valley of Musa. Musa, the *wâlí* of Majorca who represented the rulers of the island, the caliphs of Córdoba, was the owner of the estate here. He had the stones and boulders cleared from the land until the valley at the foot of the Puig des Teix had been transformed into tiers of lush pastures.

The Arabian estate fell into decline following the Christian Reconquest of the island. In its place, King Jaume II of Majorca erected a small summer residence in Valldemossa at the beginning of the 14th

The monastery and its well-tended gardens were intended to accommodate twelve monks. A special ruling allowed a thirteenth member to be admitted to the brotherhood to work in the monastery pharmacy.

The monks devoted their time to the copying of books in the days before the invention of the printing press.

century, which was presented to the Carthusians of Tarragona soon afterwards in 1349. By this time the independent kingdom of Majorca was a thing of the past; the elegant palace lay in ruins and the monks had to redevelop the site, turning it into the monastery which still dominates the most popular village in Spain today.

One of the monastery's gems is the pharmacy, which has been completely restored. All kinds of bottles and jars containing ancient remedies adorn long, wooden shelves. The religious communities of the Carthusians usually numbered just twelve monks; here in Valldemossa an exception was made to include a thirteenth who was responsible for the physical welfare of his brothers and whose realm was the pharmacy.

The permanent silence at the monastery of Jesús Natzaré was only broken by the scratching of inked quills on parchment, for the monks spent much of their time copying books. The valuable collection at the library includes many of these handwritten manuscripts.

A good number of the houses in Valldemossa are decorated with tiles depicting St. Catalina, who was born here in the Carrer de la Rectoria on 1 May 1531.

Where the upper village revolves around the disparate lovers, the lower part of town is the dominion of the only saint Majorca has produced. Highly esteemed, the "patron saint of maids" is known affectionately as *Beateten* by the Majorcans, a comparative of *Beata,* the blessed – although she has long been canonized. The parish church of Sant Bartomeu in Valldemossa is devoted to the life of St Catalina; just behind the church a Catalina fountain can be found splashing,

and her place of birth has been turned into a small chapel.

Catalina Tomàs went into service as a maid at the estate of Raixa near Bunyola. Whilst out working the fields, she built an altar of stones, had visions and performed miracles. A nobleman from Palma ensured that the devout Catalina was given a religious education and accepted at the Augustinian convent at the age of 21. Despite being asked many times, she never took on the post of abbess and died a simple nun in 1574. Through her bishop, Don Diego Arnedo of Majorca, the "secretary of God" brought influence to bear on the Council of Trent called by the Catholic church in reaction to the Reformation. She was made a saint in 1930 and lies in state in a glass shrine at the convent church of Santa María Magdalena on the Plaça Santa Magdalena in Palma, where she lived until her death. Valldemossa pays homage to the God-fearing maid with a bronze statue which stands outside her birthplace.

Majorca's only saint, Santa Catalina Tomàs, was born in Valldemossa. With this votive picture from the monastery's collection, a sailor thanks her for a safe passage home.

This is what the monastery in Valldemossa must have looked like when George Sand came here with her beloved Frédéric Chopin.

Lonely nocturnes
George Sand and Frédéric Chopin

"Monkeys" was the word she used to describe the people of Valldemossa, expressing simply and clearly that she neither held her hosts in high esteem nor felt particularly at home here: "So we were alone in Majorca, no less isolated than if we had been living in a desert; and when we had done battle with the monkeys and won our daily bread, we used to sit together around the stove and laugh at it all." Although the vacation George Sand and Frédéric Chopin spent in Majorca in the winter of 1838/39 is probably the most famous, it's also – hopefully – the least typical for the island.

There was little of the usual romanticism, idyll, lovers' bliss and paradisiacal island solitude to Chopin's and Sand's Majorcan sojourn. Yet strangely enough, it's this which seems to attract an incredible number of inquisitive holiday-makers each year. They are carted here in coaches in their thousands, eagerly searching for the spark of passion in the remnants of an illicit liaison between two famous people.

Townsfolk and farmers
Majorca was recommended to George Sand by people who believed themselves to be well acquainted with life on the island, with its people and climate. Her choice of destination was, however, a banal mistake which was sadly to become a tragedy. To start with, everything seemed fine; at first, the writer brimmed with enthusiasm for her temporary home. The country and the people were ideal for her "honeymoon" with Chopin. In her first letters she championed the locals as being the perfect example of people who had maintained a healthy simplicity and an unadulterated character – a romantic misunderstanding.

How rapidly the views of the sophisticated, worldly-wise George Sand changed. The Baroness Dudevant, née Amandine Aurore Lucie Dupin, and her companion Chopin had to leave their lodgings at Son Vent in Establiments near Palma after only a few days, as the landlord feared he could catch tuberculosis from the indisposed composer. The couple also had to pay for the entire "contaminated" furnishings which the landlord had burnt. In the remote village of Valldemossa, where they sought refuge, the people of the Majorcan hinterland spurned George Sand's predilection for wearing men's clothes and found her taste for cigars and pipes "unfeminine".

What really irritated the conservative mountain dwellers was not so much Sand's

When Chopin looked out from his monk's cell, the trees were bare. The Majorcan mountain winter was extremely detrimental to the ailing Chopin.

mode of dress but the fact that Madame had settled herself down in what only three years previously had been the working monastery of Sa Cartoixa de Jesús de Natzarè, with her two children, 15-year-old Maurice and 10-year-old Solange, her lady's maid Amélie – and a lover six years her junior.

As a punishment they were sold turnips and potatoes at extortionate prices. George Sand wreaked her revenge; in her memoirs, Un hiver à Majorque (A Winter in Majorca), available at every souvenir shop in town, she branded the villagers greedy thieves. The book – a tirade of hatred against the people of Valldemossa and a declaration of love to the scenery of Majorca – is by no means a spontaneous record of her journey, nor was it even written at the place where the events took place. It was put on paper three years later in 1841 as a caustic reminder of an ill-fated period in their lives.

Madame Sand went around Valldemossa in men's clothing and smoked cigars.

In *Winter in Majorca* George Sand noted down her impressions of the island for generations of readers to come.

The spirits of music

The Polish composer and French baroness had met in Paris and fallen in love a few months prior to coming to the Balearic island. They had planned their winter vacation in Majorca as a kind of honeymoon, yet their stay ended in disaster.

On 13 February 1839 they more or less had to flee the island. The cold, wet winter in Valldemossa was extremely detrimental to the health of the ailing Chopin. He coughed and shivered his days away in the unheated cells at the monastery whilst his energetic mistress undertook long walks through the unspoiled, wet mountain countryside. Despite the inclement conditions, Frédéric Chopin managed to compose many of his wonderful *Préludes* with numb fingers on an untuned

That Chopin visibly deteriorated both physically and mentally here is something the monastery prefers to conceal from its visitors.

immortalized composer on its mahogany base, allow daring but nervous fingers to brush across the ancient chairs, take a peak out of the little window – and find themselves back outside.

Cells 2 and 4 are the ones crammed with cultural mementos which await the paying guests. In all truth, they probably have no connection whatsoever to the romantic fiasco. It is more likely that the two lovers spent those distant winter months in cell 3. Access to these rooms – each cell consisted of three chambers – is prohibited. The walls which allegedly witnessed Chopin and Sand in intimate embrace remain out of sight, although they alone could attest to the unhappiness experienced here.

Chopin's condition caused Sand great anxiety: both his physical and mental state. His imagination roamed a place which at the time was a popular setting for the Gothic novel: "The monastery had been full of phantoms for him even when he felt well. But he never complained; I had to guess what ailed him. Once, when my children and I returned from our nocturnal prowlings among the ruins we found him, at ten o'clock, sitting at his piano pale as death, with haggard eyes and hair standing almost on end. It took him quite half a minute to recognize us. Then immediately he made an effort at laughter and played us the sublime things that he had just composed – and at the same time revealed to us the terrible, nerve-racking ideas that had forced themselves on him in his hours of loneliness, grief and terror."

During the composer's time in Majorca, three different doctors diagnosed the weakening Chopin with consumption and predicted an early death. The determined George Sand refused to accept such a condemning verdict. Chopin also mocked the prophesy, living another ten years before he died of tuberculosis in 1848.

When he did eventually fall seriously ill, Sand nursed him selflessly for many years. She remained true to her motto of "I love therefore I am!" which had also marked her relationship to the famous composer, even if

piano; one of the pieces, the *Raindrop Prelude,* conjures up the winter weather of Valldemossa. His own Pleyel piano was not released by customs and arrived a day before he left Valldemossa. Both pianos are on display at the former Carthusian monastery.

Hoards of culture-hungry tourists – in the 1990s about 300,000 per year, half the total number of inhabitants on the island – shuffle past both instruments through the two cells that were supposedly inhabited by George Sand and Frédéric Chopin. They gawk at the few contemporary paintings, etchings, letters and original documents, among them the *Winter in Majorca* manuscript, admire the cerebral bronze bust of the

there was "no active eroticism" between them, as she later admitted.

In honor of the composer's work a Chopin festival is held once a year in the summer months of July and August, bringing first-class virtuosi from all over the world to the little village in the mountains.

Chopin composed at the monastery, yet his own piano only arrived one day before his departure.

Son of Light
Archduke Ludwig Salvator in Majorca

The Majorcan album of anecdotes includes the tale of a farmer who in 1873 set off for Son Marroig to catch a glimpse of a supposed madman, of someone who had paid an inordinate sum of money for a plot of stony land in the precipitous northwest of the island the farmer considered completely worthless. He found his lunatic sitting contentedly on a stone, drawing: none other than Archduke Ludwig Salvator of Habsburg, cousin to Emperor Franz Josef of Austria.

At the time, the *S'Arxiduc* as he was called in *Mallorquí,* was just 25. Four years previously he had published his first book on Majorca, on the insects found on his beloved Balearic island.

Ludwig Salvator of Habsburg preferred Majorca to life at court in Vienna. He had an Italian marble pavilion built at Son Marroig.

To the curious farmer, the archduke was probably just another idiot with more money than sense who, for God knows what reason, had decided to live a life of idleness on an island, without getting anywhere near to understanding its hidden secrets and true significance. The farmer's opinion would have been shared by the court in Vienna – who would have been just as misguided in their assumptions.

For Ludwig Salvator and Majorca were to build up such an intimate, detailed and in all respects extraordinary relationship that today we can only shake our heads in reverent wonder. During his lifetime he was awarded the honorary titles "Famous Son of the City" and "Famous Adopted Son of the Balearics" by Palma and the island government and almost every village has a street named after him. It took a while, but the island finally came to understand the man who loved it so.

A Mediterranean Habsburg

The archduke had come to Majorca because he didn't belong anywhere else. Although his name and title suggest otherwise, Ludwig Salvator was not deeply rooted in the imperial and royal regime of his noble cousin. German was just one of his two native languages; he was born into the silky light of Tuscany and not under the wet skies of Central Europe, the year being 1847 and the place Florence. Ludwig Salvator was the fourth eldest child of Grand Duke Leopold II of Habsburg-Tuscany, who had married a daughter of Francis I, the king of Two Sicilies, the royal Archduchess Maria Antonietta.

The first twelve years of the archduke's life in Florence were the only ones spent at a permanent home in the bosom of his family. The Garibaldi revolt then swept through Italy, forcing the grand duke and his brood to flee to Brandeis near Prague.

This marked not only the end of a childhood relatively untroubled for his social class but also of the freedom from Vienna. Ludwig Salvator was sent to the Theresianum in Vienna where he shone in many subjects and especially in his remarkable talent for languages. At the university in Prague he not only studied law and philos-

The main home of *S'Arxiduc* was the Son Marroig *finca* near Deià, now a museum.

ophy as planned – which in itself was only just about acceptable to the Viennese court – but also the sciences and archeology, as if he could postpone the next inevitable phase in his education.

As third in line to the imperial throne he was earmarked for a career in the military. He had inherited the command of the 58th foot regiment at birth and was now scheduled to attend the Sankt Stefan military academy in Vienna to train as a cavalryman. Yet Salvator, who took after no-one in his family, who with his defiant streak had dropped out and swam against the tide, instead completed the "high sea master's certificate for long journeys" – miles from the sea. Vienna was shocked.

A bride in flames and Majorca

To try and force the black sheep back to the fold, the emperor made the 19-year-old archduke governor of Bohemia and Moravia in the Prague Hradcany castle. During a military parade, which Ludwig Salvator had to inspect as commander of the 58th foot regiment, a terrible accident occurred. His bride, Princess Mathilde, was so bored on her balcony that she tried to smoke a cigarette without anyone noticing. Her dress caught fire; layer upon layer of skirts and petticoats burned, turning Mathilde into a living torch, with no time to undo laces,

The archduke (back right) – with his three elder brothers – often had a faraway look in his eyes.

bows, and hooks and eyes. She died a terrible, agonizing death.

Perhaps out of love for Mathilde or perhaps because this was the final proof that the life he was expected to lead was not for him, the archduke took the tragedy as the grounds for doing something for which there was no word in those days; he dropped out. Illness came to his aid; the palace doctors prescribed that he go south for a change of climate to cure his asthma.

Thus he first came to Majorca as Count of Neuendorf in 1867, barely 20 years old, drinking up the simple life on the island like a man dying of thirst. He was intoxicated by it, spellbound, and fell hopelessly and blissfully in love with the mountains of the Tramuntana, the cliffs along the bays and the steep coastline, the never-ending blue of the sky and the sea, the ancient olive tress, the young girls working the fields – and their male counterparts. Two years of travel and study passed in this paradise, with Majorca the focal point and Ludwig Salvator's book on insects the result.

Years of departure and arrival

However, he wasn't settled – yet. His restiveness, coupled with the lack of a place he could

Salvator had the ruinous manor house of S'Estaca turned into a Moorish palace for his mistress, Catalina Homar.

call home and where he felt he belonged, compelled him to set off around the world time and again. For Ludwig Salvator, travel must have been a mixture of passion and enjoyment on the one hand and almost an addiction, an uncontrollable restlessness, on the other; in a letter he called this unrest his "demonic urge to travel". He wrote of his "affliction" at greater length in *Um die Welt ohne zu wollen* (Around the World – Involuntarily), published in 1881.

Yet wherever he was in the world, there was always one place which embraced him like a lover, which awoke in him the desire to be allowed to return, which made him feel human: Majorca. He thus came back, began exploring the country and buying up land in the northwest of the Serra de Tramuntana. He chose a place called Son Marroig as his main home, a *finca* with a defensive tower and thick walls protecting the estate on the side flanked by mountains and romantic, dreamy loggias and terraces which let in the light of the south on the side looking out across the sea. He had a marble pavilion shipped in from Italy and erected at Son Marroig with a view out towards the Na Foradada peninsula. Here he would sit and

listen, enraptured, to the *bufador,* the roar, thunder and crashing of the waves on the rocks. Son Marroig is the only one of the archduke's three estates open to the public.

Then came Estaca, which at the time of Ludwig Salvator's purchase was a derelict manor house. He had it torn down and built in its place a gleaming white Moorish palace for the love of his life, complete with decorative merlons. Estaca now belongs to

American actor Michael Douglas and his Majorcan wife who – unfortunately yet understandably – don't take kindly to inquisitive visitors.

His last acquisition was Miramar, which still belongs to his family and is used as a weekend retreat and hunting lodge. This is where Ludwig Salvator spent the rest of his days, in a residence worthy of his title and status, in a fantasy castle of Marès stone and marble, in a dream-come-true built by an eccentric but contented figure living in self-imposed Majorcan exile.

Naturally nature
One of the most distinguishing and remarkable traits of the *Arxiduc's* character was his rapport with living things. Unable to harm any plant or animal or see it destroyed unnecessarily, he took up the cause of nature. Unlike the spirit of the age, which loved to see nature controlled and kept in check, nothing would have been more alien to the archduke than to landscape his bit of Majorca into an ordered design. On the contrary: if he had to lay out paths, then he made sure that they blended in perfectly with their surroundings, becoming almost

Time and again a "demonic urge to travel" enticed the cousin of Emperor Franz I of Austria away from Majorca to explore the wide world.

invisible. He patrolled and protected his stretches of forest as if they were areas of top security.

He was particularly fond of olive trees. In his book *Die Balearen* (The Balearics) he wrote with an enthusiasm verging on euphoria, very different from his usual matter-of-fact, descriptive observations almost devoid of comment: "The olive trees in Majorca grow very old and it is not uncommon to come across *Olivares* which surely date back to the 16th or 17th century. Mature trees take on the most adventurous, knotted forms, often intertwined with one another and almost always hollow, yet still full of life, hence the saying that it is impossible to kill an olive tree. Some reach a considerable height; the largest I have found on the island is near Palma and is called the *S'Olivera de sa Pó* (the olive tree of fear), a name which may have been generated by some superstition or other." Ludwig Salvator's fascination with and respect for these mystical trees was so great that he wouldn't allow ancient specimens which no longer bore fruit to be felled or even pruned.

His attitude to animals was similar. Horses on their way to the slaughterhouse and dogs too old to be of any use to their owners were rescued and paid for by the archduke. Aged mounts stumbled around the paddocks on his estates where jaded hunting dogs were allowed to pant away their last hours in peace and quiet. For Ludwig Salvator, nature was not something which man should attempt to master. The way he managed his land in Majorca shows that he felt at one with his surroundings and saw himself and his dominions as a small part of an expansive, magnificent, erudite whole. His landscape-friendly masterpiece around Son Marroig, preserved in all its unspoiled beauty as if under a glass dome, was later turned into the first nature reserve in Majorca, the Son Moragues Park.

Catalogs, caravan routes, and terms of endearment

Leaving nature to do as she wishes was only one of the achievements of the archduke's sojourn in Majorca. His other was to describe his natural environment and everything which lived and breathed in it. A born

scientist and explorer, Ludwig Salvator was compelled to note down everything he found out about his surroundings, everything he studied, observed and analyzed. New expeditions fuelled by his "travel demon" took him away from Majorca on his steamer yacht *Nixe* and a new book returned with him. He had most of his works published in Prague, not with the idea of selling them, but so that he could give them away as presents.

His best-known work, a compendium numbering nine hefty volumes in its original size and entitled simply *Die Balearen* (The Balearics), earned him a gold medal at the 1899 World Exposition in Paris and today fetches almost its weight in gold in antique shops. With this work, incredible for its dimensions alone, Salvator has left a memorial to himself.

The books describe the Balearic Islands in all disciplines of learning then practiced down to the tiniest detail: geography and geology, flora and fauna, agriculture and industry, stock breeding and forestry, the tax and traffic systems, art history and administration. One of his main areas of attention is directed to the inhabitants of the island and their way of life. Whereas in his observations of the smaller islands of Ibiza, Menorca and Formentera he concentrates on the essentials, with Majorca he seized the opportunity to perform a detailed anthropological,

For Ludwig Salvator, nature was something to be preserved at all costs. He permitted neither the felling of olive trees nor the shooting of aged animals on his lands.

The archduke's masterpiece, his nine-volume compendium entitled *Die Balearen* (The Balearics), was the result of 22 years of detailed study.

ethnographical and social study. Physical build and character, hygiene and education, language and science, religion and superstition, local costumes and customs, family life and festivals: nothing escaped the vigilant, Argus-eyed archduke.

Ludwig Salvator was naturally not one to favor the use of platitudes and assumptions; he was totally adverse to generalizations and negligent comments. In a businesslike manner he pertinently worked his way from plant to plant, from animal to animal, omitting neither the special steering mechanism for luxury vehicles nor the Ibizan version of an agricultural implement, describing a peasant girl in her Sunday best with the same dedication as a high-ranking priest in his splendid vestments. Where words were not enough or images could not be formed in the mind of the reader, the archduke had illustrations, minute architectural sketches and engravings made from his own drawings. Scenes from life in the

Sweet Nothings and Terms of Endearment in the Language of Friuli.

Sissy and Artemis pay a visit

Whilst the archduke was busy nurturing his literary bent, at the court in Vienna the wildest rumors were being spread about the drop-out "Don Balearo". His nephew, Archduke Leopold Ferdinand, gossiped about Salvator having established "a kind of harem", living "like a patriarch" in a simple country house "with his many wives and children, who run around half-naked and at midday are whistled to the table to partake of the family meal" by the archduke himself. Empress Sissy was sent to Majorca to see what was going on. She remarked: "What I have built in Corfu is nothing compared to this." What else she saw she chose not to mention in Vienna, even after her second trip to Majorca, accompanied by her favorite deer, Artemis. The unhappy, tamed empress, who spent her entire life wrangling with the Viennese court, was the only member of the royal household to understand, even admire, Ludwig Salvator's nonconformity, courage, desires – and his living his life as he saw fit.

What Sissy discovered at the archduke's would have caused even greater scandal in Vienna. Ludwig Salvator, whose life in Majorca was heavily dependent on his friendship with the inhabitants of the island and moreover on his liking for Majorcan

country, appliances for the house, farm and field, furniture, entrances, courtyards and even working animals are depicted in words and pictures, as lifelike as photos in a photograph album, in a unique, graphic inventory of the island at the close of the 19th century which was the first of its kind. Thumbing through this catalog of the Balearics, totally absorbed and with perhaps a tinge of astonishment, you may ask yourself just how the archduke came to compile such an authoritative work. Was he like one possessed, lost among piles of notes and slips of paper labeled "Don't forget!"? Did he hunt and hoard information with Central European precision in an

attempt to bring some sort of order to the effervescent variety of the Mediterranean? However he did it, one thing is certain: Salvator was an extremely disciplined, determined and conscientious author. If he hadn't been, this book would either not exist at all or only in measly fragments.

He spent 22 years working on *The Balearics,* during which he was also compiling at least 20 other titles, among them *The Caravan Route from Egypt to Syria* and *A Flower from a Golden Country* or *Los Angeles in South California.* He mentioned his love of Majorca in over a dozen books and also dealt with such obscure topics as

The archduke always brought the materials for at least one new book back with him from his travels.

The deed of purchase for *Nixe,* previously called *Hertha,* is on display at Son Marroig.

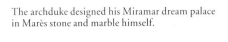
The archduke designed his Miramar dream palace in Marès stone and marble himself.

women, was indeed living happily together with several different ladies, all of whom bore him lots of children. Far from disowning them, as would have befitted his class, he gave them property and real estate from what he possessed. On one occasion he even took his one true love, Catalina Homar, with him to Vienna. The daughter of a Majorcan carpenter made a big impression on the decadent, bored courtiers of Austria, despite extreme reservations on their part; women as natural, simple and as wonderful as Catalina were a great rarity in their lives.

Catalina Homar, the love of his life
Yet once the couple had departed, the court exploded: "He even brings her here, his concubine; she can't even read and write!" Couldn't. For this is just one of the things the girl from Majorca learned from the archduke on their countless travels aboard the yacht *Nixe,* other skills being Italian, German, French, Greek and Arabic and how to run and manage his properties and vineyards. Like her teacher, she too received a gold medal at an exhibition in Paris for her

When Salvator met the carpenter's daughter Catalina Homar, she was unable to read or write. During their relationship, which was hushed up by the court in Vienna, she learned several languages and managed the archduke's estates in Majorca.

malmsey wine. Tragically, the archduke was unable to refuse her her one big wish, a trip to the Holy Land, where she caught leprosy. Back in Majorca, she had to endure years of terrible suffering before she died. In 1905, a year after her death, Salvator dedicated his book *Catalina Homar* to her, written in *Mallorquí* and the first of his over 50 works published at that time to sport his full name on the cover.

From light to darkness
The archduke's own end neared with the outbreak of the First World War. The emperor ordered him to leave Majorca post haste, with hardly any of his belongings, and to go back into exile to where he was first driven as a young man: to Brandeis near Prague.

As if he had left his soul in Majorca, the archduke deteriorated within a year and died in 1915 without having been able to resolve the tragic contradiction of his existence. Ludwig Salvator avenged himself in death; he left almost everything he had owned to his Majorcan secretary, close friend, and lover, Antoni Vives, and a legacy to a certain Antonietta Calafat who claimed to have been his partner. His family – probably unable to act otherwise in the political and diplomatic chaos of the Great War – also had a lesson to teach their errant relative; the son of light, who was born in Tuscany and found happiness in Majorca, was laid to rest in a dark, cold Capuchin vault in Vienna.

Near Esporles, the Tramuntana region appears in all its wild beauty.

Life upstairs, torture downstairs
Esporles and Sa Granja

From Palma, the road runs dead straight to the main road village of Esporles. Evergreen orange trees, gnarled olive trees and almond trees blossoming in February line the way. In Esporles, an avenue of plane trees forms the boundary between the Vila Vella (old town) and Vila Nova (new town). Tradition-conscious residents settled around the 13th-century church in the old part of Esporles, where all the public buildings are to be found. Their farms, houses and plots are larger than those of the "newcomers" of the 18th and 19th centuries in the new town to the south. The latter part of Esporles was built round a former *alqueria* or Arab estate and its well, and originally agricultural and factory workers lived here.

Nowadays Esporles is mainly a dormitory suburb for people working in the capital, Palma, only 9 miles away, but the former social distinctions between Vila Vella and Vila Nova can still be noted in summertime village festivals. In the tradition-minded part of the village solemn ceremonies and high masses are the focal point of holidays, whereas in the more recent part there is but one main aim,

namely to pay as Epicurean a homage as possible to Bacchus in pleasant company. Every family prepares toothsome treats for the holiday and then goes feasting round the neighborhood until the early hours. The refined, polite behavior of the Vila Vella resident is out of place here. In the Vila Nova, they like it rude and ribald.

Despite the split in the village, the population is considered collectively on the island

as a breed apart: old town or new, anyone who first saw daylight in Esporles is something special – or so the natives say. Here, only pitying glances are left for the poorest of the poor born on the plain of Pla or somewhere like that. "A slow digestion" plagues the people of the plain, they claim. Presumably the proud mountain folk mean the plainsfolk don't fly off the handle as easily as is habitual in their home village.

And indeed the people of Esporles are famous, or rather infamous, throughout Majorca for their aggressiveness. This reputation dates back to an incident in a dispute over water rights in the 18th century, involving the village and the Pauline monks who lived on an estate half way up the hillside on the edge of the village. The authorities awarded the monks the use of the precious water from the Canet de Sa Granja. On the day when the clerk of the court served the monks with the favorable judgment, a group of women from Esporles descended upon the assembled men and pelted them not just with hard words but

The museum *finca* of Sa Granja is set in a national park cultivated for centuries.

hard rocks as well. The outcome brought no change in the judgment, but injuries among the monks.

Dire dungeons

Initially still dead-straight west of Esporles, the road suddenly begins to twist and turn among the hills. Beside the former Arab estate of Alquería Al-Pic, it passes through a fertile valley which rarely runs short of water even in summer. Romans once strolled here in the shade of closely planted trees and savored the joys of cool springs bubbling from the ground. Today, the old estate is called Sa Granja, and presents not only one of the loveliest gardens on the island, laid out in the romantic English fashion, but also a folk museum. As in Els Calderers near Sant Joan, you can visit the converted mansion and see the carefully restored interiors and a wide range of exhibits relating to everyday life on a Majorcan estate.

When the Catalans conquered the island, Sa Granja passed to a knight called Nunó Sanç, who ten years later signed it over to a group of Cistercian monks. He soon regretted it, and demanded it back, but failed to take into account the Church's lack of respect for the law where their property was concerned. The monks totally refused to give up their monastery, drew swords to defend the estate and came out victorious. The new masters installed bare cells in the huge property, and didn't sell it until over 200 years later, to a private family. After several changes of owner, Sa Granja passed into the possession of the Fortuny family in 1665. Over the following century or so, they turned it into their summer residence, and altered, extended and blocked up the once spacious country house so that by the 18th century Sa Granja had become a warren of walls with countless corridors, rooms and halls. This is just how visitors see it today.

The splendid main house with its numerous halls, rooms and chambers has been furnished partly with antiques, partly with just old furnishings to make a museum of local Majorcan history. In the Florentine

Originally a monastery, the great house was rebuilt several times. This dainty loggia gallery was constructed in the 17th century.

Room, whose magnificent furnishings in no way fall short of its Florentine predecessors, is a glossy array of ornate Louis XV tables and seating. The tools in the toolshed and utensils in the kitchen do not gleam with such mellow gold, but nonetheless give a good impression of life on an estate that employed over 100 people in its heyday.

Twice a week, weaving women and rope-makers, potters and embroiderers in traditional dress give true-to-life demonstrations of old, almost forgotten craft skills. Even copper basins are created as visitors watch. In the inner courtyard folk groups play, sing and dance. In the restaurant, traditional culinary delights are served such as pear

In the former estate kitchen it looks as though the cook could return any moment.

bread, homemade cheeses and wines or the famous *bunyols*, doughnuts fried in oil. Those who would prefer to enjoy the splendid gardens in peace should therefore avoid Wednesdays and Fridays. This still does not mean missing out on bread, wine and other tasty samples of Majorcan cuisine.

One place where the sights are not live re-creations or performances is the cellar, where three torture chambers have been installed. A rack, a chair studded with nails and other instruments of torture bear witness to the highly painful examinations people were exposed to here in idyllic surroundings. Above ground, Sa Granja and its gardens are lovely, but all the more terrible are the Inquisition's subterranean dungeons of doom. Walking through the cold dungeons hewn out of bare rock leaves

many visitors with a feeling of oppression. You are glad to get out of the somber torture chambers to return to the dappled sunlight and walk through the gardens around Sa Granja and their running water.

In the spacious living rooms of the *finca*, the lords of the manor surrounded themselves with oriental carpets and Majorcan furniture …

… upstairs, painted silk wallpaper and dainty groups of seats create elegant intimacy …

… on cold winter nights, warmth was provided by a *braser* (brazier), a pan of coals within a wooden stand, for the covers under the canopy …

… a smith with his own workshop dealt with repairs for the house or the farmyard …

… the wool from the sheep on the estate is washed and dyed in large tubs …

… in the washroom, laundry from the whole estate is relieved of its dust and dirt from the fields and wrung before drying.

It took nearly 800 years for the Christians to reconquer the Iberian peninsula from the Moors, moving from north to south.

by	800
by	900
by	1062
by	1150
by	1220
by	1238
by	1266
by	1450
	1492

the north were hammering out further victories. By 1045 they had retaken Asturia, Navarre, the Two Castiles, Aragón and León. 200 years later the Balearics and large parts of West Andalusia were regained. Only Granada held out against the Christians until 1492. Finally it also fell, to the Catholic Kings, Ferdinand II of Aragón and Isabella I of Castile, who carried the true faith against the heathen and the torches of the Church against hell fire.

What they conquered was a three-nation, triple-culture, triple-religion state. It contained over 200,000 Jews, most of them merchants and bankers since money dealing was forbidden to Christians, and about a million Muslims, mostly artisans and peasants. Together they formed an economically powerful middle class, who had to be kept in

In 1487, Isabella I of Castile's confessor Tomás de Torquemada was raised by Pope Innocent VIII to the office of the first Grand Inquisitor of all Spain. Backed by the Catholic Kings Isabella and her husband Ferdinand II of Aragón, the large-scale hunt began for enemies of the true faith.

Under the yoke of the cross
Reconquest and Inquisition

Invading hordes and lightning attacks from foreign armies, lengthy sieges and humiliating capitulations have been a feature of Spanish history since antiquity. The first thing the invaders – Phoenicians, Romans, Vandals, Moors, and lastly Christians – always brought with them was their religion, sometimes with force, sometimes tolerating other beliefs, sometimes in ecumenical harmony. Many an occupation led to a cultural revival in Spain, others to economic prosperity. But none has affected Spain's history and self-image so enduringly as the Reconquista.

The word literally means "reconquest" of course, no more, no less. The reality was a chapter of horror and force, suppression and intolerance lasting centuries.

The sword and the cross

After the invading Moors defeated the Visigothic king Roderic in 711, they swept triumphantly up the Iberian Peninsula, crossed the Pyrenees in 720 and marched north. In 732, somewhere near Poitiers, Charles Martell, grandfather of Charlemagne, managed to stop and roll back the tide. But south of the Pyrenees, with the temporary exception of the Balearics, Spain remained Moorish. And around the same time the first dogged maneuvers towards reconquest began. In 722, a legendary commander called Pelayo first defeated the Moors in battle, at Covadinga in Asturia.

While the Moors were constructing some of Europe's finest cities, mainly in the southern half of Spain (Seville, Córdoba, Toledo and Granada), conquering the Balearics and applying themselves to the economy and culture, mostly in peace with Jews and Christians, Christian armies from check if the new Christian rulers did not want to lose face with their supporters. It was mainly the Jews who suffered, having been the target and victims of envy, resentment and persecution since the 13th century.

The fire and the cross

What had fermented so long in the nation's soul was now institutionalized by the new rulers. In 1478, the Pope replaced the medieval tribunal in Aragón by the Holy Office, i.e. the Inquisition. Personally appointed by the king, the inquisitors were above the contemporary justice system and had both temporal and religious powers plus an army of informers and bodyguards. The "painstaking" examinations were strictly secret, and after the condemnation, the executed victim's property was shared out among the crown, the Inquisition and the accusers – the perfect motivation for denunciations and slanders of all kinds.

Organizer of the Spanish Inquisition was Tomás de Torquemada, the model for Dostoyevsky's Grand Inquisitor, who doubted even Jesus's orthodoxy. Previously confessor of the ruling couple Ferdinand and Isabella, in 1483 Pope Sixtus IV raised him to the rank of the first Grand Inquisitor of Castile, which in 1487 Pope Innocent VIII upped to the Grand Inquisitor of all Spain. In the eleven years left him until his death in 1498, he exercised his power mercilessly, criss-crossing the peninsula in his feared black coach from trial to trial. It is estimated that during his rule, nearly 2,000 people finished up at the stake.

In the early 16th century, when the Inquisition was beginning to spread across the rest of Europe, the first Inquisitor reached Majorca, selecting a house in Lloret in Pla as a residence. His mission was to "root out heresy". Heresy was anything not 100% Church-approved.

The Jewish population was left with a choice between the devil and the deep blue sea: emigrate – but where? Or be baptized, and stay. But even that did not protect the 50,000 or so *conversos*, also called *xuetes* on Majorca, from persecution. As virtually no-one believed in their renunciation of the faith of their fathers, it only needed someone to claim that a *xueta* had secretly prayed to Yahweh to sign his death warrant. In Lloret

in the 17th century, a group of 250 *xuetes* were arrested and handed over to the Church police, the *Curia Militar*. A juicy catch, because once they were condemned, the Church could swallow up their entire possessions. Around the same time in Palma, there were mass burnings in the *xuetes* quarter of Call, which were celebrated like a public holiday by frenzied crowds.

Anyone that fell into the hands of the Inquisition had little chance of escaping alive. Executions like the one in this painting by Pedro Berruguete were the order of the day.

Soon the Muslim population was the target of attacks. Likewise faced with the choice of the Cross or exile, around a million were baptized. But even here, it did not even

To extort confessions, the jackals of the Inquisition were not afraid to use torture. They exhibited boundless imagination in devising horrible new implements of torture such as can still be seen in the basement of Sa Granja.

help the *moriscs*, the converted Muslims, to eat pork publicly in order to be free of suspicion. In the 16th century, the Inquisition expelled 300,000 *moriscs* and confiscated their property for Church and crown.

The policies of the Inquisition were so successful because they turned the Christian population into informers and traitors under the cover of their spiritual salvation. Anyone who denounced others basked in the supposed safety of a pure soul. Supposed, because Christians were not safe either: the very suspicion of witchcraft, dreadful offenses like blasphemy or copulating with animals or suspicious knowledge of herbal remedies led directly without trial or discussion to the torture chamber or the stake. Obsequious friars served the Inquisition as supernumerary morality police, as did the Loreto nuns in Lloret de Majorca. How many victims they handed over to Church police for conviction in torture chambers like that on Sa Granja is not known.

In Majorca, many stories are bound up with these inhuman institutions. Many of them are made up, many are legend and rumor, like that concerning the well at the entrance to Lloret. An underground labyrinth of passages and paths was supposed to lead from it, dating back to the time of the heresy persecutions, so that Jews could escape more easily. In Palma, there are similar stories of passages under the Castell de Bellver and the Jewish quarter of Call; indeed, some have been found. Most of the other stories are all too true and provable, because the Church tribunals, town clerks and authorities kept punctilious records about everything.

The Inquisition reigned in Spain with fire and sword till the 19th century. It was only decided to abolish it in 1813, when the National Assembly met in Cádiz because of the guerrilla war against the Napoleonic occupation. But it took until the Second Vatican Council of 1965 for Rome itself to catch up with this and rename the Sanctum Officium. Instead of the Congregation for Roman and Worldwide Inquisition, it has since been the Congregation of Faith. Only then did the Church relinquish the Inquisition.

Sharp iron spikes pierced the arms of the victim, to loosen his tongue.

This French woodcut of 1541 shows how the Inquisition aimed to convict a suspect: with the victim chained hand and feet and slung up, the torturer poured water on a cloth over his face. The captive would very soon suffocate to death in agony.
Apparently uninvolved, a clerk of the Holy Inquisition keeps minutes of the "examination".

The village of plenty
Banyalbufar

Antiquity knew of Seven Wonders of the World, whether for the very size of buildings and monuments constructed by human hand, or because, like the Colossus of Rhodes, they seemed to defy the known laws of physics, or because nature and artifice had been blended in astonishing and harmonious fashion. The Hanging Gardens of the Assyrian queen Semiramis in Babylon, if she existed, achieved a miracle of the latter kind, and the sight of the terraced gardens at Banyalbufar is reminiscent of it.

Undoubtedly their creator deserves the greatest of admiration. In the case of the Babylonian gardens, there was at least a named builder, if mythical, which is more than can be said for Banyalbufar. For a long time, the official version was that the gardens were solely the product of the hand of Moors expert in landscape architecture. A new interpretation, according to which the original rock-slinging inhabitants began to clear the gentle slopes, came into fashion in the last decades of the 20th century in tandem with a renewed search for a Majorcan identity and new Majorcan national consciousness. Still other sources consider it possible that the Phoenicians saw yet another opportunity here and used it to boost their flourishing Mediterranean trade.

A European dessert wine: malmsey from Banyalbufar

Certainly it was the Moors who perfected everything they found here during their 300-year rule. They were also the ones to name the place and its garden: *bany el buhar* means the "vineyard by the sea". As the Prophet forbade Muslims wine, they did not drink it. However, cultivate it they certainly did, of that there is no doubt.

In fact, wine was made here from Moorish times until the late-19th century collapse of the Majorcan wine industry, mainly from the malvasia grape, which produces a sweet, scented dessert wine that sold like hot cakes all over Europe in its day. A banquet or grand dinner party was unthinkable without a glass of malmsey from the Canary Islands or Banyalbufar. Shakespeare's Falstaff praises this splendid wine, and contemporary writers reported that the Duke of Clarence drowned in a "butt of malmsey" in 1478, in the Tower of London.

Archduke Ludwig Salvator also extolled the wine for its savor and health-giving benefits, though perhaps His Grace

Like the tiers in a theater, the terrace gardens drop down towards the nearby sea.

S'Arxiduc was not unprejudiced in this. His lover Catalina Homar was in charge of the vineyard on his estate and won a gold medal at the Paris Exposition with her malmsey. It is said that Majorca even owes its reconquest to malmsey, at least in part. The wine from the seaside terraces was supposed to have been one of Jaume I's main reasons for recapturing the island. At any rate, Banyalbufar malmsey thereafter became a favorite wine at the court of the kings of Aragón.

Controled abundance brings walls to their knees

The Moors first made the best of the protected position of Banyalbufar, in a cleft in the cliffs with a gentle incline to the sea, by inserting level areas, the terraces, in the slopes. The stones and topsoil gathered thereby were reused elsewhere on the slope – the stones to build dry stone walls below

Above: Boat owners can only reach the beach at Banyalbufar via steep steps.

Below: Collection basins ensure that surplus water is not lost.

Despite its proximity to the tourist magnets of Deià and Valldemossa, the area around Banyalbufar has retained its seclusion.

each field that supported the precious earth and checked the flow of water downwards.

These parcels of land are crisscrossed with ditches, conduits and channels, not to mention rectangular and round underground cisterns that get their water from the caves of Puig Planicía. The water runs on the overflow principle from the source cistern into the first field, whence it is distributed along branches through the plantations, if possible without evaporation losses, then runs together again at the lower end of the field before running over into the next field below. At the end of the road, the water reaches the village, where it feeds the overflow from the fields into wells and underground cisterns.

Though it may all look like child's play, in fact powerful forces of nature are at work here, and the system only works as long as the stone walls are kept continuously in good shape. In the 20th century, some farmers have tried using *blocs* (industrially made cavity blocks) instead of labor-intensive drystone walling, but it did not work. The blocks crack under the pressure of the water and earth more quickly than the traditional drystone walls, which are in themselves elastic.

In the 19th century, whole vineyards were abandoned, both in Pla and Banyalbufar. It is only now that the reculti-vation of the slopes for malmsey is slowly under way again.

When the vineyards in Banyalbufar had stopped producing – except for some malmsey for domestic use – the big land-owners had to sell large tracts of the 2,000 or so terrace gardens to landless peasants, who since then have grown mainly tomatoes and potatoes here and thus ensured that the "hanging gardens" of Majorca remain part of the landscape.

They are not much disturbed in their work. The tourist routes are concentrated on Deià and Valldemossa a little further up the coast, mostly passing Banyalbufar and the nearby Estellencs without a second glance. Only the Mirador de Ses Animes, the Watchtower of the Souls outside Banyalbufar, attracts their interest, as it provides one of the most splendid views over the Tramuntana love affair of mountain and sea.

So the village has stayed a village. Although the day has long passed when all inhabitants lived only from fishing and working the land, the island's new wealth – tourism – has been doled out only in small portions. Here it is mainly Majorcans who seek quiet and seclusion, which few places on their island offer any more. Banyalbufar has nothing to hide and little to show off. A great house has survived from the days of the

Water runs down the natural incline from one field to the next via a skillfully constructed system of stairs and canals.

large landowners, the *Baronia*, whence the valley was ruled up to the 15th century almost absolutistly – the entire population of the place was subject to the civil and penal jurisdiction of the lords of the Baronia.

The closely packed stone houses of the place do however feature some fine semi-circular arched doorways, while village life is centered on the old-established cafés like the Marisol, which has adopted Banyalbufar's leitmotif and seems to hover over the sea on one. The very fact that the place has "little to offer" means that it demonstrates the inter-dependency of nature, commerce and agriculture.

Below: Meditation Majorcan style, nestling between sea and mountain.

Right: The tower of Mirador de Ses Animes seems to hover above the sea.

Heavenly love apples
Tomatoes from Banyalbufar

In August, when fruits have reached their peak of maturity, country women still sear vast quantities of tomatoes with onion and garlic to produce *sofrit*, the "mother of all Spanish sauces". After 15 minutes in the pan, the mixture is poured into large jars and later serves as a basis for numerous sauces, rice dishes, and stews.

Even if nowadays no-one attributes aphrodisiac qualities to "love apples" any more, the local cuisine is inconceivable without tomatoes, because, unlike in large parts of Europe, "love apples" were never banished from the menu in Spain.

This may be due to the fact that it was a Spanish voyage of discovery that found

At first glance, the "love apples" near Banyalbufar look like vines.

them. After all, it was Columbus who returned from his expedition to America around 1500 with two "apples" which would achieve great importance in the gardens and kitchens of Europe. However, whereas "earth apples" or potatoes immediately caught on, tomatoes had a bumpy ride. The intense scent that the ripe fruit exuded and its slightly sweet, immensely aromatic taste irritated the taste buds of Europeans used to rather bland foods.

The Spaniards were not so skeptical about the plant. They adopted the Aztec name *tomatl* forthwith, henceforth *tomate* in Spanish, and began to preserve, cook, and

Suspended strings of tomatoes adorn the walls of a Majorcan pantry like a red curtain.

fry the ripe fruits, or even eat them fresh off the plant. However, on Majorca tomatoes have been cultivated only since 1840, after the vine-pest wrought such devastation among the vineyards as to leave the great terraces laid out by the Moors looking a picture of horror. Scarcely anything was left of *bany al buhar*, the "vineyard by the sea" to which Banyalbufar owes its name.

This is why, since the mid-19th century, after production had been destroyed elsewhere it is the cultivation of the fleshy fruit that has ensured Banyalbufar its economic survival. That was when Ferran Cotoner, Marquis of Cenia, decided to extend cultivation, after trials had shown that tomatoes flourished in the soil and sun-drenched climate of the coastal region. The farmers changed the course of the old Moorish irrigation ditches, the *síquies*, and installed great numbers of reservoirs for fresh water on and between the terraces.

Today, tomatoes in all colors, shapes, and scents have become indispensable for Majorcan cuisine. In Banyalbufar both bush tomatoes, which near the sea take on a slightly salty flavor, and the milder vine tomatoes are cultivated. Bush tomatoes are best for sauces, passata, purée, and juice, while the slightly meaty beef tomatoes are used for salads. The smaller, yellowy-red juicy *ramellet* tomatoes

are dry-cultivated, i.e. without water. As they bruise easily, they are strung on strings or *ramellets* and hung up decoratively in the larder or kitchen for storage.

Well-ripened tomatoes have an intense aroma and high nutritional content. Besides being rich in Vitamin C, they contain a lot of beta-carotene, a preliminary stage of the important Vitamin A. The human body can utilize it only in combination with fat, which is where the tomato's best friend, olive oil, comes into play, the ingredient that dots the savory i on every tomato-based dish.

Pa amb oli, bread with olive oil and tomato, is served for breakfast, as an aperitif or between mealtimes. Simple though this bread recipe may sound and is to prepare, there are opposing views as to how to make it.

Stringing tomatoes on to a thread looks like a peaceful occupation for mild afternoon hours.

Pa amb oli

Bread with olive oil (serves 6-8))

Ingredients
8 slices of *pan moreno*, 1" (2 cm) thick
4 bush tomatoes
1 clove of garlic, according to taste
best quality olive oil
salt

Toast or bake the bread, drizzle with olive oil and rub with half a bush tomato. Salt, and drizzle on a little more oil. Serve at once. This is how *pa amb oli* is most commonly served, but other versions should be tried.

Pan moreno, the dark, unsalted mixed-flour bread, is the best basis for a *pa amb oli*. However, there now follows the fundamental philosophical question about *pa amb oli*, about which Majorcans and Catalans can talk for hours, viz. should the bread be first drizzled with olive oil and then rubbed with a sliced *tomàtigues de ramellet*, or should the tomato be rubbed in first and subsequently drizzled with olive oil?

Perhaps it may be difficult to conceive that there is a difference between the two, but these are indeed two variants that cannot be compared. There is also the view that it is not tomato or olive oil that should first come into contact with the bread but a peeled raw clove of garlic that is rubbed over the bread.

Ponent

Santa Ponça. The conquerors moved on, heading overland towards nearby Palma, and only when they had taken this did they worry about the part forana, the countryside and coast.

Dangerous for settlers

Ponent was important not for its striking natural resources but strategically: anyone setting sail from the Spanish mainland towards Palma had to pass it. Considerations of this sort made the small port of Sant Elm so appealing to Jaume II, son of the Conqueror, that in 1279 he approved a highly exotic take-over clause. He had a hospital for seamen constructed, because only then was the previous lord of the port, Bernat Basset, willing to vacate. But even with a seaman's hospital Sant Elm attracted no further particular investment. On the contrary. Like at other Ponent harbors, the population had neither the money nor the inclination to create a cozy nest by the sea here. A harbor was of course necessary, but also a risk. Sant Elm, Port d'Andratx, and Santa Ponça

Below: All kinds of protected flora and fauna live on Illa Sa Dragonera – except dragons.

Classy despite the crowds
Ponent

The name Ponent means "sunset", derived from the sun descending into the sea, often accompanied by a mild breeze but in winter by an occasional destructive hurricane-force westerly wind. As capricious as the wind, splendor and poverty of both past and present times are closely juxtaposed in the extreme south-west tip of the island as in almost no other region of Majorca.

Until far into motorized, industrialized modern times, the extreme south-west tip of the island belonged to the losers of history. It looked enviously across to Palma and its flourishing commercial and cultural life, just a stone's throw away. It saw merchant ships and merchants from every country of the Mediterranean and beyond pass by the Illa Sa Dragonera, Dragon Island, in the direction of Palma and its large, safe harbor. To the north, the view was blocked by the Serra de Tramuntana, while in the south and west only the sea licked and nibbled at its bays and beaches, washed ashore pirate hordes and missing fishermen, flotsam and jetsam from sunken vessels, and conquerors.

Only once was Ponent itself the center of Majorcan history, for a brief interlude, and even then only because breakers prevented the planned landing elsewhere. In 1229, Jaume I, the Conqueror, set sail for Majorca with 143 ships. A noble called Riudemeya was the first to spring ashore on the beach at Santa Ponça to drive the royal standard into the sand at the spot where a stone cross now records the event. This achievement gained him a knighthood and the land around

Previous double-page spread: A flock of gulls welcomes the fleet of fishing boats into Port d'Andratx. Elegant sailing boats in the background testify to a peaceful co-existence between entrenched fishermen and offcomer boat-owners.

were exposed to raids from pirates until the late 17th century, so that, as in the case of Sant Elm, they must have lived out of suitcases from time to time and even left the place for lengthy periods. Only in the 19th century was the port populated again, and has since retained its special appeal of remote diminutiveness.

Despite being surrounded by the sea, the people in Ponent always lived with at least one eye to the landward. The sea alone would not feed them, but nor would the precipitous land towards the foothills of the Tramuntana. To have a chance of survival, the best had to be made of both. The two main peaks of Ponent, Puig de l'Esclop (3,041 ft / 927 m) and, towering over everything, myth-laden Puig Galatzó (3,369 ft /1,027 m), rise directly behind the coastal strip. Holm oaks and pines grow in the valleys and hollows, but the Moors added other useful plants such as prickly pear, almonds and olives. Later on, orange and lemon groves were also planted in sun-drenched, wind-protected valley locations, which made the horta of Andratx a rival to the "Golden Valley" of Sollér.

But wherever man was not at work channeling, tilling or cattle-herding, the slopes remained the reserve of some notable inhabitants – mountain goats run wild that had evinced no desire to return to their stalls in the villages at summer's end; mushrooms that found an ideal microclimate in the shade of pines and holm oaks; herbs for

Above: Near Port d'Andratx, the Torrent des Saluet has become an open-air boat house.

Below: The port of Andratx is considered one of the prettiest in the Mediterranean.

household use and to make schnapps – long the medicine of the ordinary man; and smugglers and runaway prisoners who found hideouts in the isolated heights and caves and yet remained close enough to the sea to launch into the wide world if need be....

The curse of the oppressed

...and if we can give credence to popular tales, many a lost spirit, some accursed, some prankish. The latter are goblins that frighten horses and spit into milk churns, move furniture and yet are still supposedly descended from angels. The most famous and not very amusing spirit is the Comte Mal, who rides out at night on a green horse on Galatzó in an aura of fire. He is the wicked soul of a historical figure, Ramón Zaforteza, who was lord of a large estate on Galatzó in the 17th century and mercilessly exploited its ordinary inhabitants. When disputes arose, he murdered them without further ado. The curse on him is consequently a kind of collective judgment by those who could not defend themselves against him during his lifetime. Anyone wanting to see the green glow on Galatzó for himself can now do this from one of the wicked count's former mansions. In Son Net, dominating the village of Puigpunyent, a luxury hotel opened at the end of the 1990s.

On many of the shoreline promenades in Ponent, pedestrians, joggers and cyclists can enjoy the dialog of sea and sky.

The best weeks of the year

The new luxury hotel on Galatzó, perhaps overdone in all its splendor, represents a new development, a rethinking in Majorca's most important industry – tourism. After the errors of judgment during the first great ecstatic boom in the 1960s and subsequent collapse in the 1970s, the Majorcans have realized, just before the Millennium, that the two best weeks of the year should be characterized by class rather than mass. The Ponent commune of Calvià is famous throughout Europe for just the opposite – unadulterated mass tourism – for some years it was a dream holiday destination, and very soon thereafter a stigma and deterrent. Because what the folk of Calvià permitted by way of high-rise hotels and deafening discos, tacky shops and snack bars at its beaches in Magaluf, Peguera and Santa Ponça did indeed turn Calvià from one of poorest into one of the richest places in Europe – but not a happy one. Five years before the Millennium, with numbers still rising, 1.5 million visitors set the tills ringing – and the alarm bells.

And so at the eleventh hour Calvià woke up, just as it was drowning in rubbish and its beaches had become alcohol-soaked roughhouses and more and more cheap hotels were closing because they could not keep up with newer, higher-value rivals. The Basque mayoress of Calvià, Margarita Nájera, has since then had 15 hotels torn down, barred new projects and made environmental education the commune's main subject. Both she and her comrades-in-arms know Calvià will remain a mass destination – but it is they, wise with the painful wisdom of past mistakes, who will decide which mass and at what price, for a commune whose administrative center, old Calvià, lies 6 miles inland, untouched by all this.

Protégé under dragon guard

Places like old Calvià show class, as does the small town of Andratx, whose name is often associated and confused with that of its port, Port d'Andratx, because the latter is quite special. Here, so close to Calvià, a jewel of the Mediterranean has developed and survived that has shunned mass tourism, shrill souvenir shops and crowds heading for the beach. Its policy is not one of selflessness, because it is based instead on the well-lined wallets of guests and settlers, and the absence of beaches popular with the masses. This is where sailing folk and yacht owners come who, after a good day at the tiller, want to savor a coffee or a cocktail in pleasant, tasteful surroundings on a well-laid out marine promenade, before making off back to one of the villas on Cap de Sa Mola. Another extreme, perhaps.

But even here the locals hold all the strings when it comes to ensuring a calm sea and plentiful catch for the coming year, with divine help. Once a year the fishermen of Port d'Andratx send their patron saint, Nostra Senyora del Carme, out to sea decked with flowers and candles, for her to use her charm and protecting hand, and put in a good word with the powers of the sea.

The Mother of God will then also catch a glimpse of Sa Dragonera, the unpopulated Dragon Island where Noah's Ark is sup-

Above: In the gardens of Ponent numerous types of fruit and vegetable flourish. In spring it is the fruit trees that vie with the almond trees to present a spectacle.

Following double-page spread: Scarcely credible but true. The romantic cove of Portals Vells lies close to Calvià and its concrete jungle of hotels.

posed to have tied up in order to repopulate the land. And where divine might has thus arranged the affairs of Nature, man has wisely refrained from disturbing creation. Sa Dragonera is a nature reserve – yet only a few bays away from the concrete blocks of Magaluf and Peguera that are reflected in the sea at the sundown of Ponent.

In the bright sunlight, Puig Galatzó does not seem as threatening as Majorcan legends would have us believe.

Ghostly figures and nightmares
Legends on Majorca

Narrow, steep alleys where every step demands that you think again and slow down twist between the stone houses of Puigpunyent on the slopes of Puig Galatzó. The village owes this prominent peak not just its name – Puigpunyent means "pointed peak" – but also its reputation. Many people get horrible creepy feelings here at night, and not without reason, because Galatzó, at 3,369 feet (1,026 meters), is Majorca's magic mountain. Even in daytime it seems to deceive when you look at it. The snow shining right at the top is only the sharp, limestone peak.

Most harmless are the *dimonis bonets*, the goodnatured demons that loaf around here. Small goblins that get up to all kinds of nonsense, they steal plates from the kitchen, disarrange the furniture, untie the dog, piddle on the crops and borrow the horses so that they bolt with riders and carts in pure panic. Apparently the wicked beasties were once respectable angels – but then so was Lucifer. They certainly did not learn much from it, and even the relics of St. Urban the Martyr, which made their way from the catacombs of Rome to the parish church of Es Capdellà, can't instil sense into them.

Probably the best-known ghost of Majorca haunts the foot of the mountain, the *Comte Mal*, the Wicked Count of Formiguera on his green, fire-spitting steed. That his soul cannot rest is due to the special nastiness that distinguished the former lord of the area, Don Ramón Zaforteza, during his lifetime. He squeezed his subjects dry with excessive tax demands, and when they

Around Mallorca's Magic Mountain, Puig Galatzó, good-natured goblins get up to mischief and an evil count rides restlessly abroad – so popular legend has it.

turned to the law against him and got their rights, the Evil Count lost no time in murdering their spokesman with his own hands. He paid a bitter price: since his death in 1694 he has had to ride restless and unsettled round the south side of the mountain – right through the Reserva del Galatzó, one of the loveliest natural parks on the island.

En Rotget's behavior was altogether different. Following the example of Robin Hood, the notorious bandit robbed the rich to give to the poor, presumably to stop their mouths in both senses. In all his daring exploits, the highwayman trusted in the power of his amulet, which dangled round his neck even in sleep. He was only careless once. During a *festa* in honor of Our Lady of

Lluc, he handed the talisman to a delightful woman, and was promptly seized. No-one went to the assistance of Rotget, who defended himself furiously; probably his generosity towards the poor was only a legend.

The story of *Drac de na Coca* probably also goes back to a real incident. The town of Palma was once plagued by a bloodthirsty dragon that swallowed children and tore the arms and legs off adults. One late evening Sir Bartomeu Coch passed through the town. As his steps echoed around the empty alleys, he felt a curious sense of being observed, and found two glowing eyes pursuing him. As behooved a colleague of St George, he drew his sword heroically, and turned to chase the monster, cornered it and defeated it in a hard fight in the quiet alleys of the town.

Realists of course insist that it was just the sad story of a lonely crocodile. Probably

it arrived in the Balearic island as a baby crocodile on board one of the large vessels from its homeland in Africa and did no more than keep itself alive in the sewers of the town until it made the mistake of acquiring a taste for human flesh. Today the embalmed body of *es Drac* can be admired in the Museu Diocesà in Palma, besides a painting of St George.

Left: Amid all the invisible inhabitants, Mallorcans of this life have also made their homes.

Below: Almond blossom lends the surrounding area additional magic.

Fruit with spikes
Prickly pear

The conquerors' ships returning from the New World must have looked like floating fruit and vegetable gardens on reaching Spain. Besides the numerous plants whose fruits are nowadays an indispensable part of our daily diet, they also had a strange, spiky bush on board bearing extremely delicious fruits – the prickly pear.

Majorcans baptized the prickly plants *figues de moro*, Moorish figs, while the Moors called them Christian figs. They are valued to this day as ornamental plants, and residents planted hedges of *Opuntia* round their properties to keep out unwanted intruders, human and animal, with their spines. The wildly profuse stems turn to the sun, reminiscent in shape of impertinently erect, curious elephants' ears.

In former times, cochineal insects were bred on opuntia stems because their dried larvae provided carmine-colored dye for cosmetics and drinks. Up to the 19th century, Mexico exported many tons of the sought-after dye to Europe, until large tracts of opuntia were planted in the Canary Islands and breeding cochineal insects became one of the islands' main sources of income. After the development of artificial aniline dyes towards the end of the 19th century the market collapsed. On Majorca, the breeding was never taken seriously anyway because the competition from the Canary Islands, Algeria and Central America was too great.

Two kinds of prickly pear are known: besides the normal, "real" prickly pear *Opuntia ficus barbarica* with its pale, short spines there is also *Opuntia dilleni*, which is easily recognizable from its spines (up to three inches long) and lemon-colored flowers.

The fruits of the real opuntia are partly yellowish-red, sometimes also whitish. *Figues de moro* reach their greatest length of 2–4 inches (5-10 cm) in August and stand out clearly on the outside edges of the "ears". Prickly pears have an extremely palatable orange-colored or red fruit flesh, and at harvest time are eaten raw in great quantity. They are also popular for making jam.

If the fruit is consumed raw, the numerous seeds are also edible. Often, the fruits are picked while still rather unripe and kept for eating at Christmas. Picking is done with a special pair of tongs made of wood with which the fruit is held and twisted until it breaks off the stem.

Instead of barbed wire fences, hedges of prickly pear keep intruders out.

Prickly pear in blossom looks like decorated elephants' ears.

Sorbet de figues de Moro

Prickly pear sorbet

To get at the juicy, fig-like flesh of the fruit, the skin has to be removed very carefully around the sunken navel, because the skin conceals hundreds of tiny, almost invisible prickles with dangerous barbs which soon lodge in the tongue and can easily nest there for days. These bristles, called glochids, can also cause inflammation, against which only camels, which are passionate consumers of prickly pears, are really protected with their leathery tongues. The safest thing is to buy already prepared fruits for sale in summer in the market or beside the road and eat them on the spot.

Ingredients
1lb (500 g) peeled prickly pears
1 oz. (30 g) of sugar
3–4 tsp. lemon juice
cava wine

When peeling the prickly pears, it is advisable to wear gloves to guard against the spines. Purée all ingredients together and sieve. Freeze in an ice-cream machine or freezer cabinet. Take out 15 minutes before serving so that the sorbet softens a little.

The bristly fruits are often carefully removed unripe from the stem with a pair of wooden tongs.

Monks and dragons
S'Arracó and the Illa Sa Dragonera

You cannot go further west on land. The S'Arracó Peninsula looks out over the Majorcan Channel to the rock of Pantaleu and Dragon Island, Sa Dragonera. Beyond, the Mediterranean separates Majorca from the mainland. The Moors settled this peninsula with *alquerias*, small estates, to cultivate almonds, figs and prickly pears between the pine forests and the sea.

Very little has changed in this landscape. The village of S'Arracó, as delightful as the name of the nearby valley Sa Palomera (dovecote), likewise seems difficult to arouse from slumber. Amazingly so, because the teeming tourist centers of Port d'Andratx and especially Calvià are only a stone's throw away and yet seemingly infinitely remote.

Somewhat outside it lies the former Trappist monastery of Sa Trapa, where despite secularization in 1835 the marble Madonna can still be admired that the French monks brought here in the 18th century. In 1820, they left the monastery to an uncertain, unoccupied and eventually fire-gutted fate until in the late 20th century it was bought at auction by the environmental group GOB (Grupo Ornitológic Balear) and the Amics de la Trapa and reconstructed. They were able to get Sa Trapa and its surrounding countryside protected, and now look after the numerous seabirds that nest in the cliffs beneath the monastery.

A dragon island, whichever way you look at it

Given good weather and a degree of sporting enthusiasm, one could easily swim from the lovely fishing harbor of nearby Sant Elm to Sa Dragonera, but it is still easier to take one of the regular boats from Port d'Andratx or Peguera.

One explanation of the name, the profane one, claims that from the air the outline of the two and a half mile long island looks like a dragon's head. The other is that after the Flood, a storm huffed and puffed Noah and his Ark this way.

What Noah actually wanted, after dumping his son Ham and wife on the coast of Africa to start populating what later became Ethiopia, was a nice new place to live in the Mediterranean area, and he had already lined up the coast of Valencia when the storm upset things. The whole enterprise had nearly foundered when an island like a buffer in front of the Balearics saved the Ark from capsizing. Noah gratefully left Japhet's son Drag behind on this island together with his wife Onera, who called the island after their joint names.

There were soon playfellows for the many children they reared here: little lizards that slipped out of the eggs they brought along. In a flash, the lizards had populated the island and its larger neighbor Majorca. Thus the Drag-Oneras created not just the name of the island but also that of the lizards – *dragons.*

Nowadays two automatic lighthouses grace the uninhabited island. The smugglers and pirates moved on long ago. The island is a nature reserve, so that except for the handful of visitors nothing and no-one disturbs the interplay of the local fauna and the thick carpet of herbs, mastic and pines.

The former Trappist site of Sa Trapa on the Majorcan "mainland" is, like the Illa Sa Dragonera nearby, a nature reserve.

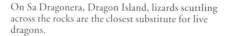

On Sa Dragonera, Dragon Island, lizards scuttling across the rocks are the closest substitute for live dragons.

Monsters of the deep
Fish and seafood

*Te conozco bacalao
aunque vengas disfrazao*

"Even if you are disguised, Master Cod, I still recognize you", sings the fisherman in an old song, and many sea creatures look very much as if in fancy dress. With its flat head and slightly open mouth, the angler or sea devil looks rather stupid. With the lamprey, you wouldn't be able to tell which aperture was actually staring at you, even if it wasn't dead already. The still living lobster obviously has problems with its outsize claws, reaching out ineffectively towards unattainably distant squid. The swordfish has already surrendered his sword, and the multi-legged spider crab looks as if it would be better off in a securely closed terrarium than on a tray in a market stall.

Visiting the fish market is one of the most impressive experiences of a trip to Majorca. Every fishing port, but especially Palma's Mercat del'Olivar, has a wonderful display of the rich haul brought back by hard-working fishermen on their nightly expeditions out to sea. Perch, eels, brace, sardines, tuna, mackerel, Mediterranean sole, dogfish, rays, sea bream, anglers, mussels, crabs, lobsters, crayfish, prawns and barnacles are neatly lined up, priced and offered for sale. Customers are not slow to come forward once a glance into the still clear eye has reassured them the catch is recent.

It is often claimed that the seas around Majorca have been fished out, but the wide selection on offer in the island's markets proves the contrary. There is for example the *jonquillo*, a tiny almost transparent little fish that is dunked in batter and then fried in deep fat. The fine white flesh of the *lluc* or sea pike is represented on every menu, with the tender gill cheeks being a particular delicacy. The *cap roig* or redhead is also fairly common in Majorca.

A glance at the clear, glassy eyes of the fish is enough to check: Majorcan fish lands fresh on the dish.

The yield of the sea is cut into salable-sized portions with a large saber.

Squid, or *calamars*, is served either in its own ink or stuffed with all kinds of delicacies, no limit being set to the cook's imagination. Raisins and almonds, mince or a purely vegetarian filling can be used; however garnished, *calamars* taste good and soon drive the rather rubbery, deep-frozen product back home from your memory.

If freshly caught fish is not available because St. Peter has sent the fishermen a storm, Majorcans don't lose heart because they have a 2,000 year old tradition of preserving fish and seafood. They open a tin of preserved anchovies or *anxoves* or fetch dried cod from the pantry.

Among the seafoods are the *musclos* or acorn barnacles, which grow to a length of 3–5 inches (7-13 cm) when they are ready for the market. The smaller venerids which dig into the sand with their fluted shells, the sword shell, purple fish and cockles are no longer rarities on a good menu. Oysters, which contain minerals and are eaten raw from the shell, are not to everyone's taste, although aphrodisiac qualities are attributed to the queen of seafoods.

Among the crayfish, the European crayfish or *Palinurus elephas* is especially popular. Also known as the spiny or thorny lobster, the reddish or purple crustacean can be over 18 inches (50 cm) long and weigh about a pound. It lives on rocky seabeds, which abound around Majorca's coasts, where it can feed on sea urchins, small squid and shellfish. As the crayfish seeks out precisely the things that the gourmet himself appreciates in a meal, its flesh, bringing the savor of the pure sea, is particularly enjoyable.

Don't try a moray if you suffer from snake phobia. The reptile-like creature can reach six feet, but, provided you have no aversion to it and trust yourself to eat it, has a firm, fatty flesh that tastes good. Likewise the lamprey, a fish-like vertebrate with nine apertures on each side, one for seeing, one for smelling and seven for gills. Up to 18 inches (50 cm) long, lampreys cause many people to recoil because their eel-like exterior is certainly not appetizing.

Other odd-looking specimens are the *peus de cabra*, which means "goats' feet" in Majorcan. An inch or more long, these barnacles cling to rocks and cliffs. Covered in long protective carapaces, they are boiled and, when eaten, an orange fluid spurts out. In appearance, they are reminiscent more of extraterrestrials' fingers than a delicacy. Provided you wear easily washable clothes, these strange creatures are a pleasure to eat, and they fetch high prices in the markets. Swordfish or *emperador* resembles tuna and like the latter is generally treated as a steak. Sea devil, or *rap*, has only recently become fashionable. Previously its rather flat body shape was found repulsive, but then the discovery was made that its firm white flesh is very delicate and can be cooked in a variety of ways. It is for example delicious grilled on a spit with tomatoes and peppers.

Another Majorcan fish specialty is the rare *raor*. The first specimens of this highly prized fish with its fine flesh are eagerly awaited by fish freaks at the end of summer. As the *raor* likes to bury itself in the seabed, it is difficult to find. *Raor* tastes best when it is only briefly seared in olive oil and served direct.

Set out on a bed of ice, fish and seafood nestle in transitional peace in Palma's Mercat del'Olivar.

Fresh fish is brought in plastic trays straight from the boat to the market hall …

… where it is sorted out "by family". The fish-like lampreys are not the epitome of beauty …

… while the "queens of seafood", oysters, reside on china plates, clearly distinguished from other lesser species …

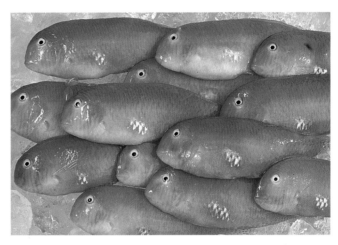

… and some specimens of *raor*, only caught in stormy weather, as if they were literally struck by lightning. A large family is that of the …

…prawns. The smaller members, shrimps or *camarones*, can be eaten whole, uncooked …

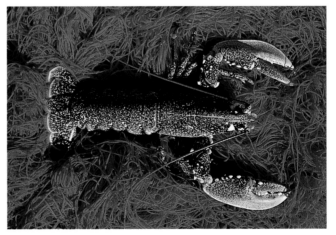

… while the delicate flesh of the lobster is only ready for consumption when its armor has been cracked.

A restful sleep after the anarchy
Andratx

"Andratx, Roman *Andrachium*, is inhabited mostly by seafarers and shows kindness and prosperity to quite a special degree. Happy, content faces smile at the onlooker from every house; it is just one of those places where anyone would be glad to settle." What Archduke Ludwig Salvator wrote in 1867 seems basically just as valid today.

Because, though but three miles from its latterly famous and popular port, Andratx has remained a little country town that, at the foot of Puig de Galatzó, seems to have slept out the end of the 20th century like a Sleeping Beauty and is in no hurry for a prince to waken it with a *besada*, a kiss. And rightly. Even though, unlike its harbor, its position largely protected it from the obligatory pirate raids, Andratx experienced such strange events in the course of its history that it has certainly earned a little rest. A bad

Left: In the cemetery of Andratx, the dead lie for five years in close proximity to neighbors in other mortuaries before they take up their final resting place under the soil.

Below: The outer wall of Castell Son Mas contains a petrified pirate gazing out to sea. He is Chaireddin Barbarossa, who did indeed fail to break in here in the 16th century.

idea of the Conqueror, Jaume I, left this pearl of Ponent, tenderly embedded in lush orchards, exposed to despotism and subsequently anarchy.

Two heads are better than one ...?

Andratx was one of the parts of the island granted to the Church after the Reconquest, in this case to the Bishop of Barcelona. In 1323, the Church and the royal house of Majorca reached an agreement about Andratx according to which both institutions had equal rights in all respects, whether it was enacting or repealing laws, passing judgment or distributing water. Nothing but trouble came of this, right down to the 17th century. The Church said this, the state decided that the inhabitants finally stop paying taxes to anyone. If the tax collector came anyway, they drove him away summarily, if necessary with force. And the violence spread. Judgments were rarely even handed down in Andratx, let alone enforced.

The most famous case is that of the multiple rapist, murderer and robber Jaume Esteva, alias Teliyer. For his crimes, he was buried alive at the state's behest in a burial niche – stupidly, on Church land, so that the Church commuted the punishment to a ridiculously trivial one and let him out – not because it wanted to protect criminals but just to exercise its right to disregarding the law.

Castell Son Mas was a refuge for Andratx residents during pirate raids.

Maneuvers on God's acre

These days, the trim little town offers the visitor its massive parish church of Santa María, the cannon-protected Castell de Son Mas and the half peculiar, half macabre sight of the cemetery. In Andratx tradition demanded that, if at all possible, the deceased should not be simply buried in a coffin. That was for poor folk. Instead, the deceased was initially interred in one of the little mortuaries which are packed closely together here, giving mutual support and company. They are covered with semi-circular tiles arched against each other which are appropriately called "monks and nuns". Only after five years are the remains of the coffin and bones cremated and the urns permanently interred in one of the grave niches. However, as the incidence of deaths did not always fit in with this ingenious system, it could occur that mortuaries stood empty, in which case they were used, eminently pragmatically, for other purposes, preferably as hidey-holes for smuggled goods.

Majorca's loquat
Fruit from round the world

With hindsight, the storm that drove Isman al-Khaulani's vessel ashore on Majorca seems to have been a gift of the gods. Not at first glance – that of contemporary Majorcans – but at the second, ours, we who know better. Al-Khaulani was a Mozarabic merchant, that is to say one who had adopted Islam. He was on his way to Mecca for the *hajj* or pilgrimage when foul weather struck and forced him to land. While his boat was being repaired, he took a good look round Majorca and discovered two things: this island could be a garden of Eden if it were done right, and it had wretched defenses that would not resist a well-organized invasion.

On his return to Córdoba, al-Khaulani told the Emir of both these circumstances, and got the commission to conquer the island. He carried it out in 902, and took over the first post of governor on behalf of the Emirate – a historic moment for the island, not only politically. After all, the Arabs helped Majorcans to improve their existing irrigation system such that the Majorcan economy flourished in the following centuries. Apples and pears, cherries and peaches, apricots and pomegranates were all more or less unknown on the island previously, but took readily to its fertile soil and prospered mightily.

Later, when Spanish and Portuguese seafarers traveled almost the entire world,

One vigorous snip and the fruit's umbilical cord to nature is cut, and the fruit is on its way to Majorcan fruit bowls.

pineapples, grapefruit, lemons, clementines and mandarins followed, but also exotic fruit such as the *nesola*, the Japanese medlar or loquat. Their refreshing fruity fruits resemble yellow plums, and are among the few fruits that are ripe early in the year. The peach-sized bright red kaki on the other hand can only be enjoyed in late autumn, when the trees have already shed their leaves.

Figs ripen in August, after which they are dried and kept for winter. The prickly pears (opuntia) in contrast, called Moorish figs by Christians and Christian figs by Moors, have nothing to do with the Arabs but come from America. Opuntia have had an interesting career. They were earlier used mainly as cattle feed, but the ripe cactus fruits are now harvested, peeled and eaten fresh.

Scented lemons can be harvested when the tree is still a tender two-year-old.

The deep red fruits of the strawberry tree (*Arbutus unedo*) are often processed to make jams and liqueurs.

Pomegranates occupy a special position in Majorca's rich fruit bowl. Right from the first they were considered a symbol of love and fertility. The edible parts are the wonderfully juicy bitter-sweet seeds; their aroma has a touch of blackcurrant to it. They are hidden inside the fruit, like the tangy orange flesh of the external seed shell. The seeds are also used to make the celebrated sweet grenadine syrup.

A *cremadillo* or Majorcan punch is as inconceivable without oranges and lemons as a *sangria*, so however small the kitchen garden, a lemon tree is a must. It is cared for and looked after from day one, until after two years not only bewitchingly scented flowers but also the first fruits develop, which are then picked fresh and bright yellow straight from the tree for the kitchen.

A further star of island produce is the much larger melon. The largest spherical or oval fruits come from Villafranca, where there used to be an annual festival in honor of the juicy fruit together with a Melon Queen. However, since for very understandable reasons the womenfolk were not too keen on becoming Miss Melon, the organizers did the politically correct thing and allowed only the melons to compete at the Festa dels Meló, with prizes for the biggest and the heaviest fruits.

Costelletes de porc amb salsa de Magranes

Pork chop with pomegranate sauce
(serves four)

The combination dates back to Moorish times, but whereas the Arabs used lamb, the Majorcans mainly use pork.

Ingredients

4 pork chops or roast of equivalent size
Olive oil and pork lard
1 large vegetable onion, diced
1 tbs. white wine vinegar
large glass of dry white wine or *Vi Ranci*
1 stick of cinnamon
Seeds and pulp of 2 large ripe pomegranates
salt, white pepper from the mill

Sear the chops in olive oil and pork dripping on a high flame. Add finely diced onions. Roast in preheated oven for 20 minutes at 180° C, constantly basting it with its own juices. Pour over wine vinegar and white wine. Add stick of cinnamon and pomegranate seeds and simmer once more in the oven for 15 minutes. Salt and pepper. Switch off oven and leave the dish to stand for 10 minutes inside. Before serving, cut the meat from the bone. Serve on a serving dish in slices.

Majorcans make no attempt to compete with South American banana exporters. They eat their home-grown bananas themselves.

The heavy, tomato-like kakis are ripe and aromatically sweet when they yield to slight pressure.

Exclusive and yet hospitable
Port d'Andratx

Until late into the 20th century this port with its view of Sa Dragonera and, on a clear day, even a glimpse of distant Ibiza, was a trading center where no-one lived willingly. But only if the products of orchards and vegetable beds could be successfully shipped from Andratx did peasant farmers have any chance of an income. In the heyday of piracy, this port was therefore kept small and unimpressive so that in case of an attack it could be quickly abandoned without agonizing over the losses.

There is no trace of this any more. The onetime ugly duckling floats on the water like a proud swan. Once a necessary but uncertain evil, the port is now one of the loveliest in the Mediterranean. When the first great run of northern European migrants with well-filled wallets came seeking refuge from the cold, buying plots in sunny Majorca, within no time Port d'Andratx had become a big but still classy fish in a small pool. Unlike its neighbors specializing in mass tourism, both immigrants and parish officials always kept an eye on appropriateness of scale. Along the two-mile coastline towards Cap de sa Mola villas and second homes were built which for all their opulence blend discreetly into the rocky slopes, or at least the older ones do. Thus, any local who for centuries had owned a worthless, barren plot of land now reaped a unique opportunity for a magnificent deal.

No hotdog stalls or trinket shops

The little port has adjusted discreetly and tastefully to the needs and standards of its new residents. A large marina offers sanctuary to floating dreams. In the lanes, one row back behind the seafront, there is hardly any traffic, modern traffic-calming being in place.

Neat cafés line the shorefront, doing it with Mediterranean flair without needing to resort to cheap pottery and beach slippers. The untrained visitor will have to hunt for postcards and suncream because he won't trip over them as in nearby Peguera and Magaluf. And bathing costumes, rubber ducks and fishing nets are pretty pointless because there is virtually nowhere to swim. Port d'Andratx is for boats and strollers, a piece of maritime Majorca where the soul can quietly relax, if it can afford a seat in a café.

Above: In the port of Andratx there is always a lot going on. Fishing boats return from their daily trip to the fishing grounds, while leisure skippers polish decks and brass.

Right: Offshore at Port d'Andratx, the fishing fraternity have a go at the sea population, and not only with nets. For crayfish and related crustaceans they have special traps anchored to the sea floor.

Opposite: Calvià is just round the corner and yet could not be further. In Port d'Andratx, tourism has found a discreet, unobtrusive mode. Both European yacht owners and local fishermen profit equally – and are jointly proud of Port d'Andratx's reputation as the "prettiest harbor in the Mediterranean."

The fishermen and the Virgin
Sea processions on Majorca

The night of 17 July: the whole harbor is a sea of lights, while the mild air and a slight onshore breeze, a starlit sky, brightly lit yachts and the light from street lamps, torches and houses lend the evening a wonderful atmosphere of magic, as in a dream. On the water, countless *llaüts* bob up and down, all equipped with torches, the reflection of their flames rippling back to the quay on gentle waves. One in the middle is particularly lavishly rigged out and illuminated; it carries a figure of the Virgin, and is slowly driven out of the harbor with the other boats, lightly rocking, on to the open sea.

Almost all the ports of the Balearics have nocturnal ship processions around the nights

of 15 July. Because in matters of faith the fishermen know they are in good hands: their guardian angel, the Virgin Mary, in this case the Blessed Virgin of Mount Carmel in the Holy Land, watches with tender but firm female hand over their welfare. To constantly renew her goodwill for themselves, they hold this annual festival in her honor, and although relatively few families live exclusively from fishing nowadays, they have remained true to tradition. In Port d'Andratx the celebrations for the *Mare de Déu del Carme, Carmen* in Castilian, last three days, but the great nocturnal procession is the high point.

First, the Mother of God is placed on her pedestal and decorated all over by the

The Blessed Virgin of Mount Carmel protects fishermen on the high seas. So that she does not forget her duties, a great festival is celebrated in her honor every year.

The Virgin sails out to sea on a festively decorated *llaüt*.

the whole summer in humble huts on the shore separated from their families, because the daily walk to the sea cost too much effort and time.

On 29 June, shortly after Trinity, the figure of the saint is carried down to the sea for the Sant Pere procession and fixed to a richly adorned boat, which casts off immediately, followed by all the other fishing boats, so the procession can be continued out at sea.

Year after year, the faith of the fishermen is reasserted on the high sea in this unique parade. It is accompanied by traditional songs and prayers of supplication, during which time gradually all the catching equipment and finally the water itself are blessed, so that the fishermen will find rich fishing grounds and return home safely – like the floating processions this evening.

fishermen's wives with flower arrangements and candles. Her parade mantle is dusted down, the crown buffed up. Meantime the menfolk decorate their *llaüts* with garlands of flowers and gay lights. Eventually, everyone gathers in the church to hear the seafarers' liturgy, which was written when the fishermen first combined as a guild and elected the Blessed Mary of Mount Carmel as their patron. That was in the 14th century.

After mass, the men carry the Madonna on their shoulders out of the church. It is counted a great honor to be able to shoulder the divine burden at least part of the way. When the Mother of God has been carried around the whole harbor, she is carried on board an exceptionally splendidly adorned *llaüt* and sails out in the evening breeze, followed by the other boots wound round with garlands of lights and flowers, to pacify the water and its harsh force with her grace and beauty.

Hope for St. Peter's blessing

Port d'Alcúdia celebrates the festival of its patron saint Sant Pere (St. Peter) without torches and Bengal lights. St. Peter was once a humble fisherman on Lake Galilee, and has therefore been patron saint of seafarers and fisherman and guardian not only of the pearly gates but also of the weather.

However, for Majorca he has an additional special importance.

The feast of Trinity the week after Whitsunday used to mark the beginning of the fishing season. This was the day when the fishermen, laden with bags of provisions and accompanied by friends and relatives, trekked through the mountains down to the shore. For centuries, many fisherman who actually lived inland were forced to spend

The procession is accompanied by a brass band with cheerleaders.

Wild goats,
mild poppies
Es Capdellà

As the name Capdellà, "Cape of the Furthest Point", says in Majorcan: there's nothing more to the west. Not at least as understood in the mountain region of Calvià. That a mountain village should contain an unmistakably maritime term such as Cap in its name has seafaring reasons: in 1717 Antoní Barceló was born in Galilea, very close by. He went to sea and soon moved up from the rank of simple sailor to the Royal Defender against Corsairs and commander of the Spanish fleet. With part of his very large income he endowed a parish church in Es Capdellà, not Galilea. The church in Galilea he did have renovated, but the seadog christened the village with his new church Cap.

As it intends to honor his name, it blends into the hillside as picturesquely as if it were riding on lapping waves. Away from the main roads, the village follows its own rhythm. In the gardens of the houses,

Opposite: Untroubled by traffic chaos and a long way from the sea, latter-day corsairs in Es Capdellà take to their bikes.

Below: Esclata-sang is braised and enjoyed where it is found.

washing fills with the wind, much as the sails of a *llaüt* do in a breeze. Around Capdellà of course the prey are four-legged rather than submarine. No contest; S'Alqueria is hunting terrain, not a fish pond. But sportsmen are much more likely to find goats reluctantly allowed to run wild in their sights rather than majestic stags and timid roedeer. In accordance with tradition, goats are allowed to graze freely, relying on them sticking with their leader and going with the

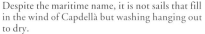

Despite the maritime name, it is not sails that fill in the wind of Capdellà but washing hanging out to dry.

herd. Unfortunately, they do not always do that, instead scattering in freedom over the pastures over 2,000 feet (185 meters) up and bringing into the world the next generation of completely wild mountain goats.

In November, after the first heavy rains, mushroom hunters go a-stalking in the woods, in their rucksacks a bag containing a pan, garlic, pork fat, salt and pepper and a few bush tomatoes. They are hunting *esclata-sang*, a mushroom of the milk fungus family. Sweating the ingredients lightly together in the pan, they make a delicious mushroom fry, because *escalata-sang* must be eaten quite fresh – and where fresher than where you find it?

The woods on the high ground of the south-west can also turn up other finds: herbs for *herbes*, Majorca's herbal liqueur, and the opium poppy, *Papaver somniferum*, called *cascall* in Majorcan. This remedy for pain and sleeplessness is obtained from bushes about 2'6 inches (80 cm) high, or more precisely from the flower capsules, which are cut crossways five times to release a thickish white juice. Watered down as a mouthwash, it is a splendid remedy against toothache.

Herbs in the bottle
Palo and herbes

The European Union has dealt a savage blow to *palo*, which means 'stick'. The dark herbal spirit, which is part of any good Majorcan meal, has been officially devalued by the bureaucrats. As with the famous *ensaïmada* buns, the Majorcans wanted to protect the designation of origin of the sweet brandy and so approached the Awards Commission in Brussels.

The bureaucrats of the Commission promptly delivered a shattering no to the liqueur producers' suggestion. In the notice of refusal it says that the stamp of quality cannot be issued because some ingredients, such as for example gentians and cinchona, did not grow on Majorca and therefore had to be brought in from other regions. *Palo* could not therefore be a drink completely

originating in Majorca and was therefore not worthy of protection. No doubt more than one bottle of the dark liqueur was downed to make this nasty document digestible.

Palo did not always feature just as an aperitif or digestive in Majorcan pantries. In the 16th century, when malaria was carrying off many a Majorcan, a cocktail of cinchona and gentians was introduced by the Countess of Chinchón as a proven means to fight the fatal fever. However, as the brew had a pretty foul taste, it was soon refined with cane sugar, nutmeg, and, some say, carob, then matured for a year in oak barrels for the dark-brown brew to develop its unique taste.

Thus, *palo* was ready for its grand

Right: The basis of *palo* is cinchona.

Below: To round off the unique flavor of the drink, additional ingredients find their way into the pot.

Herbes and *palo* are almost as popular as souvenirs from Majorca as the famed coiled *ensaïmada* buns.

tion. No doubt during pirate raids which plagued the island between the 14th and 17th centuries, the brave defenders strengthened themselves with a stiff tot of the stuff for Dutch courage's sake – certainly the modern *moros i cristians* "postludes" in Port de Pollença or Port de Sóller can't do without it.

entrance. Its hour came when the bell tolled for wine. Directly after the vine-pest *Phylloxera* had devastated vine stocks in the 1890s, the Majorcan herbal liquor was promoted from a mere aperitif to a complete substitute for table wine. With an alcohol content of 22 to 38 per cent, it does moreover have a little more bite than wine.

The island's most famous herbal liqueur is *herbes*, which has no problems of origin. All the herbs used in it grow on the island. Pliny was familiar with it 2,000 years ago. Writing about its predecessor *hierbas*, he reported that it contained 100 herbs and was used effectively against disease. After all, Majorcans are quite at home in their herbal gardens and have certainly always employed herbs such as rosemary or thyme against ailments as much as an aromatic taste improver.

And long before antipasti with tomatoes, mozzarella and basil marched triumphantly across Europe in the colors of the Italian national flag, that particular herb was already much appreciated on the island. As to how many of the aromatic taste-bearers a really good *herbes* should contain, minds do not think alike. Many opine that a *herbes* is perfect with five different ingredients, others think twelve is the happy medium, while perfectionists demand at least 26 plants of different kinds in the olive-oil colored drink for it to unfurl its characteristic aroma.

At any rate, along with mint, rosemary, hyssop, lavender and myrtle one herb must always be present – anise. The basis for aniseed liqueur is the colorless or pale yellow essential aniseed oil from the fruit of *Pimpinella anisum*, which has a spicy smell and sweetish flavor, and is mixed with herbal extracts. Experimentally minded brandy distillers add the aroma of oranges or lemons, to add a distinguishing touch to the liqueur. Nowadays *herbes* is available in three versions for most tastes; *seques* or dry, *semiseques* or medium dry and *dolces*, sweet.

The effects of *herbes* are beneficial for both body and soul, as has been known since the 13th century. In its 40 or so "revolutions" the possibility cannot at least be excluded that it works on the mind. Whether it stimulates, excites or dulls is, as with every medicine, a matter of the appropriate dose.

The famous Majorcan philosopher and missionary Ramon Llull was apparently far from spurning the occasional glass of *herbes* during his long stay on Mount Randa before losing himself in spiritual thought. He enthusiastically extolled the drink as medicine and recommended regular consump-

The "illuminating" drink gleams a poisonous green in the characteristic bottles.

From Cinderella to Princess
Calvià

At the end of the 20th century it is difficult, if not impossible, to imagine that the southwest tip of the island was once a Land's End, and that only smugglers used to feel comfortable between Palma Nova and Fornells, because they would find safe hiding places for their goods; that otherwise only lonely rocky bays with fine sandy beaches dallied time away in the weak ebb and flow of the Mediterranean tide and that for centuries people in Calvià hardly knew how to fill the next family supper bowl .

They were fisherman and peasants, exposed to one of the most inhospitable landscapes of Majorca. The little they had they inherited by the division of property:

Above: Once the poorest commune in Europe, Calvià has become the richest. The magic formula for this success lies back in the boom years of tourism. Give visitors – in this case, a mainly British sun-sand-fun public – what they want. Not until the 1990s did Calvià take a more critical look at itself.

Left: Majorcan props for photos to take home: "We were there (even if we didn't see much of Majorca)."

the eldest son got the farm, and all the other children the uninteresting bits of land on the coast – an irony of history, as would become clear only a little later. Their area had only made history once, they thought, and that brought feudal rule and poverty. It was at Santa Ponça the Christian *conquistadores* landed in 1229 under King Jaume I to conquer the island and drive out the Moors.

Ten tourists for every Majorcan

Seven hundred years later a new invasion lay at the gates of Calvià, up to then one of the poorest communities in Europe. Ever since the "primeval" tourists George Sand, Frédéric Chopin, Archduke Ludwig Salvator of Habsburg-Tuscany, and the Austrian Empress Sissy left for home with tales about the sunny delights of Majorca, an initial trickle of tourists has been turning into a flood. Britons in particular started visiting the island after Winston Churchill spent a holiday in Port de Pollença.

Before that, in 1905, the island authorities saw the need for an office to promote tourism. 30,000 visitors a year was more than the island could absorb without action being taken. The first hotels were built in Palma, and in and around Port de Pollença. After the Civil War and the years of starvation came the economic boom years, even in Franco's Spain, and the ever-resourceful, business-minded Majorcans, who had had invasions before, made a virtue of necessity.

Majorcan connoisseur and historian Jesús Rodríguez explains it like this: "Majorcans responded to these new, relatively moneyed invaders with a balanced attitude of half welcome, half indifference. They made the visitors' stay easy and pleasant, but took no part in their doings, which ran contrary to their deeply conservative customs."

In 1950, 100,000 tourists landed on Majorca. Ten years later it was 350,000, and by 1966 the magic figure of one million had been surpassed. As a non-EEC country and shunned dictatorship on the edge of Europe, Spain was considered more than a bargain compared with other regions. But the size of the demand dramatically outstripped supply.

Majorca's population increased tenfold to 600,000 under the lure of the new wealth, many of the immigrants coming from the poor regions of the Spanish mainland, particularly Andalusia and Murcia. In 1950 there were 8,200 hotel beds in Majorca. Nearly 50 years later, around 6.2 million tourists slept in 390,000 hotel and apartment beds – a quarter of the Spanish total.

Every fourth visitor goes to Calvià and the beaches of Magaluf, Peguera, Santa Ponça, and Illetes. When the boom began,

Calvià's history at a glance, put together in a tiled picture. Key dates: first populated 400 BC, arrival of the Romans 123 BC, conquest by the Moors 902 AD (it says 904 in the picture).

On the right, an overview of the wealth of flora and fauna from which the commune lived for

centuries before and after the Christian reconquest in 1229.

Center, above, the picture shows Calvià's great moment in history: Jaume I's troops landing at Santa Ponça, which belongs to Calvià, and driving his standard into the sand.

the Calvians did not shilly-shally; their bays were close to the port and airport of Palma. No-one had ever built anything here. Now they built hotels. Owners of piecemeal legacies of beach plots now struck it rich. Mostly family businesses sprang up with around 300 beds, because the team of father, mother, and children and a few seasonal hands could not manage more.

In the 1960s, wage and social security costs were low, so that many of these new hoteliers could expand without the quality of service suffering. They offered fresh-cooked food with ingredients fresh from the

Right: Come as you like is the rule. In the high season, nothing remains of the rigid, seemly dress code of yesteryear. Guests must feel at ease and not be confronted with local preconceived value judgments.

market, personal care of guests and everything still cheap.

"I still remember how my father was the manager of our first hotel on the Playa de Palma and looked after the reception," recalls Luis Riu Jr., president of the Riu hotel chain, a Majorcan enterprise with more than 80 hotels (1999). "My mother worked in the floor service and the reception. Grandfather was responsible for technical maintenance and purchases, grandmother for laundry and the floor service."

Families like the Rius and the Escarrers, founders of the Sol Melià hotel chain with

Below: Cala Portals Vells belongs to Calvià commune. Its concrete towers and round-the-clock entertainment are just round the corner, but nonetheless minor escapes from everyday reality are possible even here. Sporting boats at anchor bob up and down, a reminder that the water needs to see action too.

over 250 hotels (1999), and the Barcelós with their tourist empire, which includes 44 hotels among other things, swam with the tide of fortune. Once guests started flying in aboard charter planes, wanting to rent cars and make excursions, communes like Calvià were scarcely able to keep up with the high-rise hotel blocks, approved and thrown up in haste until they formed a wall of concrete segregating land from sea. The personal service and good food likewise had to give way to mass production. Quick profits were too attractive, and high demand pushed up prices for basic food-stuffs.

Europe's richest commune in crisis
The oil crisis of the 1970s brought it home even to Majorca's visitors that the golden times were over. Caterers paid off waiters, seafronts atrophied, sewage plants remained absent, road-building stopped. Small hote-liers had to quit, numerous high-rise hotels changed hands several times, rarely being renovated in the process.

And scarcely anyone anticipated what would soon happen in the principal village at the foot of Puig Galatzó. Basque-born Margarita Nájera married a Calvian, and after she had looked her fill at the humble beauty of the stone-built village and the

On the eastern border of Calvià commune, at Port Vells, things seem rather quiet, even if guests enjoy the same liberal ways as at Peguera and Magaluf.

nouveau riche blessings of the beach communities, she stood for mayor, and in 1991 was duly elected.

A Basque teaches Majorcans to protect their country
The new mayoress of by far the richest commune in Europe knew one thing clearly: things could not go on like this. Tourists on cheap packages were often drunken vandals.

131

Refuse had to be collected five times a day in Calvià to cart away the tourists' droppings. "Majorca will always have an ecological problem, with too little water, too much rubbish and too much dirt in the streets, unless Majorcans and tourists alike change their ways," says Nájera. Tourism yes, but to a bearable extent and with quality. As it used to be in Majorca.

Measures were passed for 15 dismal hotels, gruesome concrete blocks from the boom time of mass tourism, to be blown up and in their place inviting beach promenades laid out. Her administration re-classified 1,500 hectares already scheduled as building land as natural landscape worth protecting. That did not make her friends among the property speculators, but it did win the "European prize for environmentally sustainable urbanism" in 1997, jointly with Stockholm and Heidelberg.

"In Spain, environmental politics and environmental awareness are still in their infancy," explains Nájera. "But thanks to the long-standing solid example of more enlightened cultures, we've got a head start." Conditions such as 1996, when drinking water had to be brought in by ship, must never be allowed to arise again. In Calvià, "where we must and want to be a step further forward," since 1998 "gray" water has been used in toilets, in other words, water that has been cleaned in the communal purification plant but not to the final, drinking water standard.

Calvià is on its way. In Calvià's shore communities, hotels still crowd together side by side. Magaluf is a British mass reserve, Peguera speaks German, and lonely coves are history. But things are progressing in a model way. In Calvià even the sea is swept now. Every day, a small *llaüt*, the typical

In the old village of Calvià, center of the administrative district, mass tourism has still to make a mark. Only the neat and tidy image indicates that hunger and poverty have long become alien terms.

boat of the Balearics, sets off early in the morning along the south-west coast of Majorca and fishes plastic bottles and bags, rubber shoes and battered coolboxes out of the sea. Even mass tourists shall have clean water.

Right: Once a day a community *llaüt* collects rubbish from the sea. The careless and irresponsible treatment of nature in Calvià is over.

Below: Even in Calvià the idyll is just round the corner – dreamy coves like this protect themselves against the storm of holiday invaders by confronting the sea with cliffs rather than beaches.

Raiguer

Majorca-off-Sea
Raiguer

Shortly after the last winter rains have given the earth one final good soak, the almond trees on the gentle sloping foothills of the Tramuntana mountain chain offer their first buds to the sun. A few days later, clouds of white and pink blossom have settled on the trees, filling the clear pre-spring air with a delicate fragrance. On such days, it is still so cold in the evenings that in many stone villages a quite different aroma fills the lanes, generously supplied from the same source, as almond shells of the past harvest are burnt in household fireplaces.

Once *primavera* has finally prevailed over the short Mallorcan winter, the farmland turns into a sea of blossom, scent and color, though unlike in neighboring Pla, it is scattered over hillsides and valley hollows. Raiguer switches between two worlds; between the headlong gallop of the Tramuntana and the comfortable amble of Pla.

In summer, every vehicle on the curving, narrow country roads is transformed into a composition of dust and glistening light. On the drystone walls and the façades of the bright yellow Marès stone houses lizards defy gravity in the search for the best place on the sunny side of life for cold-blooded creatures; crickets and grasshoppers launch into a months-long concert in the olive groves, apricot and carob plantations and the brown-burnt fields, interrupted only by the dry cracking and banging of the almond harvest.

Only to fall silent in autumn, when cool swathes of mist transform the fields into magic landscapes at eventide. Or even more enchanted scapes during the daytime, if nature so wills it, and much wetter than mist. At Campanet, the chalky soil is so porous that a decent downpour is enough to transform the red soil between the trees into a regular lake in the twinkling of an eye. *Fonts ufanes*, proud springs, is what Mallorcans call this phenomenon, which has

nothing to do with either springs or with the traditional tale of subterranean water courses from the distant Pyrenees.

Shoes and wine ...

For most holiday-makers, Raiguer is a must item during a proper visit to Majorca any time of year, because this is where a whole series of the most popular tourist souvenirs come from.

Inca, the geographical center of Raiguer, welcomes thousands of visitors every day. During the day, they flood the shoe and leather goods factories and their direct outlets, looking for a bargain that will be more use at home than the three hundredth soap dish made of shells. Shoes from Inca are well-known and famous throughout Europe. The high-quality workmanship promises durability, certainly until the next visit to Majorca, and in matters of fashion Inca shoemakers have no need to hide their faces behind their Italian colleagues from Milan and Florence.

Since founding their own guild in 1458, the shoemakers and furriers of Inca have handed on their skills from generation to generation. And they are, at least on this scale, the only craft that has flourished in Inca to this day. Around 1600, there were already 150 craft workshops at work in this centrally placed town founded by the Romans. They ranged from cobblers to weavers, carpenters and smiths to potters. Eight lawyers ensured that everything was above board.

And, with almost the same soil under their feet as neighboring Binissalem, the good folk of Inca also turned to wine-growing. However, unlike their neighbors, wine-growers from Inca were unable to pick themselves up after the vine-pest disaster of 1890 and replant their stocks. But enterprising as they had always been, they

Previous double-page spread: Whereas the wind has powerful work to do on the sails of the old windmill behind Santa Eugènia, the agaves have nothing to do except bask in the sun.

Below: In Raiguer, agriculture and industry both have their hands full. Even so, time needs to be made for a bit of snail tempo.

found a new use for the disused wine cellars. In these naturally cool *cellers* they left only the huge tuns in place, half walled up in the lofty walls, brought in tables and chairs and installed cooks and created a form of gastronomy that is quite unique in Majorca, obstinately unsuited to hotdogs and the clichés of the mainland. Meanwhile, Mallorcan wines flowed from the tuns as before, though now of Binissalem vintage.

Fifty years after the vine-pest made short work of all the wine stocks and desperate wine-growing colleagues had afforested their fields with promising almond trees, the latter wine area got interested again. The only reputation it had to lose was a bad one, because when the whole of continental Europe was without wine nearly a century earlier and indiscriminately bought everything that resembled fermented grape juice, Mallorcan wine-growers made their great killing – the majority with frightful skullsplitters. But conditions are good in Binissalem and neighboring Santa Maria del Camí; adequate precipitation, a short, hot summer, and soil with the right mixture of chalk and sand such as wine needs. It's slowly getting about in Majorca that today's Binissalem wines from the traditional Manto Negro grape and above all the skillful blends of Cabernet and Tempranillo can do more than increase the sales of aspirin.

The border territory between the Tramuntana uplands and the plains of Pla carries water in its name – Raiguer. Windmills like this one at Campanet pump it out during the day so that the extensive plantations do not run dry.

… clay whistles and carvings

Further towards Palma, in Marratxí, the oddest symbols of Majorca are produced, the *siurells*. Not actually in Marratxí, because that is only a name for the combined villages of Sa Cabaneta and Pòrtol, the two pottery mini-metropolises of Majorca. At first glance, the *siurells* – Joan Miró was so keen on them that he collected them avidly – seem to derive from the avant-garde, experimental brain of a post-modernist artist, but that is an illusion.

These clay figures, which depict peasants and all kinds of creatures, are mostly painted white and dotted red and green. At the base or plinth a small whistle is hidden, on which it is anything but easy to play even a single note – even for the makers. Whether they were a Moorish children's toy or a medieval flirting device remains unclear. But one thing is clear: they are witty, a little askew like their whistles, and as appealing as they are useless.

Don't jump to conclusions from the name! Biniamar is not "Bini-on-Sea" but an old Moorish settlement named for the "sons of Omar". In late medieval times a fortified site developed. Better safe than sorry.

Two other Mallorcan bestsellers also come from Raiguer, and both from the same village: Consell is not only the home of the typical *pa moreno*, the unsalted dark bread of the peasants, but also of a very suitable topping, the *camaiot* sausage. A spicy mixture of blood, meat and fat bacon embedded in thick rind, it has cast off its calorie-rich villainous image in a new wave of Mallorcan pride.

Peasant life between self-determination and suppression

Being some way from the sea, this region was always blessed with a special, almost continental climate, with enough heat and rain for a flourishing agriculture. So fertile and lush are the pastures on the slopes of Raiguer that for example 14th-century peasants from Selva fought stubbornly to be their own masters. At any rate, with some success. Around the commune of Caimari they could plant carob, almond trees, and olives at their own initiative, breed black Mallorcan pigs and – an almost unheard of concession for the time – even own their horses.

In Lloseta on the other hand the villagers had to endure serfdom in its worst form for several hundred years. Granted in the course of the *repartiment* – redistribution of land under Jaume I – to a Catalan baron and declared a county by his heirs in the 17th century, Lloseta could have rejoiced in one of the finest aristocratic palaces, the Palau d'Ayamans, were it not for the most degrading punishment facilities installed by the lord in front of it – gallows, stocks and a hanging cage, to make great offenses out of minor misdemeanors.

Struggling for freedom, 1,500 feet up

Raiguer has its share of historical and fateful locations. In Alaró it is 1,640 feet (500 m) up, and nowadays displays only the remains of plundered masonry. The castle hill is nonetheless extremely attractive for its strategic setting – a splendid panorama allows every movement on the surrounding plains to be seen from afar, and the vantage point was probably used as a lookout from Majorca's earliest days. When the Moors came to the island, the first Christian inhabitants sought refuge here and held out eight years against the subsequent siege.

More than 300 years later it was the turn of the Moors to barricade themselves in against the invading Christians. But despite adequate supplies for a long, stubborn war of confrontation, matters took an unexpected turn after a short siege. The commander and governor of Pollença, El Benehabet, surrendered, convinced that, given the Christian superiority, nothing could be achieved but a bloodbath on both sides.

Sails for the wind and silence for dissonances

Purely civil functional buildings adorn other hills in Raiguer: unlike in Pla, windmills serve not to pump water but to grind cereals into flour. Three especially fine authoritative specimens on Mount Putxet loom over the village of Santa Eugènia. Only one of them still has sails for the wind to turn or strum its Aeolian harp.

But that's no problem. The center of earthly music is not far. ACA, the foundation for contemporary music, has taken up residence in an old farmhouse in tiny, sleepy Búger huddled between two hills. It was exactly what its founder Antoní Caimari needed: the singing peace of Raiguer for the weird harmonies of his highly esteemed three-tone music. So as not to dampen the spirits of village inhabitants all at once, ACA also gives concerts with classical programs. After all, Raiguer and its harmonious beauty are much too generous to allow for nothing but dissonance.

Raiguer? What's that?

In villages such as Búger or Moscari, where mass tourism could not be more distant, where at best a few scattered foreigners spend up to

Above: "Proud springs" is what Mallorcans call this impressive display of natural forces. Heavy downpours of rain flood the porous chalky soil near Campanet knee-deep in a flash, changing picturesque almond plantations into raging torrents of water.

a week at a time in one of the golden yellow stone houses, where the village bar is the social center and only Mallorcan is spoken, a question for advanced Majorca connoisseurs needed clarifying. All the names of districts in Majorca have a meaning. They refer to points of the compass or the direction of the wind, or, as in the central plain of Pla, the type of landscape. Only Raiguer doesn't fit the pattern. What does the name mean? In the Nou bar in Moscari the question fills an evening. The football match that blares from the TV from the upper corner of the bar, as everywhere, is forgotten. It seems at any rate that Raiguer has something to do with dampness, precipitation or irrigation, this much is agreed. Whether it comes from Castilian *regadero*, where gardens are sprinkled, or Arabic is not clear; no-one knows. However it may be, they say, Raiguer is the center of Majorca in a double sense: a nodal point and heart, something of everything, only – since the land reform of the 1990s, which gave Alcúdia to Pla – a land without sea, alas.

Following double-page spread: Mass tourism in Raiguer has fixed touchdown points: the shoe factories in Inca, the potteries in Marratxí, the vineyards in Binissalem. The farmland at the foot of the mountains is meantime just passing scenery, and looks quite undisturbed.

Below: Visible from afar, the church of Sant Llorenç looms over the town of Selva in the heart of Raiguer. The loss of their town charter in 1301 induced inhabitants not to stand idly by while the owner of large estates asserted his privileges, and their stubbornness was to some degree successful.

Where the clay whistles
Marratxí

On the last day of June, eyes, ears, and noses have much to do in Marratxí. That they are not disturbed by the irritating buzzing, whizzing or especially the chomping of mosquitoes is all thanks to the local saint, Sant Marçal, the patron saint of animals, who watches over all the creepy crawlies, and on his feast day forbids mosquitoes access, or so local legend has it.

In the Pòrtol part of the town, all restaurants fill the summer air with the smell of rabbit with onions, and all the potters put out their wares on the street, because Pòrtol is Majorca's leading center for ceramics. A strange piping and fluting, sometimes rather asthmatic, sometimes masterly, fills the lanes and streets.

Responsible for this are the most typical of all Majorcan ceramics, the *siurells* that Joan Miró so delighted in. These are archaic-looking figures up to 15" (40 cm) high, mostly depicting men and women in hats, but also dogs, horses, horses and riders, bulls or donkeys. They are painted white and apparently randomly provided with red and green dots. And they all have a little clay whistle in the base, which with difficulty produces a note - and funnily enough, many of the makers are unable to play their own *siurells*.

Where the *siurells* come from remains unclear. Some ethnologists believe, very obviously, these are an ancient Moorish toy. In Majorca, the popular view is that the

At the end of June, the pottery stores in Marratxí are cleared in honor of Sant Mascal. A particularly interesting sight are the droll *siurells* with their green and red dots.

Phoenicians imported the little whistles, as they did in similar form in Sardinia, Crete, and Ibiza. Others consider them a flirting device going back centuries: if a young man presented his beloved with a *siurell*, she could show her views without a word: if she dropped it and smashed it, he'd lost. If she played *siurell* notes, he'd won.

Earthenware soup bowls, Moorish ceramics, and Andalusian intruders

Pòrtol's potters do of course produce other no less practical objects. The rural population of Majorca has used earthenware crockery for cooking and eating for centuries. Only the triumphal march of plastic combined with a weakened sense of tradition caused a lot of trouble to the established pots and plates business in the mid-20th century.

Scarcely a half century later, markets and potteries are once again overflowing with *greixoneres*, full-bodied cooking pots made from brown clay, plates, cups, whole dining and coffee services, serving plates, bowls and teapots. In Majorcan, clay is *fang*, and at the *Fira del Fang*, the ceramics fair of Marratxí in the last week of March, all kinds of Majorcan pottery wares can be admired. In Pòrtol itself, the potters working purely as craftsmen are found somewhat out of the center. One of the *olleries* (potteries) called Can Vent even uses a donkey to drive the clay-mixing machine.

Majorcan general-purpose and everyday ware is a plain reddish brown and simply glazed. A somewhat more luxurious variant possesses a decoration of simple lines and dots, mostly in dark green, dark blue and yellow. However, as Majorca has not only red but also white clay, the markets and potteries also sport decidedly good-looking, colorful china as well. The white clay was originally used to make roof tiles, which in Majorca are shaped like pipes slit lengthwise

In old times, every household had cooking and storage crockery made of earthenware.

and set in alternate concave and convex rows.

With this tough but nonetheless handsome clay, master potters produce all conceivable kitchen and household utensils on their wheels. Typical of Majorcan china are large flower patterns in red and blue tones, reminiscent of Michaelmas daisies or sunflowers. Very widespread are also plates

After a few decades dominated by plastic, the potters in Pòrtol and Sa Cabanete have their work cut out for them.

with sun and moon "portraits" adorned with the Majorcan names of the four main winds and arabesques - ornamental, purely abstract patterns in the Moorish tradition, which forbids any representation of living beings.

Meanwhile, mass tourism with its enormous demand for souvenirs has resulted in great quantities of pottery from the mainland being sold on the island, mostly from Andalusia and the Toledo ceramic centers of Talavera de la Reina and Puente del Arzobispo. They include enchanting pieces, of course, but anyone wanting genuine Majorcan pottery need only turn the desired object over to check. The origin has to be labeled underneath.

Lace bonnets
and hempen soles
Costume

With wide-brimmed straw hats pulled low over their foreheads, groups of women still make their way to the fields even today, carrying hoes and rakes. The *palmito* is tied under the chin with colorful ribbons, and under that women frequently wear a scarf tied at the back, often sewn out of dark material, just as their smocks and skirts remain generally dark blue or black. The simple clothing of female agricultural laborers has scarcely changed since Archduke Ludwig Salvator described it. That may be because the clothing was the result of practical considerations rather than the latest fashions. The broad brim protects against blinding light, the scarf absorbs sweat, and dark materials look dirty less quickly than light materials.

But apart from agricultural gear, things have happened in clothing. Ludwig Salvator was already able to report in the last quarter of the 19th century that the costume "is only worn by the occasional older person who has remained faithful to patriotic tradition." That is even more true today. Majorcans may at first glance look somewhat more

A long plait is a traditional part of female dress in Majorca. It hangs down under the lace coif to the hips.

classic than their northern European holiday guests, but the current fashion here too is basically international. Local costume is taken out of the cupboard only on festive occasions.

These days, you are most likely to come across men in broad knee-length breeches and women in ankle-length skirts with brightly colored aprons in a folk group.

Shortly before the turn of the millenium, the fine lace cloths, *redosillos,* are also still popular with the young female majorcans, though only for special occasions.

Then colorful cloths embroidered with plant motifs, the *mantó,* catch the eye from afar, while the men wear a broad single-color sash, the *faixa,* round their hips to dance and wear knee-length socks under the wide

Around 1930, it was quite normal on Sunday to get the traditional costume out of the cupboard.

often hangs to waist length. These days, women and girls with modern short hairstyles can buy such Majorcan plaits in their hair coloring at the hairdresser's or folk costume shop.

Archduke Ludwig Salvator also mentioned in his description that poorer people go barefoot almost all year round, but these days bare feet are only seen on the sandy beaches. *Espardenyes*, espadrilles with hemp soles, have put an end to shoeless lives, but the expression *gent d'espardenyes*, "espadrille people", still means poor people. The simple espadrille meantime has been wafted to the top of the social ladder, finding its way into the royal household in Madrid, because Queen Sofía regularly buys *alpargatas*, fiber sandals, during her traditional summer holiday in Majorca.

trousers. For both men and women, there is always a straw hat.

That the costumes emphasized the figure was also noted by the Archduke: "Majorcan women almost all wear a *gipó*, a close-fitting black bodice which shows slenderness of build to advantage; it is open at the front and is closed with pins." The *gipó* was not a festive garment but traditional women's clothing that was also worn to work.

On holidays, jewelry was added, as is still the case. In religious processions and other ceremonial parades women's clothing flashes everywhere with gold buttons and chains. "Among the most common articles here are the shirt and gipó buttons, which total 16 pieces to make up a *botonada* (row of buttons), and if decorated with gold and precious stones they cost up to 160 frcs," a huge sum at the time.

The *mantó*, a richly embroidered fringed shawl made of finest silk, is a feature of female costume all over Spain, as in Majorca. These often hand-made shawls are real prize pieces, though the versions in souvenir shops are generally industrially made and therefore less valuable. In general, the longer the fringes, the more expensive the cloth; hand-embroidered *mantó* can cost a small fortune.

Part of women's local costumes on the island are white, roughly shoulder-length coifs of lace that cover the head and frame the face. "It is called *volant* when it is soft and closer to the neck and rounded in front, *rebosillo* if it is starched and spread over the shoulders like a bell and falls to a point over the breast …" Underneath it, women wear their hair tied in a long, simple plait, which should at least peep out under the coif and

Hat on for the field, off for church – folk festivals mix the two.

Nymphs and bandoleros
Santa Maria del Camí

Ali cost 70 *libras mallorquinas*. That at any rate is what the receipt dating from 1518 says, certifying the sale of Ali, a 22-year-old slave. It is exhibited in the Museu Balear, the private museum of the Conrado family located in the Convent dels Mínims, the former Minorite monastery at Santa Maria del Camí – the Monestir de Nostra Senyora de la Soledat. On show is a jumble of all sorts of things from numerous landed estates and times, and also a collection of historical documents including letters, marriage certificates and contracts of sale for all kinds of things, including Ali. Perhaps the purchaser hoped Ali would discover a spring on his land, because rural superstition attributed this skill to Moorish slaves.

Moved from near Palma to Santa Maria in 1682, the monastery is in the center of town. That Santa Maria itself is *del camí*, 'on the road', should be taken literally. In Roman times there was a crucifix here and a rest station, which the Moors left where it was, making the place one of their principal settlements and calling it Canarossa. After that, the *carretera* from Palma to Alcúdia via Inca, the old main road of the island, ran right through the middle of the town. Today, the Palma to Inca freeway passes close by, so that everyone gets a glimpse of the massive main church. The foundations have been there since 1246, but the church is of Baroque period and unmistakable, particularly because of the sturdy belltower with its blue, almost truffle-shaped pointed crown.

An idiosyncratic detail in Santa Maria del Camí betrays what makes the inhabitants tick. Again and again you see a branch of pine over the doors, in various stages of drying and turning brown. They are a natural indicator for fermentation and thereby of the aging of wine, because almost all families grow wine for household use and store it in the cellar. They are quite aware that they can no longer compete with

Weapons are no longer traded in the market at Santa Maria del Camí. The lethal-looking folding knife only slices pumpkins in half.

Binissalem, five minutes away as the crow flies, but they are not willing to abandon their own viticultural tradition..

Where more than nymphs and highwaymen hide out

Being remote from the world, this valley was a refuge for bandolers or gunslingers. Grouped into militias, they carried out an absurd mini-war on behalf of two feuding families and fell upon anything and anyone to obtain their daily bread, weapons and clothing. The havoc they caused sometimes got so out of hand that the community set up an armed civil defense: on Sundays, all men between 16 and 60 who were fit and had weapons had to take part in shooting practice in the village fields.

If we are to believe the poet Joan Rosselló, both they and the bandits were watched – by supernatural beings, because above the valley floor is a hidden cave where,

Above: In Coanegra Valley bandits roamed freely in the 17th century. Residents did their utmost to keep house and farm barricaded.

Left: A pine bough over the door indicates that wine is being fermented within.

says the poet, nymphs dance round a fire. Unfortunately they stole the firewood from the god of the cave, who was so annoyed about it that he changed them into doves.

Reality comes full circle here, because the grotto was found in the 18th century by someone whose mule disappeared under a heap of pigeon excrement. A closer look revealed it had "found" the entrance to the cave, which lay concealed under such a "nymphish" heap. Once a week, on Sundays, the owner of the land allows visitors to find out for themselves who is now living in the huge grotto.

Playground of the winds
Santa Eugènia

Two superlatives, a local mountain and an emblem, distinguish the small, sleepy little Raiguer town of Santa Eugènia and its associated neighboring villages of Ses Coves, Ses Alqueries and Ses Olleries (the latter's very name indicates its main industry: potters make pots from clay). Santa Eugènia itself has a saint in its name, but oddly enough has neither a church nor a monastery. Only a Madonna from Lourdes watches over the spiritual welfare of the villages from the "Lourdes cave" on the road from Santa

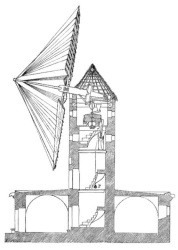

Eugènia to Ses Olleries. On the other hand, Santa Eugènia has two cemeteries: one Catholic, and beside it, since 1978, a Jewish one, the only one in Majorca.

But none of this is responsible for the fact that Santa Eugènia is well-known everywhere. Three purely functional and wholly practical secular buildings have made it

Left: Until the 19th century, windmills only ground cereals, as the conical roof indicates.

Below: Thanks to the inventiveness of a Dutch engineer, windmills were re-equipped to pump water for irrigation.

famous – the windmills that crown the local hill of Putxet and no doubt would have been a special challenge to Don Quixote if he had ever sought Dulcinea in Majorca. Like thousands of other mills on Majorca, they could say more about local life than is told in many a civic chronicle.

In Santa Eugènia's case they are corn mills, recognizable by the pointed top, their line-up in exposed formation on the top of the hill and the fact that they have no collection basin beside them where in water mills precious water is stored. Santa Eugènia lived mainly from cereal farming even under the Arabs, grinding its own corn with wind power so it was ready for sale.

Flour, tobacco, and other powders

In the best preserved of the three, the Molí de Can Camarada, you can still see how the oldest type of Majorcan windmill worked. Since the 15th century such mills have operated by a vertical and a horizontal cogwheel interlocking to drive the millstone below. If need arose, mills of this kind also shredded tobacco, refined gunpowder to explosive quality, and crushed dry clay to dust.

Since engines have replaced wind power, many old windmills are now either sailless or the sails dangle unused.

Not until the 19th century did Majorcans begin to apply this principle to agriculture's number one problem child, namely the ready supply of water. Up till then, donkeys and mules had trodden endless circles around Moorish *sínies* to pump water from the depths of the limestone soil. In Archduke Ludwig Salvator's day, there were still 4,000 *sínies* on the island, and near Sóller there are still around 70 such draw wells at work.

A Dutchman liberates the mule

Water mills in Majorca were a Dutch import. In 1847, Paul Bouvij, an engineer from the land of windmills, converted a cornmill into a water mill. To do this, he swapped the grindstones for cogwheels and a crankshaft, to generate the necessary lift. Outside, a collection pond was installed for the water, so that on windless days the fields could be irrigated from the stored water. The mills still had sails like the old corn mills, but a control fin, which enabled the mill to follow the wind, was not installed until around 1870. Soon countless similar water pumps were installed on the favorite playgrounds of Majorcan winds, Pla, Raiguer and Migjorn.

Both water and cornmills are distinguished by their type of sail: on the *molí de vela llatina* they are similar in shape and material to the sails of traditional *llaüts*. The *molíns de graellat* are blown by the wind through wooden lattices nailed and screwed to the wheel frame. Mills with "flower wheels", the *molíns de ramell*, catch the wind

149

This stump of a windmill does not indicate what kind of sails were used to grind corn.

A "flower wheel" windmill like this one catches the wind in fan-shaped wooden blades.

This corn-mill revolves by means of the *graellat*, a wooden lattice without canvas coverings.

This water mill undoubtedly used to have wooden blades fixed to the wheel. Now it is bare.

A latticed corn mill like this usually stands on higher ground. It does not need to be near the ground water.

In full sail, windmills like this with *vela llatina* sails, though without the sea below them, were best placed to exploit windpower.

Until windmills took over the job, precious water was extracted from underground with *sínies* like this by mule power. They were still used in Ludwig Salvator's day, as the illustration (right) of one near Palma shows.

with wooden boards arranged like a fan, and have a cousin mostly painted blue and white (the colors of wind and sea), the *molí de ferro* with sails of sheet iron.

Performance without fuel or muscle-power

Common to all is the enormous pumping power. Without fuel or muscle-power, they can shift up to six and half US gallons (24.5 liters) of water per revolution, i.e. up to 127 US gallons (480 liters) a minute. It was only when petrol and diesel engines came in the 20th century that windmills had to yield to progress – but not for long. The first oil crisis reminded farmers of the trusty old

sailed friends, and at the end of the 20th century the island government provided grants for re-instating Majorca's emblems. And with success; now, over 1,000 windmills revolve on Aeolus's playgrounds, and not just for decoration.

Furthermore, they are also the first thing that modern visitors see when flying in to Es Prat, Palma's airport – a sea of windmills, many of them revolving elegantly and untiringly in the wind, while others rise from the field like decayed tooth stumps. Many mills are full size, but their sails hang despondently idle. Some even once pumped dry the huge field on which Majorca's airport now stands. Constant, dignified, they are as simple as they are cunning in their operation, which has changed but little ever since the meticulous observer Archduke Ludwig Salvator of Habsburg-Tuscany drew a cross section in his Balearic diary.

Bread, sausage, and the appropriate utensils
Consell

Like many other settlements in Raiguer, Consell also dates back to shortly after the Reconquest by the Christians in the early 13th century. It was built on the estates of a former Moorish farmstead called *conxell*. By the 17th century, provision had also been made for the spiritual welfare of the peasants and artisans, initially with a simple chapel; later, in 1720, this was expanded into a church, the Mare de Déu de la Visitació, Our Lady of the Visitation, which refers to Mary's visit to her cousin Elizabeth. By then, Consell was already an active, busy place with more than 400 inhabitants, mostly

Right: The peasants of Consell have not had to worry about their spiritual welfare since 1720, when their Madonna was given a proper church.

Above: Traditional specialties like *pa moreno* and *camaiot* enjoy great popularity.

peasants but also decidedly skillful and inventive artisans and cooks. Consell has devoted a small but charming local history museum to them.

The cooks and bakers of Consell for example not only established a fine art and reputation for *pa moreno*, the dark, unsalted bread of Majorca, over the whole island but also created *camaiot*, a worthy rival for *sobrassada*, the sausage spread with paprika. This specialty food processes pig's blood (naturally from a native *porcella negra*), bits of meat, fat bacon, spices and salt into sausage and, if traditionally made, it is pressed in a thick rind rather than a sausage skin. Like many foodstuffs from simple peasant cuisine, *camaiot* was frowned upon for its high fat content during the 1960s and 1970s when the modern "healthy eating" fad reached even remote rural areas, but as the fashion changed 20 years later, it recovered its status, and now sales are better than ever.

Mixers and stirrers in peasant kitchens
In Majorcan cuisine, spices, cloves of garlic and cold sauces such as *allioli* – garlic

Only the rough work is done by machine in this workshop making wooden utensils. For salad spoons to sit nice and smoothly in the hand, they must be carefully sanded by hand.

mayonnaise – are crushed or stirred not in a mixer but traditionally in a mortar made of stoneware or, better still, olive or holm oak. Wood stands the pressure of the pestle better than the rigid, brittle stoneware, and a hard, smooth wood like olive is very easy to clean.

Mortars of this kind have been produced by the turners and carvers of Consell for centuries, along with all kinds of other

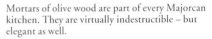

Mortars of olive wood are part of every Majorcan kitchen. They are virtually indestructible – but elegant as well.

household equipment and furnishings. The aim of a good woodworker is always to produce the desired design if possible from a single piece of wood. Adding bits, gluing, doweling and screwing are considered either second-best or a concession. Basically, woodworkers work like sculptors, who can tell from the block of marble what sculpture lies within, sense its elasticity and inner tension by touch and carefully liberate the figure from its outer casing of redundant stone.

In Consell, wood craftsmen have long passed the level of simple turned spoons, forks and mortars. Wooden-handled folding knives whose design resembles curved Arabic daggers are as much virtuoso pieces as the richly decorated chests and practical but sophisticated bread bins to keep the number one bestseller, the *pa moreno* (*pan moreno*) fresh and to hand.

Crisp, crusty, nourishing
Pa moreno

According to a Majorcan fairy tale that Ludwig Salvator records in his collection of stories, a shepherd from the well of Ses Basses was pursued by Moors, but always managed to escape them by using his head. They had already failed to catch him several times before they cornered him in a cave and told themselves hunger would have to drive him out and that, this time, they could definitely catch him. But the shepherd laughed at them through a hole in the cave, showed them a loaf of bread and explained what he was doing: "I'm cutting the bread," he said, "I'm cutting half of it." And so it went on until in the end he showed them how he had cut all the individual slices. At that, the Moors lost heart and said: "He's got bread for a fortnight, he won't come out, and we can't catch him." And they went away and never came back. Since that day, the cave has been called *Cova d'escata pa*, the Cave of Bread Parts.

Right: In earlier times, corn was laboriously ground by hand between two stones. The mill is now driven by a motor whose feed pipes look like Medusa's locks.

Above: Ready to bite into – fresh dark *pa moreno*, the basis for the popular *pa amb oli.*

Bread used to be kept in hanging baskets like this.

If Arab pirates had indeed been as gullible as those mentioned in the story, then Majorca would certainly never have been so devastated by corsairs as unfortunately happened in many coastal towns. The Moors in the tale certainly belong in the realm of fantasy – but the bread was definitely *pa moreno*.

Nothing happens in Majorca without *pa moreno*, the nourishing rye bread whose color distinguishes it from the widespread white bread. The large bakeries, especially in Palma, with their huge output of white bread, almost persuaded Majorcans to forget their basic foodstuff. Only when a degree of prosperity arrived with tourism and a desire arose to revive traditions did they recall their *pa moreno*. A not inconsiderable factor has certainly been the diet-consciousness of tourists, who today invade the island instead of pirates, and prefer the firm dark bread to the puffy white.

Unfortunately, rye bread was once partly responsible for one of the island's worst diseases. It is easy to understand how desperate Majorcans were when they discovered that eating it caused ergotism poisoning resulting from eating ergot, a fungal disease of rye, which carried off a lot of people in the 10th and 11th centuries. They prayed long and hard to St. Antony for help, until they finally discovered that their sufferings– vomiting, diarrhea, and gangrene of the fingers and toes–could be avoided by picking over the corn more carefully before grinding.

Fortunately those times are past, and the incomparable smell of freshly baked *pa moreno* wafts from all bakeries. Baked without salt but with rye flour, yeast, and water, Majorcans add a small quantity of wheatmeal to the bread before it is pushed into the oven, which gives it its characteristic color and a taste stronger than the pallid white loaf. A good dark bread must of course be baked in a wood-fired oven, otherwise the crust will not be crisp and crusty. Bakers in Consell are particularly good at it. Their *pa moreno* is reckoned the best on the island.

Pa moreno is the basis for the widely popular *pa amb oli*. For this, a thick slice of fresh crusty bread is rubbed with garlic and a very ripe tomato and finally drizzled with olive oil. A basic Balearic food, *pa amb oli* represents a perfect symbiosis of the most important Majorcan products – bread, tomatoes, and oil. After this favorite starter comes the *sopes*, a stew, once a poor man's food. Here again, thinly sliced *pa moreno* plays a central role. The slices sit at the bottom of the *greixonera*, the earthenware casserole, where they are drenched in a tasty vegetable broth and returned to the oven.

That the *pa* in this classic dish features large is evident from the name: the slices of bread themselves have likewise been named *sopes* or soups. Thinly sliced, the dried bread can be bought in bags at every bakery on the island, but of course preferably in Consell.

It needs a wood-fired oven for the crust of the bread to be really as crisp as it should be.

155

Poverty and deprivation
Mancor de la Vall

Even if Massenella is not far, for the inhabitants of Manicure all good things came to an end at all times. Located on the edge of the Serra del Norts, the 2,103 ft (641 m) of Puig de Suro is the highest you can get within the commune boundaries of Mancor de la Vall.

Inca, one of Majorca's industrial centers, is only 3 miles away – but seems to belong to a wholly different world, because the lifestyle of Mancor and its atmosphere are scarcely those of today. The little village at the foot of the Serra de Tramuntana seems a Sleeping Beauty, especially in winter when the white sheet of snow covers the landscape. A lonely country road leads into the village and on up to the Santuari de Santa Llucia – where, as from all mountain monasteries in

Majorca, a wonderful view can be enjoyed, as is readily apparent. Its church is the most humble and plainest of all rural chapels built by the Christians after the Reconquest; first documented in 1348, it was for centuries the parish church for Mancor and Biniarroi until Sant Joan Baptista was built below in Mancor de la Vall. The relics of the martyr Probus found their last resting place here, besides those of the Marquès de Palmer, who donated them to Mancor after a pilgrimage to Rome.

The Romans felt quite at home in Mancor, and cleared oak, burnt blackberry brambles and planted a great number of vines on the rocky slopes and in the fertile valleys, which flourish here exceptionally well thanks to a special microclimate. Winters are unusually cold by Majorcan standards; it often snows, and rains a lot; summer days are hot, only at night does it

When a thick layer of snow covers the terraces and tree tops, the landscape of Mancor de la Vall looks even more magical and remote.

turn markedly cool even in the warm season. It is ideal for wine-growers, but an abomination for frozen north Europeans. So far, Mancor has been spared mass tourism.

The irrigation arts of the Moors enabled hemp, flax, vegetables and pulses to be cultivated. Livestock bred included goats and sheep, cattle and horses. The large estates of the Christian conquerors were farmed by tenants, who lived with their families in splendid houses and sublet the worst fields to peasants less blessed by fate.

For everyone else at that time poverty was written large in Mancor, as everywhere in Majorca. By far the largest group of land workers were day laborers, who were always employed just for sowing and reaping. Their income depended on the benevolence of their lords and the size of the harvest brought in. Even the annual *Romeria Santa Llucia*, the pilgrimage up to the Santuari de Santa Llucia on Easter Monday, did not help much there.

Only in the 17th and 18th centuries did some of them get a chance to become tenants or subtenants of the worst land. Many seized the opportunity with both hands, just to have a place to live and work. Thus a *roter* class came into being. The land allocated to them had in part still to be cleared, hence the name. *Roturar* in Castilian means to make cultivable.

Before the *roter* could plow their fields, however, they had first to collect stones by the hundredweight. The larger stones served as building material for their humble dwellings, which in fact looked more like shelters than human habitations, but in which the whole of life was carried on.

For most *roter*, these were probably better living circumstances than when they were day laborers. Living space, barn and stalls were all in one, often with only a thin mud wall separating the humans from the ass, sheep and poultry. The roof was supported on a frame of substantial almond and olive trunks coated with sandstone and mud. A fireplace in the corner provided warmth, and tiny slits allowed air and light in, because there was no money for larger glass windows. A straw-filled palliasse on a

beaten clay soil was all the *roter* could afford as beds. There was no money for other furniture such as tables and chairs from their meager income, after the rent had been paid.

"It was always bread that dwindled rather than hunger, and they could clearly hear the rats scuttling round in their stomachs," it says in the Majorcan fairy tale of the seven-hued pony.

People, asses, sheep, and hens all had to crowd into a smallish space. The most important supplies dangled in a basket hanging from the roof.

Roter farmers built primitive accommodation in the fields, using drystone walling techniques.

Only a narrow entrance allowed daylight and fresh air into the drystone-built house.

From skull-splitters to top wines
Binissalem

If we are to believe Pliny, the Romans could not get enough of the wines of Majorca. In the first century BC, he praised the wines of the Balearic islands, and there seems to have been a brisk trade in ships carrying Majorcan wine to the Roman Empire. Regardless of whether they liked the taste, they nonetheless basically diluted their wine by half with water. Furthermore, they considered a meal without *garum* to be simply inedible, and exported to southern Hispania in return unimaginable quantities of this ancient equivalent of Worcester sauce, made of anchovies and decomposed fish, rotted in the torrid heat of the south and fermented. Spicy stuff, OK – but delicious?

The reputation of Majorcan wines, which inevitably reflects on those from Binissalem in Raiguer, was not and is not very high. Majorcan wines were frequently drunk at the courts of Aragon and Castile, especially malmsey, as is confirmed by order lists from the 14th century and impatient threats when a consignment was late. However, other chronicles remark sourly that the adulterated vinegar the Catalans cobbled together after the Reconquest of Majorca made holes in the table tops. Indeed, in many villages, the wine store is called *Can Vinagre* even today; the vinegar house, where wine is sold in the customer's own plastic bottles from great vats of wine, and it is a matter of luck whether you take away an astonishing vintage or a skull-splitter.

During their 300 years on Majorca, the Moors brought wine-growing to its prime. Places like Banyalbufar might be called "the little vineyard by the sea", while the area in and around Binissalem was recognized as having the soil, the volume of rain and the perfect microclimate for wine. Of course, they made very little wine, drinking it being banned by the Prophet after all, but did produce table grapes and the raisins that are indispensable for Arab cuisine.

Sheep, goats, and cows in the vineyard
Binissalem had to wait until the 19th century to gain a reputation for wine all over Europe. Until then, peasants had always trod the grapes for wine, but that was mainly for domestic or local use, or possibly export to the mainland. At any rate, viticulture was so important to Binissalem's economy that in

The vine stocks of Majorca produce roughly 1 million gallons (4 million liters) of wine per annum. The great wine-growing center is Binissalem in the heart of Raiguer.

the 14th century wine-growers did not hesitate to launch a mini-war against the newly installed great landowners. The latter were letting their livestock roam freely, so that sheep, goats, and cows wandered in and out of vineyards as they wished, feasting on grapes and vine leaves. The indignation of the Binissalem vintners reached a point where the governor of Majorca intervened in 1419 and passed a law forbidding livestock breeders to allow their animals to graze in vineyards, olive groves and wheat fields unless expressly permitted by their possessors. It also threatened slaves and prisoners with 50 lashes if they helped themselves in the fields.

Above: In spring, a carpet of meadow flowers grows up under the vine stocks.

Right: The classic Majorcan grape variety is *Manto negro*, though experiments are being made with Cabernet Sauvignon and Tempranillo.

Above: The dedication of this church in Binissalem is to Our Lady of the Rubies. Perhaps a local ruby red wine is used for communion.

Left: The town has set up a monument to its principal industry in front of the church.

Except for the parish church of L'Assumpció, first documented in 1247, and its magnificent altarpiece, and the two urban palaces of Palau Can Gilabert and Can Antich with its elegant loggia, Binissalem does not offer much to look at architecturally, except for the charm that wine centers exude almost automatically. Even so, the 19th century writer Joan Cortada depicts contemporary Binissalem in such glowing terms as if it were paradise. He even assures us that in and around Binissalem there were so many vine stocks that they wound round olive trees, twisted round oaks and carob trees and penetrated the woods.

A little yellow beastie brings rise and fall

The explanation is obvious: Cortada, who died in 1868, must have lived through the first years of the gigantic wine boom in Binissalem. Because when the tiny yellow vine-pest *Phylloxera* set out on its devastating travels in France in 1863, demand rose in any area not affected by it. The parasite reached Portugal in 1871 but spared Spain, but went on to Germany, Switzerland, and in 1875 Italy. Within a few years, the island of Majorca had become all Europe's hope for a glass of wine.

In Porto Colom, the harbor of Felanitx, the quayside had to be extended for the 60 gallon (225-liter) tuns to be loaded quickly and efficiently. Coopers could hardly keep up with the demand for new bordelaise barrels. The harvest of the vineyards was sold even before buds appeared on the stocks. Europe bought wine, irrespective of the type of quality, and paid any price. Binissalem very quickly became very rich. Showy houses were built, and even in Petra and Felanitx anyone with a few pesetas to spare bought a piece of land and planted it to vine. But the dream did not last, and awakening was bitter. In the late 1880s, the little yellow pest reached Majorca, and that was the end of the vine stocks.

Starting over with almonds
In despair, peasants planted almonds in the devastated vineyards, because almonds promised stable prices and a constant market. It is a stability that ultimately they have relied on too long. At the end of the 20th century, the exhausted almond trees are no longer capable of producing rich crops, and the competition in cheaper production countries with younger tree stocks is also on the move.

The shock of the rise and fall of Majorcan wine went so deep that almost 50 years passed before the first hesitant attempts were made to grow wine again on

Majorca. The new wine-growers had to overcome not only the *Phylloxera* trauma but also the very modest reputation their wines had acquired during the European wine drought in the previous century.

But the basic conditions are good: in Binissalem, which has the only DOC (*Denominació d' Origen Controlada*, official certificate of origin) in the whole Balearics, both soil and climate are right. Currently Majorca's output is over 1 million US gallons (4 million liters) of wine per annum. The new wine growers have planted mostly the *Manto negro* variety, which despite difficult processing produces balanced red wines.

Even though electric presses are available, many wine-growers work traditionally. Connoisseurs say that only foot-pressed wine has the right aroma.

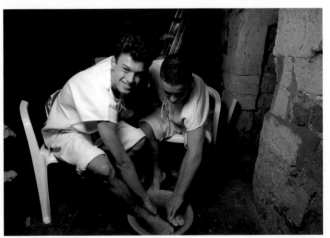

Scrubbing will not help. After many gallons of treading must, the feet remain blue for a few days.

At the grape harvest festival in Binissalem, a sample of the new vintage is offered to the Mother of God.

Could a better match be conceived? Wine and dance and a lively public to celebrate a juicy harvest.

Learning to walk with Manto Negro

The Ribas winepress in Consell, part of the Binissalem DOC, proves that Manto Negro wines corrode neither tables nor stomach linings. On the contrary. The vineyard has worked out the right blend of Syrah, Cabernet Sauvignon, and Tempranillo grapes (the latter being very popular in mainland Spain) with results well worth sampling. Fruity, elegant Ribas wines can be drunk young, but nonetheless improve with age.

The rising star among the red wines is currently Anima Negra, black soul, produced by a young wine-growing team in Santa Catalina near Andratx. The wine is heavy, almost black, full of content and with a marked nose and body; it will no doubt cause quite a stir.

The firm of Ferrer in Binissalem dates back to 1931, and has made a new reputation almost exclusively with Manto Negro. In his exemplary wine cellar, José Luis Roses Ferrer has succeeded in producing a strongly individual local red wine using traditional craft techniques and without any fashionable flummery.

In Porreres in Pla, Jaume Mesquida has developed a Majorcan Sparkling wine, *cava* and an outstanding red wine that fetches a good price, which at least shows the winegrower knows his stuff.

Goats, as wild as possible

Like all wine-growing centers worldwide, Binissalem is most interesting at harvest time. In Majorca, harvesting hands insist on getting *fideus amb cabra* to eat, which is goat meat and noodles. The best meat is tangy, and comes from wild goats.

The insistence on goat meat goes back to an ancient Mediterranean tradition: in antiquity, a goat was ceremonially sacrificed

to Dionysius, the orgiastic god of wine. Thus at harvest time, villages like Binissalem are filled with the fragrance of pressed grapes, the first fermentation and the intense smell of simmering goat meat – even if things are no longer quite as idyllic as described by Ludwig Salvator from the days before the major attack of *Phylloxera*. He paints an exceptional genre picture: "The peasants can be seen on their way to the vineyards very early, and only return home at sundown. The women mostly sit on the cart in a confusion of clothing, while the men steer the beasts, the children run happily ahead and the girls as they go improvise a dance in the dusty road to the rhythm of the songs they sing. And everything is stained red from the purple juice, women and men, cart and all, as if at a Bacchanal."

Barefoot but wearing hats, wine-growers and their helpers still harvested the wine at the end of the 19th century. Even infants went along to learn.

Opposite: Work is not over after the grapes are picked. Regular sampling is done to establish when the wine from the large tuns can be transferred to the smaller barrels.

Right: Binissalem is Majorca's only controlled label. The abbreviation DOC guarantees the wine's origin and quality.

Below: Having earned themselves a terrible reputation in the 19th century, wine-growers are now able to offer top-quality wines again.

Some Majorcan wine estates

Bodegas
   Franja Roja SA José Luis Ferrer
   (since 1931)
   Conquistador 103, Binissalem
Bodegas i Vinyedos
   Antoní Nadal Ros. (since 1988)
   Finca Son Roig, Binissalem
Hereus de Ca'n Ribas SA (since 1711)
   Celler de Ca'n Ribas, Consell Celler
   Jaume de Puntiró (since 1981)
   Plaça Nou 23, Santa Maria del Camí
Santa Catalina (since 1984)
   Ctra. Andratx – Capdellà, km. 4, Andratx
Bodegues
   Miguel Oliver
   Font 26, Petra
Bodegues
   Jaume Mesquida
   Vileta 7, Porreres

Forgotten oppression
Lloseta

Invasion after invasion, new ruler after new ruler, centuries of bondage: the Palau d'Ayamans in Lloseta is an especially vivid memorial of feudal oppression. It has also become a popular destination for day-tripper groups passing through Raiguer and Pla. It would seem the collective memory of this picturesque village, with a whole row of grand houses, has erased memories which for centuries were synonymous with unbridled despotic autocracy. Many think Majorcan fatalism is to blame, others concede that a great part of the tradition is oral and has been lost in the course of history: don't let's talk about that any more.

The rule of terror, blessed from above

In the case of Lloseta, this is particularly serious, because the palace of Ayamans, with its lovely gardens and extensive suites of rooms, represents a reign of terror such as one would not wish on one's worst enemy, and one that lasted over 200 years. In 1232, Lloseta and its population were granted by Jaume I to Don Arnoldo Togores, one of the king's loyal servants during the Reconquest. Henceforth, Don Avnoldo and his descendants had the right to dispense justice in all matters relating to the serfs of Lloseta – and injustice.

Left: Busts of petrified feudal landlords and their ladies, set in relief, medaillons, look down on the rank and file of Lloseta from Aiamans palace.

Below: The Count of Aiamans and Baron of Lloseta and his family lived in this splendid Renaissance palace, surrounded by the poverty of their serfs.

In 1634, King Philip IV bestowed the title of Conde de Aiamans (Count of Aiamans) and Baron of Lloseta on Miquel Luis Ballester i de Togores, a descendant of Arnoldo who finally instituted a reign of terror. In the main square, the Plaça Major, the lord of the village set up stocks, a pillar from which a huge cage was suspended wherein the accused or condemned were displayed to be pilloried, and alongside that, as a permanent fixture, a gallows for good measure.

The Count treated his wife on the same "principles". He lived with her in his town palace in Palma, at number 5 in the Carrer de Portella, which today is home to the Museu de Majorca. After the Count had married his wife, Margalida Despuig, he obviously treated her just like his serfs. She fled, and sought refuge from her husband in the convent of Mary Magdalena. The Count would not allow his wife to escape. He stormed the convent, seized his wife, and henceforth incarcerated her at home until the poor, luckless woman was finally murdered by bandits in 1651.

Beside the hardhearted Count's palace in Lloseta – a particular attraction for tourists

In the park, vases with allegories provide a dreamy atmosphere.

Above: An idyll in the middle of the village. The lords of Lloseta created an oasis of feudal splendor on the model of French gardens.

Below: Nowadays, the magnificent park is a public attraction. A veil of silence is drawn over the past.

because of its splendid park – stands one of the island's few really large factories, the cement works, which still provides 90% of the building materials used on Majorca. The local rhizopods also deserve a mention, because there are millions of them in Lloseta. They are found more than 330 feet underground, petrified in the Eocene age over 37 million years ago, in the thick so-called nummulite layers.

Broadcast-minded inhabitants
A century ago, Ludwig Salvator counted "1,195 inhabitants and 412 houses" in Lloseta, "the latter being all single-story and painted white." Now antennas and even a broadcasting studio have been added. Since the 1980s, the Ramón family have operated a private TV station. Ad-libbing, as it were, they broadcast within a range of 6–7 miles (9–11 km), refusing to be intimidated by the ban on broadcasting. Open up again, new frequency, good evening, here is Channel 7. Over and out for Lloseta.

A savior from famine
St. John's bread

No tenir un pa a la post, not even to have bread. Probably every language has a version of this Majorcan expression for unimaginable famine. This is because no other basic foodstuff is of such fundamental importance to our diet as our daily bread. It comes first of the requests in the Lord's Prayer, because if you don't even have bread, you might not get to the next one.

Such considerations preoccupied many in 15th and 16th century Majorca. During the great famines, like John the Baptist, Majorcans were forced to use the pods of the carob bean for their own food. They began to grind the pods to produce a modest bread substitute and thus give their bodies at least a minimal form of sustenance. In Migjorn, which was particularly hard hit, the seeds were also eaten roasted.

The area around Sencelles is ideal for the biblical trees, because they flourish best in a hot climate a long way from the coast and in the lee of the mountains. Growing to a height of over 30 feet (9 meters), the evergreen *garrover* trees like the company of olive and almond trees, but they are easily distinguished from them by their dense domed shape and rich green foliage.

The Moors never conceived an ambition to plant them in plantations but more or less left the trees to themselves. Even so, it was they who introduced the trees to Majorca, because like John the Baptist they are native to the eastern Mediterranean. The fruit is also called St. John's bread, which likewise goes back to the Bible, because the pods of *Ceratonia siliqua* were all John the Baptist could find to eat in the Jordan desert.

The Greek word *kerátion* means "horn", which refers to the curved seeds of the bean of the carob. Due to their constant weight of 2.78 grains (0.18 g), they were long used as

Carob trees like the company of almond and olive trees, but can be distinguished from them by their dense, deep-green foliage.

units of measurement for gold, silver, and precious stones, and the Greek word *kerátion* developed into our modern term *carat*.

The fruits hang on the branches in great clumps. They are green in winter, turning nut brown and then chocolate colored as they ripen. The tough skin of the 4–12 inches (10-30 cm) long pods or carob beans contains a sweet pulp, which begins to ferment shortly after maturity, at which the tree begins to exude a sweet, pungent fragrance.

Harvesting takes place in September. As is done in many places with olive trees, the branches are banged with pipes or sticks so that ripe clumps of fruit fall off and can be collected. The edible fruits are rich in sugars, starch and protein, and have always been used to feed livestock.

In the 1930s a plant was opened to process the fruit industrially. Ersatz coffee was made, but the fruit was also still exported as animal feed. Carob has been used as a cocoa substitute and in the production of alcohol and sweet foodstuffs since the early 19th century. It became so widely used that it was included in traditional Majorcan recipes such as curd pudding or *cassola de brossat.*

Packaging also sometimes lists carob flour among the ingredients as a thickening agent, as this flour is among foodstuff additives qualifying as an "emulgator". At the end of the 20th century, carob flour acquired increased importance, for use in the production of both diet foods and natural foods. And many stressed-out people who can't take caffeine are now returning to the once despised coffee substitute based on carob flour.

The rumor persists that Majorca's brandy distillers would use carob beans to make *palo*, a thick, sweet herbal spirit. The distillers totally reject the insinuation and assert that carob would only be used along with wood for heating at the brewing stage.

At harvest time, the brownish-violet pods, which generally hang from the branches in clumps, are pulled off the branches with shackle hooks.

Cool cellars, hot soles
Inca

Faïence is earthenware with a white tin glaze. The name comes from a particularly sophisticated version produced in the north Italian town of Faienza. However, popular earthenware of this kind was known in the Middle Ages and the Renaissance, as now, by the name of majolica, which came from Majorca, where the major center was Inca. The place was famous for the fact that its potters knew how to make faïences equal to those of Faienza, and had done so since Moorish times and well into the Renaissance.

And as the earthenware came from Majorca, it was called "majorica", later amended to "majolica". Spanish tin-glazed tiles or *rajoles*, which continued the art of Moorish potters, were the direct forebears of Majorcan and subsequently Italian and Central European majolica tiles.

None of this is evident in Inca nowadays. Even Ludwig Salvator did not find any ceramic workshops at work, and was only able to report hearsay on the subject. The fame of the place for ceramics is as much history as the medieval Jewish ghetto that Inca once possessed – the only one on the island besides that of Palma.

Nowadays, other things are more important in Majorca's third largest town. "Inca has two inns," Ludwig Salvator commented laconically in 1867, and had no more to say. That has radically changed. Nowadays there are least two convincing reasons to visit Inca. One is to make an extensive and leisurely tour of the overexpensive factory stores of the shoe and leather factories, and secondly to take refreshment in a *celler*, one of the semi-underground restaurants in a former wine-cellar. There are a lot of these.

Yet Inca, which – as prehistoric finds from the area prove – was a proper settlement from the earliest times and served the Romans as an administrative center, has more to offer than hot soles and cool cellars. The parish church of Santa Maria la Mayor in the center of the small but classy old town bears witness to the fact that Inca was rich before tourist buses arrived. Its 13th-century foundations stand on the site of the old Islamic mosque, even if the body of the present church is the result of rebuilding and extensions of 18th-century date.

Inca's main church, Santa Maria la Major, stands on the foundations of a mosque. This was already a flourishing industrial settlement in Moorish times. Inca was noted from early medieval days for its majolica ware.

ations of air pressure. What could they do with them after the destruction of the vines?

Nowadays chefs cook traditional Majorcan cuisine in the *cellers*. No paellas, no truita, but loin of pork in almond sauce, snails with paprika sausage or the typical *sopes mallorquines*.

Unsalted *pa moreno* is always on the table, with *gató d'emetlles amb gelat* to follow, almond cake with almond ice. Word of this has long got around not only among Inca's 23,000 inhabitants but in Majorca generally, and visitors from all over come and join the feast in *cellers* in the old craft town of Inca in the heart of the island.

Inca's cuisine always knew how to care for both body and soul. This delicatessen, whose 19th-century decor is more like a ballroom than a store, packs all the specialties of the island into a very small space.

The builders had the expertise to get the best out of the light yellow marès stone, for example constructing an arcade under the eaves and elegant tracery on door jambs and windows. Inside, the baptistery chapel contains the only surviving *torn* on the island, a wooden winch which was used to submerge the bawling infant during baptism.

A further holy site in Inca is on Puig d' Inca (988 feet). There is supposed to have been a chapel here even in Moorish times where today the Ermita de Santa Magdalena is open for prayers.

Majorcan morsels with natural air conditioning

Over a glass of good Majorcan wine and tidbits from Majorcan cuisine, *Inqueros* will proudly relate the history of the local *cellers*, because Inca is famous for them. As in nearby Binissalem, wine has been grown here in some style since the 17th century. Here as elsewhere, the vine-pest wrought havoc in this major industry at the end of the 19th century, and Inca's citizens

preferred henceforth to rely on other skilled occupations from their great repertory, especially leather working of all kinds.

However, the erstwhile wine-growers almost all had cellars in town, in whose cool, shaded recesses wines could be stored in giant tuns untroubled by heat and upsetting fluctu-

As Inca is no longer the wine-growing center it was, the semi-underground storage vaults have found a new use. Surrounded by venerable giant tuns, local chefs of the town serve up the finest traditional Majorcan dishes in these *cellers*.

Majorcan medley
Vegetables on the island

During Lent you see individual Majorcans stooping at the side of the roads and along the banks of streams. The explanation of this odd sight is that they are collecting wild green asparagus because, after all, fasting in Lent still means eating something. The young asparagus is prepared in a variety of ways. An advantage is it does not need peeling, only washing and chopping before it is braised, steamed or preserved.

Asparagus is of course only one of Majorca's vegetables. The island's markets indicate how wide and colorful the range is, presenting the whole variety of Majorcan produce, grown mostly in market gardens in the vicinity of villages. Such *hortes* were always set up for preference in regions that could be easily irrigated.

Plants that flourish include golden yellow corn (maize), densely leafed artichokes, crisp lettuces, tightly furled cauliflower, fragrant chili peppers, huge spring onions, purple aubergines, sharp onions, tender asparagus, unprepossessing beans, light green leeks, and finally the "paradise apples" or tomatoes.

For Majorcans, it is very important for all vegetables and fruit to come from Majorcan soil and not be imported from the mainland, even if the latter can sometimes be half the price. The price differential is due to more difficult cultivation conditions on the island. The soil is very chalky, which slows down the absorption of important minerals. This combined with the constant shortage of water means that fruits are basically smaller and cannot compete with European norms.

Inside it is different. Majorcan vegetables are that much tastier. This is very evident in the tomatoes, which have become indispensable for Majorcan cuisine and are found in all colors, shapes, and fragrances. The famous *sofrit*, the most important Spanish sauce, is made only with the smallest and best.

Along with the brightly hued fresh vegetables, pulses are also important. One of the oldest is *fava* broad beans, which belong to the pea family and are robust annuals. When the beans are small and tender, they form the basis of delicious dishes. Particularly worth trying is *Fava pelada pagesa*, a white-bean stew with salted rib of pork and bacon. Or just a vegetable stew.

Onion harvesting without tears on Majorca.

Sopes Mallorquines

Majorcan vegetable stew

Ingredients for four portions

5–7 oz (150 to 200 g) *sopes*
(thin slices of dried *pa moreno*)

¹/₂ Savoy cabbage

¹/₄ cauliflower

1 leek

3¹/₂ oz. (100 g) sugar snaps or peas

3¹/₂ oz. (100g) runner beans or French beans

1 large vegetable onion

2–4 cloves of garlic, chopped fine

2 tomatoes, diced

7 fluid oz. olive oil

1 tbs. pork lard

2 cups of meat or vegetable stock

1 tsp. sweet paprika

1 small sprig of large-leafed parsley,
chopped small

Despite the implication of the word *sopes*, this is not a real soup. *Sopes* are wafer-thin slices of dried *pa moreno* bread sold in a bag or loose in any bakery. *Sopes* are laid out in the *greixonera* as a base. The cooked, half-dried vegetable stew containing ingredients that vary according to season – as long as Savoy cabbage is included – is spread out on top of them before the dish goes into the oven for a final simmer.

Cut all ingredients into pieces of equal size and have ready. Heat the *greixonera* (or a cast iron container) with olive oil and the pork lard. Briefly sear the onions without browning. Add the leek and stir. Now add the garlic and diced tomato. Simmer the mixture at low heat to reduce it slightly. Then stir in the Savoy cabbage and beans and top up with two cups of hot meat stock. Immediately add the peas, cauliflower, and teaspoonful of paprika. Simmer for about 10 minutes at low heat.

Place the *sopes* (dried bread) in the same *greixonera* to fill the bottom, pour on the vegetable brew, and sprinkle with parsley. Put in a preheated oven (300°F, 150°C) and simmer for 10 minutes.

Universally popular cauliflower is grown in Majorcan vegetable gardens as well.

Tender shoots of green asparagus move from the wayside into the pan unpeeled.

Aubergines and peppers form the basis of numerous Majorcan dishes.

Majorcan beans may be smaller than elsewhere, but they taste better for it.

171

Shoes for the world
Inca

That walking and living was easier wearing shoes was known in the dawn of prehistory. Feet were swathed in animal skins stuffed with straw, feathers or wool against the cold, and in the course of time, the wearers learnt to make soles wear-resistant and add the weirdest of fastenings to produce the maximum comfort and vertical equilibrium. The Romans swore by sandals with complicated laces, while the Orientals went for unheeled slippers with tips turned upwards. Except for lightweight summer shoes, the West took the latter as its model for "proper" shoes.

In Italy, Florence is a byword for good shoes. In Majorca, possibly even in Spain, a comparable reputation graces the little town of Inca, and has done so since 1458, when the shoemakers of Inca set themselves up independently of the guilds of Palma. In the heart of the island and surrounded by farmland, Inca had been made a *vila* by royal decree, and was on the way to becoming the most important town in Majorca after Palma. In feudal, post-*Reconquista* Majorca, the only way to achieve independence at work was to adopt a craft. Craft industries were not subject to meddling by landowners because land was not needed. And a *vila* like Inca, which had civic status, had a chance to take control of its own trade.

Guilded shoes

Thus in 1458 the shoemakers of Inca set up their own guild and drew up their own statutes. At the same time, their members had a wish to place their work under the protection of a patron saint. Unfortunately none of the disciples or the papally approved martyrs was a shoemaker. The shoemakers fell to studying the legends, and finally plumped for St. Mark.

This was because St. Mark had just arrived in Alexandria to become bishop when his shoe fell apart. A Jewish shoemaker named Aniano began to repair the shoe for him. Unluckily he stabbed himself with his awl while working; Mark miraculously healed him, which so impressed Aniano that he became a Christian. Thus Mark is still the patron saint of shoemakers.

The shoemakers in Inca were not left to themselves, however, even if today theirs is still the most important industry in the town. In 1600, the town boasted 64 shoe and furrier workshops, 31 weavers and spinners,

A relief showing members of the shoemakers' guild or *el Collegi d'Honorables Sabaters* at work.

As in the time of the great Antoni Fluxà, a template is worked out so that the upper can be cut out complete.

In the next step, the insole is glued to the pre-prepared upper and sewn for extra strength.

The bottom sole is then stuck on to the insole, to form a single unit with the rest, and likewise stitched.

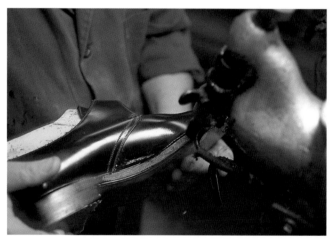

Unevennesses are then eliminated and small patches of glue carefully removed. The *sabater* now polishes his work for the first time.

Finally, the upper is stitched once more from above, to last (almost) for ever.

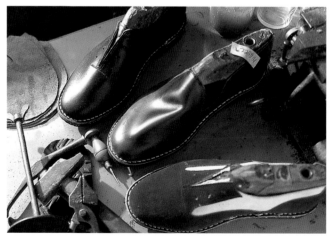

The result: three finished shoes, which with their pairs will no doubt soon walk off the shelves.

A Lottusse emblem is printed on the sole before the process of stamping and sewing the sole begins. The highly stylized lotus blossom is a protection against misuse of the brand name.

29 carpenters, 22 smiths plus sundry potters and tailors. Eight lawyers settled here, to look after all the contracts and administration that the craftsmen required.

Inca's shoemakers' guild set out its economic and ideological aims in its statutes. Shoemakers were safeguarded by a kind of common social insurance fund, competition was kept under control and the best possible sales opportunities were ensured for all. At the same time, members of the guild were obliged to behave decently in public so that Inca's shoemakers could stand out not just as excellent shoemakers but also as valuable, reliable members of society. The guild was financed from members' contributions, including a levy that all *mestre*, or master craftsmen, had to pay when employing an apprentice. The common purse of the guild paid for members' funerals, supported their widows, and also paid out for guild festivities and pious masses.

The guild, called *Collegi d'Honorables Sabater*s, was quite independent of the town, and very early on began to draw up criteria for training young apprentice shoemakers. A first step was to determine that training for a *sabater* should last at least four years. In 1640 this was extended to include a further four years as a journeyman before the young shoemaker could open a workshop of his own and train his own apprentices.

The modern planned business

The shoe business flourished, though in the mid-16th century the co-operative had to be reorganized because the shoemakers' guild had divided itself into two groups. One produced just rough working shoes for Majorcans, the others sought the trade of the gentry but unfortunately were not technically up to it. The result was that Majorcan customers turned to foreign suppliers and imported their shoes from anywhere but the island.

The master cobblers came together and decided to break the guild into three. The first group, the *mestres d'obra grossa*, masters of rough shoes, devoted themselves to producing robust working shoes. The masters of the second group were called *mestres d'obra fina* or *primeters*, or shoemakers for quality work, who specialized in walking shoes, while the third group were the *mestres tapiners*, who made only top quality women's shoes.

An epidemic of plague struck the island in the 17th century, carrying off many Majorcans including some *sabaters*, even though it is still said today that the epidemic did not ravage the cobblers so badly. At any rate, the plague hit demand. Majorcans had bigger problems than just the purpose and shape of their footwear. For some decades, shoemakers only produced to order for the limited Majorcan market. Often they spent the summer on the land, and only in winter took their seats by their *brasers* (braziers) outside the door to produce sundry pairs of shoes.

Modern quality products

In 1836 a local artisan called Antoni Fluxà realized that the guild was once again facing oblivion and needed drastic restructuring. He called some shoemakers from Inca to a meeting at his house, where they decided on a reorganization of the shoe co-operative and the promotion of exports.

Inca could no longer afford to coast along supplying just Majorca or at best mainland Spain. Shoemakers no longer thought in terms of individual pairs but began to make lasts and copy every model in quantity. They organized themselves into groups, had certain models patented and busied themselves setting up a network of wholesalers and middlemen.

This paved the way for the first shoe factory, even though it would take years for the factory to actually open its doors. Besides local outlets, the artisans of Inca now also exported abroad, principally to the Philippines and Cuba. For many ex-Majorcans who had left their island in the 19th century and found a new home in the "Pearl of the Antilles", shoes from Inca possessed great symbolic value. They represented a piece of home you could even walk on. When both colonies were lost in 1898, the market again dipped, but eventually the top three businesses, the Fluxàs, Gelaberts, and Payeras, installed machinery and went over to industrial production.

Work procedures were standardized and organized in series. But for a shoe to really fit and sit comfortably, all the parts have ultimately to be assembled by hand. The machines can help with cutting out, speed up and strengthen gluing processes by means of pressure and heat, and press the shoes to shape and give them a high polish. In between these procedures, the shoe passes from one skilled hand to another, because only hands can feel irregularities, only eyes notice color defects, bits of glue or torn thread in the sewing.

Then as now, the shoemakers first cut or punch out the upper and pare the edges. The next step is to cut out the soles, stamp them and spread on the glue. Subsequently upper and sole have to be brought together by sticking the upper to the insole, after which the upper and the insole are sewn to the bottom sole. These through-sewn shoes are still considered the best and most durable.

The most famous brands for the international market are Camper, Yanko, and Lottusse, which very quickly became successful. Lottusse can incidentally be easily recognized from the abstract lotus blossom stamped on the sole.

High-value shoes for world-famous designers are still produced in Inca and Llucmajor by firms which, after many structural crises, have specialized in niche markets for high-value, labor-intensive fashion shoes. Despite their handmade shoes, the average Majorcan is thus once again confronted with the cheap offerings of other countries where production costs are much lower.

Although industrial Inca has meanwhile blossomed into the third largest town on the island, the reformer of the shoe trade has not been forgotten: in 1952, a memorial to Antoní Fluxà was set up in Llucmajor.

A monument in Llucmajor honors Antoni Fluxà, who opened the way to the world for Majorcan shoes.

The key to control of the island
Alaró

Remnants of *talayots*, Roman pottery, and Byzantine coins of Constantine V together with a host of Moorish relics have been found in the ground, but above it not much is left of the fort of Alaró except a few feet of walling. Beneath it, the hill which gave it its unique strategic position is as massive as ever.

The traces of this fort in all major conquests of the island are of course anything but faded or buried. Anyone who could vanquish it, set on its eyrie a dizzy 1,640 feet (500 m) above the village of Alaró between Puig Mayor and Massanella, had the island in his grasp. But that was no easy matter, as anyone who makes it to the top in peacetime, up the bumpy cart track by car or on foot, will appreciate – an attacking army would be presented to the defenders of the fort totally exposed, almost suicidally, as if on a huge serving dish. The fort of Alaró, unsurprisingly, was considered impregnable. Or nearly so. Only treachery and despair could make it vulnerable.

Besiegers besieged

When the Moors occupied the island in 902, according to Arab chronicles, the *runes*, i.e. the non-Arabs and northern peoples, held out against siege in the fort of Alaró for eight years and five months. Possibly the besieged were descendants of the Iberian people who had presumably lived on the island since the 11th century BC, and had already given the Romans splitting headaches with their catapults. The Romans had found them relent-

Once considered impregnable, the castle of Alaró has had to yield to the ravages of time. In the 10th century, the islanders resisted the Moors for eight years from here. When the Moors themselves came to be ousted, they gave up almost without a struggle, in the belief they did not have a chance.

less, stubborn warriors, and nothing seems to have changed by the time the Moors arrived.

The Moors in turn sought refuge here against the invading troops from the mainland when Jaume I began to reclaim the island for Christian rulers in 1229. He and his strategists feverishly debated how to get a handle on the tricky situation at Alaró and storm this impregnable castle, but it took over two years before the encircled Moors surrendered.

Their commander, the governor of Pollença and Inca, El Benehabet, could no longer hold the famished fort and yielded to the Christians in 1231. As a reasonable man, he did it without letting it come to a heroic and necessarily bloody last stand, which later earned him the reputation of a traitor.

A symbol of freedom

The true age of the fort is enshrouded in the darkness of history. The evidence has vanished with the fortifications. The present ruins date from the later Middle Ages, being last restored in 1320.

That was just a few years after events that etched themselves on Majorca's collective memory, enshrining the castle as a symbol of freedom. In 1285, King Jaume II left the island for a short while. His absence tempted his rival Alfonso III of Aragón – the son of his brother, no less – to conquer the island for his kingdom. Majorcans loyal to King Jaume II fled to the castle and for a long time defended themselves successfully.

Alfonso III nonetheless tried to persuade them to give themselves up, but their leaders En Cabrit and En Bassa responded with mocking ditties: "We know here no *anfós* (halibut) that bears the title of King of Majorca but only one *anfós*, which you eat with sauce."

The subject of their derision vowed to burn the knaves once he had taken the castle. And so he did. The two Majorcan national heroes were impaled alive and roasted. Admittedly, Alfonso's shot misfired: he was excommunicated, and the two nobles were

Left: Some 1,640 feet (500 m) up, both defenders and attackers could keep almost the whole island in view.

Below: Where sheep are here looking to the right was the scene of another decisive event in Majorca's history in 1285, when Majorcans fled to Alaró to escape the Aragonese invaders. Two of them paid with their lives, but nevertheless gained their country for an independent monarchy.

With the Tramuntana behind it and Pla at its feet, the fort of Alaró was more than just an important strategic point. Anyone who had this area in his power usually had the whole island in his grasp.

lauded as martyrs, *els Sants Màrtirs*, and buried in the cathedral of Palma.

The castle is still defended, and sometimes very painfully. In the rockface below the old watchtower is the Cova de Sant Antoni, a cave full of stalactites, which tempts daring climbers to clamber down to it. If they are lucky, access is untroubled. If not, they encounter a herd of vicious wild asses whom nothing can buy off.

Some 1,640 feet (500m) below, the village of Alaró did not interest the warlords,

Today, the castle and its historic remains are back in the care of nature. Only walkers and sheep pass this way on tours of conquest.

but other "strategists" made its history rather exciting, quite independently of the castle.

Freebooters of the mountains

In the late 17th and early 18th centuries, *bandoleros* (bandits) found Alaró the perfect hideout. The law was a long way away in Palma, and the road to Alaró was slow and difficult, while the surrounding mountains abounded with discreet hidey-holes for booty and supplies. The bandits could thus assume jurisdiction, collect taxes and levy tolls and just generally take what they liked or seemed useful. Thus for a considerable time they freely plundered and persecuted with impunity.

At the same time, the altitude of Alaró created a niche in legal Majorcan trade, making it an important trading center for mountain produce. Huntsmen and breeders sold the skins of their animals here, while charcoal-burners brought charcoal into the valley in huge leather packs on their mules. Meanwhile, peasants from Alaró discovered that mulberry trees and consequently silk-worm breeding prospered here, and where silk is made, embroiderers and weavers are not far away. Olive trees also found the mountain climate congenial and provided excellent olive oil, so that the name of Alaró became chiefly associated with this product. And also with

brown coal, which was mined from 1920 to 1987 down almost 4 miles (6.5 km) of tunnel.

Alaró lights up

Then in 1901 the Perelló brothers, owners of a soap and oils business, gave Alaró something that even the capital Palma did not have at the time – electricity. After initial resistance from fellow citizens, who consid-

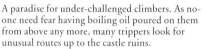

A paradise for under-challenged climbers. As no-one need fear having boiling oil poured on them from above any more, many trippers look for unusual routes up to the castle ruins.

ered it a devilish invention, with the help of the town council and a few progressive neighbors the brothers got some street lighting installed as well as lighting up their factories and houses. The first hundred street lights were the talk of the island, and people came from all over to see the "wonder of simple light" with their own eyes. Progress in the matter of electricity also brought progress in the media: Alaró was later home to Majorca's first free radio in the 1950s and a private TV station in the early 1980s.

In the 17th and 18th centuries, its very remoteness made Alaró an important trading center for products from the mountains: charcoal and skins, silk materials and smuggled goods changed owners here.

Ardent husbands
Charcoal-burners in the mountains

In past times, a cloud of charcoal smoke used to hang over the mountains of the Tramuntana range in winter like a fine, almost invisible cover. In the villages, the smell of slow-burning wood was only noticeable to sensitive noses, but in the early 20th century up on the peaks there was a smoldering and a stoking at almost every road junction. Drifting smoke greeted every walker and passer-by immediately they entered the charcoal-burning realm. It was the heyday of the charcoal-burner.

The silent and reserved figure of the charcoal-burner, who spent most of his life like a hermit, features in both the songs and the tales or *rondaisses* of the Balearic island. The mythology of the Majorcan mountains is inconceivable without the dark charcoal-burner.

There is of course a reason for this: on Majorca, but especially in the towns, where many a builder simply forgot that one day winter would come and therefore included no fireplaces in his plans, wood-based fuel was for centuries the only method of cooking and heating. Mules carrying huge leather packs slung on each side were loaded with the precious black substance and

Right: Only rarely does the occasional mountain *sitja* nowadays smolder away to produce charcoal from boughs and tree stumps. In the early 20th century, this sight was very common in the mountains.

Above: A stone ring with a cover of twigs and straw forms a charcoal kiln.

Once the *sitja* is stacked up, a thick layer of earth dampens the burning process and ensures the characteristic sweet smell.

trudged all the way to the center of Palma with the indispensable winter fuel.

No fire is without smoke, however, and the freezing, fireplace-less towns invented all kinds of utensils to warm themselves without the risk of suffering severe smoke poisoning. The magic formula was called embers, and there were all kinds of warming appliances based on these, depending on requirements.

Ironing was done with glowing charcoal placed in cast-iron irons, while damp sheets were warmed up with a warming pan likewise filled with embers. A container on a long wooden handle, the pan was passed between cover and sheets several times before people went to bed. The *maridet*, literally "husband", as this variant of the hot water bottle was called, was probably used principally for older single ladies. Sometimes old ladies carried their *maridet* – in the shape of a cast-iron receptacle filled with embers – by its handles to mass with them, to assist

the poor circulation of their feet in the cool church interiors during the lengthy service.

Many households still have a *braser* (brazier), a metal pan filled with embers and secured under a round table. During the cold season, life circulates almost exclusively around this *camilla* covered with a thick, floor-length cloth. Everyone who sits down at it pulls the thick cloth over the knees and thus shares the agreeable warmth that spreads beneath the table. Instead of the traditional charcoal tray, these days the heating is however electrical.

Originally, the charcoal-burners only used branches and logs that accumulated when the poor-quality timber stands were thinned out, but by the 19th century consumption of charcoal had risen to the point where estates in the mountains could only satisfy demand by weighing into healthy stands with saw and ax. And what Greeks and Romans had begun centuries earlier in the Mediterranean region now resumed in Majorca – the deforestation of great tracts of land.

Archduke Ludwig Salvator was horrified to see this process at work, and forbade the

felling of even a single pine in his woods. The former boundaries of his possessions are still distinguishable today by stands that are centuries old. In the Son Moragues national park, which lies within his former lands, some historic charcoal kilns have been restored and can be visited.

Though clearing was forbidden in Majorca in the mid 20th-century and some steps were taken then towards afforestation, it takes time for the tip of a tree to reach the sky.

Charcoal-burning as an occupation is virtually extinct. Every now and then sundry *sitjas* or charcoal kilns smoke in the oak and pine forests of the Tramuntana mountains. Although handmade charcoal is very popular despite its relatively high price, environmental awareness has developed, ensuring that industrially produced charcoal is preferred.

The few remaining charcoal-burners belong to a laconic, reticent species. They spend almost the entire year in their *barraques* (stone huts) with grass roofs, collecting twigs and boughs, and poking around in fires.

To build a *sitja*, the charcoal-burner first lays out a ring of stones, inside which he creates a firm base consisting of rich red,

In urban households, splendid charcoal braziers like this one warmed the parlor.

moist soil stamped level, called the *solera*. The thickest logs are placed in the center of the *solera*, on top of which the charcoal-burner then stacks small logs and slender boughs to make a tall pile. Finally, all this is covered with the same red earth as served for the base. Only in the middle at the top does a small opening remain for the fire to find its way into the kiln. The carbonization process begins at once and lasts 14–18 days.

No charcoal-burner enjoys deep sleep, because the wind can easily overheat the fire or else the sun puts the kiln out. Besides being light sleepers, all charcoal-burners also need an excellent sense of smell. Not every fire causes equal smoke, and fine nuances

To produce charcoal, charcoal-burners not only have to carbonize wood. They also have to build the kiln, in the old way. Only when the rushes have been correctly stitched up does the kiln work properly.

indicate to the burner how intense the heat is. For the production of charcoal, the temperature in the *sitja* should ideally remain constant. A single over-heavy sleep and the work of weeks can be lost.

A small town with independent ways
Selva

At night, the narrow, twisting road from Inca to Pollença winds through total darkness until suddenly a view opens up on an impressive panorama. Against the black wall of the Massanella massif gleams the golden yellow church of Sant Llorenç in Selva, lost in a strange trance. Despite its ponderous five arcades and the rather short and stocky tower, it appears to hang weightless over the town sleeping the Raiguer night away below it.

Work on the construction of this church must have begun soon after the Christian reconquest, at the beginning of the 14th century, even if the modern parish church is a reconstruction of the original burnt down in the 19th century.

The dice fell for Selva in those years after the victory of the Christians. Initially its hinterland around the Puig de S'Escuder served the Moorish resistance as a place of refuge, but not for long. Faced with their obviously completely hopeless outlook they committed suicide and found a lonely grave in the mountains that could not protect them.

Land to those who farm it!

Selva was granted a charter for a market from King Jaume II in 1301, and its citizens began a long, dogged struggle for the privilege of owning a piece of the fertile land around Selva themselves. Jaume II, who always had pressing need for money, sold piece after piece of land until almost the whole of Selva, including its villages of Massanella, Biniamar and Moscari, belonged to peasants.

This in turn did not please the Catalan who had been granted Selva for his services during the Reconquest, and he called in his property rights again. Whereupon the

184

Selvans took their complaint to the highest court in the kingdom of Aragón, the *Consell Suprem*, and at least regained the parish of Caimari.

Here the chalky wooded mountains, raw and massive, home to charcoal-burners and bandits, there the mild plain, with low hills, fields and meadows, divided into many individual *finques* and smallholdings – Selva and its surroundings, where Tramuntana and Pla meet, are decidedly fertile.

Hemp, cereals, fruit and vegetables, almonds and giant groves of olives and holm oaks enjoy what kept many people busy over the centuries: a micro-climate with hot summers, a lot of rain in autumn and spring, and cold, damp winters. Even the pastures around Selva are so lush and rich that the peasants bred not only the traditional pigs and sheep here but also horses.

With such good livings nearby, the bandits living in Selva's mountains from the 15th to the 18th centuries also felt particularly comfortable, as self-appointed robber partisans. Their unbridled freebooting did not even stop when their leader Guillem Oliver "Sord" was shot in 1679 and his body kept in Selva prison to forestall an honorable *bandoler* funeral. Their time only came to an end when the Bourbons disarmed all

The land around Selva is so fertile that the peasants rebelled against the great landowners in the 14th century: "We do the work, they said, we want to harvest the fruits of the work as well." Even if they did not win all down the line, they gained partial victories.

Majorca in 1716 to put an end to *bandolerisme.* In and around rebellious Selva they confiscated 154 hand guns, 19 muskets, 67 *armarins*, 6 carbines, 14 pistols, 111 swords, 111 bayonets, 5 daggers, 10 machetes, 20 short swords and 7 halberds.

Gnarled natives
Olive trees

*Son aceitunados tus ojos
y están aderezados
de orégano y sal*

"Green as olives are thine eyes, gleaming and fiery, as if spiced with oregano and salt," trills the old love song. Ardent north Europeans wooing green eyes would probably mention emeralds, but why not olives? After all, olive trees are among the oldest cultivated plants in the world.

Planting of *Olea europaea* began more than 5,000 years ago in the Middle East. From there they spread to Greece and then throughout the Mediterranean, being introduced to the Iberian peninsula by the Romans. Spanish oil was already being filled into amphorae, closed with a seal of origin and dispatched to all parts of the Roman Empire at the beginning of our era.

All kinds of good qualities were attributed to the thick, sometimes golden gleaming fluid from early days: it does wonders for the skin, improves the taste of food and reinforces the body's resistance. Latterly it has become known that olive oil is high in monounsaturate fatty acids, which reduce the risk of heart and circulation diseases, protect against cancer and prevent gallstones.

Nowadays there is a huge variety of types of olive. In Spain alone 260 different varieties are supposed to have been counted, their names depending on the color and shape of the trunk, the leaves or the fruit, the area of cultivation or the oil produced.

The greater part of the olive groves in Majorca were planted in the 16th century. The dry, chalky soils in the Serra de Tramuntana in the north-west of the island

The leaves of evergreen olive trees shimmer silvery green. They flourish best in the Serra de Tramuntana.

are particularly suitable for cultivation. This is why most of the 14,000 hectares of olive groves in the Balearics are found around Selva, Estellencs, Valldemossa, Fornalutx and Esporles. Speaking of the regular lines of trees with their leaves that look greeny gray from above and silver gray from below, the Spanish poet Antonio Machado described their appearance as combed earth, *terra pentinada*.

Business with the fluid gold was brisk for centuries until bureaucrats in Brussels decided that the acidity of Majorcan olives was too high and did not comply with the prescribed EU norm. Since then, olives have only been grown for local use and are not exported any more.

The *olivera* can reach a grand old age of up to 1,500 years, and is also considered a symbol of peace and immortality. In the course of its life, it may adopt bizarre gnarled shapes. The largest olive tree that Ludwig Salvator found on the island in 1870 was located near Palma and was called, no doubt for superstitious reasons, *S'Olivera de sa Por*, olive tree of fear. As the tree is often hollow when old but still grows with great energy, it is said that an olive tree never dies.

The grotesque deformations of the trees are not entirely natural. Older trees are often attacked by a fungus that rots the wood. Peasants consequently keep cutting out the decayed parts, so that frequently holes are sawn in the trees, generating the typical crippled growths.

A particularly fine example of a veteran deformed by the ravages of time stands in the Plaça de Cort in Palma, the square in front of the town hall. Apparently the aged but dignified tree is at least 1,000 years old. This was reason enough to slap a plaque on the tree and fill the flower bed round its base with decorative plants.

Olea europaea takes 4–10 years before it begins to bear fruit, and reaches its full yield

During maturation, the color of the fruits changes from light green to deep black.

– as it were, its prime – after 30–35 years. From about 75 onwards decline sets in and the yield drops noticeably. The long harvesting season of the *olives* lasts from September until well into February. In autumn the first still unripe green fruits are picked off, preserved in brine either whole or cut small and spiced with fennel, lemon peel and pepper pods.

The first *pansides* fall from the trees in October. They are a little wrinkled and dark purple in color. Dressed with oil, salt, garlic and bay leaves, they can be eaten at once. From November, Majorcans harvest the black olives, which are preserved in salt water for two months with salt, lemon and garlic before they are ready to eat.

The idea of preserving olives in brine came from finding fruits washed ashore on the ebbtide after they had fallen into the sea. Olives previously classified as inedible suddenly tasted juicy and fresh because the salt seawater had removed the bitter flavors. Since then, almost every family in the Mediterranean region has had its own special recipe for preserving olives.

Harvesting for oil production begins at the end of November. The fully mature fruits are by then a rich black and wrinkled. The traditional harvesting method – still in

However good they taste, it is good manners to leave one olive.

use – is called *tomar*, in which the olives are carefully thrashed out of the tree with sticks called *gaules* so that no damage is done.

Even by the 19th century, this method of harvesting was still unusual. Although the procedure was used for almond trees, in the case of olives it was normal to wait until the olives were ripe enough to fall off by themselves. Presumably it was later discovered that the quality of the oil is noticeably improved if younger olives are used.

Mostly, nets are spread out under the trees to catch the ripe fruit. They are then picked up and collected in small baskets. A good olive picker can pick the fruit of a fully grown tree in a day, which amounts to about 88 pounds (40 kg) or the gigantic number of 20,000 olives. Along with the meager wage for this arduous work the harvest helpers usually get some bottles of the precious fluid after production as well.

Manufacturing olive oil

Haste is imperative with olive oil, because in contact with oxygen the fruits develop bitters and all too easily lose their fine, slightly fruity aroma. The freshly harvested fruits are first washed and then placed on a conveyor belt to be sorted and for leaves and stalks to be removed. They are then processed in the oil mill so that they burst open. Best for this are millstones of granite because these scarcely heat up during milling and thus do not dispel the ethereal, heat-sensitive oils in the air.

The stone rollers that make up the mill rotate on a stone platform. The output

A *tafona* – the flat slabs containing the olive pomace are stacked up into a column and then pressed with a heavy beam or *biga*.

collects as mush in a broad, ring-shaped channel. A funnel is fixed over the center of the grinder. This *tramutja* provides a constant supply of olives. About 240 pounds (180 kg) is needed for each round of grinding or *trullada*.

When the juice which drains out of the paste by itself after grinding is collected the best of the oil, the *flor d'oli*, is obtained. The yield of this is very small, however, and the mush is usually further processed after grinding. The pulp arising during the *trullada* is spread over 60–90 flat mats made of coconut or esparto fiber, called *cabasses* or *esportins*, which are then stacked on top of each other to make a column in a hydraulic press or *tafona*. Using the leverage of a huge beam made of pine, the *biga*, the *esportines* are then pressed.

For best quality results, the temperature must not exceed 86 Fahrenheit (30°C), because once again heat would have a negative effect on the aroma and vitamins. About 11 pounds (five kilos) of olives are needed to produce two pints (one liter) of oil. After pressing, the reddish oil has to be cleared to separate it out from the plant juice or *alpechin*. In traditionally operated businesses the ensuing mixture is put into an overflow basin in which the oil rises to the surface because it is lighter than the pomace. During this lengthy procedure, the plant juice begins to ferment slightly, imparting its bad taste to the oil. Increasing use is therefore being made of more rapid electrically operated extractors. The plant juice is spun outwards on a centrifuge, leaving the pure oil to gather around the rotational axis of the machine. The oil is then left to stand for a few days for the natural cloudy matter to settle. Frequently it is then passed through a paper filter before being bottled and sold. Meantime the unfiltered, slightly cloudy oil is becoming increasingly more popular because of its stronger taste.

In general, three main categories of olive oil are distinguished, with the virgin oil (*oli d'oliva verge extra* extra virgin olive oil) representing the top quality for Spanish cold-pressed olive oil. This oil comes from the first pressing and may not exceed 0.035 of an ounce (1 g) of fatty acid per 3.5 ounces (100 g) of oil. *Oli d'oliva verge* is also always cold-pressed oil, but from the second or third pressing. In this case, the acidity must not exceed 0.07 (2 g) of fatty acid per 3.5 ounces (100 g) of oil. *Oli d'oliva* is either refined oil or a blend of refined and cold-pressed oil. This relatively cheap oil is used principally for deep-frying meat or fish. All olive oils are sensitive to light, heat, air and damp. If they are stored in a cool, dark dry place, they keep for up to 18 months.

The non-pressed preserved olives never survive that long. Served on small earthenware plates and offered round, the delicious green or black fruits are usually eaten up in minutes.

As olive oil is extremely light-sensitive, even decorative bottles should only occasionally be exposed to light.

After the harvest, the easily spoiled fruits are carefully washed and placed on a conveyor belt.

During the trip into the inside of the mill, leaves and stalks are removed so that only ripe fruit lands in the funnel.

The olives are quickly spread over a stone platform so that they only briefly come into contact with oxygen.

In the oil mill, heavy conical granite stones grind the olives to a dense pulp.

The paste of fruit flesh and stones is spread on circular coconut or esparto mats, which are then placed on top of one another.

Up to 90 *esportine* are stacked up into even columns.

The precious liquid is squeezed out of the *esportine* by a hydraulic press. High-value oil is produced from the first pressing.

The temperature must be constantly watched. For best quality oil, it should not exceed 86 °F (30°C).

The result is *oli d'oliva verge*. The virginal liquid runs into the collection tank.

Skills from Venice
Glass from Majorca

By around 600 BC the Phoenicians of
Majorca were already producing that delicate, transparent combination of minerals
which so elegantly accommodates wine and
even seems to improve its taste – glass. No
records exist on Majorca to tell us how the
Phoenicians learned to transform sand,
quartz and stone into glass, but archeological
finds at Artà and Alcúdia prove that they
passed on their knowledge of its manufacture to the Romans.

While the Romans knew how to make
tinted glass, it was the Moors who really
made use of the full spectrum of color – especially green, the color of the Prophet
Mohammed. In spite of the unchallenged
dominance of Christian culture on the island

since 1232, green has remained the favorite
color of many of the island's glass-blowers –
along with several others, of course. A fond-
ness too for richly ornamented, curlicued,
and arabesque forms has its parallels in the
Byzantine-influenced glasswork the Moors
introduced to Majorca.

Three workshops today are especially
famous for the perfection of their glass-
making techniques, and the brilliance and
beauty of their products: the *Gordiola*
factory at Algaida, *Lafiore* at S'Esglaieta, and
the company *Menestràlia* near Campanet.

Monopolies and bans
To understand how the products from these
factories and their working methods were
arrived at is to know the story of how the
island's historical legacy merged with the
development of craft techniques once the
Moors had been driven from the island.

The Majorcan glass-works are one of the
highlights on the island's tourist trail

Majorca's new Christian rulers naturally
wanted to drink their *copa de vi* from elegant
glassware too and, what is more, they appreciated the economic potential of the glassmaker's skill.

They therefore commissioned the
council of guilds, the *jurats*, to declare the
glassmaker's trade a monopoly. In the 14th
century glassmaking was even forbidden for
a time for ecological reasons: the furnaces
were consuming too much wood, and the
island's forests were rapidly beginning to
disappear. Account books from 1452,
however, prove that the monopoly was being
undermined by bribes and special commis-
sions – the trade in glass was apparently too
attractive to allow it to be dominated by
only a privileged few.

The unrivaled European monopoly for quality glassware was held by Murano, an island near Venice, and this position was strengthened after Damascus – once the glass-making capital of the Mediterranean – fell to the Turks. The skill of Murano's glassblowers was so extraordinary that the Doge kept them virtual captives on the island, forbidding them, on pain of death, to pass their knowledge on to foreigners.

Escape from the artistic ghetto

The Catalans had in the meantime been sending the most gifted of their glassmakers to Majorca to learn from the work of their colleagues there. At the same time they were also buying large quantities of Venetian glass in order to try and unlock the secrets of its manufacture. How they must have wished – for the sake of speed and efficiency – for someone from that Mecca of glassmaking, Murano!

Their prayers were answered: in 1600 Dermenice Barovier escaped from Murano and traveled to Majorca. In 1605 he presented himself to the *jurats* and requested to be permitted to work in the glass manufacturing workshops on the island. When the *jurats* heard where he had come from, and what he could teach his Majorcan counterparts – who were still largely working according to the medieval principles of the Catalans – they knew they had made a good catch without even having to lift a finger.

Within no time Majorcan glass-blowers were copying Venetian glass so perfectly, and were imitating its colors and patterns so precisely, that even today many pieces from this period are incorrectly listed in catalogs as Venetian. Another benefactor was the cathedral of La Seu in Palma: its rose window, which steeps the interior of the church in a spectacular blaze of color, dates from the 16th century.

In the 18th century industrial production finally forced out the smaller, but suddenly very expensive, glass workshops. Not until the tourist trade boosted demand two centuries later did glass-blowing come into its own again.

The glassblower places a lump of quartz sand in the furnace on the end of a long rod, which is also his blowpipe.

It needs a steady hand to apply new layers of rapidly cooling glass onto the basic form.

The vase starts to take shape – but it must still be finely cut, polished, and separated from the blowpipe.

Roman, Moorish, and Venetian influences as well as the islanders' own ingenuity lend Majorcan glassware its playful beauty.

Where elves go swimming
Campanet

At first sight the alluvial land around the old church of St Michael, the Pla de Tel, looks like just one more grove of olives and evergreen oaks, cast up in the fertile undulations of the Raiguer district. But when it rains heavily, as it is often does in this part of Majorca between November and April, this area is utterly transformed. Great volumes of water gush up from cracks in the porous limestone until the earth is transformed into a raging current which rampages unchecked through the trees in its path until it reaches the Torrent de Sant Miquel, where it succumbs to the constraints of a river bed. The Majorcans call this phenomenon *fonts ufanes*, proud springs. The vernacular expression is apparently an attempt to explain an otherwise inexplicable event: subterranean water from the Pyrenees, it is said, chooses to emerge from below ground here and so put an end to its secret existence. The *fonts ufanes* are said to carry leaves from certain types of trees – oaks and beeches – which do not grow on Majorca but which can be found in that range of mountains separating Spain from France. Modern science requires tangible evidence, however, and has long since dismissed this theory as untenable. The *fonts ufanes* are, in fact, large caves in the subterranean limestone – as are the Coves de Campanet, first discovered in 1945 – which overflow after heavy rain.

The mystical traditions of the region still steadfastly maintain that this is a place for supernatural events. After all, the conquerors of the island chose this spot to build their church of St. Michael – and before them the Moors built their mosque on the same site. This mosque, in its turn, was constructed on the remains of an early Christian church which rested on the foundations of a Roman temple – and that stood in a place where the original inhabitants of Majorca worshipped benevolent forest spirits and *dones d'aigua*, water nymphs who bathed in the sunlit streams.

The "proud springs" are the work of a combination of porous limestone and torrential rainfall and not, unfortunately, magic.

A happy pig meets its end
Matança

It is already the end of January and time is definitely up. If the pig is not slaughtered now, the authorities will intervene and the beast will have to be fed for yet another ten months. It has to be today. The family has come together, the daughters and sons, with their spouses and children, having traveled great distances to be here. There is no time like the present!

The butcher, the *matador* – also known as an *escorxador* – is there as well. The family has prepared everything down to the last detail, as has the *matador* himself. In a meeting beforehand everyone is reminded of precisely which tasks they have to perform. Like a nurse in an operating theater, the lady of the house lays out the tools and imple-

ments on a table in a certain order which has been handed down unchanged from generation to generation. The butcher then delivers a practiced blow to the pig – and the animal dies instantly.

Every last drop of blood is caught in jugs and bowls laid out for the purpose. The family immediately begins to cook the blood over a fire, and the liquid slowly bubbles and thickens in the pot. The skin of the pig is scalded with boiling water and then shaved. The mother of the family then selects a special knife and slices off the pig's curly tail. This is a privilege belonging to the female head of the house and is often accompanied by an obscure liturgy, such as an ancient oath stating that only she has the right to remove the pig's tail.

The butcher now takes a short break during which the vet, as prescribed by law, inspects the pig to ensure that it is in an

The black Majorcan pig, *porcella negra*, is carefully fed and tended for a whole year.

acceptable condition. The job of the *matador* does not stop with the pig's slaughter: he must also remove its innards in a correct and hygienic manner. The animals were once killed by a blow to the head, but later the practice was adopted of beheading them or slitting their throats, and then hanging them up to drain the blood. The pig is then either cut open down its spine in order first to remove the chops, or the butcher cuts open the belly to release the innards. Families once used to slaughter the animals themselves, but today it is a job reserved for the *escorxador*.

Some of the difficult jobs in the slaughtering process have to be carried out with great precision. Apart from the actual

Before the pig is slaughtered all the necessary knives and vessels are meticulously laid out as though on an operating table.

After the butcher has delivered the fatal blow, the pig is drained to the last drop of blood.

Boiling water is then poured over the pig so that its bristles stand erect.

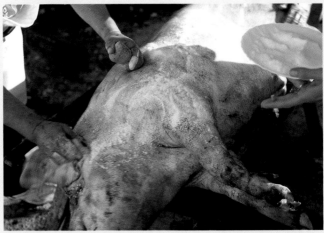

The bristles are shaved off and later used to make various types of natural fiber brushes.

During the break there is time for a quick joke: here, the pig has his ears tweaked.

The carcass is then hung in the time-honored manner and carved into individual joints.

195

The women clean the intestines.

Sausage filling – not a pretty sight for vegetarians.

In the afternoon sun the fatty skin of the pig is processed.

Anything useful is ground through the mincer.

Sausages of different types are cooked over the fire.

After the work is done there is time for a snack of *sobrasada*.

slaughter and the carving up of the carcass, this includes filling jars with pickled meat and, especially, producing the correct mixture of spices for the various types of sausage. The final combination is subject to a taste test by the most experienced of the helpers.

The allocation of tasks at the festival used to be decided by family relationship, the social status of the participants, and, of course, their relevant experience. The grandmother, for example, would be responsible for cooking the blood for the blood sausage; the older female friends of the family would clean the intestines with water and lemon juice; and the men would carry the pig to the table for slaughtering. The lady of the house was in charge of general organization. She had the (perhaps unenviable) job of deciding who should be given presents, and how much each person should receive according to their position in the family. She also determined the menu for the meal which was held after the work was over.

The food and drink offered to guests at the end of the day were ultimately a measure of the family's generosity and status. Normally there are great quantities of all sorts of meat products and offal which have to be used up quickly. Fried meats, salted sweetbreads, schnitzels, soups with bacon and meatballs often have their place on the menu. The most popular dish, however, is *frit de matança*, a stew made with fresh vegetables, potatoes, and offal.

Everything except the squeak

Absolutely every bit of the pig is either eaten or put to some practical use. Some of the meat is salted and the rest, together with the offal, is made into sausages called either *camaiots* or *botifarrons*. The *botifarrons* are the classic dark blood sausages, while the *camaiots* contain larger pieces of meat. The women sew sausage skins from the pig's own skin and even the penis is turned into a stick – formerly a useful tool for lubricating machine parts. The *pixa de porc* had an important place in the house and was often hung on the wall so that it was a constant presence – surely a matter for sexual ethnologists to speculate upon!

The children also have their duties. It is up to them to organize the evening's enter-

tainment; the absolute high point of the day's festivities for the end of this arduous day is crowned in every household with a great *festa* of music and dance. The occasion is also an opportunity for admirers of the family's unmarried daughters to get closer to the objects of their interest.

Pigs are back in fashion

There is evidence that swine were already domesticated in the second millennium BC on Majorca, and ever since then they have enjoyed enormous popularity. According to the Greek historian Diodorus Siculus, the much-feared Balearic slingers would rub their bodies with the grease of a pig after dining on its meat.

In the Middle Ages, the philosopher and theologian Ramón Llull discussed pigs in his chronicles, and later the *porcella negra*, the black pig, would become synonymous with the island's exports, its meat soon as popular as lobster from Menorca or veal from Avila in Central Spain.

For many centuries the annual slaughter of pigs in country areas was an important tradition which ensured there would be sufficient food for the whole village during the winter months. With the onset of the great boom in tourism in the middle of the 20th century, and the economic upturn which resulted, rural

traditions gradually came to be abandoned.

Fattening a pig for the household was no longer worth the effort and came to be considered a nuisance – a luxury which only romantics and traditionalists could afford to indulge in. The animals drifted out of fashion and were only occasionally seen as sucking pigs being roasted over a wood fire; only professional butchers and small industrial enterprises continued the slaughter of pigs.

As people have slowly started to rediscover their old customs, a few rural families have once again started to raise pigs, combining their slaughter in the traditional manner with a celebration. Today there is probably no better opportunity for getting to know a Majorcan family than to take part in a *matança*; these occasions reveal the very essence and mentality of the locals whose families are close-knit but where there is still plenty of personal space for each individual.

At the end of the day the entire family dines on dishes of freshly killed meat.

Harmony and dissonance
Búger

Búger is a contradictory place: though the town is sandwiched between two major population centers – Campenet and Sa Pobla – it enjoys a picturesque location on twin hills which makes visitors feel that they could not be farther from the madding crowd. And yet here, of all places, you can hear a very different music from the sort played in the Majorca of mass tourism, beaches and nightlife. In Moorish times there was a farmstead in Búger but today nothing remains except its name: Bujar de Rahal Algebel. The town's eight windmills seem to salute the visitor from afar and at least one of them still has its sails with which to fan guests who come to this remote hamlet to see the sights – and hear the sounds. It almost seems as if this last solitary set of sails were no accident but a sign that the old village was signaling to the passing traveler.

Today, the rhythms of Búger are no longer defined by the creaking of a white-washed windmill's sails in the languid Mediterranean breeze – the music of nature's chance encounter with technology. They are instead the melodious tones which emanate from the heart of a perfectly tuned grand piano, black and sleek as the wings of

a raven: Búger is now home to the *Fundació Àrea Creació Acústica*, the "Foundation for Acoustic Creation", an institution famed throughout Majorca.

Good music, after all, can only flourish away from the hurly-burly, in surroundings so peaceful that the air almost seems to

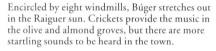

Encircled by eight windmills, Búger stretches out in the Raiguer sun. Crickets provide the music in the olive and almond groves, but there are more startling sounds to be heard in the town.

vibrate visibly over the fields as it makes way for sound. That, in any case, is the opinion of Antoni Caimari, who arrived in Búger together with his concert grand piano. In the upper part of the village he renovated an old farmhouse which has retained its exterior of natural stone and Majorcan shutters – and even its well and the vine-covered arbor in the courtyard. The interior, however, is quite a different sight. On the upper floor, Caimari has built offices and rooms for acoustic engineering, and on the ground floor all the non-supporting walls were demolished to create a concert hall which can also function as a recording studio. However, not a note escapes – eavesdroppers would be sorely disappointed and even the sheep in the fields are spared the terrors of the kettle drum – because the building has been completely soundproofed.

The inhabitants of Búger are proud of their "Foundation for Acoustic Creativity" – just so long as every now and again they get to listen to classical instead of three-tone music.

Perhaps that is not an entirely bad thing as Antoni Caimari, pianist and composer, prefers to play contemporary music: what may sound simply weird and out of key to the ears of the villagers is his passion – three-tone music – into which he weaves elements of Majorcan folk music. Nevertheless, he can rely on the goodwill of his fellow villagers. "Whatever Antoni is up to, it must be all right" they say laconically – and proudly, too, for they know that Caimari has made something special out of Búger.

In order that the townsfolk are not left out in the musical cold, the *ACA* also organizes concerts for those orthodox ears with a weakness for classical harmonies where everything is strictly arranged according to the rules of Western music with its octaves, thirds and fifths. Money for the foundation has to come from somewhere, Caimari knows – and it tends to flow more quickly in major and minor.

Playground of the Muses

Of the Muses, it was not only Terpsichore who liked the look of Búger: long before the *ACA* arrived, her mythical colleague Thalia – the Muse responsible for that "stage" we call the world – was busy here. According to the historian Gabriel Llompart, the most important document in the history of Catalan theater comes from Búger. This work is known as *Pascual* and its 200 pages describe around 50 plays from the Middle Ages and the Renaissance. Barely a detail is left out: costumes and stage sets are meticulously described, as are dramatic effects and the relationships of characters to each other. The book is truly a delight for all those interested in the history of theater, ethnology and social sciences. There is a catch, however. To marvel at this treasure of early European theater requires a trip to Barcelona: *Pascual* is housed there in the Biblioteca de Catalunya.

Antoni Caimari deliberately chose the dreamy town of Búger in which to set up his music foundation. Music has a good chance of being able to unfold in all its beauty in the tranquil surrounds of such a village. The Foundation's concert hall, its recording studio, and offices have found an unusual home in an old farmhouse.

Palma

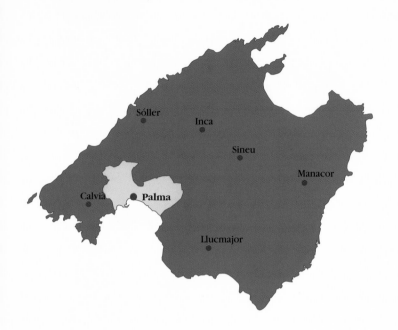

A metropolis from birth
Palma

At nine in the morning dust, litter and leaves from the streets and the last wisps of early morning haze from the sea lie across Palma like a half-remembered dream. The seats of the 100-year-old cafè Líric are still only sparsely occupied: its large espresso machine – probably as ancient as the café itself – moans and, with a resigned sigh, discharges steam into glasses of milk and cups of coffee. On the ceiling, the blades of a fan stoically make their rounds with an audible whoop. Whenever the waiters return to the counter they reach into an ashtray full of coins and throw a handful onto their tray – change for the customers. Now and again the scream of a moped or the roar of a car breaks the silence, but otherwise all is quiet on the Carrer del Mar. Palma is a late sleeper.

From the air, the city looks as though an elfin queen had dropped her fan right into the great semi-circular bay in the southwest of Majorca. The hinge of the fan would be the cathedral and its ribs would correspond to the streets of Sant Miquel, Sindicat, Sant Francesc, Sant Feliu, and Concepció. The town has only been called Palma de Majorca since the beginning of the 20th century – both the native palmesans and the *forasters*, the country-dwellers, call it *La Ciutat* – the city. So the Moorish name, Medina Mayurka, has survived into the present, along with the Roman name.

The Romans christened the town Palmeria, the victory palm, in

Previous double-page spread: The symbol of the island's capital: the cathedral of La Seu was built by Jaume I in 1230 in honor of an oath he swore before his successful conquest.

Right: Today, white doves – symbols of peace – flock around the statue of King Jaume I, conqueror of Majorca and vanquisher of the Moors.

around 122 BC when they decided to found a city on this broad, protected harbor after landing on the island the previous year. They called on the gods to protect the new *urbs*, drew up a streetplan and marked out the course of the later city walls which were to protect the population from attack.

Inside the walls, the main arterial routes were laid out in strict geometrical fashion according to the rules of Classical urban planning. One axis ran from north to south along what is today the street of Sant Roc, and the other from east to west, exactly where the Estudi-General now is.

Roman *palmesans* lived mainly from their trade in wine, textiles and oil. This Majorcan-Roman idyll survived for over half a millennium, threatened only by a plague of rabbits which required specialist assistance from Rome. It all came to an end in the fifth century, however, when the Vandals invaded the island, destroying large sections of the Roman city.

Water for an expanding metropolis
When the island came under Arab rule in 902, the Moors modified the remnants of the Roman walls to meet their needs. These desert

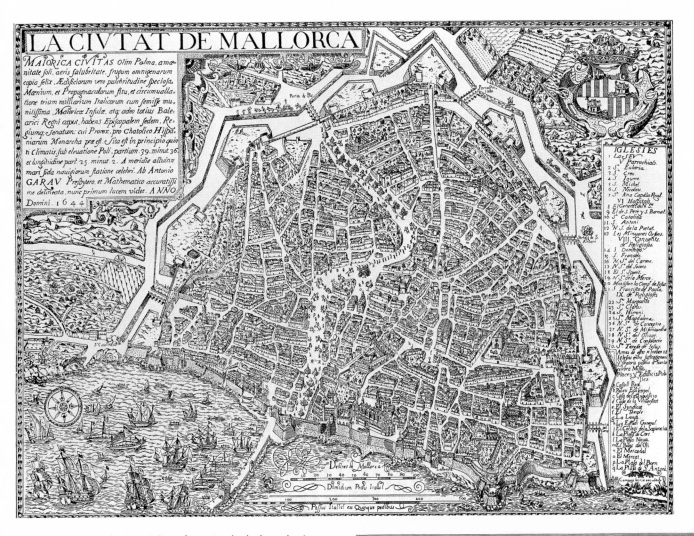

La Ciutat de Mallorca

peoples naturally had a particularly special relationship with water and this is reflected in the sophisticated supply system they built for Palma. Carried by small aqueducts, water was brought in to the center of Palma from its source, the "Emir's Spring", some five miles (8 km) outside the city. As the population expanded rapidly the course of the city walls had to be changed; for the first time Medina Mayurka, as the city was then called, grew beyond its defensive boundaries. At around the same time the Almudaina Palace was built in the center of the town.

Art and culture also prospered under the Moors. The island was home to three religions and cultures – Muslims, Jews, and a small community of Christians – who lived peaceably side by side, and became an international meeting place for leading intellectuals of the day.

The Almudaina became the seat of a literary circle, honored by the visits of illustrious Arab poets such as Ibn al-Labbana or Ibn Hamdis.

The Catalans and Aragonese completely changed the character of the Muslim city and in their blind hatred of the "infidels" eliminated almost every trace of the Arabs. Moorish buildings were either razed to the ground or converted into Christian structures.

Jaume I had barely set foot on the island in 1230 when he ordered the cathedral of La Seu to be built below the Moorish palace of Almudaina as a sign to all those approaching from the sea that Majorca was now in Christian hands. However, it had to be built on the foundations of a former mosque which meant that the cathedral was not oriented towards Jerusalem but Mecca – a particularly subtle hint from Allah of the debts Christian Mediterranean culture owed to Islam.

Above: The Cases Casasaya on the Plaça Weyler were built from 1909–1911 at the peak of the Art Nouveau era by pupils of Gaudí's.

Left: In the Carrer dén Colom – Columbus Street – well-maintained and elegant façades provide the ideal ambience for a stroll.

The course of the city walls was altered several times and moved ever further outwards – influxes of Catalan, Provençal, and Italian immigrants meant the town was still growing. In the 16th century the city's inhabitants were divided into distinct quarters: the wealthy and privileged nobility could afford to live in the protected inner part of the town, in the palaces of Sa Calatrava and in a quarter bordering on the walls of the bishop's palace and the cathedral. The Jews also lived in their own quarter, the so-called Call, a closed ghetto-like area near the church of Santa Eulària.

However, anyone who wanted to move into the city from the surrounding area, the *parta forana*, had to settle outside the city walls. Santa Catalina and Es Jonquet, previously just a scattering of houses, grew to become suburbs in their own right.

In the 15th century the bed of the sometimes violent river Riera was diverted to the west after constant flooding of what is today the Passeig Born and the Ramblas; in 1403 it had swept away 1500 houses together with their inhabitants. In 1902 the city walls suffered a similar fate. City planners thought only the demolition of the ancient walls would allow for a rational expansion of the town, which they felt was being restricted by this tight corset of stone. The zigzag *avingudas* which now surround the heart of the city were built on the foundations of the city walls.

An experience by night and by day

If today the visitor fights his way into the inner city from the encircling ring roads and is finally able to escape the traffic jams (as much a part of Palma as its cathedral), he will see *La Ciutat* for the maritime metropolis it is – a city whose Art Nouveau villas, turn of the century coffee houses, galleries, museums, and shopping arcades are the equal of any other big city in Spain.

Now and then the comparison is made between Palma and Barcelona, even if this really only applies in a few cases: the promenade of the Via Roma, for example, was renamed and is now called simply Ramblas – like its green counterpart in Barcelona, also populated by flower-stalls.

The Teatre Pricipal, in which none other than Arthur Rubinstein, Yehudi Menuhin, and Montserrat Caballé have appeared, is no less a venue than the Liceu opera house in Barcelona. Indeed, its director's strategy of aiming for a healthy mix of both challenging and entertaining music has met with considerable success. It sometimes happens that the world-famous Catalan soprano, Montserrat Caballé, enchants an audience one evening with her arias, and 24 hours later the equally famous pop-singer Julio Iglesias takes the stage to delight his fans with catchy melodies about love and desire.

As befits a proper metropolis there is also plenty for those who prefer pleasures of a different variety. They begin their evenings with a good meal before having a drink or two in the Carrer Apuntadors or traveling to the western quarter of Es Terreno to dance the night away in Tito's, the home of techno.

During the day Palma is an ideal place to stroll about. The promenades of Passeig des Born, Ramblas or Sagrera, lined with palm and plane trees, evoke an almost tropical ambience. The casual visitor can be forgiven for asking himself whether he is still in Europe or on a Caribbean island with its soft, eternally mild and spring-like air. The fruit and vegetables on offer are certainly not unlike those from tropical regions, and whoever casts his eye over the fish and seafood for sale in the city's three market halls is bound to have the feeling that he is looking at the bounty of the seven seas rather than only of the *mare nostrum*.

From the Passeig dalt Murada, directly in front of the cathedral, the spectator's eye travels over the Parc de la Mar with its palm trees, artificial lake and modern sculptures, past the Club Náutic with luxury yachts from all over the world, and up to the Castell de Bellver which watches over the city like a sentinel from its pine covered hill. The westernmost part of the capital is marked by the Moorish towers

Above: The light of the past illuminates the fabulous chamber of the Teatre Principal. Here one can revel in all the luxuries of velvet, gold, and music.

Left: Tourists can enjoy alternative transport in Palma too. This carriage tours the shoreline promenade of the Platja.

of the harbor, Porto Pi, where mighty oil tankers lie at anchor a discreet distance from ferries and the floating hotels of cruise ships.

Light and shade in the old alleyways

The center of the city is full of light. The former Moorish palace of Almudaina, which was extended after the conquest of the island by the Christians, is today the official Majorcan residence of the Spanish king Juan Carlos I and his family – if they are not gliding over the gentle Balearic waters in the royal yacht, or enjoying a beach holiday at their summer residence, Marivent, on the Cala Millor.

Directly next to the Almudaina is one of the most beautiful cathedrals to be found anywhere – La Seu – whose dazzling windows transform daylight into all the colors of the rainbow.

In the jumble of streets in the old town, where cobblestones and asphalt cover even older Arab and medieval routes, the finest examples of civic architecture in Palma can be seen. Half-open doorways afford a glimpse of the town's patios, the interior courtyards of the old city palaces with their stone archways and wrought iron balustrades; often there is a fountain in the middle, and almost always tubs full of cascading flowers.

Between the doors, the sumptuous Art Nouveau buildings practically invite the eye to scramble over their façades, ornamented window frames and balconies. Palma has much to offer in both religious and secular architecture. The airy, columned cloister of the monastery of Saut Francesc, renovated at the end of the 20th century, captivates the viewer with its profound tranquillity: in the middle of the hustle and bustle of the city it is a haven of peace and contemplation.

Beauty like this needs to be protected and preserved. Both the city authorities and residents are aware of this fact and have acted to maintain their historic buildings. The old town has had care lavished on it with not so much as a crack in the plasterwork of privately owned city mansions. This is partly due to the financial incentives offered by a municipal foundation to those owners willing to restore their own properties. But owners of large properties in the city also renovate their houses out of a sense of self-preservation. Every time a crumbling building in Palma is pulled down and the earth is disturbed by bulldozers, traces of the Roman or Arab past are found. Such discoveries are immediately a signal for heritage conservators go to work, and this effectively puts an end to any attempts to continue construction.

But it is not all wine and roses for Palma's architecture. The conservationists seem to have skirted the *barri xino*, the "Chinese quarter" east of the Plaça Major, as scrupulously as do most visitors and the locals themselves. In this district, many houses have not seen

The shade of the bookstore in the Clinica Dental is a particularly pleasant place to browse.

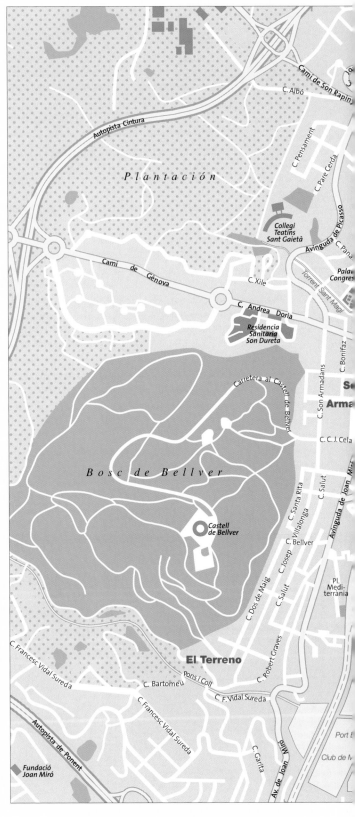

The former course of the city walls is instantly recognizable on the map. Marked out in yellow here, a ring of boulevards today traces the route of the former city limits. The Bellver Castle far to the west of the town is also easy to locate. The central point towards which the entire city is oriented is the cathedral which sits right by the water. Rather than facing Jerusalem, it is angled to the southeast towards Mecca.

© 1999, Studio für Landkartentechnik

Above: Behind these seemingly indifferent walls in the Old Town, delightful enclaves await the visitor: the town's patios.

a coat of paint in decades and the gloomy, unsettling impression of the area is emphasized by the tiny stores and sinister warehouses tucked away in side streets, the graffiti-covered walls, and the hordes of wild dogs and cats that roam about through the piles of trash.

The city of artists and designers

In Roman times it was not Palmeria but Pollentia, today Alcúdia, which was the fashion capital of Majorca, and its exports reached to the farthest corners of the Roman Empire. Of course, things have changed since. The reputation of La Ciutat for beauty is not just because of its rich tapestry of churches, monasteries and palaces:

Palma chic is as popular in Spain as fashion from New York is in the US, or Milan in Italy.

The city can also boast the highest number of art galleries per square foot in Spain – not even Barcelona comes close to approaching Palma. In the Via Veri reputable couturiers put their astronomically expensive designs on display, while south of the Avinguda Jaume III there are rows of leather goods boutiques and shoe shops in whose windows internationally known brands such as *Camper*, *Yanko* and *Lottusse* from Inca are exhibited like crown jewels.

In the Carrer Argentaria, the street of the silversmiths in the former Jewish quarter of Call, precious stones sparkle alongside Swiss watches, filigree silver goods wait alongside massive signet rings for interested customers. Book worms browse in old bookshops for works on the city's history, and connoisseurs of art feel faint at the prospect of having to make a choice between galleries; to calm their anguished souls they usually make the world famous *Fundació Pilar i Joan Miró* in Calamajor in the west of the city their first stop.

Surrounded by architectural travesties in a uniform mud-brown – monstrosities which conceal thousands upon thousands of apartments within their concrete frames – in 1993 the artist and his wife constructed a monument to their life and work which is as architecturally daring as it is artistically convincing. It features clear lines in a bright, almost white, Marès stone under a star-shaped roof used for collecting rainwater, and is flooded with the Mediterranean light which pours in through narrow windows slits.

Some of the incomplete paintings, drawings and letters by the famous artist and architect give the impression that this grand master of Spanish surrealism has just put down his pen and brush for a minute and gone out for a quick *café amb llet* or coffee with milk.

The wise visitor will wait for another day to view the Collecció March, a museum of contemporary art owned by the March foundation and – like a visit to the Miró exhibition – another absolute must. One can only absorb so much, after all, and time should be given to reflect on the impressions gained at the Miró foundation. This artistic digestion process is best aided by a trip to the Castell de Bellver: nowhere else is the view of Palma as breath-taking as it is from up here. It is at its best in the afternoon when La Seu is slowly shrouded in a gentle golden light, appearing like an enchanted

mountain on the other side of the bay. Behind it live 350,000 people, more than half of all Majorcans, in their mansions and tower blocks; by day they are blanketed in the roar of traffic but by night they are festooned and cradled by the lights of the city, reflected in the inky blackness of the sea.

Above: A unique panorama over the city is revealed from the Bellver Castle.

Opposite: Via Veri: a street of galleries and designer stores with post-modern marble façades and medieval pavements.

Following double-page spread: The popular Forn d'es Teatre below the Plaça Major has more to offer than just a beautiful Art Nouveau façade. *Ensaïmadas* are served here in all conceivable dimensions, from the size of a silver dollar to that of a wagon wheel.

A song in stone
The cathedral of La Seu

Majorca's liberation from the Moorish "heathen" almost came to grief at sea: when Jaume I, just 20 years old, cast off for the island in the fall of the year 1229 with 20 000 men and 143 ships, the flotilla quickly got into such distress that the young king feared the towering waves would drag the ships and their crews down forever. During the three- and-a-half-day crossing there were several occasions when he thought his hour had finally come. In those days it was widely accepted that in such circumstances there was only one thing to do: swear an oath. Consequently, Jaume pledged that if he were to succeed in driving the Arabs from the island he would express his thanks for God's providence and mercy by erecting a cathedral upon it. This cathedral, swore the seasick king, would be built on a massive scale – perhaps the biggest the world had yet seen.

Jaume the Conqueror was lucky. He not only arrived safely at the island, he was also able to defeat the Moors. As a God-fearing Catalan, he did not to forget his promise when he celebrated his triumph on New Year's Eve 1229, and soon set about putting his intentions into practice. A decision on a site for his offering to God was quickly made: Arab architects were experts at selecting suitable locations for their places of worship, and the hill by the sea where the Palma mosque had been built proved perfect for their Christian successors. The spot had another advantage – the Muslim mosque could be seen from far out at sea, so by erecting his house of God on the same site Jaume underscored the victory of the true Faith over Islam.

This expression of Christian triumphalism does not bear closer examination however. Probably because they were in a hurry, Jaume and his architects had not stopped to consider the location for long enough. They had intended to show the superiority of Christianity by building on the foundations of a mosque, but in so doing they created one of the great historical paradoxes. Anyone kneeling at the altar in Majorca's cathedral does so in the direction of Mecca like a Muslim and not, as should be the case in a Christian church, facing towards Jerusalem.

The cathedral, 360 feet (120m) long, has all the appearance of a mighty siege castle.

Tourists like to view the cathedral by settling on the 'Costa de la sev' steps.

He had wanted to create columns so fine and of such a filigree appearance that it would appear as if they transcended the laws of statics. But although it was to be a house of God, the building was still bound to the laws of nature, a fact which became apparent when the first two columns were tested by allowing them to carry part of the roof: they quickly began to buckle like blades of grass under the immense weight, and threatened to collapse completely. There was no choice but to widen their diameter by eight inches (20 cm) to a total of five foot six inches (1.68 m). Nevertheless, in relation to their height of more than 66 feet (21 m), they are among the slimmest load-bearing columns in the world.

In 1389 the builders completed work on the south door, the Porta del Mirador, whose pointed arches are lavishly ornamented with animal motifs and gargoyles. Hope was renewed that work on this architectural masterpiece would soon be finished, but at the end of the 15th century part of the ceiling collapsed and work was put back by several years.

The minaret from the former mosque survived all the construction activity for several centuries and was a constant reminder of the island's former glories; it wasn't until the 16th century that it was finally converted into a belltower. At 150 feet (48 m) in height, its proportions are decidedly modest in comparison with the other dimensions of the cathedral.

When money for building work became scarce, all levels of society – starting with the bishops and the cathedral chapter, the royal house of Aragón and the nobility right through to the merchant class – had to dig deep into their pockets to ensure that the church could be completed. In 1601 these donors could finally breathe easy; the main façade was finished, the masterpiece had finally taken shape and was essentially complete. A new series of disasters, however, constantly set work back by several decades: in 1851 an earthquake destroyed the west façade and it was rebuilt in a Renaissance

The two towers of the western façade were not finished until the 19th century.

Construction on this Palma landmark, which some have described as a lion lying in wait and others as a watchful sphinx, was quickly begun. The king and his architects hastily drew up plans and the foundation stone was laid as early as 1230. This sort of speed was deemed necessary by Jaume for fear that God might become angry if he did not fulfill his vow.

In the first phase the mosque was torn down to the foundation walls, the minaret being initially spared the demolition hammer. The architects erected an apse facing south-east and this was consecrated in a ceremony in 1269. Although the plans for the church were prepared in such a short space of time, construction work soon became bogged down: neither Jaume I nor his son, Jaume II – nor indeed many later kings – were ever to see the building completed.

Pressure on the pillars and on the donors

The first of the 14 slim columns which support the roof of the nave were completed in 1389 but the ambition of the architect, Jaume Mates, was soon to rebound on him.

style which jarred with the otherwise Gothic building. In 1857, and again in 1906, storms damaged the rose window, and several other windows were destroyed by a bomb dropped in 1936. La Seu never did become the largest cathedral in the world – not even the largest Gothic cathedral. Other architects built other churches on an even greater scale such as the cathedrals in Seville or Cologne.

But there are no lack of superlatives for La Seu, His Own, as it is known. It is considered the most joyous church building in all Spain, and it is no coincidence that La Seu is known as the "Cathedral of Light": the morning sun falling through the rose window, with its glass dating from 1236, drenches every nook and cranny of the interior in a light which looks as though it were freshly copied from a rainbow.

A hesitant Art Nouveau
This carpet of light is the work of no less a man than Antoni Gaudí, the master of

Elevation of the cathedral of La Seu from Ludwig Salvator's book on the Balearics.

The *oculus maior*. Covering almost 350 square feet (100 m²), the rose window is one of the largest Gothic stained glass windows found anywhere.

Modernismo, the Spanish variant of Art Nouveau. At the end of the 19th century Joan Campins i Barceló, the Bishop of Majorca and a man of modern views, thought the interior of the church was in need of refurbishment. Because Catholic liturgy was by then moving away from displays of pomp and ceremony, he wanted to liberate the Cathedral of Light from the ballast of previous centuries and adapt it to more contemporary trends.

Campin i Barceló was an enthusiastic disciple of Art Nouveau and he knew immediately whom he would entrust with this task: he met with Antoni Gaudí, who had established his reputation with his work on the cathedral of La Sagrada Familia (The Holy Family), and whose projects evoked as extreme a response as do those of the English architect Sir Norman Foster at the end of the 20th century.

Gaudí paid Palma a visit and looked over the cathedral, critically inspecting the Baroque altar and leaning against the delicate piers to examine the way the light fell through the windows according to the time

of day and prevailing weather conditions. For three years he studied and sketched until he finally presented his design in 1904 and work could begin. For ten years he labored without interruption until suddenly, from one day to the next, he simply decided not to finish the contract.

Why Gaudí suddenly lost interest in this ambitious project is not quite clear today. It may be that he was sick of the constant criticisms the Majorcans made of his plans. For ten years laymen, architects, and members of the church alike had attacked him, claiming that he was acting more like a revolutionary than a restorer, and that he should stick with the skills he had learned in his profession. He should, they said, place himself at the service of his Creator rather than attempt to outdo God.

The result was that Gaudí sullenly withdrew into the role of the misunderstood artist. The bishop was at his wits' end: the cathedral had exhausted 15 generations of architects and still it was not properly finished. Gaudí's ecclesiastical clients tried once again to persuade him to continue, but the Catalan architect stuck by his decision.

A chance for fame

Finally, when almost all hope had been abandoned, a glimmer of light appeared at the end of the tunnel. Joan Rubió, one of Gaudí's pupils, offered to complete the work together with his colleague, Guillem Reynés.

The two men began work immediately; the controversial project, which their teacher had already abandoned, offered them the chance of achieving fame. On the other hand, they risked arousing people's ire with their ideas, a state of affairs which would lead to their careers ending almost before they had begun.

Their first step was to remove the Baroque retable in order to open up the view through the church to the chapel of the Trinity. They also moved the choir from the center of the nave to the presbytery so that light could fall unhindered through the great rose window, a feature which had always been at the heart of Gaudí's concept of opening La Seu up to the light. In different parts of the cathedral Rubió and Reynés covered windows and lamps with colored glass from Catalonia and in doing so transformed the cathedral into a spectacle of color.

The area around the bishop's throne near the apse was also fundamentally remodeled. More than 5000 hand-painted and glazed tiles from the Majorcan workshop of La Roqueta were decorated with olive branch motifs so realistic they looked as if they would start fluttering with the next breath of wind; the olive branch tiles were positioned so as to wind around the 55 coats of arms of previous bishops.

The marble altar was crowned with an enormous canopy hung below the *oculus maior* – the almost 120 square yards (100 m²) of the great rose window, one of the finest in Gothic architecture. The old 14th century gilded canopy had to be moved to achieve

When the sun falls through the rosette windows into the interior of La Seu, the church reveals its greatest charms and is transformed into a cathedral of space and light.

this, and it was given a new home as a daring decoration over the Portal del Mirador.

The altar itself was restored and carefully set back in its original position.

And there, above the altar, is probably the most breathtaking use of art that was ever seen in a Catholic church – a great suspended ring like a candelabra decorated with fishing nets, sails and other rigging and looking as though it were floating on the waves of a mystical sea. Hundreds of lightbulbs illuminate the work which is intended to depict the miracle of transubstantiation during the Eucharist.

Although the crucial renovations in the cathedral were carried out under the direction of Joan Rubió and Guillem Reynés, they are still attributed to Gaudí. There are few references in the relevant literature to the magnificent work of these two architects; whether for marketing reasons – Gaudí's name has a greater cachet than two of his unknown pupils – or for reasons of negligence, Rubió and Reynés have been denied elevation to the Olympus of architecture.

Left: The massive crown-of-thorns baldachin by Gaudí is suspended over the main altar in the presbytery.

Inset: Hundreds of light bulbs light up this work of art which is surmounted by a crucifix.

Cults and commerce
Easter procession in Palma

The first spectators begin to make themselves comfortable on their wooden benches at midday; they grope about in their bags bringing out opera glasses and water bottles, and begin fanning themselves to cool the heat of their excitement. Spectators too, it seems, have to be thoroughly prepared for the annual *Processó del Sant Crist de la Sang*, the procession of the "Holy Christ of Blood". As with life, so with processions – whoever arrives late is punished. In this case the penalty is being condemned to observe the passage of the *coufraries*, the island's fraternities, from two or three rows back in the dense crowd.

The spectators seated in the front rows have already long since gone through their "procession" and made their "sacrifices": every year tourists and locals stream into the island's tourist offices for days on end to try and obtain tickets for seats from which they can follow the most important Easter procession in the island's capital. For the city, the effort certainly pays off – employees

in the tourist information office on the Plaça de la Reina have to flex their fingers to stave off cramp after all the counting of banknotes they are required to do. And in the cafés, bars and restaurants in Palma there is also the odd peseta or two more in the till than usual. The fact that International Regatta Week is held in Palma's harbor during *Semana Santa*, Easter week, is not exactly bad for business either.

Some time in the late afternoon of Maundy Thursday the patience of believers and spectators is rewarded. The first to be seen are the officers of the *Coufraria de la Sang*, the Brotherhood of Blood, who have led the procession since the 16th century. Several of their more privileged members are allowed to carry the extremely heavy platform on which stands a black figure of the *Sant Crist de la Santíssima* carved in wood, together with a crucifix and baldachin; the float approaches slowly, swaying from side to side as the men struggle under their burden. Directly behind them is the statue of the *Verge dels Dolors*, the Virgin of Sorrows. All the other fraternities must wait several hours until the oldest of their number has finally begun to move on from the hospital church, the Capella de la

Santíssima Sang, behind the General Hospital. It is not until the *Coufrares de la Sang* has begun the long march past Palma's most important churches and the cathedral that the other *coufraries* may follow them. Fraternity members are clad entirely in black, their floor-length cassocks ending in a black hood. Black eyes glint through the slits made in their conical "witches' hat"; chains rattle on the feet of some members and wax drips incessantly onto the streets from the candles and torches they hold. They make a terrifying sight, looking like something from the dark days of the Inquisition, or as if they had just escaped from a movie about the Ku Klux Klan.

The fraternities which follow, although not shrouded in eerie black, are no less uncanny. Some of them wear white robes bearing a startling red cross reminiscent of crusaders. Others have had to dispense with their candles because they are busy beating themselves with chains and leather whips – even though the Pope has forbidden any public displays of penitential self-flagellation. At the same time, someone carrying a cross – a so-called *natzarè* – sinks exhausted to the ground in front of the cathedral. In view of the midday heat, no one knows for sure whether this collapse is serious or feigned – until the *natzarè* suddenly gets to his feet and continues on his way.

And that way is long. It is not until the early hours of Good Friday morning that the procession numbering several thousand penitents – both male and female – returns to the Capella de la Santíssima Sang. The wax from their candles, meanwhile, has long since run into the cracks between the paving stones and hardened.

Opposite, top: The shrine weighs around a ton and it is a privilege to be allowed to carry it during the Easter procession.

Right: All the city's fraternities take part in the procession of the Holy Christ of Blood.

Opposite, bottom: With their hooded faces the penitents have a warlike appearance.

A steadfast rock in the currents of time
La Roqueta

Two years had yet to pass before Spain's best known artist and architect, Antoni Gaudí, was to follow the call of Majorca's bishop Joan Campins i Barceló and redesign Palma cathedral. But in 1897 Pedro Juan Aguiló Forteza – known by his nickname, Cetre (falconer), in reference to his surname Aguila (eagle) – was already dreaming of inspiring the greatest artists in Spain to work on his ambitious project La Roqueta, ("little rock").

Cetre wanted to set himself up with a ceramics factory and just outside the city, in Son Espanyolet, he bought a factory whose 9530 square yards (8500 m2) suited him perfectly. At the same time he bought a shop in the heart of Palma, in San Miguel Street, in anticipation that the factory's high quality work would have to be displayed and sold somewhere. Pedro reveled in his fantasies: the greatest artists of his generation would create designs for his company, and the factory would become known far beyond the bounds of the island.

The entrepreneurial spirit was in Pedro's blood, so to speak. His father had for a long time been obsessed with the idea that Majorca should have its own railway, and he eventually became a co-founder of the Sociedad de Ferrocarriles de Majorca, the Majorcan Railway Company.

The business concept of his artistically talented son, Pedro, fell on fertile soil. At the turn of the century ceramic tiles were not being produced on Majorca because the undisputed market leaders in Europe were the British and French. It was high time, therefore, that the ceramic arts which had been brought to the island long before by the Arabs were revived and the market stimulated.

Once the plant had been purchased and installed, Cetre immediately set about hiring designers. Today, it is not known exactly how many there were in the 21 year history of La Roqueta. He employed a full-time draftsman, Vicente Llorens Rubí, who had studied design in Valencia. Llorens designed numerous works such as the beautiful Art Nouveau ceiling for the Aguiló family's house at Porto Pi: 81 tiles sumptuously decorated with birds which seem to be flying up

When *Modernisme* was flourishing, tiles from La Roqueta were no longer exclusively used for interiors. Over time, Art Nouveau façades also began to be decorated with the factory's imaginatively designed products.

into the branches of a tree. This work of art can today be admired in the Museu de Majorca.

Partly supported by his father the owner of the business worked as well, designing wall and floor tiles and decorative items. The factory began to flourish, and it was considered chic and modern to have the walls of one's kitchen, corridor, dining and living rooms decorated with tiles, vases or plates bearing the La Roqueta hallmark.

And then there was Gaudí …
At the same time as La Roqueta the Spanish version of Art Nouveau, *Modernisme*, was making waves in Barcelona with its playful use of color, sinuous forms and especially for its variations of Moorish and Gothic formal elements. The works of the movement's pioneer, Antoni Gaudí, in particular had come to define the style of the era.

The work he had begun on the cathedral of La Sagrada Familia in Barcelona – the project which was to dominate his career – split art critics into enthusiastic supporters and those who contemptuously dismissed

Since the "little rock" factory was disbanded, several examples of its work have been exhibited in the Museu de Majorca such as these tiles by Gaudí.

Tiled allegorical figure on the Casal Barceló.

A tiled bird rises into the air.

Roqueta then changed hands several times until it was finally bought by the industrialist Joan March in 1918.

At that time, however, March had not yet discovered the advantages to be gained for himself or his business from an association with art; it was not until many years later that he attempted to achieve social recognition as a patron of the arts. Without batting an eyelid, therefore, he dismissed the company's artists and craftsmen. Where once the name "La Roqueta" had signified the miraculous transformation of clay into works of art, it now stood for the production of soap and oil.

the architect for his unrestrained fantasy.

When work on the Palma cathedral finally began, the factory was inundated with contracts. More than 5000 ceramic tiles planned for the redesigned presbytery by Gaudí's pupils Rubió and Reynés had to be painted with olive branches and coats of arms, and then fired.

But this was not the end of matters. Gaudí worked on various other projects as well as the cathedral. The Casal de Forteza Rey on the Plaça Marquès del Palmer, with its ceramic reliefs and glittering, colorful façade featuring luminous tiled flowers, has been compared with Gaudí's other masterpiece of domestic architecture, the Casal Battló in Barcelona.

Cetre's dream of making La Roqueta famous had long since come true. The factory's products were not just used for imaginative interiors – more and more houses in Palma were decorating their façades with skillfully made tiles from his workshop. One of these masterpieces is the Casal Barceló on the Plaça de Josep Maria Quadrado 9 from 1902, which is decorated with an allegory of the liberal arts designed by Vicente Llorens. The first two floors feature an ornamental tiled wreath with a floral motif, but the really sensational work is a series of tiled images between the windows on the fourth floor. Five of the six liberal arts are depicted here: painting and sculpture, music, architecture

and literature. Although the sixth art – dance – is missing from this line-up, the Muses have acquired extra followers from the ceramics and textile industry.

Soap and oil – the end of La Roqueta
The successful period of the factory's history continued until 1910 when Cetre had to give up the business for health reasons. *La*

The Casal de Forteza Rey has been compared with Gaudí's magnificent Casal Battló in Barcelona.

Azahar
The Moors on Majorca

In 1838 Chopin could still be impressed with the "Arab appearance" of Palma – presumably more obvious then than it is today. The Moorish influence on Majorca has survived longest however in its place names: Algaida is derived from the Arabic word for "forest", Deià from the Arabic *daia* for "village"; Binissalem and Raixa are Arabic in origin too, while Banyalbufar meant the "vineyard on the sea". Even if the historical remains of Arab architecture on the island are sparse, traces of the Moorish era, or at least the spirit of Islamic culture, can be found on almost every corner.

For over three hundred years, this island in the heart of the Mediterranean flourished under the Moors. As soon as the Arab conquerors realized what sort of paradise the island's fertile soil and ancient cities could be transformed into, they brought over their best urban planners, scientists, artisans, and engineers from their North African homeland.

The curiosity of a pilgrim

If the legends are to be believed, the island's heyday began with a storm. The merchant, Isman al-Khaulani, a Muwallad – or Christian who had converted to Islam – had embarked on his *hajj* – a pilgrimage to Mecca – when the journey was interrupted by a storm, and he was stranded on the shores of Majorca. He was forced to spend several weeks on the island before he was once again able to board his ship, and he used this time to inspect Majorca thoroughly and spy out its defenses.

After he had returned to Spain he described to his master, Emir Abd-Allah of Córdoba, Majorca's beauty in the most glowing terms, not forgetting to mention that the island's defensive system was less than adequate.

He quickly convinced the Emir that it would be a simple matter to turn Majorca into a province of al-Andalús, the Arab empire of

Ein junger Maure.

Above: A young Moor in traditional costume.

Left: Within the space of just a few years the Iberian peninsula came under the rule of the Caliphs of Damascus, and later those of Baghdad and Córdoba. The green arrows show the campaigns of the Moors; and the various shades of red mark the territorial gains of the Christian reconquest.

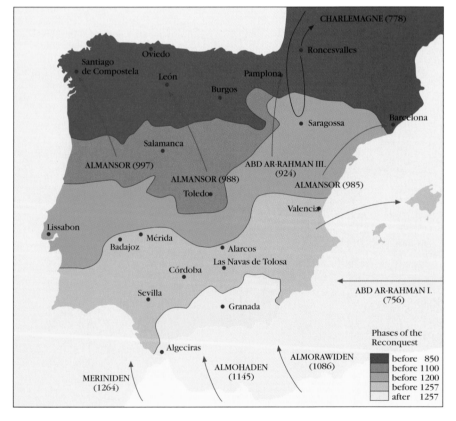

the Iberian peninsula. The Emir then charged al-Khaulani with the conquest of the island, which he led successfully in 902. He was also appointed its first *wâlî*, or governor.

The first thing that al-Khaulani did was to make a closer inspection of Palma, which was to be called *Medina Mayurka* from then on. Extensive building work was necessary to convert the city into a center worthy of Islamic life; his next step therefore was to order the construction of the Almudaina, the Government Palace which was built right by the sea. The Moors were also concerned with the physical well-being of their subjects and around the middle of the 10th century they erected the Banys Árabs.

These Arab baths, like those of the Romans from whom the principle had been adopted, were not only meant to purify the body but also the spirit and, above all, to promote social interaction. The baths were one of the most important meeting places for both men and women – though they were strictly segregated by sex of course. Here, one could talk about the family, forge plans and conduct business deals. If a conversation became too heated, one could move from the *caldarium*, the steam bath, to the *tepidarium*, where tempers could cool off a little in tepid water. The skylights in the vaulted roof, which was supported by twelve columns, allowed warm sunlight to fall onto the bathers below.

Al-Khaulani died in 913, a year after his "superior", Emir Abd-Allah. Some of the Moors now found commerce, agriculture, or crafts – work in general – too demanding. There were quicker, more comfortable and more exciting ways of getting at other people's money – and their attentions turned to the sea and to piracy. Al-Muwaffak came to power in 947 when he succeeded al-Khaulani's son, Abd-Allah, and he decided to devote himself to the lucrative business of becoming a pirate. What is more, he did this with official approval, gaining some notoriety in the process: until 969 his Arab fleet used Majorca as a base from which to ravage Christian maritime traffic along the entire Catalonian and French coasts until finally hardly a single captain dared to sail there.

While the island's rulers were thoroughly preoccupied with piracy, the civilian population pursued more peaceful interests.

A gold coin from an Almohad hoard: legal tender on Majorca from 1203 to 1229 AD.

During the period of Moorish rule Majorca experienced a second great cultural ascendancy. Muslims, Jews, and a small Christian minority lived together in peace. The "fine arts" were encouraged at the court of the Moorish rulers in the Medina Mayurka (Palma) which attracted poets and musicians from the Arab world. This old illustration from the Siliman Namé (Saray Library, Istanbul) shows such a musical soirée at the court of a caliph.

Artisans developed the famous art of hand-painted ceramic tiles which became known to history as majolica. Engineers perfected the island's irrigation system, greatly increasing the fertility of the soil and introducing Christian residents of *Medina Mayurka* to the pleasures of fruits, vegetables and spices which were previously unknown to them.

The Majorcans were awe-struck by the orange groves in the Moorish *sulliar* (the "Valley of Gold" near Sóller) and intoxicated by the scent of their fruit, if only because of the poetry of its name: *azahar*.

They also grew to love *al barkuk*, the apricots, peaches, pomegranates, and almonds and they were able to observe how pine nuts, caraway, and raisins found their way into the Moors' cooking pots to lend strong-tasting meat dishes a milder and sweeter flavor. The island's Moorish masters prepared dishes of exquisite quality and were eventually able to convince the native Majorcans that such good cooks could not possibly mean them any harm.

Generally the new rulers did not interfere in Majorcans' lives. They were able to continue practicing their beliefs unmolested and if there were any deeper communication problems they simply turned to the adherents of the third faith on the island – the Jews – and asked them to translate. Life during the main period of Arab "foreign rule" was, like everywhere else in the world, not necessarily a Golden Age but it did pass peacefully.

Too far removed from the Emirate of Córdoba – to which the Balearics belonged – to play a role in internal political quarrels, the Majorcans led an insular existence in the truest sense of the word. When the islands passed to the southern Spanish kingdom of Dénia a century after it was conquered, a new governor arrived who was still more tolerant than his predecessor. Ali ibn

Mujahid even recognized the Bishop of Barcelona as the spiritual leader of Majorca's Christians, and allowed the induction of priests and the exercise of ecclesiastical offices.

A short period of independence

For a while the Balearics made the most of being far from the centers of Islamic power in al-Andalús. The islands increasingly developed a reputation for not being concerned with political developments on the mainland, and of living in their own world in conditions they had created for themselves. One *walî*, al-Mu'tada, even went so far as to proclaim an independent Kingdom of the Balearics in 1076; until 1093 coins were minted on the island with his

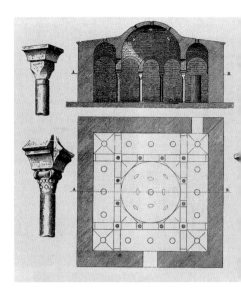

Above: Details of the columns, the floorplan and elevation of the Banys Àrabs from Archduke Ludwig Salvator's book on the Balearic islands.

name, and all previous currency was withdrawn from circulation in order to demonstrate the island's autonomy.

During this period of splendid isolation however conflict amongst the different Moorish kingdoms on the Spanish mainland was growing. Moreover, Christians were conquering more and more of the Arabic *taifas* – the 20-odd principalities into which the Moorish empire had splintered – and were encroaching ever further south from their strongholds in the north of the country. Initially, Majorca was not the main focus of interest as the islands' Arab masters on the mainland had their hands full with other problems; these distractions helped to create the climate for an independent Moorish kingdom in the Mediterranean.

The new ruler, Moxabir, was not so naïve as to believe that these ideal conditions would remain unaltered forever; he ordered walls built in order to protect the city from possible Christian attacks.

Obviously the providence of Allah guided him in these endeavors, for in 1114 an

Left: Al-Khaulani transformed Medina Mayurka into a flourishing center of Islamic life. The Arab baths, which were built later, were intended to purify both body and soul.

army of Pisans and Catalans embarked on a common crusade against the Islamic pirates of Majorca who had virtually brought maritime commerce in the Mediterranean to a standstill. Their first siege of Palma was unsuccessful, but in 1115 the allied troops of Catalonia and Pisa managed to occupy the city and "liberate" 30,000 Christians.

Victory seemed certain when last minute reinforcements of Almoravids reached the island from the mainland: the commander-in-chief of the Christian alliance, Ramon Berenguer III, was forced to flee and Majorca was once again in the hands of the Moors. In 1203 Almohad rule began in Spain and the group of islands was once again integrated into the Moorish empire.

What had previously been a central characteristic of Islamic rule – religious tolerance – completely bypassed these fanatical warriors. Understanding of differing points of view was not their forte, though such scruples did not prevent them from retaining the practice of piracy. If the Almoravids were more intolerant to other religions and cultures than the Moors before them (they carried out forcible conversions to Islam, for example), their successors, the Almohads, were even more devoted to a rigid Islamic fundamentalism. Perhaps this narrow-mindedness contributed to the dogmatism of the "Christian" conquerors which was seen when they so zealously set about destroying every sign of Arab culture after retaking Majorca.

The last Moorish governor to live in the Almudaina was Abu Yahia Muhammed ibn Ali ibn Abi Iman al-Tinmalali and he too came from a long line of pirates. During his period in office three mosques were built in Palma, a city which now numbered some 80 000 inhabitants. The largest of these mosques was situated where today the cathedral stands.

On New Year's Eve 1229 Jaume I., King of Aragón and Count of Barcelona, finally marched into Palma, celebrated his victory that very night. At number 7, Carrer Estudi General there is a relief showing the last *walî* handing over the keys of the city to Jaume I.

Although three more years were to pass before the last pocket of Moorish resistance was wiped out, the remarkable combination of high culture and utter barbarity, of science and piracy, scholarship and slavery which had defined the Moorish period on Majorca finally passed into history along with Abu Yahia. From now on the Moors were assigned the peripheral role of pirates who, based in Algiers and North Africa, menaced the coasts of Majorca until well into the 16th century. The Battle of Lepanto on 7 October 1571, in which the Christian "Holy League" destroyed the Ottoman fleet (Cervantes, the author of Don Quixote, lost his left hand in the fighting) brought this threat, too, to an end.

Remembering and forgetting

For the island's new Christian conquerors, tolerance was obviously a foreign word. Anything which even remotely reminded them of Arab rule was destroyed. In Palma only the foundations of the Almudaina Palace, the Banys Àrabs in the Carrer Serra and an arch, the Arc de la Mar – previously the Almudaina arch in the walls below the Almudaina Palace – have remained.

Traces of the centuries-long peaceful occupation of Majorca are exhibited in the Museu de Majorca. They include a valuable Almohad hoard of coins and jewelry which was hidden at the start of the 13th century when the Moors were under threat of an impending Christian invasion.

Majorcan interest in renovating remnants of their Arab heritage extends beyond the glass cases of museums as well. A Moorish tower in the city walls of Puig de Sant Pere was presented to the inhabitants of the town in the early summer of 1999. From the enclosed scaffolding of its upper deck, the view takes in the modern city and its harbor.

The most evident signs that Arabic high culture is still alive in Majorca are not those objects carved in silver or stone, however. Majorcan cooking has a distinctly Eastern touch, and there are also over 4000 words in the Spanish vocabulary which are Arabic in origin from, *alcaldes* (mayor), *talaies* (watch-towers), and *jardi* (garden) through to *sínia*, or draw-well.

Below, left: A Moorish arch with added living quarters spans the Carrer Almudaina in Palma's old town.

Below, right: Ships were able to sail directly to the Almudaina under the arch of this bridge.

Indoors and out
Palma's Patios

> The patio is the Promised Land
> in one's own house.
> (Majorcan saying)

The tradition that began at the Trevi fountain in Rome and which can be found anywhere tourists and fountains meet ought to be encouraged in Palma as well. That, at least, is what the two sons of the Comte d'Espanya believe. If they could only convince their many visitors that it would bring them certain luck to throw a coin into the fountain in their courtyard, they could sneak back later on to fish the money out and all their pocket money problems would be solved.

Their father, the count himself, stands in the entrance to their house at number 12, Carrer de la Portella and, with a friendly smile, responds to visitors who inquire about the history of the house. The chain over the doorway to the house, for example, which was hung there as a sign that an illustrious member of the Royal family had once set foot over the threshold (it is said that years ago the father of the Spanish king, Juan Carlos I, stayed here overnight).

Of course, the *Comte* cannot offer this kind of service every day, but he certainly does at the end of May, during the "week of the open patio". Although Palma's *palaus*, or better residences, are simply inconceivable without patios, the curious visitor needs a tenant or owner to open the door the other 51 weeks of the year if he wants to look into the inner courtyards. The exception is if the *palau* in question accommodates the offices of lawyers, official organizations, or museums; these patios are open during office hours and are generally supervised by friendly staff who will gladly take the time to indulge in a *explicació*, a chat about the history and fortunes of the building.

The patio door: the messenger of family news

In earlier times the patios were generally open to anyone who wanted to freshen up after a journey and make themselves comfortable in the cool, flower-filled courtyards, or simply to escape from the hustle and bustle of the street. If entry to the courtyard was barred for some reason, perhaps because there had been a death in the house, the door was left ajar to show that a visit to express condolences was expected shortly. If, however, the door was left wide open and decorated with flowers, it was a sign that there had been a wedding or that a child had been born.

The social encounters that led to weddings and births were also made in the patio, for the landing that connected the wings of the first floor, the *estudi*, had a particular function. Normally it served as the office for the man of the house, but he would often turn a blind eye if his sons used the *estudi* for a romantic rendezvous. If the stones of the patio could talk, who knows what stories they could tell of love and intrigue, conspiracies and plots? As a transitional area between the private life of the house and the public life beyond, the patios were ideal settings for such scheming.

In the patio of the Palau Marquès de Vivot for example (also known as the Ca'n Sureda), number 4 Carrer Ca'n Savellà, there was once a meeting of conspirators. This house was built by Joan Sureda i Villalonga, the first Marquès de can Vivot, in 1230 and boasted a magnificent library of around 10 000 volumes. In 1711, the Marquès's successor incited a conspiracy in favor of the Bourbon dynasty during the War of the Spanish Succession.

Above, left: The family coat of arms hangs resplendently over the entrance to the Ca'n Berga between two balconies topped with balustrades.

Below: The Can D'oleza from the 16th century was classified as a historical monument in 1973.

He was arrested and imprisoned in Barcelona but allowed to return when the Spanish war ended in a victory for the Bourbons and Philip V was named king at the Peace of Utrecht (1713–1715). The rectangular courtyard is divided by arcades into six sections and the dark passageways lend the patio a sinister and mysterious atmosphere: a stage well-suited to conspiratorial gatherings.

A Roman idea, preserved for centuries

The patio is as Mediterranean as the siesta and olive oil. The Romans built their *villae* around an *atrium*, an inner courtyard open to the sky, usually with shady arcades around the outside and a cooling fountain or well in the middle. The patio enabled people to

indulge in a fundamental requirement of Mediterranean life – remaining outdoors without also having the outside world peering in as an unwelcome guest. Palma was no exception to this rule. By the time the Arabs conquered the islands in 902 they had already incorporated the essential features of Roman housing with its cool, shady courtyards into their way of life. After the reconquest of the island in the 13th century, the Christians continued this tradition of interior courts decorated with greenery and fountains.

The patios became important when the layout of Palma with its narrow, winding streets began to take on a Gothic shape. Because neighborhood life could not realisti-

Through the arcades of the splendid courtyard of the Ca'n Berga the view opens up to the sky.

cally unfold on the streets and it simply was not comfortable to stand around outside the house, residents arranged their houses around a central courtyard. A small, wood-paneled doorway with a pointed arch opened on to an inner courtyard in the Gothic style with a stone stairway leading up to the second floor. The stairway itself featured geometric patterns and was as richly ornamented as the window frames. On the floor above this there were garrets or a loggia supported by columns.

From the ground floor one could enter a garden behind the house – located in the central yard of the whole block of houses – through a wooden gate.

In the 15th and 16th centuries the courtyards and façades became influenced by the Renaissance but never lost their original Gothic character. The house of Ca'n Catlar at number 7, Carrer del Sol clearly illustrates this: built in 1556 by Pere Abrí-Descatlar i Valentini, one of Philip II's generals, it was Palma's first Renaissance style house and its opulent façade is today one of the glories of the city. Both house and courtyard combine elements from the Gothic and Renaissance styles: the gallery on the top floor and the main portal with its pointed arch are clearly Gothic, while the five windows of the

second floor with their columns, panels and lintel decorated with knightly symbols are Renaissance. In the 18th century Guillem Abrí-Descatlar became the Marquès de Palmer and his descendants still live in the *palau* today.

Not until the 17th century did the houses of the city's dominant class undergo a radical change. Palma had become prosperous from its trade with Italy and the small, unprepossessing houses of the inner city were slowly transformed into magnificent monuments; there were fierce but unspoken competitions between neighbors to erect the most beautiful and most lavishly ornamented house.

The residents extended and ornamented their patios, and enlarged the small doorways. Columns of marble or the native Marès stone with luxuriant capitals seemed almost to do away with the conflict between the support and its load. The greatest change was seen in the stairways: stone balustrades decorated with geometrical patterns now yielded to skillfully made banisters of wrought iron.

An example of this development can be found in the house of Ca la Gran Cristiana at number 5, Carrer dela Portella which,

The Ca el Comte de San Simón, built between 1854–1856, shows evidence of French influences.

Lit from above: the simple, modest patio of the Ca'n Pasqual.

When the wrought-iron gate is opened, the visitor can risk a look into the patio.

Some courtyards can only be seen during the "Week of Open Patios": this *palau* is occupied by the Fundació Barceló.

The coat of arms below the balustrade and bright tubs of flowers in this light-filled patio mark it out as a private and intimate setting.

because it has been home to the Museu de Majorca since 1968, is open to the public the year round. This originally Gothic building was redesigned in the 17th century by the first Comte d'Aiamans and Baron of Lloseta, Miquel Lluís Ballester i de Togores. Despite its present name, "House of the Great Christian Lady", there was a time when the mood here was anything but Christian: because the Duke's wife wanted to leave him, he locked her in the house until she was finally murdered in 1651 by bandits. The building has only been called Ca La Cran Cristiana since the 19th century – the former owner, Catalina Zaforteza i de Togores, was a renowned Carlist and a deeply pious woman. She too was unlucky in life: during the rule of Isabella II (1833–1868) she was

arrested along with other Carlists on a charge of conspiracy and exiled to Sóller.

The process of industrialization in the 20th century meant that the old quarter of Palma became the victim of creeping neglect. Buildings which had once been home to entire extended families were converted into several small apartments and businessmen built offices or shops on the ground floor. The status of the former owners of these residences is today often only indicated by the names of once powerful families or famous Jewish scholars.

But back to the Comte d'Espanya. Some decades ago, he relates, a skeleton was found under the paving in the patio. According to legend, a servant had been an unwilling witness to a murder centuries before and had

then had to pay with his life. Winking and grinning broadly, the duke claims that he can often get no peace at night because of all those souls who have died in the house and who rise up knocking their brittle bones together like dice players – especially, he says, when there is a full moon and all the little heads of kings and devils on the façade of Isabella II's house next door add to the din by coming to life!

Between two religions
The Xuetes

Qui va a Liorna, ei va i no torna.
He who goes to Livorno will never be seen again.
(Jewish saying)

For almost 300 years Christians, Jews, and Muslims lived together peacefully on Majorca. Everyone was free to exercise their own faith: synagogues were built next to mosques and churches beside the temples of other religious communities. If the Christians did not understand what the Arabs were saying or trying to say to them they called on the multilingual and well-educated Jewish community who acted as cultural and linguistic interpreters.

But the Jews were not just masters of the art of translation; they were also respected artisans and scholars. In Palma they worked in the Call district, the southeastern quarter of the old town, as silversmiths, tailors, dyers, cobblers, physicians, book illustrators, cartographers or armorers. Today the street names – such as the Carrer de S'Argentaría in which the Jewish silversmiths plied their trade – are reminders of these professions.

Jewish silversmiths had their workshops in the Carrer de S'Argentaría.

Even after Jaume I celebrated his conquest of the city on New Year's Eve, 1229, the life of the Jewish community continued on its quiet course. The Jews of Majorca were considered some of the most prosperous in the entire Mediterranean region and, because they were so dependent on Jewish money, the Christians of the island did their best not to offend them. The Catholic rulers came time and again to request a "cash injection" from Jewish financiers, and a large part of these loans was used to finance the Reconquista, the reconquest of the Spanish mainland by the Christians – an undertaking which consumed vast quantities of money.

But in the middle of the 14th century the life of the Jews changed dramatically. Majorca came under the rule of the house of Aragón and that nation's unpopular king, Pere IV, imposed high taxes on the Majorcans which simple peasants and tradesmen were not able to pay.

There were outbreaks of discontent at Aragonese rule and the peasants revolted against the leading aristocratic families on the island. Instead of attacking those genuinely responsible for their suffering, the outraged populace – as so often happens – looked for a scapegoat, and – as so often happens – this scapegoat turned out to be the Jews.

Readings from the *Haggada* are held on the first two evenings of the Jewish Easter festival. *Haggada* means "tale" and it describes the Exodus from Egypt. *Golden Haggada*, Spain, 14th century, parchment, 8 ¹/₂ " x 6 ¹/₂" (23.3 x 19 cm), British Library, London.

First they were accused of manipulating the value of coins and therefore of being responsible for the poverty of Majorcans, and then, as was to happen throughout Europe in 1350, they were charged with spreading the Black Death.

Mendicant friars poured oil onto these flames by inciting the people with venomous, anti-Jewish sermons. On 2 August 1391 the Christians stormed the Call – one of the largest Jewish communities in southern Europe and home to 2500 people. Large parts of the quarter were destroyed in this pogrom and at least 300 Jews were killed by the hysterical masses. Many Jews fled into the nearby Almudaina quarter while others decided to convert to Christianity when they were faced with the choice of "baptism or death". Wily churchmen also offered Jews financial incentives by promising to reward their religious conversion with money: some Jews accepted the offer and were baptized. True to the saying "Tell me your name, and I'll tell you who you are", they purchased names from well-established Christian families in order to prove that they had become "real" Christians. Lists of the original Jewish names and their new Christian counterparts were prepared in order to make it easier to redeem money pledged for this change of identity.

From Jew to Xueta

To all intents and purposes the converted Jews practiced the Catholic faith – while continuing to pray secretly to Yahweh in seclusion at home. They had to be on their guard, however. The informers of the Inquisition lay in wait everywhere and their ecclesiastical masters were happy to credit any accusation that a Jew was still exercising his "pagan" faith: when Jews were found guilty on charges of heresy their property automatically passed into the hands of the Inquisition.

As Christians, many converted Jews outdid the Pope in their displays of piety. Out of fear of being persecuted, they even ate pork which was forbidden them by Jewish dietary law, and this is one of the explanations put forward for the word which came to be applied to converted Jews – *xuetes*. It is claimed that the term is derived from the Majorcan word *xuia*, meaning bacon.

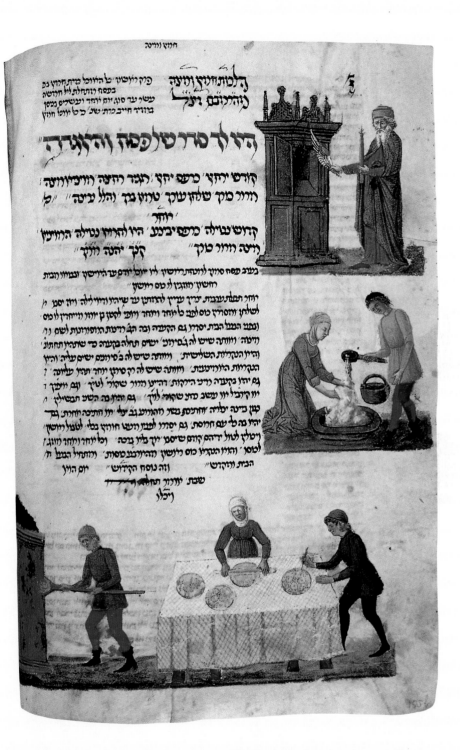

This illumination from the 15th century shows Jews preparing *matze*, or unleavened bread, which is eaten during the festival of *pessach* in memory of the exodus from Egypt. *Rothschild miscellanies*, North Italy, 1450–1470, parchment, 8 1/4," x 6" (21 x 15 cm), Israel Museum, Jerusalem.

An alternative explanation is obtained by reference to the old Majorcan word *xueta* meaning Jewess.

Often, the *xuetes* simply decided to leave their beloved homeland forever. In the first half of the 16th century, Italy was one of the main destinations for these refugees. Rome and the Papal States had offered to accept the Majorcan Jews but, as so often in history, this gesture was not inspired solely by charity. The Jews were thought to be rich and Christians on the Italian mainland were keen to have a sizable chunk of that wealth for themselves. Apart from Ancona and Pesaro, Livorno was a popular destination for the exiled Majorcan Jewry.

Palma's list

The list on which, hundreds of years earlier, the old Jewish and the new Christian names had been entered "suddenly" turned up again one day in 1755 and this promptly sparked a new wave of persecution against 85

The expulsion of the Jews from Spain in 1492.

The public interrogation of heretics by the Spanish Inquisition was unquestioningly accepted by the population at large; Lucas Valdés' auto-da-fé fresco in the church of Santa Maria Magdalena, Seville, shows large numbers of people taking part in such an event.

families with names such as Aguiló, Bonnin, Cortés, Fuster or Miró.

Even in the 20th century this list – which seemed to be jinxed – came close to causing a crisis: in 1942 a group of Falangists from the State Fascist party paid a visit to the bishop of Majorca and demanded that the list of names be handed over. The then bishop, Campius, refused to part with the document for he knew it would have meant sending between 40 000 and 60 000 descendants of converted Jews to their deaths: the Falangists had intended deporting them directly to Nazi concentration camps.

Traces of Jewish life in Palma today

Today, *xuetes* are in a better position than they ever were in the past and are much more highly regarded as an "ethnic group": indeed, there is little to distinguish them from "normal" Majorcans apart from the fact that they perhaps show greater respect for senior family members and that their family units are even more close-knit than is usual in Spain. As in earlier times they are respected for their abilities and connections in the financial industry, be it in banking or the stock market. They occupy leading positions in many areas of the economy and are also represented in the regional government.

Towards the end of the 20th century a Jewish community was again reestablished on Majorca; and like any other legal entity, of course, they are now entitled to purchase land. As Catholics, *xuetes* themselves do not belong to the Jewish community. In 1987 the first synagogue on the island since the days of the Inquisition was consecrated.

Street maps of Majorcan towns are full of names of Jewish origin, and even the great rose window in the Palma cathedral – in whose kaleidoscopic triangular structure the figure of a Star of David can be made out – is evidence of the importance of Jewish life and religion for Majorcan culture.

Everyday life can produce evidence of this sort as well – such as the six pointed star of the *crespell*, a sweet pastry developed by the Jews which is popular throughout the island as well as in Italy.

After being expelled from the Iberian peninsula in the 15th century, many Sephardic Jews emigrated through Italy and North Africa to the Ottoman Empire, where they were welcomed by Sultan Bayazid II. In Greece, the larger cities of the Turkish Mediterranean coast and Palestine, substantial and culturally active communities of Jews sprang up which were still attracting newcomers well into the 18th century.

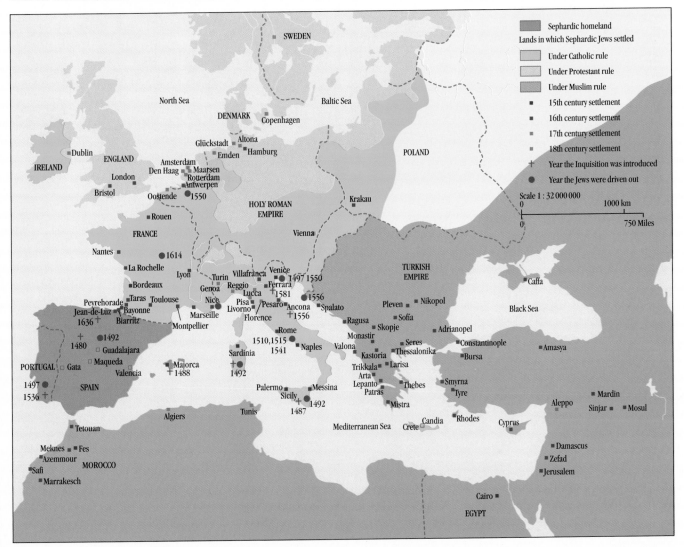

The world in rhumb-lines
The Jewish Cartographers of Palma

Of course – a world atlas! King Pere IV of Aragón (1336–1387) had thought long and hard about the kind of present he could give to win the favor of King Charles V of France, a man who was known as "the Wise" for his love of art and literature. It should, of course, be decorative and pleasing to the eye, but educational as well. After long consideration it finally occurred to him: a map of the world was just the thing for a king with such a large library.

The king did not dally so long in choosing whom he would commission to produce this work of art. Pere IV had conquered Majorca in 1343 and in the 14th century the island was the center of nautical knowledge: the most famous cartographers

lived and worked in the Jewish quarter of Call in Palma. Their knowledge of the planetary system and the shape of the earth had been learned from the Arabs whose learning far outstripped that of the more narrow-minded and parochial Christians.

The "family firm" of Abraham and Jafuda Cresques was given the task of drawing a *mapa mundi* or world atlas. It was to be a decorative work suitable for a library rather than for travel on the high seas. After two years the map, which was to become famous as the "Catalan World Atlas", was finally completed in 1377. King Pere IV himself thought it the pinnacle of the cartographer's art when he first saw it: it was, he claimed, the most beautiful thing he had ever laid eyes on.

The Cresques had not only drawn a map of the Mediterranean, they had also extended it to include the entire known world as well as illustrating the cosmos: it

The second page of the world atlas: a depiction of the four seasons and the twelve signs of the zodiac.

featured an astronomical-astrological wheel with the earth in the center and the individual heavenly spheres around it. The most innovative aspect of the map was that it not only showed the coastlines of countries along which sailors had groped their way for centuries, but "rhumb-lines" as well – direct lines which could be followed by a ship across the high seas in order to shorten considerably the duration of a journey. The use of rhumb-lines at sea also increased the risk of travel because this was in an age in which compasses were still at a primitive stage of development.

The finished work comprised six pages and Jafuda, Abraham's son, had recreated the Mediterranean, the former Roman Empire and Africa in illustrations of astonishing precision.

A precise survey of all these coastlines was impossible in those days for political reasons, and the incredible accuracy of their map can probably be explained by the two cartographers having access to an older map produced in Roman times. Around 20 BC Roman mapmakers under Augustus had meticulously surveyed and mapped the entire Empire, work which their Majorcan colleagues were then able to build on several centuries later.

Jafuda's father, Abraham Cresques, brought the maps to life with his bright illustrations and annotations. Father and son had set themselves the goal not only of creating a true and accurate representation of the earth but also of its people and their ways of life. The tiny, tight-packed letters, the legends, comments and drawings, all seem designed to fill any gap which might exist both in the map and in the body of human knowledge.

There are stylized representations of African cities on which white, blue and red flags are fluttering; and majestic rulers are seated on thrones beside tents in which nomads shield themselves from the desert sun. Off the coast of Majorca the sailor Jaume Ferrer sets sail for Senegal, thus earning himself a monument on the Plaça de les Drassanes which the city of Palma erected to him shortly after this brilliant achievement. Majorca's

The Majorcan cartographers devised …

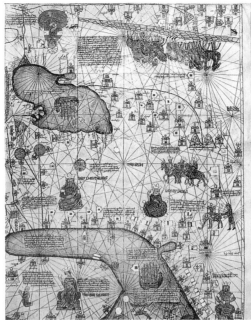

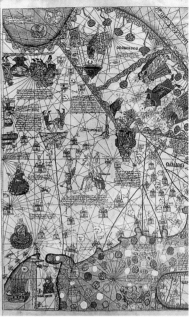

sailors had become foremost amongst Europe's explorers and this had led to the island opening up a trade in gold with the Empire of Mali.

Realism, however, no longer applies to the geographical depiction of the rest of the world. Northern Europe, Asia, and Arabia were all distorted, as were the illustrations dealing with life in these parts of the world. In their visual description of Asia, a part of the world still unknown to Europeans, the cartographers could not fall back on any

… a complex web for dividing up the world.

previous work as they had for the Mediterranean. Only the writings of explorers such as Marco Polo (1254–1324), Sir John Mandeville (1300–1372) or Ibn Battuta (1304–1369) made any reference to the location and coastal form of the continent. Here, too, there is no lack of Siberian caravans, pygmies or kings. Elephants raise their trunks into the air beside pictures of kings while the Three Wise Men present the Christ child with their gifts. In the Indian Ocean Chinese junks glide about through pearl-fishers who do battle with sharks. A text explains that the "inhabitants of the 7548 islands of the Indian Ocean are savage, drink seawater and live on raw fish."

For his part Jafuda Cresques soon had to take his leave from the fish of Majorca – which he almost certainly did not eat raw. After he had converted to the Christian faith, he was called to work at the school of Henry the Navigator in Portugal where, as Jaime Ribes, his maps laid the basis for the Portuguese sea route to India. After rounding the Cape on his journey to India from 1497–1499 the sailor Vasco da Gama was then able to see for himself whether there really was anything to the Majorcan's rumors about savages.

An extravagant tribute to the tourist trade
Palma's Gran Hotel

Once upon a time … there was an age in which foreign tourists on Majorca were seldom seen. The few who did visit the island may have described its beauty in ecstatic terms, but it was not until the 19th century at the earliest that the first delicate buds of tourism began to appear. Gradually, more and more travelers were lured to the island. Most of them had to contend with the fact that they were not as wealthy as the Archduke of Habsburg-Tuscany and so, unlike Ludwig Salvator, they could not afford to maintain a country estate for their accommodation.

There was a pressing need for a first class hotel to cope with the growing demand from the mostly prosperous European tourists for quality accommodation. After some discussion a decision was reached and a contract signed and sealed: the Gran Hotel was born.

The architect Lluís Domènech i Muntaner, a pupil of Gaudí's, was commissioned with the building of this 1200 square yard (1000 square meter) complex; artists Joaquim Mir and Santiago Rusiñol painted seven enormous murals in the dining room; and an order for hand-painted tiles from the famous *La Roqueta* factory was also placed.

The hotel set new standards for the provision of heating and electricity. In an age when gas and oil lamps were still the norm, the

hotel's generators produced enough energy for its 150 rooms, which were warmed by steam heating. Not all the rooms had their own baths, but that was by no means unusual in those days even in a luxury hotel.

The big day finally arrived on 3 February 1903 when the Gran Hotel was solemnly and ceremonially declared open. The 250 invited guests, among them well-known families from Palma like the Marquesos del Palmer

At the start of the century the pace of life in Unió Street was tranquil: today it is one of Palma's most lively thoroughfares.

or the Villalongas, were spellbound by the beauty of the building; the guests' reaction was significant because these members of the nobility themselves lived in the city's most magnificent *palaus*, or mansions.

In their dedication speeches speakers vied with each other to offer the most lavish

The hotel closed its doors in 1975. The wrought-iron balcony on the upper floor can only be admired from the outside today …

… and the same applies to this oriole window with its stained glass and the stucco crowns on its parapet.

praise of the building: the hotel was, they claimed, a hymn in stone and Majorca could now finally be said to have made full contact with European culture.

Shortly after the dedication a small information booklet was published which can be considered the first travel guide to Majorca. In its 80 pages the hotel's directors described for the benefit of "the visitor who wishes to remain on the island for several days" the excursions and city tours that could be made on the island. In 1928, when a bath in every room was slowly becoming a standard for high priced accommodation, the Gran Hotel was modernized for the first time and boasted 120 rooms, 50 bathrooms, an elevator and a spacious lounge.

But this symbol of luxury and wealth quickly began to show its age: in the Thirties, at the time of the Great Depression and the Spanish Civil War, the hotel went into decline.

In 1941 it was in such a poor state that it was scarcely worthy of the name "hotel", and most certainly not the adjective "gran". Nevertheless, it dragged itself along for many years, hopelessly antiquated and without any prospect of getting the necessary cash to carry out a thorough renovation, until the hotel was finally compelled to close its doors in 1975.

But this was not to be the last of the Gran Hotel: a foundation run by the Catalan savings bank La Caixa took pity on it, restored its original Art Nouveau façade and transformed the building into a cultural center, where visitors could admire Majorcan art from the turn of the century. More importantly still, the former hotel was declared a world heritage site by UNESCO. In the café where once Archduke Ludwig Salvator chatted with his friend, the painter and poet Santiago Rusiñol, one can now relax with a drink and sink into a daydream about the good old days.

Above: One can drift off and dream of the old days in the Gran Hotel's tastefully renovated café.

Below: The façade of this hotel built in 1901 is the most splendid example of Majorcan Art Nouveau. Looking at the *belle epoque* paintings one almost feels transported back to the days before the First World War – "the Good Old Days."

Palma's promenade—which is the fairest of them all?
Born or Ramblas

In October 1403 a river, made a raging torrent by heavy rainfalls, destroyed 1500 houses and claimed around 5000 lives. This tragic incident occurred, according to the city chronicles, where today the Ramblas, Unió Street, and the Passeig des Born make their graceful way through the middle of the city and down to the Almudaina Palace and the sea. The villain of the piece, the river Riera, was moved further to the west before it was diverted for the last time in 1620 to follow the course that it does today.

The old riverbed, however, was an unwelcome legacy for the city planners: what were they to do with the path which the river had cut right through the town? This question signaled the birth of the Passeig des Born and the Ramblas, the two boulevards which ever since have competed for the honor of being not only Palma's but Majorca's most beautiful promenade.

The Born, a square which was extended to become an avenue, begins on the Plaça del Rei Joan Carles I. where a fountain in honor

Above: The Ramblas were scenes of lively activity even during Archduke Ludwig Salvator's day.

Left: Up the stairs, down the stairs: one stairway leads to the Plaça Major, another runs down to the Ramblas.

By day one can saunter along the bright, overflowing flower markets of the Ramblas …

… or take pleasure in stocking up on the very best confectionery in a *xocolateria*.

of Queen Isabella II once stood; it was destroyed in the so-called September revolution of 1868.

Today the site is marked by an obelisk under whose crushing weight four small turtles groan – or would, if they were not made of stone.

Directly opposite *café amb llet* can be had in the Bar Bosch, an institution amongst the capital's bars. To win a seat in one of its wickerwork chairs is a matter of honor for tourists and locals alike, although the prices charged are certainly not warranted by the dubious pleasure of drinking coffee amidst the thundering traffic and asphyxiating exhaust fumes. When the writer Robert Graves patronized the bar in the 1950s it was quite probably a great deal more comfortable – and cheaper.

On the other side of the road the Baroque façade of the Palau Solleric, also known as the Ca'n Morell, was for decades covered in a thick layer of plaster; since 1995 though it has regained its 18th century glory.

Today the building is a gallery which features the work of Majorcan artists, and there is a café on the ground floor where coffee is served somewhat more sedately than in the Bar Bosch. The bustling activity of the neighboring newspaper kiosk is also an invitation to while away the hours in detailed study of the day's events.

Those who can eventually manage to tear themselves loose are then free to stroll leisurely down the middle of the Born in the shade of its plane trees in the direction of the

Plaça Reina; benches are carefully placed to allow the odd rest. The very end of the Born is marked by a fountain and it is here that the Hort del Rei begins, an attractive park with fountains in the Moorish style.

Once a year, during the city festival at the end of February, the Born is anything but tranquil. The entire length of the avenue is flanked for several days with seating for spectators and the median strip is turned into a sand-covered track for horse and coach races and jousting. A medieval market is set up in the Hort del Rei with craftsmen and jugglers competing for the attentions of passersby.

The Ramblas – actually the Via Roma – can be reached from the Plaça Major via a street of stairs. The broad crowns of the plane trees form a thick canopy covering the entire promenade. Palma's main boulevard was redesigned several times before it finally attained its present form with its stone benches; the Saturday market has drawn traders and customers since the second half of the 19th century. The Ramblas also has some very special decorations to offer on non-market days: at the daily flower market virtually everything on the island that has an attractive blossom or fragrance is up for sale.

Both sides of the street are lined with magnificent 19th century houses, but in front of them there is scarcely any room for

cars to park or even move. For this reason the Ramblas, once the broadest street in the city, is much more peaceful and attractive than the Born. The nuns of the convent of Santa Teresa still live today in this atmosphere of urban tranquillity, completely removed from the hurly-burly of city life. Not even couriers or delivery services can get a glimpse of the nuns' faces, thanks to a revolving door at the convent gate: the convent's seclusion is absolute.

The four small turtles seem almost to groan under the weight of this obelisk which marks the start of the Born.

The baker's home
The Old Town

Just go into the Calatrava quarter in the heart of Palma and follow your nose, and you will be bound to get to the bottom of that mouth-watering smell; it seems to lead you on around the corner from the Ca'n Miquel when suddenly you spot where it is coming from: the "Forn de sa Pelleteria", a bakery named after the street in which it stands. Inside you will find its portly owner, Miquel Pujol i Ferragut, enveloped in the delicious smells from the rings of dough he is forming for *ensaïmades*; then again, he may be making the famous Majorcan *coca*-pizza, or even *cremadillos* – puff pastries – filled with custard or angel's hair, a type of pumpkin purée. Sometimes he will even slide a batch of *sobrassada frita amb mel* into the oven, an adventurous combination of ingredients in which hot paprika sausage is softened by the addition of honey. This, of course, is assuming that he is not sitting on the next corner, taking some fresh air and chatting with the locals – as every worker knows, there has to be time for a break too.

Miquel Pujol i Ferragut has worked at his oven for 34 years.

Like a proud father Miquel puts his arm around the *forn* in the bakery's vault-like front room. "This oven is as old as the hills – built 400 years ago. The business was founded in 1625 and my grandfather bought it in 1914 after he had worked for several years in Argentina to save the money." Customers can admire Miquel's venerable ancestor in a faded black and white photo that occupies pride of place in an old glass cabinet in the shop. He is pictured in South America with a cart painted with the sign *Panadería Argentina*, "Argentinean Bakery".

Miquel has known and loved his home of Sa Calatrava in the Old Town of Palma ever since his birth in 1937. The quarter was once the center of Jewish business life in the city: the streets have names dating back to the ancient guilds – such as *Blanquers*, tanners, or *Pelleters*, furriers – which refer to the days when the district resounded to the activities of industrious Jewish tradesmen. The excellence of their crafts is still on show today – in the Middle Ages, Jewish gold and silversmiths filled the streets with the dull gleams and the moonlight glimmers of their gold and silver wares. Today the jewelry stores alternate with antique shops where the heavy, dark wooden furniture typical of Majorca competes in the display windows with Tiffany lamps from the mainland. Now and again an old *menora*, a seven-armed candelabra and an essential item in every Jewish household, can be seen. World-famous cartographers once worked on the Plaça Sant Jeroni. There is even the possibility that our baker, Miquel, has a famous ancestor in his family tree. "The first admiral of the United States navy was called David Ferragut, and he may have been one of my

forefathers." Is he sure? "No one knows for certain."

Miquel unlocks his shop at five o'clock in the morning. "Bakers have to get up early. When I was young I had already taken the first lot of *ensaïmades* out of the oven by the time the others came past the *forn* on their way home after a night on the town." In a quarter which still lives as if ignorant of the big city around it Miquel continues to keep alive certain rituals with his friends and neighbors; at six in the morning they turn up, a little unsteady on their feet after the exertions of the night, but still fit enough to get the requisite cup of hot chocolate down and do honor to Miquel's *ensaïmades*. Miquel pretends to make a fuss, mumbling things like "They're nowhere near ready yet" or "Just let me work and come back when the shop's open." But that, too, is all part of the ritual, because these night-owls always end up with their delicious pastries, straight out of the oven. After finishing their Majorcan hangover cure, Miquel's customers head off to bed and he is left alone once again with his oven.

Perhaps he grins, thinking about his own youth when, instead of standing by the oven stoking the fire, he could leave his flour-covered apron hanging on its peg and go and seek romantic adventures of his own. He obviously found what he was after, for he soon married and continued to run the family business together with his wife.

"Now my sons are involved as well. Perhaps one of them will want to take over the bakery." In view of the almost hypnotic devotion with which his oldest son works the dough, it is unlikely that Miquel will have any worries about finding a successor for the *forn*. Even retirement has its rituals in the close-knit Calatrava quarter. Miquel will join those respectable gentlemen who sit outside in a cozy group of friends on a bench near the Hogares de Temple – the former oratory of the Templar Knights – on the Plaça del Temple; they pass their days philosophizing about Palma, Majorca and the world – and are all the while enshrouded in the seductive odors coming from the *forn* around the corner.

The narrow streets of Palma's old town have a cozy, homey feel.

Top-flight pastries
Ensaïmades

The 3 October 1996 was a momentous date for Majorca. From that day on only *ensaïmadas* from the island had the right to bear the official name *"Ensaïmada de Majorca"*. This seal of quality was urgently needed because successful products like these are immediately susceptible to being "pirated" and copied in a market economy.

Bakers on the Spanish mainland had sought to profit from the Majorcans' success by taking a slice of their "pie", and this meant that some of the famous pastries were beginning to appear in the ovens and on the

Dancers in native costume and the cathedral of La Seu illustrate the classical packaging for Majorcan *ensaïmada*.

sales counters of Barcelona and Valencia.

The islanders' feathers were considerably ruffled and they were not smoothed until the new seal of quality was officially approved. The affair however has left something of a bitter aftertaste for the island's bakers: the Majorcan monopoly on *ensaïmadas* is only valid for the basic recipe (which is coated with icing sugar) and one of its variants, the *cabell d'angel* (angel's hair) with its filling of puréed pumpkin.

But as unequivocally as the islanders might fight for the copyright on the *ensaïmada*, the origins of this sweet-tasting roll remain ambiguous and obscure. Such historical uncertainties are often a welcome opportunity to enter into a passionate debate to settle the matter once and for all. Some will argue that the Jews invented them first, but their opponents reject this claim out of hand by pointing to the use of lard in the *ensaïmada*. After all, they exclaim, the *saïm* in the name refers to pork dripping – a quite impossible ingredient in a Jewish recipe!

The Arabs, too, shun pork but it is said that they did bake a type of pastry with the name *bolems dolçes*, and that this was the origin of the island's traditional yeast-risen pastry. This claim however merely encourages supporters of the first theory to counter-attack by saying that the Jews were making a sweet pastry called *bulema* long before the Arabs came to the island!

While this debate fascinates the Majorcans, tourists to the island pay it no mind – they tend to be too busy carrying the carefully packed pastry boxes with their tasty cargo onto the airplane. On average, 40 official *ensaïmadas de Majorca* leave the island on every charter flight, according to an equally official survey by the Balearic regional government.

The *ensaïmadas* were important enough for Archduke Ludwig Salvator to mention them in his study of Majorca: *"Ensaïmadas* of greatly differing sizes and values are produced. Those eaten at breakfast are usually sold for 3, 4 or 6 centesimos de escudo (around 8, 10 or 15 centimes). A larger sort on which they may place thin slices of sobrassada and bacon, small pieces of carabassât (pumpkin preserved in sugar), or chunks of sobrassada – or sometimes without anything else – are usually consumed as a snack during the day or for lunch as a dessert."

Even today *ensaïmadas* straight from the oven are an integral part of the Majorcan breakfast and are present on every meal table as a dessert. But irrespective of when they are eaten they should always be warm, for only then are they truly at their best.

Ensaïmada Lisa

Simple *ensaïmada*

Ingredients for 40 medium-sized ensaïmadas

2 lb. (900 g) sugar
9 eggs
6 ³/₄ lb. (3 kg) flour
9 oz. (250 g) pork fat
3 oz. (80 g) yeast
1 ³/₄ pints (1l) water
icing sugar

Mix together the yeast, a pinch of sugar, some warm water and one tablespoon of flour. Place the flour on a level surface and make a well in the middle. Knead the yeast mixture, sugar, eggs and water into the flour to form a smooth, elastic dough and leave to rise. When it has reached twice its original volume it should be thoroughly kneaded once again and rolled out into a very thin rectangle with a rolling pin.

Now comes the most important part: brush the dough with warm pork fat and roll it inwards from the longest side. Leave it to sit for another hour before rolling the coil into the shape of a snail. Place it on a greased baking tray, cover it with a cloth and allow it to sit in a cool place overnight. Bake in a pre-heated oven at 360°F (180°C). Coat with icing sugar just prior to serving.

The ingredients of *ensaïmada* – pork lard, yeast, flour, eggs, and sugar – surround the finished product.

The yeasty dough, basis for the *ensaïmada*, is thoroughly kneaded and then left to rise until it reaches twice its original volume.

The dough is brushed with pork lard and stretched in such a way that it can be rolled up along its longest side.

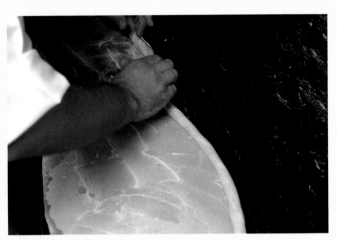

The dough is rolled inwards along its entire length to form a coil of constant diameter.

The dough must be allowed to rest once more before it is wound into its characteristic snail shape.

The pastries are finally laid side by side and baked at 360°F (180°C).

243

A master from Felanitx and stone from Santanyí make a Gothic jewel
Sa Llotja

From the Puig de San Pere, a small hill west of the Old Town, narrow streets run down to the oldest fishing and shipbuilding quarter in the city, the Barri de la Llotja. The focus of this district always has been the Plaça Drassana, the square around the wharf which faces out to sea. The first buildings on the coast are situated behind the square, and these three-storey houses are today some of the most popular restaurants and cafés in Palma.

The Spanish conquerors redesigned parts of the harbor opposite in the 13th century: they extended it, built an artificial mole and reinforced the defenses with new fortified towers. In the Middle Ages and the early modern era, Palma's harbor was an important stopping point for merchant ships sailing between Spain and Italy. Some people traveled in precisely the opposite direction – like the seafarer Jaume Ferrer who is commemorated by a monument on the Plaça de les Drassanes. In the 14th century Ferrer explored the West African coast and came back with such important information that it soon found its way into Jafuda Cresque's famous *Atlas Català* along with reports by such adventurers as Marco Polo and Ibn Battuta.

Just a few steps away from this monument is one of the masterpieces of Gothic architecture: the maritime trade exchange of Sa Llotja. In the Middle Ages these exchanges were lavishly decorated; they were, after all, symbols of the wealth of a trading nation and naturally had to be displayed to best advantage. As gratitude for their support in the re-conquest of Sardinia, Majorcans were granted the right to levy taxes on all their imports and exports. Part of this income was used to extend their defenses, and with the remainder they were able to finance the building of a magnificent exchange. In 1426 the renowned architect Guillrm Sagrera from Felanitx was commissioned to build the Llotja in 12 years for 22000 llibras. Several

delays meant that it was not until 1450 that this imposing structure, built of costly Marès stone from Santanyí, could be dedicated by local traders and the merchants' guild, the Collegi de Mercaderia.

Today, the Llotja is considered one of the great examples of Catalan Gothic architecture. The building's corners are marked by four octagonal towers; the façade on the

Above: The crenellated gallery with its octagonal towers lends the Christian maritime exchange a certain Moorish flair.

Opposite: A peaceful idyll in Palma's fishing harbor with the Llotja's crenellations basking in the afternoon sun; fishermen were mending their nets in the same way when this maritime exchange was being built in the 15th century.

sides has three of these towers and the front two in order to render its appearance less severe. The upper section is surmounted by a crenellated gallery strongly reminiscent of the architectural style of the Moors but which was also a contemporary structural element. In those days city walls, castle ramparts, and fortified churches required battlements and corner towers from which attackers could be seen and fought without the defenders exposing themselves to enemy fire. Gargoyles stretch their necks out over the façade below the battlements, and over the main entrance an angel in a magnificent cloak ushers visitors into the building which has now been converted into an exhibition hall. Inside, three aisles rise up airy and tall, and they are bathed in the same gentle light from nine windows with pointed arches.

Nine piers without capitals twist in sensuous spirals up to the roof. Only the lack of organ music and smell of incense indicate that this is not a cathedral erected to display a community's wealth, but is still a monument built by a once flourishing maritime economy to commemorate itself.

"At present the Llotja is used for storing grain and pulses and as a result it is filled with sacks," wrote Ludwig Salvator at the end of the 19th century; "… it is to be regretted that this lovely building, which is one of the jewels of the city, should not be devoted to a more noble purpose. The Llotja's little garden, with its fountain in the middle and various palms, is separated from the narrow square in front of the Escuela de la Llotja by railings; this old chapel has a Gothic portal with the year 1600 inscribed

on it, a Renaissance rose window and a bell-gable with a pointed arch ... Abutting the Escuela de la Llotja is the old house which once belonged to the Consulado de Maor, or Palma's merchant classes. On the seaward side there is a splendid Renaissance hall formed by five segmented arches resting on round columns and between their square bases there runs a balustrade with spiral balusters... From here the whole harbor can be seen. The entire building is set off by a small tower provided with a modern clock and topped by a bell."

On the other side of the street, the Passeig d'en Sagrera, fishermen still sit mending their nets which shimmer in every conceivable shade of blue. The flags of the Balearic islands flutter in the afternoon breeze on the Consolat del Mar, the former court of maritime trade; this ornate late Renaissance building from the 17th century with its five-arched loggia and late Gothic chapel is the residence of the president of the islands' autonomous government. On certain occasions local voters and taxpayers, and selected other guests, are allowed to enter the interior of this democratic palace and see for themselves what cool and noble splendor their contributions are financing ever since it became a home for civil servants rather than a school for sailors and navigators.

In the evening it becomes more peaceful down by the shore in Sa Llotja. This is the time of day when everyone streams through the maze of winding, narrow streets to the nearby section of Carrer Apuntadores, which the visitor must suspect is trying to break some kind of Majorcan record for its density of bars and restaurants. Some of these establishments entertain their guests beneath smoke-blackened ceiling beams, or in atmospheric old vaulted cellars from the days when fishermen would swig from tankards and merchants from throughout the Mediterranean would come to drink to their successful deals.

Opposite, top: Taking a stroll under the palms on the Platja de Palma, Palma's exotic shoreline promenade.

Opposite: The 17th century Consolat de Mar, directly behind the Llotja, was formerly the seat of the maritime court.

Right: In the Llotja district freshly caught fish land directly onto diners' plates.

Ahoy, Your Majesties!
Regattas in the bay

PRINCESA SOFÍA

Watchers of the Spanish royal family can recognize the signs: King Juan Carlos I exchanges his tailor-made suits for Bermuda shorts; his wife Queen Sofía dons a headscarf to protect her hair from the wind; the Prince of Asturia shows up with three days' growth on his chin; and the Infantas, Elena and Cristina, sport baseball caps and sunglasses. Suspicions are confirmed by the fashions worn in the rest of the Bay of Palma de Majorca where sporting white rules the day. This trend can only mean one thing: the King's Cup, the Copa del Rey-Trofeo Agua Brava – Majorca's most important sailing regatta – has begun.

For five whole days at the end of July the venerable Royal Sailing Club of Palma, the Real Club Náutico, is transformed into a center of international sailing. The Royal Regatta is part of the circuit for the Spanish, European, and world championships; the crucial difference with this race is that since 1981 the royal family have also taken part. The King is traditionally at the helm of the yacht *Bribón*, and the Infanta Cristina races aboard the *Azur de Puig* with her cousin, Alexia of Greece. Prince Felipe changes both ship and crew frequently: as heir to the throne he is not allowed to appear too partisan. The same goes for his older sister, the Infanta Elena, who in 1999 signed up to the *Casera* together with her

husband Jaime de Marichalar and the youngest skipper of the royal family, their son Felipe Juan Froilán. Juan Carlos I took part in Olympic yachting races in Kiel, Germany in 1972. It comes as no surprise then to learn that two members of the royal family were also Spanish team members at successive Olympic Games: the Infanta Cristina in Seoul in 1988 and the Crown Prince in Barcelona in 1992. They are all sailing after the example set by Queen Sofía's brother, Constantine, who won the gold medal in 1960 in Rome.

Opposite: Palma hosts royal regattas twice a year: the Princess Sofía Cup and the King's Cup.

Above: King Juan Carlos I, Queen Sofía and the Crown Prince Felipe applaud the victors of the Princess Sofía Cup.

Below: A forest of masts rocks in the breeze in front of Palma's Passeig Marítím.

A city with small town charm
Santa Catalina and Es Jonquet

On the Plaça Vapor, "Steam Square", fresh washing flutters merrily in the breeze on the terraces, on the balconies of the white, two-story houses geraniums hold up their bright red blossoms to the sun, and a coppersmith provides the appropriate background noise, hammering cheerfully on his pots and pans. In the residential quarter of Es Jonquet Palma is more like an Andalusian village than a busy city, except for the scraps of *Mallorquí* blowing along the alleyways, and the smell of *sopes* and *frit* from the kitchens of the restaurants and bars.

Four picturesque windmills with their sails bent by the wind mark the borders of Es Jonquet just across the harbor mole. Further up, on the other side of the street of Sant Maggí, the winding alleys of the Santa Catalina quarter twist and turn up the hill. In these parts of the town, close to the harbor, the people who made the sea their livelihood or made the necessary equipment – fishermen and boat-builders, netters and ropemakers – used to live and work.

In the 16th century the population of Palma grew rapidly; above all, the capital attracted craftsmen, for there was work in plenty. When the medieval heart of the city could no longer hold any more people within its protecting walls the newcomers were forced to set up home outside, and they joined the other older inhabitants in the *eixample*, the extension.

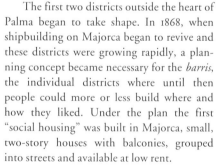

The windmills opposite the harbor mole can be seen from "Steam Square" in Es Jonquet.

The first two districts outside the heart of Palma began to take shape. In 1868, when shipbuilding on Majorca began to revive and these districts were growing rapidly, a planning concept became necessary for the *barris*, the individual districts where until then people could more or less build where and how they liked. Under the plan the first "social housing" was built in Majorca, small, two-story houses with balconies, grouped into streets and available at low rent.

By the early 20th century the working districts were full of colorful, pulsating life. There was a rich selection of *tavernes* and *cellers*, where the men from the rope workshops met the factory workers and fishermen. The centerpiece of Santa Catalina was the market hall, the Mercat de Santa Catalina. It is the oldest market in Palma, and the fishermen's wives were selling what their menfolk had

This district was not intended to have tall buildings. All the houses are at most two storeys high, but they are well preserved and "romantic".

caught here even in Arab times. Today the Mercat is regarded as the best and friendliest market in the city. The local people mingle with the star chefs from the island's best restaurants and hotels as they all scrutinize, sniff and finger the pyramids of fruit and vegetables, the ice boxes full of fish and seafood or ask the butcher to cut off a sliver of sausage, *fuet*, for them to taste. Then there is always time to finish off the shopping with a coffee in the market bar and have a chat with the *arravalesos*, the people from the suburbs, as they are still known.

Tobacco Smuggling – A Life-Saving Resource

Work has been underway for some decades now to renovate old and slightly dilapidated buildings in Santa Catalina and Es Jonquet, and some have actually been turned into hotels for tourists and people from the city center who are tired of the noise and bustle and are attracted by the dreamy, but vital charm of these districts. A tourist office has settled down comfortably in the old wash house, where block soap and the scrubbing board were employed to deal with collar edges and oil spots until well into the 20th century, disco music resounds from one of the old mills and the small taverns have grown into top-class restaurants. Even the façade of the legendary Bar Cuba directly on the border between Es Jonquet and Santa Catalina has been restored.

This used to be the center of Majorca's tobacco smuggling, some say. Others are still grateful to the two brothers from the bar, for in the 1950s, when tuberculosis raged in Palma, they brought the scarce and miraculous penicillin from Tangier to Majorca and saved many people's lives.

The houses in the former outer district have been undergoing restoration for some years now.

The old buildings on the Plaça Drassana exude the charm of an Andalusian village.

Prison with a view
Castell de Bellver

Jaume I conquered Palma on New Year's Day 1229, and he wished to set a monument to himself and his troops. A new building, apart from the cathedral, was to symbolize the might of Christianity rising over the Muslims and subjecting them finally and forever. The location for his symbol of power was quickly found: it was the hill of Bellver, which rises almost 365 feet (113 m) above the town, an ideal position for the project. But some decades were to pass before building work on the castle began, and Jaume I did not live to see it completed.

For it was not until 1300 that an architect was found who seemed adequate to the task and could realize the ambitious project. Pere Salvà had already converted the Almudaina Palace and he seemed to be the right man. For nine years 70 men worked tirelessly on the great fortifications. In 1309 their work was finished and the new king Jaume II could be well satisfied with the result.

The ground plan of the Castell de Bellver is unique in Spain for, unlike most of the fortresses, it is circular. The castle is built around an inner courtyard and the two storeys surrounding the court are also rounded. The arcades of the lower story are Romanesque, the columned walk above is Gothic. From outside the complex looks completely impregnable, but the two-storey loggias with their playful columns surrounding the inner court radiate sheer joy and delight.

The castle is surrounded by a moat 13 feet (4 m) wide and it has three towers that rise above the round keep, while the fourth, the Torre de l'Homenatge, stands outside the

The circular keep rises 368 feet (112.60 m) above Palma.

circular structure and is linked to the castle itself by a small bridge that used to be a drawbridge. The entry now is via the terrace on the second story. This used to be a strategic lookout post, for one can see for miles into the country behind and out to sea from here.

Inside the *torre* a flap in the floor leads down into a cavernous space with only a small rectangular window on one side. It was used later as a dungeon, and the prisoners were thrown down from a height of 16 feet (5 m). It is the notorious *Olla*. There is also said to be an artificial system of caves beneath the castle, the Coves d'Avall, created for the removal of the earth during the building work. The legend says that the wicked witch Joana used to poison her victims with figs down here.

The Tomb of Freedom

At the beginning of the 19th century the most famous prisoner in the history of Majorca was held in the Castell de Bellver. He was the lawyer Gaspar Melchor de Jovellanos, one of the most influential spirits of the Enlightenment in Spain. After studying law and theology in Oviedo in Asturia, de Jovellanos, who was born into a noble family in Gijón in 1744, was first appointed criminal judge in Seville in 1767 and later rose to be court judge in Madrid. He was also a major dramatist of the Spanish Neo-classical period, but when he published a daring work on land reform the conservatives started a vindictive campaign against him.

When Manuel de Godoy, Duke of Alcúdia, was appointed Prime Minister of Spain under Charles IV fortune changed for de Jovellanos, and he was appointed Spanish Minister of Justice in 1797. However, he soon came into conflict with the unreliable Godoy, who was then only 25 – he was the queen's lover as well as the king's favorite – and next year he had to retire to Gijón. When he ventured to oppose Godoy, who supported the French, directly in his *Apologia* and speak out for a liberal policy, this was the last straw for the Royalists.

In 1801 the supporter of the Enlightenment was put in prison – first in the Carthusian monastery at Valldemossa, and a year later in the fortress at Palma. He spent his time here writing – as well as a new curriculum for the island's schools, which he drew up upon the request of the Societat Mallorquina Ecònomica D'Amics del País, (Business Association of the Friends of Majorca), he also wrote a description of the castle and his life as a prisoner, particularly the tower where he was imprisoned, which he called a "living tomb".

De Jovellanos remained a prisoner in Palma for seven years altogether, until 1808. This must have been a great physical strain on a man of 57, quite apart from the mental stress. The contrast between the prison, with its impenetrable towers, and the magnificent rooms built for the royal family must have been forced upon the prisoner anew every day. He lived behind iron barred windows, within damp walls and eternal semi-darkness; he suffered icy cold in winter and the heat of summer, while the royal apartments and their light arched walks radiated calm and rest. Nevertheless, he never despaired of his fate, but wrote descriptions of the building and his surroundings in his books and letters. One of the "poetic letters", as they are called, that he wrote in prison is ironically dedicated to "life in seclusion". Which may have moved him more, when in spring he looked at the hill on which Castell de Bellver, Fairview Castle, is built – joy at the beauty of the richly blooming carnations and lilies covering the hill, or sadness that he might possibly never be free again to smell their wonderful scent? But he was able to do so at least in the final years of his life, for after the fall of Godoy in March 1808 he was released, at the age of 64. He had three more years to live, and he died on 27 November 1811 in Vega in Asturia. During these three years he played a major part in organizing the War of Liberation against Napoleon's occupation of Spain, but he did not live to see the victory.

The same year in which de Jovellanos was released from prison – and Godoy dismissed from office – new prisoners came to the castle, large numbers of French soldiers and officials who had been taken at the Battle of Bailén on 19 July 1808. It was the first major victory for the Spanish troops in the War of Liberation. Eighteen thousand men were taken prisoner and had to be distributed between a number of prisons, so some were brought to Castell de Bellver. Nearly 6,000 of them died in the next few years on the Illa de Cabrera, 11 miles (18 km) off the coast of Majorca.

The French were not the only prisoners in the Castell. There is still a plaque still to show that in 1817 the British General D.L. Lacy was shot here, condemned to death as the leader of a Liberal uprising that failed. The castle also held prisoners during the Spanish civil war, from 1936 to 1938, when the Nationalists imprisoned more than 800 Republicans here. In 1931 the castle and the woodland belonging to it were made the property of the City of Palma, and today the Castell de Bellver holds Palma's Historical Museum. This includes the collection of classical sculptures built up by Cardinal Despuig.

The writer and politician Gaspar Melchor de Jovellanos was held prisoner in the Torre de l'Homenatge.

Secret connections
The Pope, the Knights Templar, the French King and the secret passages in the castle

The Castell de Bellver has many secrets and many legends have grown up around it. Dark deeds have been done within its walls. The visitor to its dungeons, dark, dank holes known as the *olla*, will easily hear in imagination the chains rattling, the prisoners screaming or praying and the guards barking commands. In 1391 some of Palma's Jews were burnt at the stake on the walls of the castle and during the Inquisition the condemned were apparently tarred and feathered on the wall before being thrown to their deaths below.

Cruelty was not the privilege of the rulers, the ruled were no less ruthless. In 1521 the rebellious men of the Germania, the craftsmen's guilds, stormed the castle during the "carnival riots" and slaughtered all its occupants. And in the depths of the hill evil lurked: a wicked witch is said to have enticed innocent people into her caves, the Coves d'Avall, and then killed them with poisoned figs.

Quite right, of course, for any castle worthy of the name. Like the secret doors that turn soundlessly on their hinges, back stairs that give access to other chambers through pitch dark twisting passages, and secret tunnels linking the castle with the outside world. Castell de Bellver has all these. One legend says that there used to be a veritable labyrinth of secret passageways between the castle, the cathedral two miles (3 km) away and the Calatrava quarter to the east, started by the Knights Templar. And in the second half of the 20th century archaeologists did indeed find parts of a passage leading from the old El Temple building, the former seat of the Templars in Calatrava,

Left: Until around 1900 the finest group of palm trees on Majorca stood behind this round arched gate.

Below: Knights Templar accused of heresy being led into prison (illustrated book, 14th century).

to the Almudaina Palace, and they suspect that it led on to the castle.

Money makes the world go round
Naturally the Knights Templar will play a part in any medieval adventure story, for their successful conspiracies and effective means of keeping their affairs confidential made them one of the most important secret societies in the western world, and many people still believe that they influenced politics behind the scenes. Originally the Order of the Knights Templar was founded in 1119 by Hugo de Payens in Jerusalem to protect Christian pilgrims, who were visiting the Holy Land in the 12th century.

The name "Templar" comes from the former seat of the order on the Temple Mount in Jerusalem, where King Balduin

had given the Crusaders part of his palace in 1118. Officially the society was called the Order of the Poor Knights of Christ, but poverty was not their main concern, for the order spread rapidly throughout Europe, as far as Portugal, and the knights became a major power factor with settlements in all the places of strategic importance during the crusades; above all, they owned banks.

Wherever these crusaders came they acquired, through skillful trading and money-lending, land, buildings and capital, at surprising speed and probably often in dubious ways. Their power grew further when the order was made the direct responsibility of the Pope in 1139. In their white cloaks adorned with a red cross they extended their privileges wherever they settled, and generally paid neither customs duties nor taxes.

The Knights Templar exercised considerable influence in Catalonia as well, for they had extensive estates and occupied high offices, enabling them to play a part in important matters of state. This was so from 1131, just 12 years after the order was founded. Of course they took part in the Christian invasion of Majorca in 1229 – they had tutored Jaume I – and in reward for the successful repossession of the island were given 525 horses and more than 359 town houses. Even more important were large estates in Pollença, Escorca and Montuïri. The knights settled here and came to occupy a position that was at least comparable with that of a municipal administration. When King Jaume II appointed his own lord mayor in 1301 to regain control of the land, open confrontation developed between the knights and the king, for the Knights Templar were not prepared to renounce the privileges they had won.

Power makes its holder unpopular, and if money is at stake many things suddenly become possible very quickly. The Knights Templar had often been criticized for their dealings in money and their power, and serious confrontation soon evolved. Internal affairs, like the secret liturgy which was believed to center on an unknown idol, were "discovered", and fueled the mistrust of the government. The order was accused of heresy and subversion.

The French king Philip IV, Philip the Beautiful, ruled France from 1268 to 1314. When he came to the throne he was annoyed to find settlements of the Knights Templar all over his realm and he started a campaign against the monastic knights, accusing them of heresy and setting the Inquisition on them. When a former member of the order decamped to the opposing side and accused his former fellow knights of blasphemy and fornication, the door was open and strong action was possible, if the Pope could be won over to the cause.

But that was the least of the king's worries, for Philip himself had been responsible for electing the Pope. Clement V (1305–1314) was the first Pope in exile, being forced to reside in Avignon under the protection of the king of France, on whom

The Knights Templar wore an eight-pointed red cross on white robes; the serving brethren wore black or brown.

he was, of course, completely dependent. But Philip IV was waging war in Flanders, and wars cost money. So he urged Clement V to dissolve the Order of the Templars to enable him to confiscate their possessions. The Pope yielded to the pressure from the king and commanded that the order be dissolved – not unaware that at least part of their rich possessions would then come into the protecting hands of Mother Church.

In 1307 Philip IV had the Grand Master and other leaders of the Templars arrested and their entire possessions were confiscated. In 1312 Clement V finally dissolved the order and handed all their estates to rivals, the Hospitallers. At any rate, on paper, for in reality it was Philip IV and his English royal colleague, Edward II (1284–1327), who took charge of the Templars' gold.

Tunnels and Temples

In 1311 the knights' temple on the Plaça del Temple in Palma and their estates on Majorca also passed into the administration of the

Catholic Church. So the system of tunnels would have served a dual purpose. At first, it is believed, the Templars met secretly in the subterranean passages, during the time when they were still forming plans with the rulers and dealing with them. Later, when they had fallen from favor, the passages, the branches and sideways of which they had never fully revealed, gave them protection from persecution and may well have enabled them to shift a large part of their fortune to Portugal.

As the order's temple lies in the center of the Calatrava district, that is the center of

the old Jewish quarter Call, it is thought that the Jews also knew of the existence of the secret passages and used them during the many centuries of persecution by the Christians. Many scholars actually argue that there was a subterranean synagogue in Palma, where the persecuted Jews who had been forced to undergo a Christian baptism (*xuetes*) met secretly to practice their true faith. In fact, some scholars suspect that there were in any case close business ties between the Jews and the Knights Templar, for the knights' temples are close to the

The Crusaders always saw themselves as led by Christ.

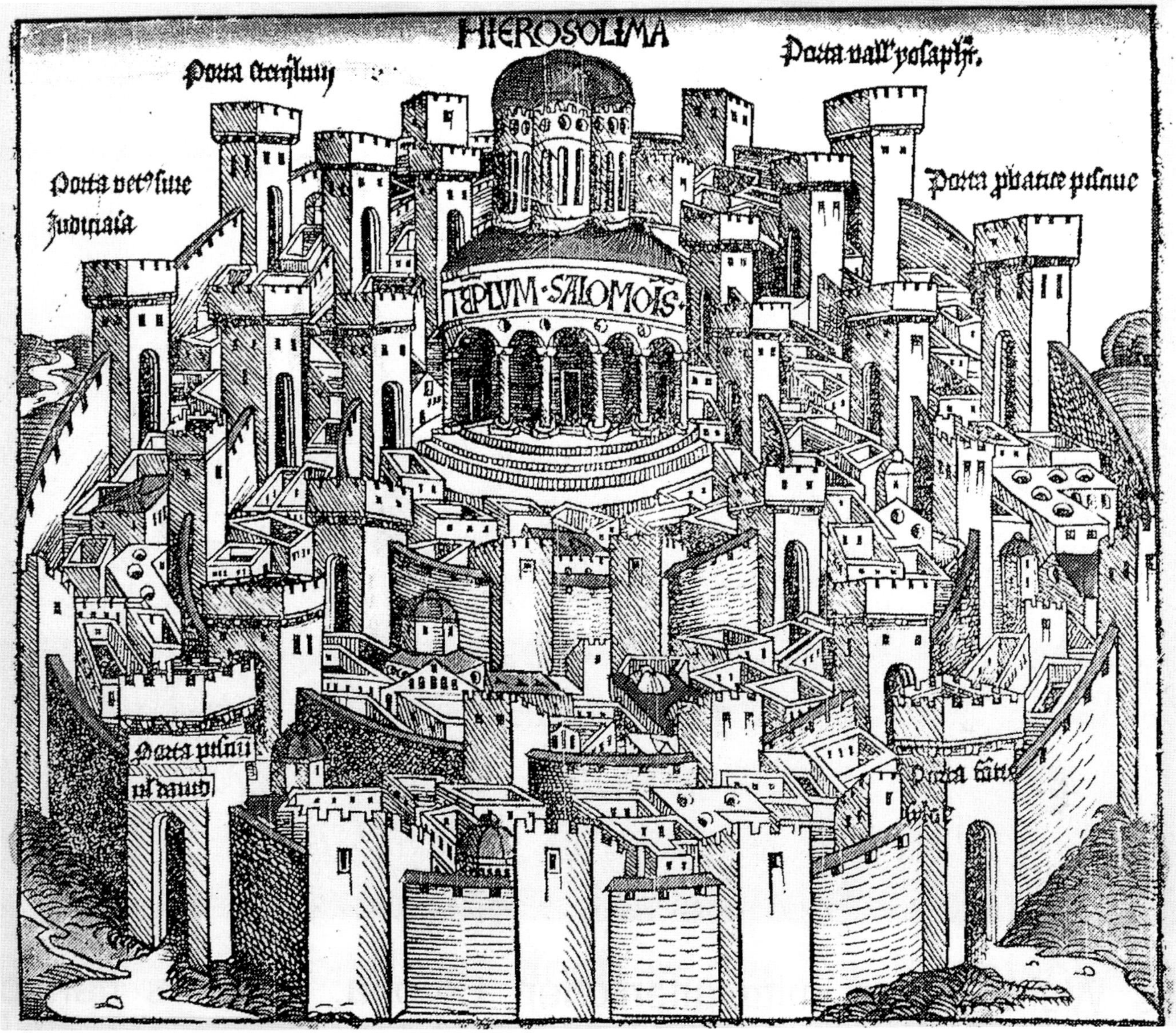
HIEROSOLIMA
TPLVM·SALOMOIS

The headquarters of the order were on the site of Solomon's temple in Jerusalem.

Jewish quarters in France and Spain as well. After all, both groups were active in banking and money lending, and engaged in brisk trade with the Orient.

As the Almudaina was used by the Christians immediately after the conquest in 1229 and the building work on the Castell de Bellver started early in the 14th century, the secret passageways leading from the city center to the castle were probably dug out at the end of the 13th century. In the 1970s a group of archaeologists discovered part of a tunnel near the cathedral, but as most of it has collapsed and the rest is full of the rubbish and rubble of centuries they had to abandon hope of continuing their excavations. Evidently the Almudaina was the point where all the passages in the system intersected.

Although it is not entirely clear exactly where the dark subterranean passage near the cathedral used by the Templars began it must have run parallel to the Passeig de Sagrera and ended at the Castell de Bellver in the Coves d'Avall caves – just where the wicked witch had her abode and did her fearsome deeds, a place from which some indeed never returned.

Refuge for the suffering and playground of the rich
El Terreno

Until the 1770s Castell de Bellver stood alone on its hill to the southwest of the city center. No one thought of living in El Terreno, the area between the castle and the coast, for even the people in Es Jonquet or Santa Catalina, only a few steps outside the city wall, were disparagingly called *arrabaleros*, suburb-dwellers.

Until the castle was built El Terreno was entirely uninhabited land near the coast, offering little more than a few fruitful meadows, big stretches of undergrowth and a hunting ground for small game. Not until 1309, when the castle was finished, did the administrators of the region, the priors of Cartoixa de Valldemossa, appoint a governor. He was to use the profit from the land and in return keep the estates and the woodland in order.

At the end of the 18th century Cardinal Antoni Despuig i Cotoner, a friend and patron of the fine arts, had his name entered as owner of El Terreno. He subdivided the land into small lots, aiming to develop it as building land. But only a few isolated houses were built, for the townspeople had not yet acquired the habit of going to the coast to relax.

Not until 1835, when an earthquake shook the city to its foundations, did the inhabitants of Palma flee to El Terreno, taking refuge in emergency huts until the violent upheavals had subsided. Thirty years later a second wave of refugees swept over El Terreno, when a cholera epidemic raged in Palma, costing the lives of more than 2,000 people within a very short time. This time a camp was set up for those who were still healthy, to prevent the disease spreading in the town. The old trees on the southwest side of the castle hill were felled as the number camping out in El Terreno grew steadily and more room was needed.

Since then a Gothic figure of the Virgin Mary, Mare de Déu de la Salut, the Mother of God of Health, has been worshipped in a little 19th century church in El Terreno. By now the name of El Terreno was familiar to everyone in Palma, and gradually the advantages of the place began to be talked about – apart from its excellent quality as quarantine station or refuge in emergencies. The first major settlement project was started in 1835 by the Societat Mallorquina Econòmica D'Amics del País, a business association, who wanted to turn this part of the bay into a residential district. But the project was not successful, and the "Friends of Majorca" had to admit that people were still not prepared to live outside the town.

The cradle of tourism on Majorca

Not until 1859, when the Ministry of Defense took charge of the area facing the sea and the first building permits were issued, were the middle-class families of Palma evidently ready for the coast. Organized building in the region began with 34 summer residences. Slowly summer holidays on the coast began to be fashionable, particularly as El Terreno, with its untouched landscape, could be reached in only an hour's coach drive from the city center.

Left: A magnificent fireworks display lights up the night sky over the town on the Feast of San Sebastian.

Inset: The flow of traffic has eased on the Passeig Maritím, and up above a swimming pool with disco awaits fun-loving visitors.

Literature, spent several years of his life in El Terreno, editing the magazine *Papeles de Son Armadans* in his residence Carrer Josep Vollalonga No. 87.

Finally in 1920 the first wave of British tourists came to the district and gradually the holiday town was complete. With the outbreak of the Spanish civil war in 1936 the British went home again, and the area lost its international flair. But the city dwellers fled to El Terreno again, as they had done in times of sickness and natural catastrophe, this time to escape the air raids of the Second World War.

After 1945 El Terreno became a popular resort for package tours, as people escaped from the factory or office for a few weeks a year to relax under the southern sun. During the day the owners of supermarkets and souvenir shops did a brisk trade, and night life flourished in the bars and discos.

Tito's – Most famous of all night clubs

In the 1940s an enterprising businessman, Capllonsch Betti, opened a night club above the Passeig Maritím, on the Plaça de Gomila, just where the Inquisition had burned unconverted Jews, whipping up mass hysteria among the watching public. Tito's soon became the most famous of all night clubs on Majorca, with a reputation spreading throughout the Mediterranean and on to America. Famous personalities from the worlds of film and music met here, as did the beauties of the night – Grace Kelly, Errol Flynn, Natalie Wood, George Harrison, Yoko Ono, Kirk Douglas, Michael Caine, Elizabeth Taylor, Richard Burton and many more, and stars like Frank Sinatra,

After 1895 more and more people began to appreciate the advantages of the district and suddenly El Terreno was the height of fashion. Anyone who thought well of themselves and had the necessary cash wanted a house in El Terreno; holiday homes were built there and people spent the weekend recovering from the stress of town life. In the early 20th century the construction of the first two hotels, the Victoria and the Mediterráneo near the Plaça Gomila, marked the start of the tourist trade. The Gran Hotel in the heart of Palma found it was facing competition, as the pioneers among the travel agents of the time could praise the "natural attractions" of El Terreno in their brochures. On the picturesque slopes between the Plaça de Gomila and the Castell de Bellver artists and writers settled beside rich citizens of Majorca – Gertrude Stein, George Bernard Shaw, Georges Bernanos, and Rubén Darío spent time relaxing here or they actually bought land and set up their own dream refuge on the Mediterranean. The Spanish writer Camilo José Cela, who won the Nobel Prize for

Film star Grace Kelly with companion.

Fashion designer Yves Saint Laurent (on left).

Pop hero John Lennon with his muse, Yoko Ono.

Josephine Baker, Ray Charles, Dean Martin, and Marlene Dietrich gave performances to rapturous applause.

One cake on a plate looks lonely, and soon a competitor appeared – El Patio, right next door. It was very successful for a time, winning prominent personalities as guests of honor and acting as a top quality showpiece. Then in the 1970s the disco wave reached Majorca and swept over it, setting new standards of night entertainment. The legendary stage shows in Tito's gave way to smoke machines and the orchestra to an 8,000 watt plant. El Patio tried to jump on the same wagon, but this time was less successful. While the new stars, DJs rapidly changing their vinyl discs, glittered next door, admired by Majorca's teenagers and their counterparts from Europe, El Patio dozed towards its less glamorous end. Tito's is still the magnet for fun-loving night birds, as they are hurtled up 164 feet (50 m) in a few seconds in the glass lifts. Up here, above the sound proofing and flickering electronic lights of the dance floor, one has a grandiose view of the Bay of Palma, its own lights flickering over the night sea to the foot of El Terreno.

Kirk Douglas

Michael Caine

Lovers of Majorcan wine Barry Moore …

… Maximilian Schell …

… and cheerful Robert Morley.

A lifelong inspiration
Miró on Majorca

"I dream of a big studio", was the title Miró used for an article he wrote in 1938, describing the many journeys and stations of his life. It was to be nearly another twenty years before he was finally able to realize his dream – on Majorca. His friend, the internationally celebrated architect Josep Lluis Sert, designed a big, light building for him near Palma, and from 1956 on Miró finally had the room and quiet he needed after the artistically highly productive but financially difficult years with the Paris Surrealists, Max Ernst, André Breton, Hans Arp and René Magritte.

That Miró, a Catalan born in Barcelona in 1893, chose to settle in Majorca is hardly surprising, for the island had repeatedly played an important part in his life. First, there were the childhood experiences in his grandparents' house, where he often spent his holidays. His mother Lola Ferrá came from Sóller. Then he met Pilar Juncosa, who was born on Majorca, and married her in 1929. The marriage was extremely happy and lasted until his death.

Finally Majorca offered the artist a refuge and protection during the difficult years of the war. When his daughter Dolores settled on Majorca with her husband in the 1950s this may well have been the final inducement for her parents to buy their piece of land there.

Majorca became the artist's final anchorage. He was now over sixty, successful, with a long established international reputation. But Majorca certainly did not bring retirement, for Miró created major groups of works here, powerful and mature ceramics, graphics and sculptures. Above all, he began to paint again, producing fascinating works after a break of many years.

This view of the artist's studio shows the creative force of his late work.

The intensive re-encounter with his earlier works was the significant starting point for this renewed interest in painting. As he at last had enough room in a studio of his own Miró spent his first weeks and months on Majorca unpacking the many chests in which he had stored his canvases and transported them back and forth between his main workplaces, Paris, Barcelona and Montroig. Surrounded by the work of more than four decades he undertook a comprehensive and rigorous review. "When I saw all these works again on Majorca I started a process of self-criticism," he said. "It was a shock, a kind of brain-washing. I was absolutely ruthless with myself. I destroyed some works, mainly drawings and gouaches. Whenever I looked at a series I put a pile aside to burn, and then

I went back to them and crunch, snap, crack, I destroyed them. There were two or three great "purges' of this nature through the years." Retracing his own artistic path, arranging and sorting his works, casting off the ballast released forces that took Miró the painter into new paths.

The landscape on the island became a fruitful source of artistic inspiration. "I find all my subjects in the fields or on the coast…", he said. "They all appear in my compositions, and the same applies to the strange hat-like shapes of the mushrooms and the seventy-seven different types of bottle gourds." Miró gave back the inspiration he received from the island. A wall ceramic fills a wall facing the coast in the Parc de la Mar in Palma, and a copy of his sculpture *Personatge*, Personality, stands on the Plaça de la Reina. Miró developed the pictorial signs that are characteristic of his work from objects he had found on his long and stimulating walks, from his encounter with the folk art of Majorca – he loved the *siurells*, as primitive as they are naive, and collected them passionately. The images he evolved from them lead serene, independent lives in the intensely colored glowing paintings. Figurations like woman, bird, world, stars or eyes people the cosmos of Miró's painting, fantastic creatures, confident and alive.

Then came important stimulus from the encounter with the young American artists. While Miró had been largely unrecognized in his own country – indeed, he remained virtually isolated – in the United States he had been regarded as one of the most interesting

European artists since his first major exhibition in the Museum of Modern Art in New York in 1941. A second and longer visit to America to receive the *Guggenheim International Award* and for the opening of a major retrospective in the Museum of Modern Art brought Miró into contact with the latest work by his young American colleagues. Mark Rothko and Barnett Newmann had been strongly influenced by the Spanish artist in their search for an autonomous, non-objective painting, as had Jackson Pollock and Robert Motherwell, but they had found their own individual way. Miró in turn studied this with fascination. The spontaneous gestural application of paint and the great expressivity of their work in particular left a lasting impression on him.

In the next few years on Majorca Miró developed a highly expressive style of painting, using a free, rapid brushwork instead of carefully contoured fields of color with form

created by line. The principle of chance that had preoccupied him since his Surrealist phase in the Twenties reappeared with new accents. He created raw, powerful, archaic pictures that are now seen as characteristic of the major works of his older period.

Above: "My pictures must be self-sufficient, like the rustling in the air or the flight of a bird, they must be beautiful and pure…". This wall ceramic in the Parc de la Mar in Palma shows Miró's organic formal language.

Left: Internationally highly regarded but never really acknowledged in Spain – nevertheless, Joan and Pilar Miró decided to set up a generous foundation, which now enriches the art scene in Majorca.

The Pla

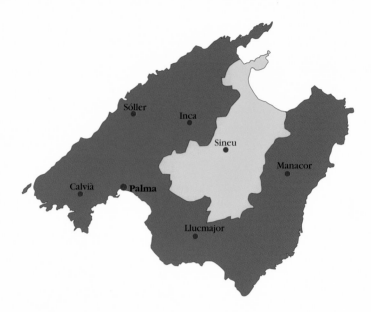

The clocks tick on, time stands still
The Pla

In summer the Pla glows in a concerted harmony of browns – from the harsh yellowish brown of the dry soil on the hills to the rich stone brown in the hollows. Then there is a reddish brown, like burnt sugar, full of cracks and fissures, baptized in fire like the inside walls of an earthen stove or the firmly trodden clay floor around the stalls where the animals seek shelter from the sun.

It is the almond and carob trees, the *rostolls*, the fields of stubble and the *guarets*, fallow fields, that form the face of the Pla, in valleys and on hills. There are wide prospects, where the land rises and falls like the waves of the sea. In between glisten green carpets of small oak and pine woods, revealing farms, cemeteries and chapels that seem to lie there asleep, as if enchanted and forgotten.

The Pla is the heart of the island and its breadbasket. The people of Majorca call it *nostra Majorca de sempre*, the real Majorca. This is the part of their island that saw conquerors and conquered, kings and vassals pass almost without visible consequences. Even the first hesitant touches of industrialization at the end of the 19th century brought little change, and the steadily growing stream of tourists who have sought out and enriched the island since the 1960s do not – as yet – seem to have reached the Pla. *Es Pla* has remained as it has always been, although everything around it has changed. So its aspect is little reminiscent of yesteryear, but for that very reason its unspoiled landscape seems to many a model for tomorrow. A slightly rosy view of the past can surely be forgiven.

The Pla covers about 17 percent of the island, but only five percent of the population live here, so it can claim the dubious honor

Previous double-page spread: The island's breadbasket glistens in a rich green in spring, thanks to the winter rain.

of being the most thinly populated part of the island. In some communities only four percent of the area is designated urban, that is, building land, the rest is farm land or forest. These people have always been farmers. And the early industries in the 19th century sought more favorable locations, where transport routes were shorter and labor and customers easier to obtain. So outside influence on the landscape and people in the heart of the island has been slight, and not much has changed in most places to today. People have always only just been able to scrape a living from agriculture here, if at all, but for most of them that was all they had.

People like these, living off and with the land, set different monuments to their culture and way of living than people who live in more fertile, richer areas. In the Pla the eye is caught, like the wind, by the windmills, and glides over their water courses and wheels. The windmills are built of Marès stone and are hundreds of years old.

For as the Pla has no natural streams, rivers or torrents, rain and ground water are the only sources available to the farmers. This part of the island needs no castles or palaces, its architecture is of the soil, defiant giver of life. Today most of the windmills and water wheels no longer pump water – many have long lost their sails. Small electrical pumps are doing the work, but they are still located in the mouth of the well or the windmill tower. The corn mills are also no longer dependent on the winds that bluster from the north through the Bay of Alcúdia into the plain; they and the towers and lofts hold the villagers' gold, their corn.

Nevertheless, these relics of the pre-electrical age still create the character of a landscape in which automatic irrigation systems have to bring the costly water to where it is needed, and they tell of their builders – people who are rooted deep in the past and have sustained their pattern of living, their customs and traditions through the centuries.

The Pla was already settled around 2000 BC. On the Balearic Islands this megalithic age, with its imposing stone constructions, is

Under the pink shade of almond trees in full blossom sheep crop the juicy spring meadows in the Pla.

known as the Talayotic Age, from the Arab loan word for tower, *talàia*, which is widely used on the islands. Some of the *talayots* are still standing. Many are multi-story towers built of blocks of stone, but their function is not known. In Costitx and near Montuïri they still seem to be watching over the destiny of the Pla as they did long ago.

When the Roman army finally conquered the Balearic Islands in 123 BC and achieved hegemony over the western Mediterranean, the establishment of the Pax Romana brought relative calm for the next few hundred years. The islands in the Mediterranean offered many Romans a welcome alternative to overcrowded Rome; others found themselves on Majorca in less idyllic circumstances, after banishment or exile. The Romans organized trade and built roads, they founded towns and set up an administration, particularly on the coasts. Even then the Pla was on the sidelines of history, and in the following centuries, too, as Vandals and Byzantines conquered the island, the coastal strips were of greater importance than the land in the center.

Only when the Moors established their rule, from 902 AD, did the situation change slightly: their *alqueries* were the first settlements of which remnants have remained. The Moorish conquerors' main

The bare tops of the fig trees stand like fearful spirits in the morning mist when the winter has stripped them of their leaves.

contribution was to build terraces and establish a skillful irrigation system in the Pla, so offering the people the first chance of a modest but independent life, not as vassals but as self-sufficient farmers. These first Moorish settlements were where many villages and large estates stand today. Unfortunately, the Reconquista, when the Christians reconquered the island in 1229 AD, ruthlessly eliminated almost all the traces of this period. Only places and names have survived, beside those that were created upon the decree of Jaume II in the 13th century – among them Petra, Sant Joan, Porreres and Algaida.

Sineu was the Pla's corn market and it was also the residence of the kings of Majorca. The palace at Sineu was built in 1309 and in 1503 it become the monastery of the strict Conceptionist order, with its vows of seclusion. The first long firm road on the island was built between Palma and Sineu, across the Pla. The markets often lay on these trading routes, and many are still there, visible traces of the time when they were trading centers and exchanges solely for the products of their region. Market places grew into settlements, settlements into trading centers and finally towns. The market at Sineu used to be the main trading center for the whole of the Pla and it is still the best known.

The Church also found its way into the Pla with the Reconquista, powerful and influential, as the many parish churches, monasteries, chapels, cemeteries and hermitages testify. Most of the churches were built on the highest point in the region, so that they dominated the landscape and were visible from afar, as in Cura, Monti-Sion and Bonany. Generally people settled directly around the church, except near the oldest church in the Pla, Castellitx, between Algaida and Randa. Only two hundred years after it was built, in the 15th century, did what is now the town of Algaida start to grow, a couple of miles northeast, probably because conditions for trade and transport were easier there.

Nevertheless, life in the Pla is still rural, the work is hard and there is little time for the idyllic. So it seems surprising to find a town

Below: Household utensils for the farmers, like this traditional clay pottery, are the main wares to be found in the Pla markets.

Above: Food for all: almonds appeal to every taste; there are also baskets full of walnuts, pine nuts, and sunflower seeds.

Opposite: A cage of lambs waiting for their new owner.

like Porreres among all the villages; it may be small but it nestles sheltered from the wind by nearby Llucmajor, which is part of the Migjorn region. In the 18th century Porreres enjoyed a remarkable economic success. While Llucmajor developed into a center of the shoe and brandy industries, linen weavers settled in Porreres, so by the end of the 18th century it was the most important town in the Pla, a quarter larger than the royal residence Sineu, which had about four thousand inhabitants.

Noble residences of generous proportions with great wine cellars, imposing gateways and stately administration buildings still bear witness to the town's former greatness. The inhabitants are not so taciturn and reserved with strangers as the people deep in the Pla, the old village heart of Majorca. Only when the Pla had suffered economic decline through the plague of vine pest, and new methods of production were started in the 19th century, did the town's brief prosperity come to an end, leaving Porreres to fall back into its role as the Sleeping Beauty, from which it had briefly awakened.

The Catalan poet Josep Pla, who visited Majorca in the 1920s, described the Pla as "beautiful, delicate, fine..., but ordinary and difficult... and then a very normal but strangely sensuous landscape". It is a list of contradictions, but they are both the strength and the charm of the Pla. It is primeval as an ox dragging his heavy plow through the hard furrow of earth, and it is also filigree, delicate as a veil in which the sunlight plays hide and seek; it is both a drum roll and a melody gently hummed in the wind.

A journey through its villages quickly becomes a journey through time: stone house after stone house stands on streets that seem deserted, old men sit in front of cafés, women stand in the doorways and gates, dogs bark in the distance, then comes the chattering of a

moped or maybe a tractor, and nearby a squeaking donkey cart with wood decades old. Outside the village the electric cables, masts and transformers disappear, becoming an unreal memory; asphalt quickly gives way to dusty earth tracks and later field paths where the tractor has left tracks like furrows in a field.

The drystone walls are endless, and they run across the Pla like a fine network. Actually a waste product, they are also an inventive solution to a difficult problem – what to do with the field stones that choke the earth and break the plow. So drystone walls separate neighbors' land, they mark community borders, and enclose farm land and hunting grounds; many welcome and bless the walker with *creus de terme*, the crucifixes where paths cross.

The *possessions*, estates, are not only the points where paths intersect, they are centers of agriculture and livestock farming. Large estates like Roqueta in María or Sa Torre in Santa Eugènia have played a major part in the Pla's economy since the 13th century.

In the middle of the sun-dried summer landscape you can suddenly come across a *sinia*, a well or cistern. It is like an oasis. Every village and every estate has a public well, to catch the rainwater or store the ground water as far as possible. Dry farming is typical of the Pla, and the main crops are field fodder and fruit like tomatoes and figs that are very resistant and need little water. For the summers are exceedingly hot and the winters are colder than anywhere else on the island except the windy heights of the Tramuntana mountains in the north. Despite the silky light the climate in the Pla has none of the gentle mildness of the Mediterranean.

Until the vine pest *Philoxera* went on its destructive path at the end of the 19th century viticulture was also important here. Particularly around Petra many farmers had devoted their land to growing vines, which was profitable. In the 1850s wine meant quick money and good earnings for the few *pageses* who had been through hard times and were quick to recognize a good chance when it came and bank on wine. For when the French vineyards fell victim to the pest, wine of any quality and provenance was in demand. But eventually *Philoxera* found its way to Majorca, after twenty profitable years, and put an end to the "happy vintages". Today young wine growers are venturing to make a new start and trying to produce high-quality wines. It is not easy, because the conditions cannot be compared with those in the mainland vineyards of La Rioja or the upper Duero, and Majorcan wine does not have the best of reputations. Most of the vineyards that were plowed up were planted with almond trees, a harvest that sold well and gave the farmers some prospect of self-sufficiency.

Only when the tourists came, from the 1950s onwards, did new life come to the Pla, although it had a different rhythm and was more hesitant than on the coasts in the north and south of the island. And now its very seclusion worked to the Pla's advantage: the summer vacationers from cold northern Europe wandered first into the village

Opposite: After the almond harvest only experts can still find something to eat under the trees.

Following double-page spread: At the end of the long Majorcan summer the farmland in the Pla glows in every shade of brown.

In April and May the poppies unfold their brilliant red and the Pla looks as if Claude Monet himself had strewn the meadows with little specks of red paint.

courtyards, curious, wondering, unsuspecting. Enchanted, they came to value the beauty and unique quality of the Pla, to love and respect its customs; they came more and more frequently, staying longer each time. They brought and created a market for rural tourism, and this in turn brought subsidies from the European Union. Finally many of them bought old *fincas*.

Now small building firms and craft firms that had been facing ruin are getting new orders. The new customers want old things, they want clay or zinc gutters, drystone walls, doors and handles like those on the rusty old models. Things that had been thought hopelessly obsolete and put away in the dusty drawers of history are being brought out again and are enjoying a new life. In many of the small craft workshops the masters of the Pla are working with the tools used by their forefathers but under modern electric light bulbs, making things that are like themselves and their land – simple, rooted in local tradition, of modest but all the more enduring beauty.

The Bread of Mercy
Algaida

The sweeping lines of this landscape and its warm colors recall Tuscany. In this gentle hilly country, with its fertile soil and pine woods between Algaida (Arabic for forest) and Randa, the oldest testimony to Christianity on Majorca – the church of Castellitx – is to be found.

While elsewhere the mosques and bath houses, town palaces and country estates of the Moors were being destroyed, the Catalan conquerors in the 13th century chose Castellitx for the location of their first church.

Evidently it was not the initial intention to build an imposing cathedral, and the church of St Peter and St Paul (Sant Pere i San Pau) in Castellitx was only granted a nave. But the entrance is adorned with a diamond-shaped pinnacle; it crowns the entrance with its pointed arches that comprises the main portal. Two hundred years later the church was given a fine Gothic altar, as a sign that the bloody age of the Reconquista was finally over. The Gothic carving of 1430 with its painted wood depicts the *Verge de la Pau*, the Virgin of Peace, seated with the Christ child on her arm; he is holding a globe in his hand.

The unusual feature of this church is that a settlement did not immediately grow up around it, or even in the immediate

Above: No village here, the church is surrounded by the gently rolling landscape.

Left: The church of St. Peter and St. Paul in Castellitx is one of the oldest on the island.

vicinity, as happened almost everywhere else. Only much later, in the 15th century, did people settle about two and a half miles (4 km) further northeast, in what is now the town of Algaida. At that time its location offered better conditions for trade and better links with other settlements.

The church of Castellitx is still an important place of pilgrimage, but technical and medical progress has overtaken its original purpose – fortunately, for earlier the people of Algaida prayed here to the Apostles Peter and Paul for protection from the plague and enough rain. Today they come in search of physical rather than spiritual sustenance: the *Pancaritat*, or Bread of Mercy, as it is known, is a public holiday which is celebrated with a hearty feast outside the church. Everyone makes a contribution, and neighbors sit down together. In the pauses between the dancing they consume huge quantities of the traditional pasties, the famous *panades* filled with lamb or a sweet filling, which every family on Majorca bakes at Easter. Two other prime items in Majorcan cuisine receive their due acknowledgment here: *robiols* and *crespells*. The former are pasties like the *panades*, but they have delicious sweet fillings of pumpkin jam or cream cheese, while the *crespells* are a way of using up the remnants. When the filling has been used up, or just because the taste is irresistible, the pastry for the *robiols* is rolled out again and cut up or cut out to make crumbly biscuits.

But this pilgrimage is not just profane gluttony. The gathering over pasties and biscuits is a kind of cookery competition for the people of Algaida; it is the opportunity to re-arrange the ranking of the best men and women cooks in the town. Everyone tastes the pasties and dishes their neighbors have prepared, and for every housewife, rich or poor, it is a matter of honor to earn laurels here.

This is mainly because Majorcan cuisine is modest as a rule. Earlier it was not possible to slip into the supermarket and buy whatever was needed. Stocks of food had to be planned for the entire year in advance, and the household budget covered slaughtering a pig, which had to provide meat and sausage for the entire year. At Christmas there was enough money to buy a capon (a castrated,

The people of Algaida use the pilgrimage to the church of St. Peter and St. Paul, as do the visitors from Pina in this picture, as a welcome opportunity to compete with each other at the "Bread of Mercy" feast, which is a communal celebration.

Between the church and the old windmill Algaida offers a large selection of restaurants that are popular all over Majorca.

fattened cock) or a chicken, and at Easter a lamb found its way into the cooking pot. These were the essential and basic items needed to maintain one's standing in the neighborhood and to enable the household to take part in the village festivities.

Robiols i crespells

Stuffed pasties and biscuits
(recipe for 8 *robiols* and 10 *crespells*)

Pastry
2¼ lb (1 kg) flour
4½ oz (150g) icing sugar
½ vanilla pod, scraped out
3 to 4 egg yolks, depending on size
3½ fluid oz (0.1 l) orange juice, freshly squeezed
10½ oz (300 g) refined lard or butter
Olive oil
3½ fluid oz (0.1 l) water

Cream cheese filling
7¼ oz (200 g) cream cheese, semi-skimmed
1 egg yolk
1¾ oz (50 g) castor sugar
zest of one orange and half a lemon

These two goodies are always mentioned together, because the *crespells* are biscuits made from the pastry, left over from making the delicious pasties filled with pumpkin jam or cream cheese.

Put two thirds of the flour on the table or into a bowl, and make a well in the center. Add the icing sugar, vanilla, and egg yolk (beaten into the orange juice) and mix, starting from the center. Melt the lard on a low heat or in a pre-heated oven and pour it at hand temperature over the pastry. Knead well, keeping the hand rubbed with olive oil to prevent the pastry sticking to the hand. Keep adding the remaining flour with luke-warm water until a pastry is formed that can easily be shaped.

Leave to stand for half an hour and then roll out, as thinly as possible for the *robiols*. Cut out little shapes with a round cutter 4½ to 6 inches (12 to 15 cm) in diameter, lay on some filling, fold over and punch together at the edges. Press a pattern into the edge with a fork. Shape biscuits about half an inch (1.5 cm) thick out of the remaining pastry and bake both in a pre-heated oven at 250°F (120°C) for about an hour.

Generally the *robiols* are filled with pumpkin jam, but cream cheese is also excellent. The ingredients for this need to be well stirred. If cream cheese filling is used the inside of the pastry case should be oiled with a small brush after being rolled and cut out.

Top: The Cossiers dances date from the 16th century

Above, left: Presumably the Cossiers were originally harvest thanksgivings or fertility rites performed like ballets.

Above, right: Good and evil clash in the eternal power struggle. The devil has to try and prevent the lovely lady from entering the church.

Bagpipes and demons
The Cossiers' dances

The dancers in their straw hats look after the beautiful lady like the apple of their eye, they circle round her trying to keep the demonic seducer away. Other men lend them support by waving colored cloths to protect the 'lady' – who is in reality a boy dressed in woman's clothes. The drama is played out in front of and inside the church: step by step the whole group moves towards the altar but the dancer dressed as a demon tries to prevent the lady from reaching the sacred spot. Accompanied by flutes, *xeremies*, the Majorcan bagpipes, and tambourines, the dancers protect her virtue and clear the way for her. Good conquers evil, light banishes darkness – happy ending Majorcan style.

The dance is called the Cossier, and it is generally performed outside or inside a church. In and around Algaida the tradition is still very much alive. The dances are performed in other places as well, like Montuïri, Porreres, Sóller and Pollença, but Algaida is the main center where the tradition can be traced back furthest.

In most other places, like Alaró, these dances were almost forgotten for more than 70 years, and they were only revived in the 1990s. This was the undisputed achievement of the scholar Xisco Vallcaneras of the folklore, music and dance department of Palma city council Escola de Música i Dances de l'Ajuntament de Palma.

The Cossiers are first recorded on Majorca in 1554. Archduke Ludwig Salvator, scion of the Austrian Habsburg family who spent

42 years of his life on Majorca, mentions them around 100 years ago; he was also aware that many variants were already lost.

Today scholars assume that the dance was formerly part of a kind of folk dance theater. Originally it would have derived from heathen fertility or harvest rites, and like many ceremonies of its kind it later found a new interpretation under the protecting and enveloping umbrella of the Church. The origin of the name *Cossier* is not definitely known, either. Some ethnologists believe it derives from the 17th century *Ball de cossis* (Clay Jugs Dance), other studies trace it back to the arrival of Scottish seafarers on the island. Phonetically *cossier* is related to *escocès* (Scottish), and a similar sound shift did indeed give its name to a folk dance performed in Madrid, the *Schotis*. This

Above: To the accompaniment of flutes, tambourines, and bagpipes the dancer dressed as a woman tries to enter the church. Her escorts have bells round their calves to frighten Satan away(left).

does derive from a Scottish dance which the Habsburgs made fashionable in Madrid.

Lost in time
Pina

Traditions can persist very stubbornly, even in the modern world. When – in 1987! – Ruth Hoggart, a British anthropologist, wanted to join a group of men in a bar in Pina she was told very firmly that she must sit with the other women. As custom required, they were gathered around the woman owner at the other end of the room, sewing, preparing food and talking about housekeeping. That is how it has always been and it still is.

Only four miles (6 km) of gentle hills separate Pina from Algaida, but the distance has sufficed to keep Pina almost completely cut off from the outside world for centuries. Even now it still lies far off the well-trodden and much traveled tourist and transport routes; it does not even have its own administration, but is part of Algaida, and so time seems to have passed by here. There has never been much reason to see the world

A guest in Pina: the anthropologist Ruth Hoggart.

beyond the village and its fields as part of village life – unless there were disputes over land rights or invitations.

For that very reason, isolated communities like Pina, whose ca. 500 inhabitants have been farmers since people settled here, are arousing the interest of researchers. For geneticists, immunologists, and behaviorists they are like fossils, in which thousands of

years of development processes can be traced and studied. This is also attracting anthropologists like Ruth Hoggart, who in 1987 chose Pina for her doctoral thesis on communities "isolated in time".

The people of Pina were a perfect subject to study. As they had been exposed to virtually no outside influence they had preserved their archaic but only seemingly simple social structures almost intact. Many inhabitants of Pina often spend months, sometimes years, and in a few cases their entire lives without leaving the village. Some have never seen the sea, they only know about it from hearsay. And to exclude any outside influence on her study, Hoggart lived as they did during her research.

Initially she lived with a family in the village to make her first contacts and get to know village life. That was not at all easy, for the family only agreed to take her because

Pina is so cut off from the world that it is a valuable subject of study for anthropologists like Ruth Hoggart.

she had a letter of recommendation from her professor. Later she had to give up her desire to live slightly outside the village, for she was given to understand that according to the village rules only people who have something to hide seek to put a distance between themselves and the community; consequently they cannot be "good people".

That was only a foretaste of the social control that Hoggart was to experience personally in the next few months. She was under constant collective observation. In a community that is mutually dependent for survival, like Pina, the borders between public and private life are fluid, if not blurred altogether.

Until a short time ago it was normal in Pina to leave the key to the house in the outside lock of the door, day and night. Anyone could come in at any time. Consequently, the villagers saw any stranger as a danger to their mutual trust, be they seasonal workers from Andalusia, drawn to Majorca by the prospect of good money, or tourists who would bring money.

One day a neighbor complained that Hoggart had had a light on late into the night. She explained that she had been working, but he would not accept her explanation. In Pina you work during the day and sleep at night, he said, it was as simple as that.

Modern agricultural machinery is not a familiar sight in Pina, even today.

The people in Pina are not really interested in the world outside their immediate neighborhood.

Hoggart learned to speak *Mallorquí* very well fairly quickly, and that made it easier for her to attend community and cooperative meetings, to observe superstitious peasant rituals and join in the traditional dancing and singing. After six months she received anonymous threatening letters accusing her of only having come to Pina to "entice" a young man away from the village to Britain.

Ruth Hoggart's study is full of events like this, more to be expected in a medieval community than one at the end of the 20th century. But the gap was felt on both sides. An 85-year old woman from Pina found it unimaginable, indeed inhuman, to live in an apartment block, side by side, and not know your neighbor.

Exotic as Pina may sound, similar attitudes apply to the rest of the island. Most of the island's inhabitants now make a living from tourism – they are familiar with visitors from all over the world but they treat them as foreigners. Very few are allowed really to come close to the people of Majorca.

Time also seems to stand still in the fields around Pina.

Bulls' heads and supernovae
Costitx

Costitx is the place where a combination of devastating circumstances was allowed to flourish for centuries disregarded, quietly and so all the more effectively. The little town of Costitx is hidden away from life on the island, and even more from world events, lying so deep in the Pla that even many people on Majorca did not know of its existence for a long time. Very few guide books mention it, and if they do it is because of an archaeological discovery dating from the prehistory of the village, not because of its charm or its sleepy remoteness.

The history of Costitx is characterized by the hard life on the land, where nothing has ever been more important than the hard labor of wringing subsistence from the soil, keeping the livestock healthy and somehow raising the children. Learning to read and write, to burst through barriers, explore the world – that was the privilege of only a few, right into the 20th century, those who were given the opportunity through the army or the Church. Lessons for the other villagers consisted merely of learning to survive and to mistrust everyone and everything that was foreign to the village. Political parties, trade unions, social organizations have never been able to gain a foothold here. The efforts of the Church in the 19th century, in this case Franciscan nuns, to bring at least some cultural life into the village with folk dance groups and Sunday schools were transformed into their absurd opposite early in the 20th century, when Church superiors began to supervise and regulate the activities. Then even the few cafés and the only cinema in Costitx disappeared. The village seemed to give up and go to sleep...

In Costitx the farmers have never had time to get an education or send their children to school. Life has always centered on the livestock and the harvest.

A lady mayor brings culture and science to Costitx

... until a woman was elected Mayor in 1987 and took office with the firm intention of waking her village up. Maria Antònia Munar is a moderate Nationalist who at the time also held an office in the Balearic government as *Consell de Cultura del Gobern Balear*, or Minister for the Arts. Her first two achievements were the Costitx Culture Center and the Museum of Ibero-Balearic Fauna, that is, for the whole of animal life on the group of islands and the mainland. Her aim was to make Costitx attractive for excursions, and to give its people a new self-confidence: "We are somebody, we have something to show."

At Maria Antònia Munar's insistence an observatory was actually built here. The remoteness of the town and the clear air in the Pla offer particularly good conditions for its operation. Four large and five small telescopes are located under three domes, enabling scientists to observe mainly supernovae, apparently "new-born", very brightly shining stars. Their discoveries are analyzed in conjunction with the Institutes of Astrophysics in Andalusia and on the Canary Islands.

The observatory is operated by the Majorcan Organization for Astronomy, but it also has another objective – to introduce young people to science. Those who are interested can visit the observatory and bombard the scientists with questions.

Above: Costitx has very clear air and was the best possible place for an observatory.

Below: The observatory contains nine telescopes, through which scientists can study movements in space.

Caps de Bou de Costitx
Talayotic bulls' heads

Costitx has even more to be proud of.
Something that is quite unique: the Caps de Bou
de Costitx. They are an extraordinary find from
prehistory that aroused public interest as early as 1895 – or
certainly should have done so. A year earlier these three
bronze bulls' heads were found on common land near the Son
Corró estate. They date from the sixth or fifth century BC, and
so they are part of the Talayot culture which is widespread on
the Balearic Islands. One of the heads is life size, the two others
are much smaller. They are all cast in one piece with strikingly
life-like details. The eyes, horns, mouths, and nostrils almost look as
if the artist had molded a mask straight from the bull.

The archeologists were also fascinated by the great similarity
between this extraordinary find and objects that had been excavated
on Sardinia and Malta, in Persia, Portugal and Greece. This suggests
that the ancient inhabitants of the Balearic islands, who have left no
written records and are always described as very primitive by Greek
and Roman writers, must have had regular contact with other
cultures even in early times.

The bulls' heads also suggest that bulls were revered on Majorca
as sacred animals, or at least regarded as having magical power. The
cult of the bull was known in the Mediterranean in earliest times.
There were bull cults in Ancient Egypt, frescoes in the Palace of
Knossos on Crete (ca. 1500 BC) show young men and women
performing the ritual "bull leap" and in a cave on Lleida on the
Spanish mainland Stone Age forefathers of the Spaniards painted
bulls, weapons and men on the walls. In Termes in southern Spain
stands what is probably the oldest bull ring, where the animals were
ritually slaughtered. It was already standing when the Romans sacked
Termes in 99 BC. Excavations have also brought to light bulls' horns
and miniatures of bulls.

But in 1895 virtually no one on Majorca knew enough to appreciate the value of the find in Costitx, which also included bulls'

horns, sparrows, and eagles in bronze, ceramics, and numerous links from Punic necklaces. Only one archeological committee urged the owner of the land to allow the scientists to undertake further excavations and to seal off the area from unwarranted intrusion. Their greatest fear was that the hope of finding gold would induce the local people to ravage the site and that valuable testimonies of the ancient time would be destroyed. But the laws at the time allowed the owner of the land on which finds were made to claim payment for the objects discovered, and in this case the owner promptly demanded the proud sum of 700 duros (3,500 pesetas). It was a huge amount, considering that a day's labor then earned at most one peseta.

The archeological society was penniless, and they did not succeed in raising the money. Helplessly they appealed to the press and this at least produced one result: they were able to prevent the bulls' heads from being sold to art dealers, and thus disappearing for ever from the island and from Spain. Two Majorcans, neither from Costitx, contacted the central government in Madrid and did manage to persuade the National Archeological Museum there to intervene and acquire the valuable find before private collectors were able to do so.

So it seemed then that Costitx had lost its emblem for ever. But Maria Antònia Munar worked tirelessly to bring the early finds that are of such significance in the history of Majorca back to Costitx – after all, she had already successfully reached for the stars. Here, too, her efforts were justly rewarded: in 1995 the Santuari Son Corró, the de Son Corró sanctuary, was restored and the impressive bulls' heads have adorned it ever since.

Stony and spiritual heights
Randa

A giant from North Africa wanted to explore the north of Europe. As he was too big to fit in a single boat, he put his feet into two different boats, put a basket full of stones on his head to keep his balance and poled himself across the Mediterranean using a long stick. Near the Illa de Cabrera a current drove the boats asunder; the giant tumbled and drove his stick into the sea bed. That is how the deep incision of the Bay of Cala Pi came into being. The basket of stones also fell off his head, it rolled thundering into the Pla and became the mountains of Randa. They do indeed look like huge blocks of stone thrown down aimlessly, with the Cura, Randa's local mountain, towering over them at 1794 feet (549 m).

Randa itself nestles like a Christmas crib in its hollow against the side of the Cura that

The monastery of Nostra Senyora de Cura crowns the peak of Puig de Cura and affords a view right over the Pla from 1800 feet (550 m) up.

Ramón Llull experienced his visions in the Sant Honorat hermitage.

Ramón (*Església de sa Immaculata Concepció i d'en beat Ramón*), a building dating from the 18th century. The altar is late Baroque, and it is dominated by a painting of the Blessed Ramón Llull, the second of the great and truly legendary figures from Randa. He was not born in Randa, any more than the giant in the fairytale, but the visions and illuminations that were the main inspiration for his controversial theories came to him in these mountains, which are often said to have magic power.

How powerful these illuminations were is evident when one climbs the Cura from Randa. Steep, stony, remote from the noise of the profane world and only exposed to the wind and the inner voice, the path winds upwards to three monasteries that were inhabited by hermits in the Middle Ages. The climb is rewarding, not only to reach the monasteries, but also for the panoramic view almost over the entire island – only the part beyond the Tramuntana mountains is hidden.

is sheltered from the wind. Like many villages on Majorca it is now mainly a weekend retreat for the descendants of its original inhabitants, most of whom have jobs in Palma. Right at the entrance to the village rises the tower of the Church of the Immaculate Conception and the Blessed

The tiny hermitage of Nostra Senyora de Gràcia nestles close to the rocks.

Above: On the monastery hill of Randa it is not difficult to feel close to heaven.

Right: Brethren of the Order of the Sacred Heart live in Sant Honorat observing a strict vow of seclusion.

Nostra Senyora de Gràcia, the first of the three monasteries, clings somewhat to one side of the mountain and looks if it was built into overhanging rock. In fact, a Franciscan monk from Llucmajor decided to lead a modest life in this remote spot in the 15th century.

Half a century later another Franciscan monk persuaded the owner to donate the hermitage to the Order of St Francis on condition that it would always be occupied. That is still the case today.

The monastery of Sant Honorat perches on a projecting rock above Nostra Senyora de Gràcia. The legend says that for a long time the only contact the inhabitants had with the outside world was a bucket on a leather strap with which they could draw up or let down communications or food. Unlike the Gràcia monastery the monks in the Order of the Sacred Heart in Sant Honorat still observe a strict vow of seclusion, devoting themselves to the study of Llullism, the writings of the Blessed Ramón Llull.

Near the peak of the Cura is the cave of Mata Escrita, named after the bushes that grow wild here with leaves dotted all over as if with script. This is where Ramón Llull wrote most of his works. In the monastery of Cura itself, which is the highest of the three in Randa, there is a wing to which unauthorized persons are not allowed access. It contains a school in which grammar and Llullism used to be taught. Founded in the 15th century, it was open until 1826, with a brief interruption. Visitors can spend the night at very low cost in one of the monastery's 30 spartan rooms and partake of the spirit and calm of this very special place. Reservations have to be made long in advance if one does not want to stand outside a closed door – in the literal sense of the word.

A small but steadily growing number of visitors come in search of a "different" Majorca, one that has to be explored on foot and will only reveal itself to those who speak a little Spanish and do not see the high rises on the coast as the incarnation of the spirit of Majorca.

Right: The first monastery was built in 1275, right at the top of the mountain which is 1794 feet (549 m) high

Below: Only the Tramuntana mountains hide the view of the sea as one looks over the Pla from Puig de Cura.

Of one who set out to break hearts and win souls
Ramón Llull

The date of the birth of Majorca's most famous son is shrouded in mystery, as is the place where the writer, missionary, and philosopher met his death. Ramón Llull was born in Palma in 1233 or 1235 as the son of a wealthy noble family from Barcelona. At first nothing suggested his later vocation, and the young Ramón seems to have cared little that he found difficulty in reading and writing and had only a scant knowledge of the Bible. He found an occupation as a page at the court of King Jaume II, and lived for each day as it came, without burdening himself with serious thought.

If Ramón, who was no doubt very good-looking, bent his thoughts to anything at all it was only if he was – by way of exception – unsuccessful in winning the heart of a lady he was courting. For apparently even as a married man with two children he could not stop seducing women from his position as a page at court – until he suddenly cut himself off without compromise from all worldly things.

The legend says that it was a woman who brought about this change. Llull was courting the most beautiful and most sought-after lady in Palma, and he actually followed her, on horseback, right into the church of Santa Eulària where she knelt to pray. The subject of his pursuit was Ambrosia de Castellano, who was married to a Genoese nobleman. After this vehement attack on her virtue she agreed, shaken, to a rendezvous.

But when they met she did not offer him love, only prayers, and this was not what Llull, the heart-breaker, wanted. He continued to press her until in a fit of despair she tore open her bodice and showed him her breast, eaten away with leprosy. "My lover is death!" she cried and apparently Ramón, who until then had been dazzled by appearances, was so deeply shocked that from that moment he abjured all physical pleasures.

However, modern Llull scholars treat this highly dramatic story with some skepticism. They believe a more likely explanation of Llull's transformation was that Jesus Christ appeared to him on the Cross five times in one night, and that he recognized this as a command to place the remainder of his life in the service of his Redeemer. Llull pondered long how to spend his life most meaningfully, and finally he glimpsed the objective he would live for from then on: to convert the Saracens and die a martyr's death for Christ. He would also write a great, comprehensive book to reveal and effectively combat all the errors of the unbelievers.

In the heavenly landscape near Randa Ramón Llull felt closest to his Creator.

After studying in Montpellier and Paris, where he also joined the Order of St. Francis, Llull visited the great pilgrimage centers of the Middle Ages, like Santiago de Compostela and Montserrat. He returned to Majorca purified and elevated, and devoted himself to self-chastisement, religious studies and his particular global view of world religions. But as he saw little prospect of achieving his object of converting the heathen without a knowledge of their language, he intended first to found monasteries in which the monks could learn the oriental languages. There was only one problem. He himself could only speak Catalan, as he had neglected his education for so long. So he donned the robe of penitence and spent nine years studying Arabic. His wife, who cannot have been entirely pleased at this change in her husband, had to employ an agent as he ceased to concern himself with his worldly possessions.

The first language school on Majorca

In the quiet seclusion of the Randa mountain and the monastery of Cura Llull worked out a concept for the implementation of his ideas, and he devoted himself to the study of languages in order to perfect his knowledge. After King Jaume II himself had approved his missionary plans the king also approved his intention of setting up a Franciscan monastery in Miramar on Majorca where 13 monks could learn Arabic. Pope John XXI was also impressed by the idea and in 1276 he gave his approval of the language school. Ramón spent almost ten years studying and writing in Miramar until he had laid down the basis of his life's work, the *Ars Magna*. Here he attempts to prove the irrefutable truth of Christianity through reason – and not simply through faith, setting the main concepts in schematic order to facilitate understanding and make proof more reliable.

In the Apostles' footsteps

When he had finally acquired the necessary knowledge Llull could be held back no longer. He went to Syria, Palestine, Egypt, Ethiopia, and Mauretania. He also worked as professor in Montpellier, where he taught the contents of the *Ars Magna*. He succeeded

Even at the age of 80 Llull had not lost sight of his elevated aims.

in opening a school of oriental languages in Rome; he studied Arab grammar in Paris and at the same time taught philosophy in Miramar. He continued to travel tirelessly, visiting Tunisia, Cyprus, Armenia, Rhodes, and Malta.

Llull has left an almost unbelievable volume of writings, which includes more than 270 treatises and novels, and at least 77 volumes of poetry. Some of his writings were in Arabic, and unfortunately these have not survived; many are in Latin or Catalan.

His thirst for the knowledge he had neglected so shamefully for nearly 30 years and his eager pursuit of scholarship became the driving force of his life and found expression in a broad range of work. Sometimes he buried himself for weeks in the study of philosophy. He vehemently opposed the principle of the "double truth" propounded by the Moorish philosopher Averroës of Cordoba, because he maintains that the truths of reason and faith, that is philosophy and religion, are contradictory. Then Llull suddenly resurfaced and produced a treatise on the philosophy of love, *Llibre d'Amic e amat*, the Book of Friendship and Love.

Or he wrote sermons to convert the heathen. Almost as a sideline he developed a compass that could apparently determine the position of ships as well as forecast storms. He believed that all knowledge and faith must be derived from reason, inventing the universal science *Ars Combinatoria*. This consists of a system of three rings that can be adjusted one against the other. On the first stand nine key words like "eternity", "wisdom", "virtue" and "will". On the second references like "greater", "smaller" or "the same". On the third are questions like "from whence", and "how". Turning the rings produces a large number of new themes over which philosophers may ponder.

In his poetry Llull was the first to use the Catalan folk language for literary work. So he was the founder of the Catalan literary language long before, in 1311, Dante ever conceived the idea of writing his "Divine Comedy" not in Latin but in Italian, so gaining the *Divina Commedia* the reputation of being the first work of world literature in a vernacular tongue.

Llull never lost his desire to travel. Even well into his 50s he was in Naples with Charles II, working out his unique plan for a crusade, which is viewed with some disfavor today. But at that time, shortly after the Moors were driven out of Spain in a campaign in which Llull's father played an active part, the sword and the Cross were regarded as the proven means of driving Islam not only out of Spain but out of Europe altogether.

Many critics therefore see Llull as the exact opposite of a theologian regarding the great world religions as of equal rank and wishing to bring them closer together; they see him as a religious zealot. He speaks of one God, and for him that was certainly only the Christian God. This is why he was filled with missionary zeal to persuade the Muslim heathen to abandon their false faith in Allah. And if he founded a missionary school, as in Miramar, where the monks could learn Arabic, this was only because he was convinced that the people in North Africa could more easily be converted in their native tongue.

So Llull the Franciscan was already a thorn in the flesh of the Dominicans during

The man who traveled so restlessly during his life found his last resting-place in a chapel of the church of Sant Francesc in the heart of Palma.

292

his lifetime. In their hatred of all heathens they regarded the conversion of Jews and Muslims as useless. Hatred, if of a different kind, also finally cost Llull his life. He was stoned by an enraged crowd of religious fanatics in 1315 on a journey to Bejaia in Algeria to preach against Islam and for Christianity. At any rate, so the story goes. For although there is a painting of the scene in the church of San Salvador in Arta it is probably only a pious legend. Other scholars believe that Llull was brought back to Majorca from Genoa at the age of 80 by a merchant and died peacefully. The story that he lived to be 100 and died in Italy in 1333 is probably untrue as well.

Ramón Llull, also known as Raimundus Lullus, has been beatified but not yet pronounced a saint. During the period of the Enlightenment the controversy on Majorca over his canonization led to iconoclastic attacks and street riots between 1749 and

1777. The whole island was divided: the supporters of the Enlightenment wanted to prevent his canonization, and their opponents were then all the more determined to achieve it. This is no longer a bone of contention; Llull is revered like a saint in Catalonia and on Majorca, where this is fueled by growing nationalism. His name day is 29 March, when his supporters make the pilgrimage to his grave in the church of Sant Francesc in Palma's old city, right next to Santa Eulària where he had his illumination, and to his monument, which was set up before the Almudaina Palace. In Lullus University students eagerly studied theology and church law until 1842, although the missionary idea gradually receded into the background.

Llull had a monastery built in Miramar where 13 brethren spent years learning Arabic, while the monk wrote his life's work *Ars Magna*.

A typical Majorcan estate
Albenya

The walls, ground plans, and building stones of Albenya, an estate lying between Randa and Montuïri, can be read like a history book that starts long before the Reconquista. There was an Arab settlement here before the Catalan reconquest in 1229. The Arab word *albenya* means "building", and even the conversion of the main house in the early 19th century did not entirely eliminate the traces of the Moorish ground plan.

The Albenya estate is still one of the largest in the entire Pla, and it has belonged to the Morell family, who are highly respected on Majorca, for generations. Today estates like this are very rarely still farmed, for farming is only worthwhile for small holders and on a self-sufficiency basis. In the 19th century the family could live by selling grain, rye, almonds, and other agricultural products. At that time maybe two dozen maids and farmhands lived and worked here; in summer their number would easily rise to more than 50, for in those days an estate like this was one of the main employers.

But by the end of the 19th century the vine pest *Philoxera* had started to undermine the entire structure of farming on Majorca. With smaller and smaller harvests the farmers were also struggling with rising taxes, wages and maintenance costs. A short time later even unskilled laborers preferred to work in the tourist industry, where they could be at least fairly sure of earning good wages.

Ferran Morell, a pioneer of the treatment of lung diseases

The doctor Ferran Morell is also a member of Albenya's Morell family. For a long time he was director of the Pneumonology Department in the La Vall de Hebron hospital in Barcelona. He was the first in the history of Spain to carry out a successful lung transplant. In the 1980s he discovered a method of treating an asthmatic fever from which the people in Barcelona were suffering. At that time the Condal district witnessed repeated waves of a severe respiratory disease, which caused some fatalities and was a mystery to the medical profession. Then Morell realized that the attacks always occurred when ships loaded with soya were at anchor in Barcelona. While the cargo was being loaded on to lorries the dust got into the air and caused the attacks.

Opposite: The Morell estate has been in the hands of the same family for generations; it is one of the largest in the Pla.

Above: As a child Ferran Morel breathed the country air of Albenya. Later he became a specialist in lung diseases and was the first in Spain to carry out a successful transplant of this organ.

Left: In summer, country houses like that of the Morell family are almost hidden by the rich natural vegetation.

295

Honey is only for the upper classes
Montuïri

Tot el món ès món, manco Montuïri: The whole world is the world, except for Montuïri. The old saying shows how remote this district once was. Today a good road leads to this Pla village, bringing the world to Montuïri in tourist coaches. The visitors admire the elegant filigree houses standing close together, with their family coats of arms above the doorway and inner courts decorated with flowers; then they shop in the new supermarket for pearls. Hardly anyone perceives the social tension hidden beneath the "picturesque" facades and the idyllic surface. But there is real social tension, for unconsciously, in the course of centuries, the traditional rules have become part of the structure of the village. As if they had been poured down the long spine of the hill all the alleys, steps and streets lead up to the symbol of the old order, the village church of Sant Bartomeu; it is as massive as the power of tradition in Montuïri.

The district around Montuïri is full of hermitages and chapels, like so much of the Pla; many stand in such hidden spots, in such close symbiosis with nature and the landscape, that tourists are overwhelmed by their "romanticism". But anyone who listens closely will hear them murmuring – the spirits of history that have withdrawn to their reserves and do not wish to be disturbed by the profane modern world outside.

This feeling of being in an enchanted world, and Montuïri's unworldly motto, are not coincidental. While Sant Joan celebrates the idyll of village life and Villafranca has taken its industriousness to extremes, Montuïri is still rather sleepy and isolated, despite the new road.

Scrape and bow to those above, tread on those beneath you senyors, missatges and laborers

At first the barriers between the great land-owners, the middle class and the working class seemed to be quite insuperable here. As in the Sicilian clans, here also the big families in each class, with their feudal traditions, each had a patriarch who had the right to intervene in every sphere of life. Be it a laborer's hire, schooling for an agent's child, or a peasant's daughter marrying – without him nothing could be done.

But most of the *senyors* lived in distant Palma. An agent, known as the *missatge*,

Even without their sails the five windmills of Montuïri tower imposingly over the town.

craftsmen, farmers, factory workers, mechanics, electricians or taken up various freelance occupations. As late as the middle of the 20th century, the villagers recount, a newly married couple wanted to eat bread with the meat paste *sobrassada*, and honey, on their wedding night. But they did not dare to buy honey, for eating honey was and has remained a privilege of the *senyores*.

This strict division between tradition and the modern world is evident in many places on the island and on many occasions – and some are very painful. Majorca has been thrust into the tourist trade too quickly for full understanding and adjustment to take place. The fashions and consumer habits of the tourists are quickly taken up by young people on Majorca, but so far there has been little integration with the traditions and patterns of thought of the island people.

managed the estate or farm for them. He occupied a middle position between the landowner, the *amo*, whom he had to inform of even the smallest event, and the farm hands. The *missatges* lived in the houses of the *senyors*, like members of the family, and they formed a tribe of their own; but of course they in turn were subject to control.

The simple laborers were the lowest class, employed at most for a week at a time on one estate or another for a starvation wage. "It was always like this, you can't do anything about it, anyone who rebels against it will starve". This simple fact, long recognized, was passed like a prayer wheel from one generation to the next and ensured that the power structure survived.

The system persisted in Montuïri until after the Spanish civil war; why here of all places has never been explained. Only the hesitant beginnings of a middle class, owners of small and middle-sized farms, could make themselves slightly independent, and even this was severely limited. As soon as it was necessary to fix prices for grain or ensure access to public wells, and so water for the fields, they had to bow to the conditions set by the major landowner. Possibly the reason for this adherence to the past is that there is no real "educational culture" here. A few biographies of saints, here and there a legal document, are all the village regarded as

worth recording. No artist, no town chronicler has ever tried to derive inspiration here.

Freedom calls – and puts an end to the old way of country life

In the middle of the 20th century news of a new booming industry even reached Montuïri. For the first time young people who knew nothing but the power and impotence of village life could learn a trade outside the village in tourism, or at least spend the main season away from hearth and home, on the island's sunny beaches, and return in the autumn, their pockets full of their own money.

But those who return from an outside world that has treated them better than their home village will despise their native village from the depths of their hearts, at least initially. And so it was in Montuïri. The young people began to rebel, they despised their local language; they no longer wanted to dance to the old tunes, sing the old songs and they certainly did not want to obey the *senyors*, who had lost touch with the world.

But the past never dies; it is not even past, as William Faulkner remarked. And the same applies to Montuïri. The old classes are still strictly separated, even today, although no one now takes it upon themselves to prescribe this, and although the villagers have long since become shopkeepers,

Quails and partridges
The stars of Son Bascos

In the 1890s the people of Montuïri had an idea that was to prove very profitable. They built up a big quail farm, and now more than 5,000 of the brownish birds are born there every week.

The farm of Son Bascos also has a restaurant, where – naturally – quails are served in every conceivable variant. *Coturnix* are tasty fried, with an onion and tomato sauce, marinated or cooked in a good measure of wine. This makes the unassuming little birds, that are only about eight inches (20 cm) long, into "drunken quails", *guátlleres emborratxades*.

As well as breeding quails the farmers of Son Bascos are engaged in another lucrative business. They breed what are here known as *reclams*: bait birds for partridges. For centu-

Above: Two hands full of feathered profit. In front the quail, *coturnix*, behind a partridge, *perdix*.

Left: Bait bird at work.

ries these beautiful earth-colored birds have been hunted in the rural areas of Majorca. Only male partridges can be used as bait, for they attract other males to fight with them. The females come up to the birds of the other sex peacefully.

To train a bait bird the farmers select a young, adaptable partridge and put it in a cage that is then hung in the farmyard near an experienced bait partridge. This enables the newcomer to learn its song. Moreover, the proximity of the veteran calms the young bird and prevents it from losing its voice from the shock of isolation. A lot of patience is needed to train a bait bird, for generally the bird cannot produce the virtuoso song immediately.

At the end of its singing course the bird is fed every day with a mixture of pre-chewed almonds and egg yolk, to enable it to develop a good resonance and a powerful voice. Some hunters only feed the bird one or two evenings before they go hunting, others regularly.

On the day of the hunt the cage with the bird is hung up in the hunting ground and covered with branches, leaving only a small opening. As soon as an attacker approaches, attracted by the powerful song, he is hit with well aimed buckshot *perdigones*. Thereupon the bait bird sings another aria, known as the "funeral dirge".

The people of Montuïri celebrate the hunt with a big feast of partridges. Then the *Fira de Sa Pergin* is held on the first Sunday in December. This is a fair at which every species of animal connected with hunting is exhibited and sold. And here the bait birds only attract human interest.

Guàtlleres amb figes

Quails with figs

Ingredients
4 quails, ready for cooking
salt and pepper
1 dessertspoon butter
1 bunch of herbs, e.g. thyme, rosemary, oregano and 1–2 bay leaves
2 small onions, finely chopped
1 dessertspoon flour
6–8 figs, peeled
7 fluid oz (200 ml) white wine
1 dessertspoon grated bitter chocolate

Wash the quails, pat them dry, rub in salt and pepper and tie into shape with kitchen twine.

Grease a casserole with butter and lay in the quails. Add the bunch of herbs, the bay leaves and onions and dust the quails with flour. Put into a pre-heated oven at 460°F (240°C) for about 10 minutes until the flour is browned. Turn the quails, add the figs, pour over the white wine and stir in the chocolate. Reduce the oven to 350°F (175°C) and leave the quails in for a further ten minutes. Serve in the dish.

The quail itself seems astonished at the huge number of potential descendants.

299

Bittersweet
Majorca and almonds

The Arabs had been settling comfortably on Majorca for some time before they became painfully aware that they missed the soft, velvety aftertaste left on the tongue by an almond tart after a huge meal.

While the Greeks cultivated the almond tree at a very early period and supplied the Romans with its nuts, the "Mohammedans' tree" was still quite unknown on Majorca. Soon after the conquest of the Balearic Islands the Moors set about changing the situation. They planted the first almond trees in 903, and started their triumphal progress all over the island, where they are now the most numerous of all trees.

Since then, in January and February each year large parts of the plain around Montuïri are transformed into a sea of soft pinkish white. *Prunus dulcis*, the sweet almond, blossoms and flourishes in more than 50 varieties. *Prunus amara* is the name of the bitter variety, whose amygdaline contains one of the most dangerous vegetable poisons, cyanide. But have no fear, before the slightly bitter taste which a delicious dessert usually leaves behind could have fatal consequences you have to eat at least ten bitter almonds unadulterated. No baker would ever use so many in a cake, unless he really had evil intentions with regard to his customers.

The farmers around Montuïri have been growing almonds for centuries, cultivating new trees in the nurseries here. After two years, when a sapling has produced at least a few hundred blossoms and the trunk has reached the necessary size, the branches are lopped and the blossom of the desired variety is grafted on. The trees reach full maturity after about ten to 15 years; 45 hard-working and fruitful years later their glory is over. The tree declines visibly and stands wizened and emaciated between its fertile neighbors.

The almond trees on Majorca are not irrigated, they grow as God created them. At harvest time in late summer the loose nuts are knocked down with sticks, landing on nets spread ready beneath. Finally the kernels are removed from the hard shells

Above: In late summer the loosely attached nuts are knocked down using long sticks.

Opposite: Budding almond trees transform the landscape into a sea of fragrant blossom.

If the almonds do not fall to the ground they are knocked off with sticks.

Then the fallen nuts are carefully gathered up and sorted into baskets.

Small twigs and dried leaves will later provide the sheep with a change in diet.

The people of Majorca use the remnants of the shells on their fires in winter and the unique scent spreads over the entire island.

Finally the almonds have to be removed from another shell.

Then they are peeled, and a soft kernel emerges from the hard shell.

302

ready to make almond biscuits, chocolate, nougat, oil, liqueur and all the many other varieties, right through to the favorite Christmas specialty, *torró*, with its nougat admixture. Children all over the peninsula have been eagerly waiting for this since long before the festive season.

There are many different recipes for *torró*, and it is a popular holiday present. The best kind is *torró fort*; it is hard and consequently difficult to bite, generally shaped like a block of chocolate, with big chunks of almonds in a white mass of egg white and honey. Taken with *café tot-sol* (Spanish espresso) and Majorcan brandy (the Soau brand) it is the peak of delight!

Gató d'ametlless

Almond Cake

A celebration meal on Majorca without this classic dessert would be unthinkable. Often almond cake is also served with almond ice cream. Originally from Valldemossa, this recipe has gradually spread all over the island. It is always worth trying a piece, for there are more recipes for almond cake (all derived from the basic recipe) than varieties of almonds.

Mix the icing sugar with the egg yolks until smooth; add the lemon zest, cinnamon and peeled vanilla. Stir in the ground almonds. Whip the egg whites until stiff, add to the bowl and mix until even. Put in a greased baking tin and bake in a pre-heated oven at 350°F (180°c) for 55–60 minutes. Leave to cool and serve on a lace plate. Sprinkle thick icing sugar on top.

Ingredients
9 oz (250g) icing sugar
8 egg yolks and egg whites, separated
zest of one lemon
1 knife tip of ground cinnamon
1 vanilla pod
9 oz (250g) peeled almonds, finely ground
oil to grease the tin
icing sugar for the top

A crisp delicacy: coated almonds

An international language and a regional dialect
Biniali

Biniali gives the impression that it is not really there – and it is not marked on many maps of Majorca. It is tiny, and lost in the course of time, seeming to dream in the shadow of the Tramuntana mountains waiting for a new chance, a new miracle. Perhaps these are the best conditions for originality to survive, for Biniali's local color has formed at least two remarkable personalities, whose hobby and obsession have immortalized its name. One is the enthusiastic supporter of a regional dialect that was almost forgotten, and the other is the selfless promoter of an international language that almost nobody speaks.

José Maria Jaquotot

At the entrance to Biniali, near the road to Sencelles, stands a house dating from the 14th century. It belonged to José Maria Jaquotot Molina, who lived here until his death in 1995. He was born into a French family at the start of the 20th century, and became one of the pioneers and advocates of the worldwide artificial language Esperanto. Jaquotot was a painstaking observer of his time, and he came to the conclusion that Majorca, with its steadily growing flow of sun-seeking foreigners, offered optimum conditions for the artificial language to spread and be accepted.

Esperanto was developed at the end of the 19th century by the Polish doctor Zamenhof. The idea was to eliminate the communications problems that have been keeping people apart since the fall of the

Before the first washing machines laundry was heavy work. Remote villages like Biniali still do not have running water in every house; water has to be fetched from the well.

Tower of Babel with a language that anyone could learn. Unfortunately, few have been interested in Esperanto, and this project in international understanding has never acquired more than a million supporters.

One of the most committed was José Maria Jaquotot. He was a member of a committee that produced regular publications and writings in the attempt to popularize Esperanto. In 1961 he founded an association, the *Baleara Esperanto Asociacio*, with Miquel Arbona, Gabriel Vida, and Bernat Rabassa. It was to concern itself with the spread of Esperanto in Spain and naturally particularly on the Balearic Islands. In the same year they managed to hold a conference in Palma for Esperanto supporters from all over Spain.

This did nothing to make Biniali less cut off from the world. Like so many villages in the Pla it witnessed a dramatic fall in the number of inhabitants at the start of the 20th century, when places like this did not get a share of the new goodies for a long time, often too long. The peasants had little choice – they either had to emigrate to Central and South America or try their luck in the new tourist trade, a chance that was difficult to assess. Whichever way they decided, they would have to leave the village. Often only the old people remained behind, many humiliatingly dependent on what those who had left could send them. The clocks ticked on but time stood still.

The tourist boom after 1960 laid the foundation for Majorca's immense wealth at the end of the 20th century, but for a long time it worsened the problems of the rural areas. Even now more than 80 percent of the Majorcans work in the tourist centers on the coast and use their native villages at most as a dormitory or weekend refuge.

Only slowly did places like Biniali recover some value, as quiet refuges for freelancers or foreigners, many of whom fell in love with the old, often dilapidated farmhouses and decided to settle here. They have lovingly and faithfully restored the old houses in the traditional Majorcan style, but very few take the trouble to learn the island language, *Mallorquí*. This development would have greatly displeased Don Francesc de Borja Moll, at least in Biniali.

Don Francesc de Borja Moll

Born in 1903 on the neighboring island of Menorca, he became the patron and promoter of his mother tongue, Catalan, a language that is still alive although for a long time it was in danger of dying out.

Catalan had been overshadowed since the 18th century, when King Philip V made Castilian – which is what most people now understand by Spanish – the language of state. The other four languages spoken in Spain were despised from then on; using them was regarded as vulgar, separatist and uneducated. Under Franco it was actually an imprisonable offense to speak Basque, Galician, Catalan or Mallorquí in public. As a result – Franco, after all, remained in power until 1975 – the following generations hardly spoke these languages. It is only thanks to the persistence of people like Don Francesc de Borja Moll that they have

Thanks to people like Don Francesc de Borja Moll Catalan is still a living language although it was suppressed and forbidden.

survived at all. He and others like him organized secret conversation groups, they spoke Catalan at conspiratorial meetings and ensured that their children had special "private tuition".

So Borja Moll became a key figure in Majorcan culture. From 1920 he devoted himself to the language, literature and politics of the Balearic Islands, publishing books in Catalan in his own publishing house. His greatest heritage is a truly mammoth work, a dictionary of the three variants of Catalan: Catalan, Valencian, and Balearic. Borja Moll was able to draw on the preliminary work of Monsignore Antoni M. Alcover, vicar-general of the diocese and collector of Majorcan fairytales, who was born near Manacor in 1862 and died in 1932. Borja Moll worked on his dialect dictionary for 43 years, only a few steps away from the house where José Maria Jaquotot dreamed of a world speaking Esperanto.

In remote Biniali of all places José Maria Jaquotot dreamed of a world speaking Esperanto.

The center of the world
Sineu

Under the bell tower at Sineu, says the legend, lies the axis that prevents the world from slipping. Far below the town four columns support the earth, only unfortunately three of them are broken, and the fourth is groaning under the heavy weight. Is Sineu the center of the earth?

Not exactly. But it is certainly the center of Majorca, geographically and historically, for Sineu was the capital of the Kingdom of Majorca from the start of the 13th to the mid-14th century. And although the little capital's age of glory was only brief, the people of Sineu are still proud of it, and of their very beautiful city.

In fact, it is not even certain that Jaume I, who conquered Majorca and so put an end to 300 years of Moorish rule, ever set his

Above: The axis of the world, says the local legend, lies beneath the belltower at Sineu

Left: The old railway station in Majorca's former capital now invites guests to linger rather than travel.

royal foot in Sineu. The royal residence is the work of his son, Jaume II, who ordered a noble residence to be converted to a palace in 1309 and ensured that the new capital acquired a direct road to Palma. Only 40 years and one Jaume, the third, later, the kingdom had come to an end and Sineu was no longer a capital city. The royal apartments on the top floor of the palace were left to gather dust, the kitchen and servants' quarters fell silent and the wine vats in the cellars stood awaiting their fate, their round bodies empty, not full of the noble liquid.

Only in the late 16th century did Philip II take pity on the town; he gave the palace a

A winged lion is the emblem of the patron saint of the town, St. Mark the Evangelist. It stands guard at the entrance to the main church, which is dedicated to the Mother of God of Angels.

face lift and donated it to the Conceptionist Order of Nuns, who still live in it today observing strict seclusion.

Were giants the first settlers on Majorca?

Very different beings dwelt in Sineu as early as 2000 BC–, they were giants! At any rate, so the people say, for an old document argues that only giants could have built the many *talayots* of huge blocks of stone weighing tons around the city. And the find of a human skeleton nine feet (3 m) long has never been explained, but it has fueled the legend. It lay right behind the church of Sineu, and was discovered in 1718 under a gravestone adorned by a rider with a lance and lettering which neither churchmen nor scholars could decipher.

It is, however, certain that some of those who settled in Sineu were Romans. Remains of Roman dwellings can still be seen and Pliny, the traveler of the Classical world who obligingly recorded everything worth knowing on his travels, mentions a place called "Sinium" on Majorca in the first century AD.

The city chronicles also record that "the crescent moved over Sineu as over the sea, leaving no traces". But 300 years of Arab rule left only the knowledge of how to sow crops and irrigate fields properly – in a society that is ultimately a farming community and produced the lion's share of the grain for the island for centuries, this was a vital heritage.

Guards from Sineu

Admittedly, Palma is the new capital, but Sineu remains unique, if only for one thing it has inherited from its time as the capital in the center of Majorca, the Wednesday market that has filled the narrow alleys around the church for 700 years. It is easy to find, just follow the people carrying bags; in any case, you are bound to hear it.

Set up like a mobile bazaar, every alleyway in the market has something different to offer. Right outside the church fruit and vegetable sellers are trying to convince customers of the value of their wares by offering generous tasters. Anyone who has forgotten to have breakfast will certainly be able to eat his fill here, except those who cannot stomach spicy pickled olives and capers the size of lentils or even of peppers so early in the morning. Better, then, to go into one of the many bars around the market, and take an *ensaïmada* with *cafè amb lliet*, coffee with milk, in a glass, naturally, another relict from the time of the inventors of bazaars.

The people of Sineu are proud of their city's past as the island's capital.

Of course, a visit to a café is an essential on market day. There are plenty to choose from, round the marketplace in Sineu.

Walking sticks of gnarled olive wood and dog collars to match – master and dog can go for a walk together appropriately adorned.

For 700 years sales of farm animals have been a key feature of Sineu market. Here guinea fowl and roosters await customers.

Every conceivable variety of olives, capers, and pickled peppers is on offer by the bucket. Tasting is allowed as an aid to decision-making.

On we go round the next corner, to find a crowd round a stall piled with table cloths and serviettes, night shirts and underpants from thongs to passion killers. Another alley is full of wood carvings and ceramics, where people spend hours sorting through piles of plates to find their favorite pattern, or play with children's puzzles, rattles and mobiles, while housewives suspiciously run their index fingers round the inner walls of a pestle of olive wood. Only one without a crack or rough spot will do, and today there's so much rubbish being made, you have to be terribly careful!

Now it is only a few steps to the heart of Sineu's market and whinnying and mooing, growling and chattering, hee-haws and grunts tell us from afar what is going on here. Our sense of smell does too. Mares with foals wait fearfully, their nostrils flaring, by the fence for release, but it does not come. Pigs hide their button eyes under their flapping ears, chickens and doves are absorbed in an endless dialogue of cackling and cooing from one sales box to the next.

But it is the donkeys that are the best sellers in Sineu, for they may be bad tempered but they can work at 20 months old, and as a farming community the Pla cannot do without these furry beasts of burden. And, hard to believe but true, guinea fowls! Their extreme timidity makes them eagerly sought after as guard fowl, for they will surely announce any intruder by cackling loudly before he has even glimpsed the farm from afar. If they have lost interest in keeping watch, or lost their voice, they will make an excellent Sunday lunch.

Those who do not care for such busy Wednesdays can find a good refuge from the market bustle in one of the cellars in Sineu, a cellar restaurant where he will certainly be offered a tasty bite and something equally good to drink. Any more requests?

The Wednesday
market in Sineu is
like a bazaar. The
avenues of stalls are
arranged in groups
of goods, and they
stretch right round
the main church.

A kingdom in the center of the world
Majorca 1276–1349

In 1997 the Kingdom of Spain had every reason to celebrate: in May King Juan Carlos had announced the engagement of his younger daughter, the Infanta Cristina, to the Basque professional handball player Iñaki Urdangarín. For months before the wedding in October nearly all Spain had almost daily occasion to celebrate the young couple's happiness. Nearly all Spain, almost daily. Because then the bomb went off. One fine summer day the King announced that he had invested the couple with the title of Duke and Duchess of Majorca.

The people of Majorca were in uproar. Whoever had heard of dukes of Majorca? There had been kings on the island; Majorca

had once been a kingdom, not a mere duchy, of which there are thousands, all over the place! The explosive announcement was quickly stated to be a hasty decision, an error in communication, which was possibly no less embarrassing but understandable. It was corrected. Cristina of Borbón and Greece and Iñaki Urdangarín were to be Duke and Duchess of Palma.

Majorca calmed down again. The storm faded as quickly as it had arisen, dropping to the usual pleasant sea breeze. Of course the royal family would never have thought of degrading a former kingdom – and that of Majorca, of all places! – to a duchy.

For it was true: Majorca has indeed been an independent kingdom. Perhaps only for 73 years, and 700 years ago, but even so! It is not the years that count in Majorca's self-esteem but the importance, the fame, and economic power this brought.

The conquest of the city of Palma is shown here on a medieval fresco; it took three months.

Spain, a patchwork quilt

1228: Spain as a state had not even begun to exist. In the 13th century the Iberian peninsula consisted of nearly a dozen different independent territories; only Portugal already had its present geographical and political borders. The central and northern thirds of the peninsula had been reconquered by the Christians from the Moors, in a campaign that was to last nearly 800 years and has gone down in Spanish history as the Reconquista. A number of kingdoms were still fighting parallel to each other against the Moors: León, Castile, Navarra, Aragón, and Valencia.

The Moors had been on the mainland since 711, and they still ruled the south, which they had divided into several emirates.

Their domain stretched from Badajoz in the west across Jaén and Murcia to the border to Valencia in the east; from 798 they had attempted to gain possession of the Balearic Islands, succeeding intermittently and completely from 902; *Medina Mayurka*, now Palma, was the capital and the viceroy of the Caliph of Córdoba was the supreme ruler.

A rich three-culture society

In domestic politics the island enjoyed peaceful coexistence between Christians, Jews, and Muslims. The Moors had introduced such successful irrigation and farming systems that the island was virtually independent because the people were self-sufficient. A well-organized administration, in which Jews and Muslims worked hand in hand, and a skillful foreign trade policy kept Majorca wealthy; it was a land full of magnificent palaces, bath houses, mosques, and libraries.

So it is understandable that the Catalan neighbors cast very envious glances at an island in so strategic a position. They were also full of hatred, for all the Majorcan emirs had a common hobby: piracy. Anything on the Mediterranean that could be taken was plundered by the sea pirates. Counter attacks by Christian pirates were always successfully warded off by the Majorcan Moors; even the Catalan Count Ramon Berenguer had to withdraw after besieging the island for more than a year. But he went on fighting with the pen, writing an account of his adventures off the coast of Majorca in a heroic epic, the *Liber Maiolichinus*. His work touched a nerve with the Catalan nobility – the desire for revenge, the desire to conquer. On the pretext of wishing to liberate their Christian brethren on Majorca from the Moorish yoke they beat the drum to summon followers to the attack and were heard.

143 ships and the plague head for Majorca

Their young king Jaume I, who was just 20, had good reason to extend his kingdom. Majorca

Until Palma fell to the Christian conquerors the king and his men had to make do with field tents. This fresco in the Palace of Berenguer de Aguilar in Barcelona dates from around 1280 and it shows King Jaume I before his tent outside the walls of the city.

was a rich prize; it would not only unite and enrich the eternally quarreling Catalan nobility, it would also free the king of their intrigues. The Church gave him the perfect alibi with its desire to drive out the unbelievers. On Christmas Eve 1228 the conquest of Majorca was decided in Barcelona, and on 1 September 1229 20,000 men embarked on 143 ships and set sail eastward.

A severe storm nearly put an end to the whole expedition, but Jaume made a vow to lessen St. Peter's anger. If his expedition was successful, he said, he would immediately start building a cathedral on Majorca. St. Peter acceded, and the soldier Riudemeya thrust the royal standard into the ground on the beach at Santa Ponca; a cross still stands there to mark the spot.

The conquest of Palma took nearly four months and it was not until New Year's Eve 1229 that the Christians succeeded in breaking through the Moors' defenses. The *wâlî* Abu Yahia said: "It is the will of Allah" and surren-

Above: Jaume I was crowned King of Aragón, Castile, Montpellier, Perpignan and Roussillon at the age of five; he was just 20 when he conquered Majorca.

Below: The map shows the political divisions in the Mediterranean after the division of the kingdom by Jaume I.

dered. The ensuing street battles and plundering transformed Palma into a blood bath, and as a result the deathly hand of the plague touched the island for the first time.

The last bastion to fall was the impregnable fortress of Alaró. Regarding the situation as hopeless the governor surrendered without a fight, to the horror of his followers. The last rebels tried to hide in the caves of Drac but the Christians smoked them out by lighting fires, and by 1232 the whole of Majorca was in their hands.

Crowned king at five, at 21 the conqueror of Majorca: Jaume I

Jaume I, King of Aragón, Castile, Montpellier, Perpignan, Roussillon, and Provence now also ruled the Balearic Islands. In keeping with his vow, he had the large mosque demolished and started work on the promised cathedral. He also divided his island among his faithful combatants and the Church, declaring around half of it his personal possession.

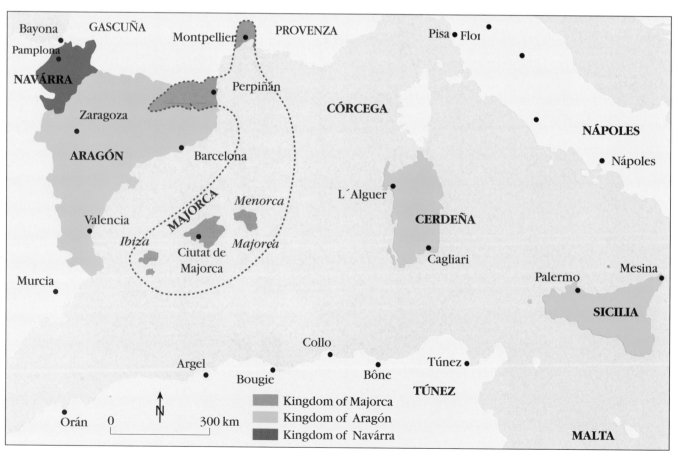

Many of his men left Majorca after a short time, selling their land in small lots to local farmers. Jaume I offered privileges and subsidies in this latest addition to his realm and immigrants came to Majorca from Italy, Roussillon, Provence, Aragón and Catalonia; the island people forgot Arabic and spoke Catalan, with the southern French accent that is still characteristic today.

The child king is beneficent and Majorca booms

Jaume I was crowned king at the age of five; at the age of 13 he was married to Eleonore, daughter of King Alphonse VII of Castile. Despite his youth he was well versed in matters of state. Once he had possession of Majorca he tried to make peace with the Moors who had remained, knowing that without their industry and profound knowledge of the island he would not get far. The Jews were also expert businessmen and essential if the new Majorca was to prosper.

Above: The beginning of the end of independence: Jaume I orders his kingdom to be divided into two after his death in 1276. His eldest son Pere becomes King of Aragòn and Catalonia, his younger son Jaume is to rule over the Balearic Islands, Roussillon and Montpellier. The sons signed this document to seal the agreement.

Below: Only under Jaume II did Majorca become an independent kingdom.

Soon after the conquest, therefore, Majorca experienced a new upswing. Piracy was rooted out for a time, and shipbuilding, weaponry, and weaving supplied the entire Mediterranean with their eagerly sought products. The new cathedral was nearly finished, the castle of Bellver would shortly be started; Majorca was enjoying a boom it would not see again until the middle of the 20th century.

A fateful testament

But then Jaume I made a mistake that would cost Majorca its freedom. He decreed that his kingdom should be divided on his death: his eldest son Pere (Pedro) was crowned King of Aragón and Catalonia, and the younger, Jaume, became King Jaume II, the first king of independent Majorca. Jaume II completed the castle of Bellver, he founded Manacor, Petra, Llucmajor, and Felanitx and made Sineu his royal residence. His sickly son Sanç I (Sancho I) ruled for only 13

313

The last king of
Majorca, Jaume
III, came to the
throne in 1324.
The kingdom
would survive for
another 25 years,
until the battle of
Llucmajor, when
it lost its
independence.

years, plagued with asthma and childless, but Majorca's prosperity continued as if of its own volition.

In 1324 Sanç's nephew came to the throne as Jaume III, but in nearby Catalonia Pere II, grandson of the "cheated" Pere I, had not forgotten the historic humiliation. In a blitz attack he took Majorca and drove Jaume III out to Roussillon. Jaume III tried to regain his kingdom in 1349, but he was not successful. He lost his life at the battle of Llucmajor and Majorca lost its independence.

Less than 150 years later Ferdinand II of Aragón and Isabella I of Castile married on the mainland, so laying the foundation for the central Spanish state. Majorca was now part

Below: Abu Yahia, the Governor of Majorca, hands over the capital to Jaume I. The relief hangs in the Carrer de l'Estudi General in Palma.

Top: This coat of arms hangs in the royal palace in Sineu, recalling the 73 years when Majorca was an independent kingdom.

of the kingdom of Aragón; it became part of Spain, and the discovery of America thrust the island, that had once been the navel of the world, onto the sidelines of history.

A gift of the Carthaginians
Capers

In the fields around the village of Llubí market gardening has flourished for thousands of years. No wonder, for the soil is fertile and the nearby Serra de Tramuntana shelters the plants from the wind. The Moors taught the people of Llubí highly inventive irrigation, terracing and conservation techniques as early as the first millennium, and so the narrow alleys in the village, with their little low stone houses, have always been a market for wine and herbs, fruit and vegetables; above all, the queen of Llubí's products, capers.

Here, too, the people of Majorca profited from the art of the Moors: by the Reconquista the farmers in Llubí had perfectly acquired the irrigation techniques used by the Arabs and been farming fruit, vegetables, grain, herbs and wine since early times. But they paid particular attention to the cultivation of

Below: Not a drink – after three months in their bottle the capers are a sharp, refreshing addition to a meal, or simply a *tapa* as a quick snack.

Right: The beautiful caper flowers are sadly only a waste product of the difficult harvest.

the little, dark green plant with its wonderful pink blossoms: the caper bush.

The *taperera*, which has given Llubí such a big reputation, probably came to the island in pre-Christian times, brought by the Carthaginians. But it is not until 1789 that capers are first recorded as a major source of income for Llubí. Nearly another two hundred years were to pass before a proper industry was able to establish itself here.

For it was only in 1977 that Joan Rosselló set up a factory, initially mainly to bottle olives, but it soon began to specialize on capers. Finally, in 1985, 63 small producers in Llubí formed the *Sociedad Agrícola Transformadora Llubinera*, with the aim of providing a better organization for the farmers on the island, and above all joint marketing. Today Llubí, with some other villages like Campos, is the main producer of capers on the island.

Capers grow on a bush whose roots can go down several yards. The *taperera* is a very hardy plant which will remain dark green

when other plants have long given up the struggle against the pitiless summer sun. The capers are harvested just before the buds open. As they are very small picking them is relatively difficult and time-consuming. Moreover, the buds are delicate and have to be handled with great care if they are to withstand being picked unharmed. That is particularly the case with young, small capers, and these are the most highly regarded – and of course the most expensive.

The capers are still picked by hand today. The work is made more difficult because the bush protects the fruit-bearing stem with thorns. The buds have to be pulled off with a quick, sure movement of the hand, and the pickers wear gloves and arm shields to protect them from the sharp thorns.

Later the superfluous parts of the plant and foreign bodies that have become mixed with the harvest while it was being picked or during the transport are carefully removed. Then the capers are soaked in vats for three months; finally the stalks are removed and the capers are sorted into sizes. They are put into glass bottles and mild wine vinegar is poured over them; as *envinagrat* they are then ready for sale and consumption.

The people of Majorca generally eat capers direct from the glass with *pa amb oli*, the famous bread with olive oil and tomatoes. But the main role of capers in their simple cuisine is in a recipe called *llengua amb táperes*, calf or pork tongue with capers, which give the dish and its sauce the necessary and special sharp taste.

Capers are an essential ingredient in a perfect dish of tongue, not only for the people of Majorca. But they enjoy the privilege of being able to use the noble fruit straight from the harvest.

Llengua amb táperes

Tongue with capers (serves 4–6)

The smaller the capers the more valuable they are; however, a few *taperons*, extremely large capers, are added to every dish, because they have a particularly strong taste. They can be the size of a thumbnail and have to be quartered. Tongue or skate with capers are the classical dishes, and those who appreciate the aroma of these little flower buds will be happy on Majorca – the island's capers are among the tastiest in the world.

Ingredients
1 calf's tongue, 2¼–3¼ lb (1–1.3 kg)
salt
pork lard
3 onions, peeled and diced
2 tomatoes, skinned, seeds removed, diced
4 leaves of sorrel, thinly sliced
2 leaves of stick celery, finely chopped
1 bay leaf
4 stalks of flat-leaf parsley, finely chopped
2¼ oz (60 g) capers
4 large capers (*taperons*)
coarse milled black pepper
cinnamon

Clean the tongue and wash it carefully. Lay it in a cooking pot, add salt and cover with cold water. Bring to the boil and cook on a medium heat for about 45 minutes. Remove the tongue, run under cold tap and remove skin. Put the stock aside.

In a *greixonera*, a traditional Majorcan clay pot, heat the lard, fry the tongue briefly with the onions and the tomatoes, then add the sorrel, celery leaves, bay leaf, black pepper and parsley and pour on part of the stock. Stew for half an hour on a medium heat. Remove the tongue, pass the sauce through a sieve or cream with an electric mixer. Add the capers and *taperons*, and a touch of cinnamon to taste. Slice up the tongue and pour the caper sauce over it.

Dark green caper bushes cover the fields when other plants have long since dried.

Symbol of transience: the flowers open in the morning and have fallen by midday.

Timing is all-important: the buds have to be harvested just before they open.

A sure swift movement of the hand is needed to pick the buds.

The small capers are the most expensive, because particular care is needed to gather them.

After the buds have been picked the superfluous leaves and stalks and other foreign bodies are carefully removed.

Red cock finds grain of rice
Sa Pobla

The foreigner surprised the influential gentlemen of the Friends of Majorca Business Association (Societat Majorquina Econòmica D'Amics del Pais) that had been founded to encourage growth in the Majorcan economy. Alexandre de Cauterac was a Frenchman, and he came with a proposal that seemed incredible: 2,500 acres (1,000 hectares) of the Albufera swamp, which altogether covered 6,450 acres (2,580 hectares), should be drained and vegetables, and above all rice, grown on half the regained land. Until then rice had played virtually no part in farming on Majorca.

The Friends were skeptical. They could hardly have imagined that today Majorcans would mainly associate Sa Pobla with rice, and rice of excellent quality. They were afraid that the underground springs that fed the

lagoon and almost the entire Pla with water would dry up. Moreover, the Napoleonic wars had taken almost all the young men away from the farms to the battlefields, and De Cauterac was French. So at that time he was an enemy; probably he was not only unwelcome on Majorca, like so many of his compatriots he would have been driven out.

That was in 1799, and that put an end to the dream of growing rice for a time. Subsequently a few farmers did try to grow rice in the Albufera, but the *arossaires*, as they were known, lived in wretched poverty; those that did not starve died of the malaria that was spreading far too rapidly in the marshy districts. This miserable state of affairs only improved when the farmers discovered at what time of day the anopheles mosquito that infects people with marsh fever is active, and then when quinine was discovered and proved to be the first effective preventive and cure.

Thankfully, for the Albufera wetlands are extremely fertile. The climate and

On Sundays Sa Pobla's marketplace is full of the scents and colors of the hinterland farms.

farming conditions are so favorable that the delicate, thin-skinned new potatoes that are so popular in the British Isles can be grown three times a year. The marshland also offers ideal conditions for rice farming. It is astonishing that this idea, which seems so self-evident, never occurred to the Moors, who were otherwise so skillful at farming, for with their efficiency they would certainly have overcome the obstacles that held up the rice project for so many centuries.

Rice growing on Majorca

For it was only after 1901 that intensive efforts were made to grow rice on Majorca, and then the project was too ambitious. It was believed that the natural sources of water in the region and the fertility of the soil could be exploited to achieve a yield per acre that was greater than that in the Levante region of Spain and the Ebro delta. It did not prove possible. The transport costs to the mainland were high, and marketing, particularly on the mainland, proved too difficult in competition with the well established products of Valencia and Murcia. In 1908 the *Agrícola Industria Balear* once more ceased producing rice.

But clearly Majorca is not like other places. The demise of the *Agrícola Industria Balear* seems to have been just the spark the "rice project" needed to get going. The owner of the land divided the rice fields up into smaller lots and sold these to the people of Sa Pobla and Mura. They in turn split up the lagoon, repaired the irrigation plant, cleaned the channels and actually created the job of "irrigator". Since then this region has produced rice in modest quantities but of very high quality.

Above: Equipment for sports fans: riders, bottle throwers, and armchair footballers will find their designer ware at the market.

Below: Quality control: You can finger, sniff, and taste on a visit to Sa Pobla's market.

A natural paradise in the north
S'Albufera

Today Albufera is a nature reserve. It covers 6,000 acres (2,400 hectares) and is still the largest wetland on the Balearic Islands; but now the area is only around one third of the size recorded by the Roman natural historian Pliny, who came here in the 1st century AD. He described red cocks and night herons being sent to Rome as delicacies.

Now that the economic possibilities of the district have been exploited, the island government is operating an exemplary nature reserve and information center. Visitors are taken on guided walks and hikes, where they have the opportunity to observe flamingos and little egrets, red cocks, black vultures and the Albufera's rare species of toads at first hand.

The products of the Albufera also figure largely in the regional cuisine. *Espinagada*, for example, is a pizza-like pie made with the tasty *anguila*, the freshwater eels found in the Albufera, and spiced with red paprika from Sa Pobla. The use of the very hot red peppers seems to derive from the time when the waters of the lagoon were still full of marsh fever and the people of the region sought to protect themselves with the disinfectant effect of the red peppers.

Around 200 species of birds use the nature reserve of S'Albufera as their permanent residence, or as an interim stage on their migratory journeys.

The fire of abstinence
The Sant Antoni Festa

Dimly lit by the flickering light of the great fire, the devils push back the long-bearded man; he can hardly resist them and can only defend himself by striking out with the Cross. Fearful, the terrifying figures draw back, but immediately launch another attack, pressing in upon their victim again and bringing him down. Again he succeeds in frightening them off with the sign of the Cross. On 16 January, the day before the feast of St. Anthony, *foguerons*, great bonfires, are lit for the first time in the new year. Masked men dance in their light, and figures of devils are burned to demonstrate victory over evil. Like the *Cossiers* dances the theme here is also about temptation and salvation, seduction and virtue. The temptation of St.. Anthony and the dangers to the spirit through the flesh are enacted, and as the ritual is performed all involved are symbolically victorious. The performance is repeated until well into the morning hours to the accompaniment of trenchant remarks.

Many legends have grown up around St. Anthony. He is said to be the patron saint of animals, especially pigs; he helps to heal the sick and can even cure an addiction to gambling. Hence the saying: "the first fire burns on St. Anthony's day and gambling ceases to hold its sway." All the legends around St.. Anthony Abad are closely connected with fire as protection against vice and temptation. The saint was born in Egypt in 251 AD and spent most of his life in the Libyan desert, praying and fasting. He is regarded as the first Christian monk, and as is seemly for such a figure was visited several times in his desert hermitage by the devil in the figure of a woman, attempting to lead him into temptation. To protect himself he lit a fire and walked over the glowing embers – pain being a weapon against lust.

Hence the custom of lighting huge bonfires in the belief that this would heal what was known as the "itching disease", ergotism, that cost the lives of many Majorcans in the 10th and 11th centuries. From then on the disease was

Playing to banish vice and sickness is hard work for the village band.

known as "St.. Anthony's Fire"; it came from a poisonous fungus that attacked rye. In the final stages the suffers had black evil-smelling and dying patches on their skin, particularly their fingers and toes, that looked like burns; they also suffered muscle cramp and mental confusion. As no cure was known the Majorcans remembered the early pictures of St.. Anthony walking over a fire, and they tried to give the devil a dose of his own medicine by lighting bonfires.

St.. Anthony's reputation as the patron saint of animals derives from his gentleness towards animals, which is evident in an almost "ecological" legend. A sow had given birth to a little sickly piglet that could hardly stand. St.. Anthony pitied the poor creature and blessed it, upon which it suddenly recovered and was able to walk. The piglet was so grateful that it followed the saint from then on. Traditionally – and with the logic of old rituals that seems so strange to us today – a pig is sacrificed to St.. Anthony on

The villagers make merry till dawn dressed as fabulous creatures that spit fire and shout pointed remarks.

The glowing fires drive out the wicked devils; then victory over the powers of darkness is celebrated with a glittering fireworks display.

17 January. Generally it has been fed so well that it can hardly walk to the slaughterhouse by itself.

The custom of the *pi de Sant Antoni*, the greasy pole, is even older. A pole is set up and well soaped; then a cock is tied to the top. Young men have to try and climb the greasy pole and get the cock; of course they keep sliding down again amid general laughter from the watching crowd.

Neighbors' Day

In the early morning hours of 17 January the bonfires on the streets of Sa Pobla have burned low and are only glimmering. The villagers, who have spent the entire night dressed as demons launching repeated fierce attacks on the saint, can rest for a few hours, while the saint and his supporters can be sure that sickness, vice and temptation have been banished from the village until next January.

But when they wake up again the next item on the program starts. The house has to be made spick and span, the doors opened invitingly wide and preparations made for a huge midday meal. For many visitors can be expected today, and there has to be enough of the Majorcan eel pie, *espinagada*, made especially for this event, for all the friends and acquaintances who will call.

Above: At harvest time the farmers help each other. Here they are gathering strawberries.

Below: In earlier years the hot red peppers were thought to protect from food poisoning.

Espinagada

Pie with vegetables and freshwater eel
(6–8 servings)

Ingredients for the pastry
³/₄ oz (20g) yeast
luke-warm water
1 pinch of sugar
1lb 2 oz (500 g) plain flour
7 fluid oz (200 ml) olive oil
salt

Filling
1lb 12oz (800 g) fresh eel
4 cloves of garlic, thinly sliced
1 bunch of flat-leafed parsley, chopped
pepper, salt, paprika powder and the zest of one lemon
7 fluid oz (200 ml) olive oil
10¹/₂ oz (300 g) freshly shelled peas
7 oz (200 g) fresh spinach, stalks removed and cut into medium-sized pieces
3 spring onions, diced
1 hot pepper cut in thin rings

The red peppers are dried and truly light the fire of St.. Anthony on the tongue.

It is traditional to eat *Espinagada* on the feast of St. Anthony, which is celebrated on 17 January in La Puebla (Sa Pobla) and other villages and towns. The people hold "open house" and all their friends, and strangers, too, are invited to try a piece of the pie and enjoy a glass of wine.

Huge bonfires are lit on the streets to warm the people as they celebrate the saint on this cold, damp day. They gather round the fire and listen to the singers, who sing pointed and impudent ditties accompanied by the *ximbomba*, an old musical instrument. The air is full of smoke and the village glitters from afar with the flames of the many bonfires. This and the singular spicy taste of the *espinagada*, burning on the tongue, are the lasting memories of the feast of St. Anthony.

The pastry

On principle any dough made mainly of white flour can be used; add approximately 7 fluid oz (200 ml) of olive oil for every pound of flour.

First dissolve the yeast in a little warm water, add 1 pinch of sugar and 1 dessert-spoon of flour and allow to rise beside a well heated oven. Put the flour on a board, make a well in the center, add the risen yeast, olive oil (hand warm) and water with a pinch of salt and knead until a smooth dough is made. Allow this to stand under a cloth in a warm place until twice its size.

The fresh eels should be cleaned, washed, the bones removed and cut in equal large pieces, if possible the day before, but certainly a few hours before they are needed. Marinate with the garlic, parsley, lemon juice, pepper, paprika powder, and olive oil and put to one side.

Roll out the dough evenly and lay it on a well oiled rectangular baking sheet so that the edges protrude. Prick the dough on the sheet with a fork. Boil the peas for about 5 minutes in a little water and then drain. Mix with the pieces of spinach and spring onion and add salt and pepper. Then fry gently with the rings of pepper in the olive oil. Spread all the filling evenly over the dough, pour over the marinated eel and bake until golden brown in a preheated oven for 35–40 minutes.

Espinagada is also popular as a covered pie; in this case make double the quantity of dough and bake for 15 minutes longer.

The stronghold on the hill
Alcúdia

First let us clear up some rather confusing facts: Alcúdiastands where the Romans founded their first town on Majorca in 123 BC. They called it the "stronghold", as if to encourage it on its way through history. But the town that now bears the name Alcúdia is the place the Romans called "Pollentia"; it is the oldest town on Majorca that has been inhabited throughout history. The little town of Pollença, only six and a quarter miles (10 km) further inland, dug the old Roman name out of the dust of history at some time and raised it to new if different heights.

The Vandals are to blame for this confusion. When they invaded Majorca in the fifth century they put an end to the *Pax Romana* and burned Pollentia to the ground. The Roman town was depopulated over-

Above: The town of Pollentia was founded in 123 BC and it was the first Roman town on Majorca. Its particular importance for the Romans was due to its geographical position in relation to Rome to the east, while Palma only became more important later, when the Romans were more oriented towards Spain.

Left: The Roman amphitheater at Pollentia, now Alcúdia, could seat 2,000 spectators and affords a fine view of the nearby bay.

night and it was never resettled. Those who survived moved further inland and founded Pollença. Four hundred years later the Moors built a new town on the hill beside the Roman ruins. The Arab word for hill is *al-kudia*, and the town is now called Alcúdia. The inhabitants used the old Pollentia as a supermarket for stones, but not all were suitable for their purposes.

Happily, for this preserved Roman remains for centuries that elsewhere would have simply been buried under new buildings.

Julius Caesar's tailor

Not all the Roman remains in Alcúdia are accessible; many are on private land, in the garden as an extra, so to speak. But Alcúdia has the most peaceful and secluded Roman theater, a perfect structure dreaming on a natural hill and seating 2,000 on simple rows of stone seats. As with many other Classical theaters, the landscape is part of the scenery; it is a grandiose view right across to the bay of Port d'Alcúdia, over the remains of town houses, public wells, sewage channels and whole streets of houses. Together with the Archeological Museum they give an idea of what a fine, bustling town Pollentia was in Roman times.

Majorca was strategically important; above all, Rome needed to subdue the Majorcan pirates who were ravaging the western Mediterranean, daring to attack not only Roman trade ships but warships as well. So in 123 BC the Senate sent the Proconsul Quintus Caecilius Metellus with a big fleet to the island to rid the region of the pirates. He was successful; indeed, the Romans do not appear to have had to fight very hard to gain a foothold on the land. Despite the feared Balearic slings – actually a tautology, for the Balearic Islands are named after the *baliarides*, slings – Rome easily overcame the slight resistance and quickly occupied the entire island. Metellus was allowed to call himself "Balearicus" from then on; he established Palma quickly in 122 BC, settled 3,000 veterans and colonists on Majorca and died in 115 BC.

Towns like Pollentia rapidly attracted Romans who were tired of the big city in their motherland, and within a short time the town began to grow and flourish.

Weavers and tailors in particular settled here, and they transformed the new town into a center of avant-garde fashion. Anyone who wanted to make an impression in Rome had to have his toga, clothes and cloaks make in Pollentia. According to historians, even Julius Caesar insisted on a *latixclavia*, a robe from Majorca.

Work on the city walls at Alcúdia was started by Jaume I in 1300; in 1660 Philip IV extended them and added a second ring of fortifications.

Outwardly impregnable, inside full of art treasures

The Alcúdia of the Moors was not allowed to leave much of the town's second great age to posterity; the Christian conquerors were too thorough in their campaign of destruction in the 13th and 14th centuries. However, a *sinia* has survived in Alcúdia outside the gates of the town in the west, that is, a Moorish waterhole operated by donkeys. Immediately behind it rise the monumental fortifications around the core of the old city. They were started by Jaume I in 1300, but it was mainly Philip IV around 1660 who extended them, strengthening them and adding a second ring of walls. The city wall is wonderfully preserved, and it includes a church to ward off invading hordes with the thrust of prayer, the church of Sant Jaume.

Inside this stone safety cordon with its guard of palms the visitor to Alcúdia can walk through art history – from a Bronze

Age grave just inside the wall, through the late Romanesque church of St.. Anne with its decorative wooden ceiling to the fine Renaissance town hall. The town also has sunny squares and quiet, half-hidden alleys, where a breath of history may well be heard and felt, if a car is not honking its way through at that moment.

How strategically important Alcúdia once was is evident from the peninsula that pushes into the sea behind the town. It is called La Victòria – those who conquered here had a decisive part of the island in their hands, and from the Talàia d'Alcúdia, a mountain 1456 feet (444 m) high on the peninsula, they had a natural look-out as far as Menorca.

Today the road leading up to the top is one on which even the car's engine will stutter a little, but the effort is worthwhile. It is also worthwhile to pay a visit to the Chapel of the Mother of God of Victory; she

Fire, water, wind and earth make the S'Albufera in the hinterland of Alcúdia a natural theater.

effectively resisted the attempts of Islamic pirates to capture her and miraculously always returned, preferring her chapel 459 feet (140 m) above the sea.

Exactly where the Romans and the Vandals came ashore to found Alcúdia or to pillage is not recorded, but it could have been where the present harbor and port now stand. Instead of Roman galleys, yachts and fishing boats bob gently side by side, and instead of elegant Roman togas from Pollentia Bermuda shorts, beach robes and straw hats fill the scene. For this is where Majorca's best sandy beaches start; they edge a bay that curves gently under the sun for more than 12 miles (20 km) down to Cap Ferrutx. Hardly anywhere else on the island does the morning light seem as magical as here, when it gently wakes the Albufera marshes in the hinterland and bathes the beach in a diffuse, red light.

You can practice every kind of water sports here, and fitness fans can cycle to Pollença, Cala San Vicent or along a scenic mountain road to the legendary Cap de Formentor – past the hotel of the same name on its magnificent site by the beach; it has witnessed grandiose events and welcomed many illustrious guests.

Right: Where the Romans once landed, yachts sway gently in Port d'Alcúdia

Below: The bay of Alcúdia attracts sun-seekers and water rats to its beach, which stretches for miles.

A battle against flies and bulls
Muro

In the 13th century Muro was a ghost town at times – the bubonic plague and marsh fever had completely depopulated it. But that was the only such period, and since then the people of this little town have lived up to its name, which means "fortification wall" – the evocation of strength, toughness and resistance.

Life here has always been dangerous. The nearby Albufera swamps with their brackish water and malaria mosquitoes brought sickness, disease and death to Muro for centuries. Anyone who could escape fled to drier and less dangerous areas.

But this always entailed another risk, namely to die of hunger, for after all, to flee was to abandon one's land, and the stretch between Muro and Sa Pobla has particularly fertile, deep black rich soil. Torn between the fertility of the soil and the deadly diseases of the region the people always came back to Muro.

To survive they needed to be well organized. After the expulsion of the Moors, who had introduced and refined crop farming, and the resettlement of the district in the

Above: Two women enjoy a moment of peace and a chat by the door.

Right: The palms cast long shadows onto the main church at Muro; it was built in the 13th century and is dedicated to St. John the Baptist.

334

late 13th century, guilds grew up in Muro, as carpenters, stone masons, smiths, bakers and tailors formed organizations to secure their incomes and to maintain sales outlets and training facilities. The main walls of the imposing church of Sant Joan Babtista also date from this time – with the dangerous environment in which they lived the people had a particular need of divine protection.

When even the traditional grain crops could no longer feed the growing population the farmers of Muro invented the system of *amitger*, a kind of cooperative in which part of the population provided material, livestock or land while the other performed the work. The yield was shared. Then when it also proved possible to drain some of the deadly marshes Muro's inhabitants acquired the reputation of being extremely industrious with a talent for organization. They are also reputed to be not exactly masters at

diplomacy. Their ethnic background may offer some explanation of this.

For Muro was already inhabited about 2500 BC; caves that were used as dwellings in the pre-Talaiotic age have survived. The ensuing Talaiot culture itself has left its typical watchtowers, the remains of which surround the town as they did more than 3,500 years ago. Coins and burial places have also been found that prove that the Romans established a settlement here, and an Ethnographic Museum in Muro proudly displays these testimonies to its history.

Left: The people of Muro formed guilds and cooperatives in the Middle Ages.

Below: What is good for man cannot be bad for sheep; they too receive a blessing.

Bull-fighting in the quarry
The Arena at Muro

At various places around Muro a very special stone, Marès, is to be found. This is a lime sandstone that was formed in the Quaternary period from compressed layers of sand. It is a light shimmering stone in warm yellow tones. Often found near the coast, it is excavated in open cast mines. Where the stone

Top: A round stone quarry was excavated especially for the bull ring in Muro and the stone was "recycled". However, the stone excavated was not enough to build the entire arena and some had to be purchased from neighboring quarries for some of the ranks of seats and stalls.

Opposite: A bull has forced the horse and rider with the lance up against the wooden fence and the situation is dangerous. The matador in the gold-braided costume hastens to his aid. The spectators, who are judge and jury in a bull fight, are protesting loudly and getting ready to shout free advice.

has been removed a hollow quarry remains and these were often used in the past to house cattle or even as a natural conservatory, for the hollows are sheltered from the wind and enjoy their own micro-climate.

But the enterprising people of Muro thought of another way of making use of an old quarry – a bull ring. As few of the quarries were dug out with this recycling plan in mind, finally, at the beginning of the 20th century, a new quarry had to be dug in the shape of an arena before the project could be realized.

A *Plaça de Bous* actually consists of a whole range of subsidiary buildings as well as the actual arena, including the stalls for the bulls, a saddling enclosure for horses, a chapel and of course the ranks of seats for the spectators. In Muro the architects of the Plaça Monumental expected to use the Marès stone that had been removed to build up the tiers of seats, while the stalls and lower ranks of seats would be cut directly out

of the rock. Stones that were not used here would be sold to cover the building and labor costs.

Unfortunately the calculation did not work out, for the stone that was removed was of lesser quality and not suitable to build all the ranks of seats. Better quality stone had to be purchased, and this enormously increased the building costs. But the trouble was worthwhile. The arena at Muro quickly became famous throughout Spain for its exceptional beauty and its position, and matadors of rank and reputation regarded it as an honor to appear here. All the stars of the 20th century, from Antonio Ordonez through El Cordobés to Espartaco and Enrique Ponce have adorned the posters of the Plaça Monumental and its light sand with their presence.

Majorcan dreams in cloth
Hemp

On Majorca the traditional two-color fabrics with geometric patterns are called *tela de llengües* – tongue cloth. They are made using a special weaving technique known as *ikat*. Unlike kilim or jacquard the warp thread here is dyed in the desired pattern and then interwoven with a white or natural thread. If only a striped pattern is desired the weavers attach various colored warp threads to their looms and add white thread.

The fertile soil of the district around Muro is better than almost any other on the island for growing a very special plant. This is hard to cultivate in the other regions that suffer from drought. The plant is hemp, *Cannabis sativa*. This has not changed for centuries, for there is still great demand for hemp products on

Majorca, even though the market has never really recovered from a blight that struck the plants in the middle of the 20th century – not *Philoxera* this time but another pest.

Preparing hemp

Hemp has been cultivated since the third millennium BC. It is first recorded in China. It was first cultivated on a large scale in India from the ninth century BC, but it only came to Majorca more than 800 years later, with the Romans. Hemp is not an easy crop to grow. It requires much hard work, and it also stinks. The seed is expensive, for hemp is a unisexual plant and will only grow if male and female shoots are planted in the

Left: The old looms were made entirely of olive and pine wood.

Below: The *tela de llengües* are also made entirely by hand on a modern loom.

338

White weft and warp threads give a white cloth. This is used for curtain material, tablecloths, and bed covers on Majorca.

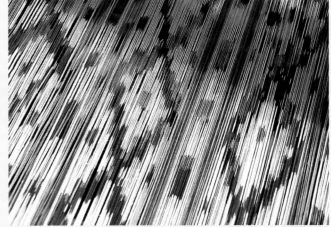

In *ikat* weaving the warp threads are dyed in the desired pattern and traditionally blue plays a large part.

The white weft thread softens the contrasts of the colors and gives the patterns a slightly blurred appearance.

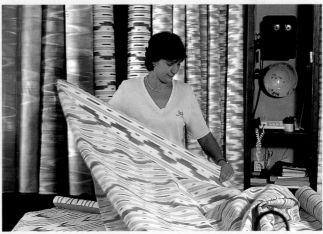

Tela de llenguës are available now in every width and color; other fibers may be incorporated, depending on the intended use of the material.

proper relationship. Once the plant has reached its full height, which is considerable at up to 13 feet (4 m), it has to be cut carefully by hand. Before the fibers can be removed a degeneration process has to set in, and this releases evil-smelling gases that can cause headaches, nausea and dizziness. So a government decree was issued in the 16th century that the air-polluting plant could only be processed at least a quarter of a Spanish mile (about three quarters of a mile or 1.28 km) from the nearest housing.

The fibers are very robust and they were formerly used to make working clothes. Even now a proper bride's bottom drawer on Majorca must contain bedsheets and tablecloths as well as towels made of hemp –

presumably *tela de llenguës* as well as natural or white cloth. These durable textiles enjoyed another boom at the end of the 20th century, after yielding for years to the advance of more "modern" synthetic fabrics that are easier to launder. Now the glowing colors and cheerful patterns of the hemp textiles are back in demand; in many Majorcan villages the old looms have been dusted off again and are creaking as the shuttles go back and forth. Apart from Muro the main *tapisseries artesanals* are in Santa Maria del Camí and Pollença, all known for the perfection of their handicraft. As a tribute to the modern age the weavers now capture the Majorcan dreams in color on looms that are wider than the traditional 32 inches (80 cm).

The people on the island do not appear to have needed the other dreams hemp can offer. There is no record of the resin or leaves of the plant being smoked for the short-lived release from the problems of everyday life. Only a cup of hemp tea is very welcome as a traditional cure for rheumatism.

Pirate, opportunist, and patron of the arts
Joan March from Santa Margalida

For more than 1,000 years people have lived in the little market town of Santa Margalida. In 1679 it was given a beautifully decorated church surrounded by trees on a little plateau above the town; at the beginning of the 20th century a liqueur factory and a few leather industries settled here, but none of this was enough to record the town in history books. It had to wait until 1880, when a son was born to a swineherd in a cottage, whose name would be linked with that of the town for all time. Joan March Ordinas of Santa Margalida became one of the richest men of his day. He was a manipulator, a pirate, and a patron. Posterity sees him as a horror and a shame but ultimately he remains a mystery. His birthplace has set no

monument to him, as is usually the case with a famous son, and if he had not created two monuments to himself, a mausoleum in the grand style in Palma cemetery and the Joan March Foundation, no one would voluntarily speak his name today.

Scruples? Never heard of them

Evidently he was born with a combination of abilities that people usually only have singly. He could twist anyone round his little finger, and where that did not work, he would buy them. He had a sense of direction as keen as a compass needle for the right place at the right time, and he was absolutely unscrupulous. He would let whole cargoes of animals owned by competitors die a miserable death in harbor before he would allow them to do business, and he had a way of always emerging as the winner. He could make maximum profit out of almost nothing, an ability he had already demonstrated in the school playground, where he did not sell

whole cigarettes but just a single puff. He was also quick to perceive how lucrative money-lending could be; if he lent anyone 10 céntimos he wanted 20 back next week.

Instead of herding his father's pigs young Joan looked around to see how best to sell the meat. At the age of 20 he had a firm contract with a sausage factory in Barcelona. He soon entered the tobacco smuggling trade from and to Algeria, buying up his competitors' carriers and crews; as a result state revenue from tobacco tax had shrunk within a few years from 50 million to 165,000 pesetas.

Parallel to these activities he set about clearing up the traditional division of land on Majorca. The old moneyed classes were beginning to decline at the start of the 20th century: the small holders could get more steady employment in industry and the farms and estates were being left untended. March bought them up, divided them into tiny lots and sold them to the former farm hands at rock bottom prices; owing to the large quantity of sales he still made a huge profit. In the course of his life he was responsible for more than 40,000 land registry entries in this way. To avoid having to pay the burdensome conveyancing charges and interest to others he set up his own bank, Banca March; it still has branches in every village in Majorca today and operates on the mainland as well.

With his business instinct and total lack of ethical or moral sense he acted as middleman during the First World War, from which he emerged immensely wealthy. For a cash sum he promised the British he would watch the movements of the German fleet in the Straits of Gibraltar. Then he assigned pilots to the German ships to take them safely into the Mediterranean. If the Germans captured one of March's cargo ships they all got a slice of the fat profit. The Germans, at a price, of course, had unrestricted access to everything they needed. And March, in addition to the income from sales on these floating supermarkets, got the insurance for the loss of the cargo. There

Joan March was one of the richest men of his time and one of the most unscrupulous.

were 2,500 of these German "shopping tours" in 1917 alone. As March had by now bought up all the shipyards on the Spanish Mediterranean coast, including the *Trasmeditarránea*, which was still operating, there was no lack of choice.

For a time March was literally venerated on Majorca for his success, and even the political Left supported him as a man who had cut off the old feudal pigtails. In 1926 they enabled him, if indirectly, to enter the Spanish parliament, the *Cortes* in Madrid. This took him into the country's governing classes. But his machinations during the Spanish civil war, if not before, opened their eyes. Here, too, March made sure he was on the right side. Although it has never been possible to prove this definitely, he appears to have helped to finance Franco's Fascist campaign with "generous" loans; and for the supplies of ore, oil and iron that were so essential for the conduct of the war, March more or less had a monopoly all over the Mediterranean.

For all his many connections, and all his classic corruption, March nearly came to grief on one occasion. He was arrested on suspicion of having murdered the son of his companion Josep Garau, but the judges were all taken off the case at the last moment. March finally fled to Gibraltar with the entire prison staff – to resume his business and emerge in the middle of the 20th century as one of the richest men in the world. No one has ever found out how rich he was.

In 1955 March decided to clean up his affairs and enter high society. For the first time he felt that money alone was not enough, so he transformed himself into a patron and set up a foundation for the arts, the *Fundación Juan March*. It was first located in Palma and later, in 1976, fourteen years after March was killed in an accident, it moved its headquarters to Madrid. The March Foundation first devoted itself almost exclusively to the fine arts, awarding generous scholarships to painters and sculptors. Public attention was drawn to its activities through costly gifts to the state, like the *Poema del Mio Cid* Codex in 1960; after March's death in 1962 the Foundation extended its activities to research programs in biology, sociology and European politics. Nearly 6,000 students and researchers have received assistance from the Foundation to pursue their studies since 1957; the Foundation itself has won national and international awards.

In 1990 the Museum of Contemporary Spanish Art was opened in Palma, the *Collecció March d'Art Espanyol Contemporani*. It now has branches in Madrid and Cuenca. As well as changing exhibitions it has a collection of 58 paintings and sculptures by almost all the major Spanish artists of the 20th century – Arroyo, Barceló, Chillida, Dalí, Julio Gonzalez, Gris, Miró, Picasso, and Tàpies. Apart from Dalí many of these artists supported the Republicans in the Spanish Civil War, and they would probably turn in their graves if they knew that their works were hanging in a museum financed by a former supporter of the Falange. The building that serves as the museum in Palma was the first branch of March's bank from 1916, and money almost certainly flowed from here to Franco.

Only tourists have to pay an admission charge to the museum, not the people who live on the island. And as if they knew that this and its commitment to the arts and sciences cannot make March any more popular with the natives, the Foundation does something to gladden the hearts of Spanish Catholics: every year it displays one of the most valuable Christmas cribs in the March Palace in Palma.

March was never satisfied with his biographers. It is said that he and later his heirs bought up all the copies of any life that could be taken seriously, including Manuel de Benavides' *El último pirata del Mediterraneo* (The Last Pirate on the Mediterranean).

Joan March founded his own bank to enable him to handle property deals at lower cost. The Banca March has a branch in every village on the island.

The church in the village
Maria de la Salut

The curious names given to the Virgin Mary in Spain, as in the village of Maria de la Salut, the Holy Virgin of Health, generally derive from a wondrous vision of Mary, as a consequence of which a church immediately had to be built. The stories are similar all over Spain, as here. To protect it from invading Moors the peasants buried a figure of the Virgin Mary that they particularly revered. Centuries later, after the Reconquista, it was accidentally dug up, again by farmers, or, as many stories go, by children.

It is usually said that the figure radiates a bright light once it has been cleaned of the dust of centuries, and it speaks graciously to its reverent finders, telling them clearly to build a church in her honor on the spot where she has been found. One of two possibilities will decide the name given to the figure of Mary, and so to the church. Firstly, the figure may be holding something that characterizes the find. In one case on Menorca, for example, she was accompanied by a tame bull, so the place of pilgrimage is called *Verge del Toro*, the Virgin of the Bull. Or, as probably here in María de Salut, her appearance coincided with a miracle. This figure of Mary dispensing health appeared most appropriately at a time when the plague was exacting a heavy price on Majorca. Possibly the sick began to recover that day, or the epidemic suddenly declined. Whatever it was precisely has been forgotten in the course of time, but the name has remained – and the figure, which certainly dates from pre-Moorish times, still adorns the main altar in her church, Nostra Senyora de la Salut, Our Lady of Health.

Another figure of Mary stands above the Baroque main portal, which dates from 1697, but this time she is not looking very charitable or as if she loved her neighbors. She stands like an Amazon, strong and determined, affirming the dominance of the only true faith as the mother of all true believers. There could hardly be a better illustration of the difference in the way the Church saw itself between the early Christian era and the time after the Reconquista.

The Church and its mercy
Villages like Maria de la Salut generally profited most from the rule of the Moors. The Arabs brought effective irrigation systems and introduced new varieties of crops like apricots, almonds and figs. There was little fear of religious persecution, for the Moorish period on Majorca was characterized by peaceful coexistence between Christians, Muslims, and Jews.

The Baroque church of Our Lady of Health is visible from afar as it towers over the little town.

For the priest Jaume Santandreu (third from right) love of one's neighbor means fighting poverty and isolation.

its power and economic structure in question. For people like Santandreu, however, everybody has the right to a life without poverty and need – so love of one's neighbor is an act of social responsibility.

So it was not long before the Church rid itself of the rebellious priest. But even after his suspension Santandreu remained a popular reformer, creating many projects for those in need in the spirit of the Gospel.

The reconquest of Majorca by Jaume I put an end to all this. Now the island and its rulers were again incorporated in the Christian church, but at first the followers of Moses and the Prophet who had remained on the island still exercised power and economic influence. If the Christian rulers wanted to stay in power they had to change the old structures quickly, if possible by law; if not, with force.

To put it simply: Anyone who was willing to forswear his false faith could stay; anyone who refused to do so was driven out, arrested or burned at the stake. The levers of power were used where society was most vulnerable; language, schooling, civil and trade rights and personal possessions were all affected. Gradually the Church took charge of them all. It set up a monopoly of education in the language of its choice, so that reading and writing became a privilege of a small, rich hand-picked elite.

Converts who were accused of heresy lost all their possessions, their houses and farms went to the Church. They were then known as "dead estates", as they were Church lands and so inalienable. They ceased to be goods that could be traded and were taken out of the economic system. But they still had to be managed and farmed, and so with its huge possessions the Church rapidly became one of the largest employers

on the island. In the 16th century the guilds required new members to prove they were "of pure blood", so excluding descendants of the Jews and Moors. In this way the Church acquired control of nearly everything on the island within a relatively short time; it was supported by the ruling classes and the Catholic kings on mainland Spain.

Basically, the Church lost little of its influence, at least in rural regions like the Pla, until the death of Franco in 1975. After the Spanish civil war the Church was a state within the state, controlling education, culture and of course morals right into the bedroom.

The Church of Liberation, Majorcan-style: Jaume Santandreu

Maria de la Salut eventually produced a very unusual son of the Church, for here of all places in the 1970s the priest Jaume Santandreu founded one of the most progressive community centers in all Spain. Convinced and inspired by the ideas of the South American liberation theologians Leonardo Boff and Gustavo Gutiérrez he set up a number of liberal reception centers for drug addicts and alcoholics in Palma.

Conflict was inevitable. The official Church had never thought much of the liberation theologians, for their attempts to free the mass of the poor from the controlling and oppressive arm of the Church called

Small pleasures: A farmer enjoys a smoke during his rest break. One of the first centers for alcoholics and drug addicts was opened in Santa Maria de la Salut.

The quiet of time
Ariany

"There is not a false note here, there are no spectacular mountains, nor dizzying ravines. The plains and flat fields flow gently over the earth, and in this scenery dwells one of the most welcome guests – quiet. It is the quiet that permits us to hear the voices of nature and the echoes of time... And that is because man and nature have never been at loggerheads here." Guillem Frontera of Ariany has wonderfully captured the atmosphere of his native village in this description, indeed of the Pla as a whole, its very essence. That is hardly surprising, for from the cemetery beside the charming domed parish church of Nostra Senyora d'Arocha, which stands on a slight rise, one has an enchanting view over the gently rolling plain.

Nothing much has ever happened here. The village of Ariany, which numbers 800 souls, occupies only a tiny place in the island's history books and the memory of its people. It is the youngest community on Majorca, for in order to enter the third millennium in independence it split off from nearby Petra in 1982; but anyone who needs gas still has to drive to Petra. In many respects Ariany is like a fly preserved in amber: of strange beauty and overtaken by the passage of time – and fairly soon forgotten.

Scarcely any other village on Majorca has been so hard hit by the flight from the land as this one. As Ariany has never had factories or traded outside the village it had and still has no jobs to offer apart from agriculture. There is no town hall, no bowling alley, no cinema to dissuade the young people from seeking their fortune elsewhere. Those who want to stay can only choose to spend what leisure remains from work in the folk dance group, on the football field or in the swimming pool. That is, if they have any

The tropical vegetation seems to stand like a wall protecting Ariany from the outside world.

work at all. Even the elegant wheels of the fine windmills around the village have ceased to pump water or mill corn, and no one has ever set them going again.

Not even tourism has come. For centuries nothing new or momentous has happened here, but many have gone – mainly to Palma and on to the tourist beaches, where they can find work and share in the pleasures and frustrations of the modern age. At most they come back to the village at weekends, where their fathers, a generation and many opportunities further back, are still wringing from the family land they have inherited the wheat, oats and rye they need just to survive.

400 years' lambs at compound interest

So it is no wonder that in a place like Ariany strange medieval customs have survived and occasionally resurface. One such curiosity from the feudal past is the *alou*, or payment in kind. It is a legal curiosity that has only persisted in this form on the Balearic Islands, and even here only in such forgotten corners as Ariany.

"To understand the *alou* you have to go a long way back in history", says Miguel Coca, Professor of Civil Law at the University of the Balearic Islands. "When the Catalans conquered Majorca in the 13th century they divided the land up among their faithful followers, their political allies and the Church. The new major landowners could sit back and enjoy the fruits of other people's labor, unless a small and remote farm did not yield enough; then they would sell it."

Right: Few young people want to live in villages like Ariany now.

Below: If a *finca* changes hands curious medieval interest claims can surface.

But they added a clause to the selling price allowing them to claim payment in kind. This would give them a direct and useful additional income from the point of sale. "It could be one lamb a year, a few sacks of corn, a cock", explains Coca. "As the *alou* was tied to the house or farm and so was entered in the land register, the claim never lapsed." For many generations it was duly paid, but then the creditors died, their heirs multiplied and spread to distant lands. Only in places like Ariany were the farms or *fincas* generally handed on from one generation to the next and rarely sold.

It may happen that someone wants to sell a *finca* that has been in the same family for centuries. Then the lawyer commissioned to perform the conveyancing is legally bound to search out all the relevant legal clauses attached to the property. A glance at the old land register will tell him that the *alou* of one lamb a year plus interest and compound interest has not been paid on the *finca* for 400 years. "The problem is",

grins Coca, "that the *alou* may have been forgotten, but it still applies. Generally neither the vendor nor the heirs of the former major landowner from the time of the Reconquista know anything about it, but it is still valid in law."

To become the rightful owner of the *finca*, the purchaser now has to redeem the *alou*, but how? "To simplify these transactions and make them acceptable the Balearic Islands have introduced a regulation," lawyer Coca confides to us. "If the heirs are unknown the purchaser is obliged to declare his will to purchase in an official gazette and allow the heirs a term of five years to claim their due; of course today it would be paid in cash, not lambs or cocks." If no claim is made the *alou* becomes forever invalid. If the heirs do come forward and make their claim they will be paid up to the date of the sale, and after that their claim ceases. "There is no point in continuing a custom like that forever, particularly if it has been forgotten for ages", says Coca.

Some lawyers have specialized in *alous*, for the mediation work can be profitable. But here, too, the devil is in the detail. If a farm was particularly unprofitable and the purchaser all those centuries ago a poor wretch with a big family, a symbolic payment in kind could be arranged. It could be the right to sit on a chair in the courtyard at any time and be given a glass of water. Arrangements of this kind reflect the value of the *finca* when it was sold, but they can hardly be expressed in modern hard currency, and certainly not in conveyancing fees.

These relics of the feudal past seem curious and obsolete today, but they reflect a harsh social reality, the almost inescapable dependence of the peasants on the great landowners. Structures like these and their subsequent effects have played a part in motivating the actions of people like the priest Santandreu.

Opposite: The sand dunes of Son Serra are part of Ariany.

Below: Pigs and hens often have lots of room to scratch, wallow, and peck on Majorca.

A taste of paradise
Figs from Ariany

"You eat them freshly gathered, large quantities are dried, partly for consumption on the island and partly for dispatch abroad. They are also used to feed pigs that grow inordinately fat on them..." The fruit whose use was so described by Archduke Ludwig Salvator of Austria in 1897 is the fig.

For before the Arabs introduced almond trees to Majorca the Romans had long since given the people a heavenly gift, the fig tree. Although it actually comes from Asia Minor, the *figuera* quickly took root on Majorcan soil and since then its white, reddish, lilac or almost black fruit has been immensely popular. Along with almonds and olive trees this offshoot of the big mulberry family can claim to be part of the vegetation that defines the landscape here today.

The fig tree embellishes the Majorcan landscape until it has reached an age of nearly a hundred. It grows to medium height and bears big light green lobed leaves that, sadly, played an important part in the Garden of Eden. It almost looks as if the fig tree is aware of the consequences of the human error that made its leaves famous, and is ashamed. For when it drops its leaves in winter it looks depressed and slightly frightening with its bare arms hanging down low.

The fruits shimmer in a yellowish green to lilac color, and the farmers gather them – in the sweat of their brow – from July to early September. Then the well ripened fruits are laid out on *canyis*, wooden trays made of staves, and left to dry in the sun. In the evening the trays are placed under a sheltering roof. Next morning the fruit are brought out again; the process of harvesting and drying is protracted and wearisome, and the whole

The fig tree bears its rich green robe every year for nearly a hundred years.

family is involved. Even the youngest children help to lay the fruit out on the trays, turn them and sort out the bad ones. As always in traditional agriculture nothing is wasted here. The livestock are glad of the extra sweets they keep being given.

Before they are finally stored the fruits, now shrinking, are briefly baked in an oven. Some farmers insist on pouring boiling water over them after about 20 days to kill off any pests, and then drying them again. The procedure is the same for all the 15 varieties of figs that are cultivated on Majorca today and differ only slightly from each other in taste.

That the fruit has become a synonym for the female sexual organs in the colloquial speech of the south is now also known in northern Europe. So the visitor who speaks the language will hardly be surprised to hear many stories about *figuges*, mostly of clearly double meaning, which have also found their way into Majorcan songs..

Right: The donkey also welcomes a fruity snack.

Below: The harvested figs are still laid out on wooden trays and left in the sun to dry.

349

From July the fig tree bends beneath the weight of its fruit, and its branches nearly touch the ground.

The fruit shimmer in every shade of blue and green, depending on how ripe they are. They are picked in September.

There are so many varieties of Majorcan figs they cannot be classified by European norms.

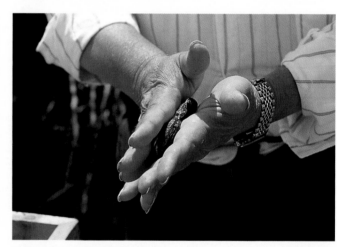

The ripe fruit are squashed before being laid out on wooden trays to dry.

Every morning the figs are set out in the sun and every evening they are put under the shelter of a roof.

After about 20 days the procedure is finished and the dried fruit will sweeten many a winter evening.

Pa de Figa

Fig bread

Ingredients
1 fig leaf
1lb 2 oz (500 g) dried figs, ground
Aniseed or aniseed liqueur to taste
4¹/₂ oz (125 g) almonds, peeled and halved
Almonds for decoration

The people of Majorca knead fig bread literally with the flick of a wrist, as quickly and skillfully as they can rhyme songs with double meaning.

The figs are first mixed with aniseed, almonds and a shot of aniseed liqueur. Then artistry is required. For in the next part of the job the unformed mass of the dough has to be shaped into a pyramid, like those in Ancient Egypt. When a satisfactory result has been obtained and the pyramid stands on the table like its namesake in the land of the Pharaohs, the work of art is set on a fig leaf that has been laid ready. Then it is decorated with almonds, but as these are pressed in the pyramid often collapses and loses its shape. Now one has to wait, for the dough must dry in a well ventilated room. Try it with a coffee or a glass of aniseed liqueur.

Dried under the pitiless sun, the figs form the basis of the classical Majorcan recipe for fig bread.

A bubbling success story
Petra

The Arabs who founded this small inland town named it "The Radiant One" after its large Jordanian counterpart. In the 1970s, however, its sun seemed to have set once and for all when the transport authorities stopped the railway line between Palma and Artà in Inca, thus cutting Petra off from the capital.

Today the township mostly attracts tourists wanting to visit the birthplace of its most famous son, Fray Junípero Serra, and the museum connected to it. Unlike this widely traveled Franciscan friar, Petra has not been blessed by good fortune: the attempts of some families to give this remote town economic significance by growing wine there were a failure owing to the boom in Spanish wines from Navarra, Rioja and Penedés. And the story of one – albeit small – economic success here also has rather a sad ending – but one that is typical for the Pla.

La Paduana – the island's oldest soda water factory

While working for a soda water manufacturer from Artá in the 1930s, the father of the Fortezza Bonnín family must have thought "I can do that, too". No sooner said than done. Together with his brother, he bought a small soda water machine: the first investment in a later flourishing business. They set it up in their grandparents' home, and the two of them laboriously filled buckets with water outside the estate and carried them up to the house. There they added carbon dioxide – and the soda water was ready for drinking. The business had got off to a start.

As demand for this artificially produced seltzer increased, some years later they moved to Na Capitana, a family property outside the village. Here, there was a spring bubbling to the surface. They expanded the business: a small one–story building on the property now housed a larger machine.

This opened up new possibilities. From then on, the two innovative brothers produced not only soda water, but also orange juice and pineapple soft drinks. After one of them had experimented long and carefully to find out the right proportions for the various ingredients, the recipes for the drinks remained constant. This brother was given the nickname El Químico, the chemist, because of the meticulous way in which he tested the different possible mixtures. One bottle of water after the other had carbon dioxide added to it before being

Large, open arches and a rose window decorate the parish church of San Pere in Petra.

Monument in honor of Majorcan peasant women.

sealed off. The brothers ordered the fruit extracts for their refreshing beverages from a firm in Barcelona, while the bottled carbon dioxide was bought in Palma.

Later, they dug a well, using a donkey to draw up the water. Now there was enough work for more than just the two brothers. A former wet nurse used to come up to the factory to wash the bottles, while a young man was employed to deliver the drinks. A time came when deliveries were not carried out by donkey cart alone: an old truck proudly bearing the name of the family company, La Paduana (The Paduan Woman), was also used. When the business continued to thrive, the donkey was put out to pasture for good and a new, modern truck was bought. It carried the inscription El Gran Poder: "The Great Power".

This had its reasons. In the 1950s the daily production of the Paduanos had risen to about 80 bottles of soda water and 40 bottles containing other thirst quenchers. When their grandmother later became ill, the two founders of the firm moved back with their children to Petra to look after her, as is the custom in Majorca. From now on, they also managed the farming land. They founded a sort of co-operative that provided

a livelihood for 12 people: while some family members were working in the fields, others busied themselves with making and selling the soft drinks. Every new bottle meant more money in the family cashbox, money that was immediately invested in expanding the business.

The "chemist", however, continued to develop new recipes for these popular drinks. The bottling plant was now situated in the hallway of the family house in the middle of Petra. The family lived and worked in rather cramped conditions, but the great demand for their products meant they were able to expand their market and increase their production even further.

Competition for the chemist

Business boomed, and the future looked very rosy – until tourism started. Tourism should really have meant a further rise in the fortunes of the two industrious brothers and their families. But vacationers also brought competition to Petra. Large companies in nearby Barcelona provided the hotels with everything they needed for their guests. Anything from bed linen and furniture to soft drinks could be delivered punctually when required. Small Majorcan businesses like the Paduanos, which had had such high hopes of tourism, were not able to stand up to such competition.

And the time came when the chemist's recipes no longer made anyone's mouth water. Especially because, as early as 1886, two men in the United States had scribbled down a recipe with the name "7X" on a small piece of paper. The mystery of this strange and wonderful brew, which supposedly once contained coca leaves, has never been revealed. But this brown-colored drink has flooded the entire world with bottles or aluminum cans bearing its eye-catching logo. Few have been able to withstand its sticky-sweet power. Not even the Paduanos.

Before the Paduanos were able to afford their first truck, a well-behaved donkey used to be employed.

Brother Juniper and the Indians
Fray Junípero Serra

"On 24 November 1713, Miguel Joseph Serre was baptized as the son of Antonio Serra, farmer, and his wife, Margarita." This simple entry in the register of the municipality of Petra does not betray the fact that Petra's greatest son, whom later generations would know as Fray Junípero Serra, had been born.

It soon became clear that José Miguel was a boy of very sharp intelligence. But Majorca, and especially Petra, with only 2,000 inhabitants, did not offer him the opportunities he needed to quench his thirst for knowledge. For this reason, parents back then either sent their children to the army early on, or gave them into the care of the Catholic church as was the case with Miguel Serra. His father had contacts to a wealthy clergyman at the Palma cathedral who promised to look after Miguel's education.

In the autumn of 1729, Antonio and Margarita handed over their 16 year-old son to this rich and learned churchman. After the boy had learnt to read and write, he attended lectures on philosophy, and was accepted into the Franciscan order on 15 September 1731. He changed his name to Fray Junípero: "Brother Juniper". He decided on this name because his namesake was a man considered one of the most devoted followers of St. Francis of Assisi, the founder of the order.

Fray Junípero soon became a fine orator. His sermons, given in churches and monasteries, were very popular; they were immediately put into print and distributed among the faithful. In 1742 he received his doctorate in theology from the Lullus University in Palma. But Junípero wanted to go further – in the geographical sense as well. As his later biographer, Francisco Palou, tells us, the young friar devoured any reports about Franciscan friars in the New World. The life of San Francisco Solano, known as the "Apostle of the West Indies", made a particular impression on him. From then on, Junípero had only one goal: he wanted to go to the New World to be a missionary to the unbelievers. He immediately began to try for a transfer to America and, in the spring of 1749, his application for a position at a missionary station in Mexico was finally granted.

Shortly after this, Junípero started out for Málaga by sea. From there, he sailed further on a Majorcan ship to Cádiz, then the largest Atlantic port in Europe. There he had to wait two and a half months before finding a berth on the ship Nuestra Señora de Guadalupe. Shortly before the ship departed, he wrote one more letter to his parents, his sister, and his cousin in Petra. Because his family could not read, he addressed the letter to his close friend Fray Francisco Serra, who was to read it to them. In this letter, Junípero does not conceal the joy that filled him at being able to leave the restrictions of his native land and follow his calling. He sent particular greetings to his

Portrait of the missionary Fray Junípero Serra in the monastery of Santa Cruz, Querétaro, Mexico.

Above: The idyllic courtyard of the Fray Junípero Serra Museum in Petra can certainly stand comparison with the patios in the capital.

Right: The kitchen of the house where "Brother Juniper" was born.

mother, as he was convinced that her prayers had caused God to direct him on this special path. He was never to see his parents or Majorca again.

On 18 October 1749, Junípero first stepped on to American soil in Puerto Rico, reaching Veracruz on 18 November after a further extremely arduous voyage. A mighty storm had driven the ship onto the coast near the port, and it was only by a miracle that the vessel did not sink. Fray Junípero, however, never had any doubts about his safe arrival in Veracruz. In accordance with the motto *L'home propos i déu dispos* – man proposes, God disposes – everything seemed

This statue in front of the Sant Francesc church in Palma shows Junípero holding up a cross as a symbol of his success as a missionary, while giving a naked Indian child fatherly protection.

to point in the one direction possible for him.

On 14 December 1749, Junípero headed off with a Franciscan friar from the order of Jerez de la Frontera on an arduous journey through the Veracruz mountains across to inland Mexico. They needed two exhausting weeks to complete this walk of 249 miles (400 km). The two friars walked 17 miles (25 km) every day, reaching Mexico City, then capital of the viceroyalty of New Spain, on New Year's Eve.

They immediately set out for the Apostle School in San Fernando. The abbot greeted Junípero with open arms and the words:

Loreto is the oldest Spanish settlement on the peninsula of Lower California. It was founded in 1696 by Juan Mariá de Salvatierra, a Jesuit. In 1770 the Franciscans set up their central supply station here both for Lower California and for their journeys to California. The "visitations" were also organized in Loreto: because the missionary stations on this 994 mile (1,600 km) long section of the coast were often widely separated from one another, the church set up a visiting service. This called on the various remote "visita" churches at regular intervals and attended to the faithful in each.

"Oh, we have been brought a juniper forest!" A few hours later, Serra and his companion were able to celebrate the New Year's mass of the year 1750 in the New World. After this, they set off towards Sierra Gorda. The landscape was so similar to the description given by the friar San Francisco Solana that Junípero was deeply impressed. Here were mountains up to 19,000 feet (3,200 m) high, surrounded by valleys in which desert-like areas alternated with tropical oases full of lush vegetation.

However, as famine reigned among the Chichimecas, the tribe that the two missionaries wanted to convert to Christianity, these people were not overly interested in new divinities. Junípero therefore first introduced them to new methods of gardening and agriculture before conveying his religious message and converting them to his faith. Because of his active help, some historians today call him the first foreign aid worker in the history of Christianity. Junípero continued his missions in the Sierra Gorda and Mexico City for 18 years.

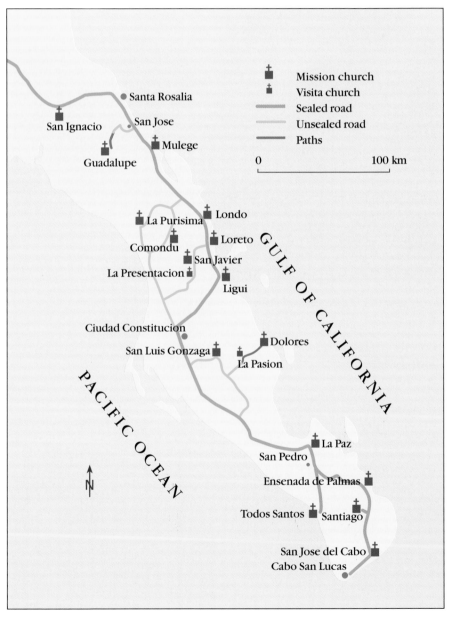

When the Jesuits were expelled from the peninsula Baya California by the Indians in 1768, the Franciscans took over the missions there. The order appointed Father Junípero to lead the mission stations in this remote region. One year later, he was commissioned by José de Galvez, a close advisor of the Spanish king, Charles III, to set up new missions in Alta California, now California. This promotion to being superior of the Franciscans in California was what finally revealed Junípero's true vocation.

The background behind this royal command was as follows: at this time, no nation had yet announced territorial claims to the west coast of North America. A competitive struggle for the region began between the Spanish, English, and Russians. Together with Junípero, missionaries and soldiers began an expedition of over 1,250 miles (2,000 km) towards the north. The journey was extremely difficult. The men had barely any food, suffered from scurvy, and were under constant attack from the Indians.

On 17 July 1769, Junípero laid the foundation stone for the mission in San Diego – only to see the station completely destroyed again by a large-scale Indian attack on 15 August. The civilian government planned a retreat. Junípero, however, never lost his belief in the success of anything he undertook. He persuaded the governor to stay on until 20 March of the following year to wait for the ship San Antonio, which had been asked to bring food and reinforcements. The ship made its welcome appearance on 19 January, and Junípero immediately began to rebuild the station.

With true missionary zeal, he continued with his work, founding 21 missionary stations within only a few years. These were constructed like little townships. In 1771, he built the missions of San Antonio and San Gabriel, followed by those in San Luis, San Francisco, San Juan Capistrano, and Santa Clara. By 1782 he had already laid the foundation stone for the large mission in San Buenaventura. The most famous of them, however, is without doubt San Francisco de Asís, founded in 1776, which developed into the metropolis of San Francisco. This mission still exists today under the name of "Mission Dolores".

The last task Fray Junípero Serra undertook before his death was to establish the

mission San Carlos Borroméo in Carmel. By this time, at the age of almost seventy, he had grown very feeble.

After his death in San Carlos in 1784, a church order came into force making him one of the key figures in the history of Christian proselytization. Five years later, his pupil and biographer, Francisco Palou Amengal, published the book *Relación Histórica de la Vida y Apostólicas Tareas del Venerable Padre Fray Junípero Serra* (Historical Background to the Life and

Fray Junípero established nine missionary stations in California. The most famous of them is certainly San Francisco de Asís, founded in 1776. Later, the metropolis of San Francisco was to grow up at this location. The mission church soon became known by the name of a nearby lake, Laguna de Nuestra Señora de los Dolores, and exists to this day in San Francisco as "Mission Dolores". The church, built in 1761 from clay bricks in the Mexican adobe style, was so solidly constructed that it even survived the serious earthquake of 1906 without any damage.

MISSIONS CALIFORNIANES

SAN GABRIEL ARCANGEL 8 DE SETEMBRE
1771

Apostolic Works of the Venerable Padre Fray Junípero Serra), a hymn of praise to his master. The admirable thing about Amengal's treatment of the subject is the way in which the author himself fades into the background, even though it is said that he, and not Junípero, laid the foundation stone of the mission in San Francisco. A hundred years later, a monument to Junípero Serra was built in Monterey, the place where he landed in 1749.

When statues of famous heroes were being set up in the Capitol in Washington, each American state was allowed to choose two of its most famous personages so that a monument could be erected to them. California chose Fray Junípero as one of its representatives. Since the 1930s, the missions have been lavishly restored and most have regained much of their former glory.

In Palma de Majorca, an institute for further education and a street have been named after Brother Juniper. In his native town of Petra, a memorial has been erected in his honor. Surrounded by palm trees, it stands in the Plaza Padre Serra and shows him deep in spiritual pose with cross raised and head bowed. There are also panels showing his life in pictures. In Petra, his house can also be visited along with the museum dedicated to him. In 1976, when celebrations were held not only for the 200th anniversary of the United States, but also for the founding of San Francisco by Fray Junípero, money came from America to support the museum, until then a purely private initiative.

Only one thing is still lacking there: an objective biography investigating the Padre's personality. For, alongside his admirers and followers, there are also critics who accuse him of having participated in the massacres carried out by the Spanish. When he was beatified in Rome in 1988, the accusation was heard that he and the monks accompanying him had killed Indians who refused to be converted to Catholicism. Since there is no record of Junípero's religious philosophy, his behavior towards the "unbelievers" has never been able to be completely clarified.

Opposite: 1,000 Indians were baptized in San Gabriel after the first mass had been held at the foot of a cross rammed into the ground.

Right and below: The various stages of Junípero's life are depicted in paintings on tiles in Petra. In San Carlos, an Indian listens to Junípero's words, while in San Juan monks and Indians work together in the garden. But were things really always so peaceful?

Country living in style
Sant Joan

A rare member of the pig family, the *Porcella negra* or black pig, is the basic source of livelihood for the farmers living in Sant Joan, a remote village on the Pla plain. The darkly colored boars and sows scour their own farmyard and the lush meadows for delicacies, their snouts pressed close to the ground. Most of them enjoy a freedom that the pink-skinned, northern European variety in their dark sties can only dream of. If there were a pig paradise on earth, then the life of the black pigs of Sant Joan would be the closest thing to it.

Until late autumn, that is. Then, on St. Martin's Day, they meet their final hour. The pigs provide the meat for all the sausages and ham that are produced on Majorca during the year, and especially for the *Festa des Botifarró,* the sausage festival, which takes place in October. The only

chance for a *Porcella negra* to escape this sad future as the star of a Sunday stew is for it to possess such extraordinary qualities that it can be used for breeding purposes.

Sant Joan does not lie on the normal tourist routes, and for this reason has retained a naturalness that is hard to find elsewhere, even in Majorca. In fact, the inhabitants of the township claim to be the sole remaining custodians of the true Majorcan character. Perhaps they are right: Sant Joan still breathes the atmosphere that was typical for rural Majorca before mass tourism arrived.

Els Calderers: A country idyll
A solid yet elegant building in the countryside, three stories high, its yellow plasterwork covered with climbing ivy, a balcony on the right side with an Italianate balustrade, a small shrine with a figure of the Virgin on the façade under the balcony: this venerable old house is called Els Calderers. The former manor was built in 1700 at the

It's proved its worth for centuries, it can't just be thrown away from one day to the next: a mule pulling its master and cart to work at daybreak.

feet of the Puig de Bonany hermitage. Almost exactly 300 hundred years later, in 1993, a Majorcan family had an idea that was both brilliant and original: why not use this old building to show what rural life in Majorca used to be like in years gone by? And so this outstanding museum came into being. Here one can see how the house owners and the servants enjoyed life in the good old days – albeit on differing levels.

A tiny statue here, a lace doily there, huge armchairs and elegant sofas, oil portraits of ancestors on the wall: all these things still show the exquisite taste of the people who used to live here. The Majorcans of old not only knew how to enjoy their wealth, but how to display it as well. The living rooms and bedrooms on the first floor bear witness to this in an impressive manner. A lace bedspread in chaste white covers a bed of

The manor of Els Calderers near Sant Joan has been a museum for old Majorcan home life since 1993.

mahogany; a lady's narrow writing table stands at the window overlooking the garden, waiting for an inspired moment on the part of its mistress. But even the ground floor, where the servants worked, was a pleasant enough place to be despite the long hours of duty. Once a month, the housekeeper proudly polished the silver cutlery and made sure all the copper pots and pans were gleaming like new. Even today, everything is still shining in her honor in the former housekeeper's room. All sorts of native animals are kept in stalls and enclosures; even a few specimens of *Porcella negra* are there to grunt a greeting to any visitors. Numerous outbuildings house curious pieces of equipment that once helped coax the fields, woods and meadows into providing food to eat. With God's help, of course, as the chapel belonging to the estate reminds us to this day.

Private museums and family kitchens: Sant Joan

In nearby Sant Joan, wealth is not quite so much in evidence. The simple farmhouses have neither scrolls nor coats of arms as decoration. A new coat of whitewash each year keeps the houses looking clean and white, and prevents the plasterwork from deciding to part company from the masonry behind it. Whoever can afford it places a wall unit of laminated chipboard in a prominent position where it can be seen by passersby, and assigns any old rustic furniture to a hiding place in a back room.

This increasingly rare traditional furniture has a history going back hundreds of years. It includes the *canterano,* a chest of drawers with three drawers, richly decorated on the outside with inlaid work. Mostly, it contains lovingly tied-up bundles of heavily starched and pressed sheets lying next to bales of *roba de llengües* (a Majorcan cloth made of hemp), colorfully embroidered tablecloths, and table napkins. Small bags of lavender protect them from any all too predatory moths. Both the chest of drawers and its contents form a part of the dowry, which is still solemnly passed on from the grandmother to the mother and then down to the daughter, each time enlarged by new items.

For a long time, this splendid mahogany furniture was seen as a sign of poverty: it meant you could not afford anything new.

Since the upsurge of national consciousness in Majorca at the end of the 20th century, fate has been kinder to the old furniture. These often handmade items have been subject to a distinct re-evaluation. They are now considered to be historical witnesses of local culture, although not all owners of such furniture are necessarily aware of the fact.

Mahogany furniture like this was once considered an indication of poverty.

People with a nose for antiques will not have much success in Sant Joan, however. Despite the traditional contempt for such "junk", this type of furniture is almost never put on sale. If someone were to sell any of it, they would be selling part of their soul as well, and spend the rest of their life grieving that they had "betrayed" part of the family inheritance for mere money.

The churns and buckets, bedcovers and sheets are more than just objects for use: they were also the measure of a family's wealth and social standing. The annual feast on St. Martin's Day was another indication of affluence, as was any money put aside, a *raconet* in Majorcan: a nest egg hidden, buried or sewn up somewhere. It was desirable to be prepared for bad harvests, sick animals, the wedding of a cousin three times removed or other such vicissitudes of fate.

The wealthier farmers in Sant Joan still divide their home up into two areas: in one, they eat, sleep, and live according to the motto "my home is my castle". The other area is the parlor. It is there for show, and even family members only enter it on special occasions. They certainly avoid going in there with dirty boots and soiled working

In many houses, new sofas and old oil paintings furnish the same room. Grandfather's best Sunday shirt and his hat collection are also essential.

Formerly, supplies for the winter used to be neatly stored on the walls and floor in vaulted cellars like these.

clothes – the lady of the house keeps a watchful eye on that. Not the least speck of dust has time to gather in the parlor; for this, the family's "calling card", is cleaned, polished and dusted almost every day.

In this room, silver ashtrays, traditional presents at weddings and first communions, try to outshine copper goblets and pewter plates. The white walls are full of landscape pictures, painted in oils, of course. Richly embroidered cloths, mostly made by the grandmother with untiring industry, protect tables and armrests from the insidious effects of wear and sunlight. Rustic furniture is not allowed here; it would be an unwelcome reminder of the time when a family had not been able to afford the factory-made chipboard wall unit.

The back part of the houses, where the farmers of Sant Joan actually live, may not be as meticulously clean, but is certainly much cozier. There is almost always a television blaring in the corner, while above it sausages and at least one leg of ham hang from the ceiling. Next to these, rows of tomatoes dangle down to dry. The chairs serve as temporary storage for ironing, baskets full of fruit or sewing things. All sorts of electrical equipment are very much in evidence in the kitchen, but there is seldom a dishwasher: traditionally, the grandmother is responsible for washing up.

Families have much closer ties in rural Majorca than in the cities. If one parent outlives the other, then he or she is taken into one of the children's homes as a matter of course. Putting old people in an old folks' home is seen as a serious violation of the Fourth Commandment to honor one's father and mother. The grandmother actively helps the housewife as long as her health allows, while the grandfather mostly spends his time playing cards in the café.

The farmers in Sant Joan are not the only ones who think it is important to display their possessions: people in the city do as well. An entrance hall with a prominent staircase serves the same purpose as the farmers' parlor. In the upper stories, the eye is immediately caught by oil paintings and brocade curtains. The curtains are often drawn aside to give the neighbors from across the way a good view of what one has. First communions or anniversaries provide welcome opportunities for inviting neighbors and friends to an opulent meal. The desire to show others how much one possesses comes from the time when many Majorcans had to emigrate to earn their livelihood somewhere else. When they then returned as "self-made" men, they proudly paraded their new-found wealth in front of those who had remained at home.

In both city and country areas, families bring out their best dinnerware for festive occasions, transforming the little-used parlor into a banqueting hall.

The sky in flames
Sa Nit de Sant Joan

Midnight, June 24, St. John's Day: in this *Nit de Foc,* "night of fire", squares, alleys, and streets are filled with huge piles of wood. No sooner has the last ray of sun sunk into the sea when they burst into flames, lighting up the night sky and turning it into a magical stage. The crackling of the flames and the hissing of the still fresh resin mixes with the sound of lively, joyful singing, while the flickering light of the bonfires seems to show the movements of the dancing people in a series of bizarre snapshots.

The background to this ritual, here as almost everywhere else in Europe, is the idea that on this night nature unfolds special powers. For one day in the year, the sun is the lord of all existence; for one night in the year, all evil spirits are without protection or cover because the period of darkness is so short.

Like many such festivals, the midsummer celebrations have their roots in heathen custom, and have been held in Majorca by Romans, Phoenicians, Moors and Jews. And, as is so often the case, the Church later had to tolerate the fact that people were going to celebrate on this night whatever happened – so it had to invent a church holiday to make the whole thing acceptable. John the Baptist, who according to the New Testament was a

few months older than Jesus, has his birthday on 24 June, close enough to the solstice, so this heathen festival became the *Nit de Sant Joan.* Only in Sant Joan of all places, however, is it still called by its heathen name of *Festa des Sol que Balla,* "Festival of the Dancing Sun".

The highlight of the midsummer festival is a ritual in which homage is paid to the sun with fireworks and drums. Most of the participants are doubtless unaware that this homage to the sun-god has been inherited from their stone-throwing ancestors of the *Talayot* culture, or is perhaps even older – but what does that matter?

During the 24 hour long festival, there is also a lot to be done to prepare for the rest of the year. In Manacor, for example, children who are one year of age or less are presented to the village community on the eve of the celebration between the split branches of a tree called *vimer* – not without some deafening crying and screaming, as can be imagined. Amongst other things, this is meant to prevent hernias.

If you take a bath in the sea at sunrise, on the other hand, you can be sure to be free of illness for the entire year. In *Majorca Magica,* Carlos Garrido writes: "If you pick a handful of St. John's wort shortly before dawn on this day and place them in a bottle together with water or olive oil, it will help as a panacea for cuts and wounds." Women who have planted 13 chick peas before midsummer's day will see how many years they still have to wait for their prince or, if they already have one, how many children they will bear him – an important thing to know.

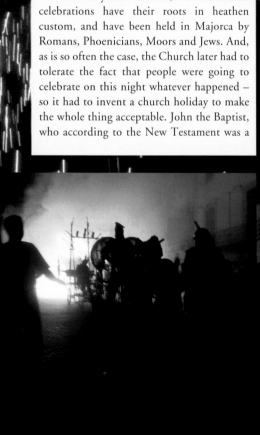

Left: On St. John's Night, anything that burns is good enough to celebrate the beginning of summer.

Right: Sparks raining down from fireworks and bonfires light up the sky during the short summer night.

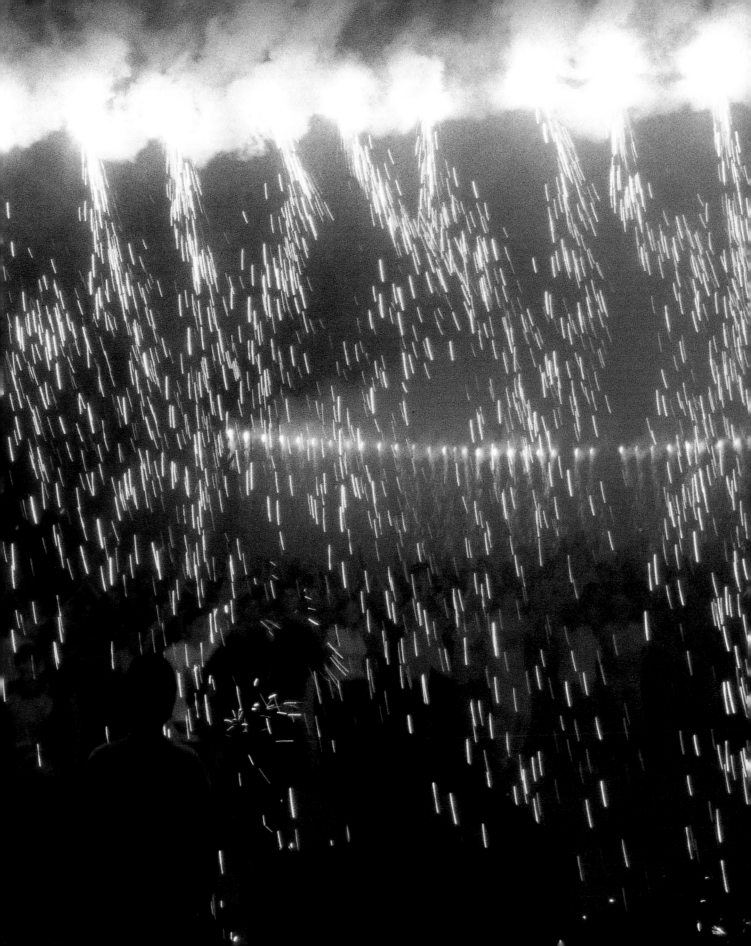

Rattling bones – in tempo
Musical instruments in Majorca

Majorcan folk musicians are to be encountered in all sorts of places. They perform at public festivals, or sometimes just for the sake of it in squares or on street corners. Tourists normally recognize the castanets one of the musicians will be holding, but the strange construction hanging around his neck is something they will perhaps not have seen before. It is a sort of ladder consisting of a number of bars lying parallel to one another. The bars are made from sheep bones that have had holes drilled in them so they can be strung on a cord. The musician plays on them by striking them with a castanet, making the bones rattle. The peculiar sound of the *ossos,* as this folk instrument is called – in other regions of Spain it is called *huesera* or *arrabel* – is enhanced when it is combined with other instruments.

A glance at the list of public holidays in Majorca reveals that the custom of celebrating different saints' days, anniversaries, pilgrimages and village festivals is alive and well. Almost every township, be it ever so small, celebrates its patron saint with as splendid a festival as possible. In the course of a year, there are numerous opportunities for *festas* with wild dancing and musicmaking, where the folk music groups with their typical instruments play an essential role.

Probably the most famous instrument of Majorca and Spain in general is the guitar, the *guitarra,* whose smaller version is also called *guitarró* . It is simply indispensable for Majorcan folk music. Another highly traditional instrument that is equally important for musical life in Majorca is the mandolin. A performance by street musicians, a *rondalla,* would be unthinkable without it. Bagpipes have traveled a long way to get here: although this somewhat out-of-tune instrument is normally considered to be the Scottish national instrument par excellence, a variant has its home in Galicia in northern Spain. From there, the *gaita* came to Majorca, where it swiftly became known as the *xeremíe* . Its crooked pipes accompany the flute, *flaviol,* the noisy tambourine and the clattering castanets, the *castanyolas,* which have become the symbol of Spanish folk music for tourists. But it would be a

Instrument maker Joan Morell specializes in making folk instruments: flutes, shawms, and *xeremíes,* Majorcan bagpipes.

The Majorcan flute, called the *flaviol,* is played using only one hand.

mistake to think that bagpipe players wear a typical Majorcan kilt when performing: men wearing skirts are as rare in Majorca as olive trees in the Scottish highlands.

Alongside these main instruments, there are several other simple, handmade ones that also have their place in folk music groups. For example, drums, *tambores,* and tambourines, *panderos* or *panderetas,* are also played. The *pandero* consists of a wooden ring with a skin stretched over it and several metal discs set into holes in the ring so they can move. When the skin is struck by a hand, the discs produce shrill metallic sounds. The *ferrets*

play the role of a triangle and are played using small metal rods.

For a long time, simple instruments were held in contempt in Majorca, becoming almost forgotten before they were taken notice of again. Today, it is possible to hear and marvel at the strange sounds that can be coaxed from mortars, *almireces,* keys, spoons, bottles, *botella labrada,* rattles, *carracas,* and bells, *cascabeles* .

Alongside these instruments for home use, professional violin making in Majorca also has a long tradition. 200 years ago, Majorcan instrument makers had an international reputation, even if they could not compete with the famous Stradivarius violins from Cremona. Their skillfully made instruments, which today are to be seen only in museums, used to be exported chiefly to South America. Because there are now a number of different music festivals in Majorca whose profits go towards a fund designed to support instrument makers, some of the workshops, such as one in Felanitx, for example, have been able to enjoy an increased demand.

Almost all Majorcan songs and dances are accompanied by instruments; only work songs are sung *a cappella.* The image of farm laborers threshing or harvesting olives with a small orchestra in the background probably

The *ossos* is an integral part of Majorcan folk music.

comes from sentimental Spanish films made in the 1950s.

But even people who do not regard folk music all that highly and view themselves rather as lovers of church music will find something to marvel at in Majorca. There are over 100 historical organs on the island, 28 of them in Palma, the capital, alone. The takings from an annual organ festival have allowed the restoration of some of these instruments, like the one in Sant Andrés in Santanyi, which was constructed by the Majorcan organ builder Jordi Bosch in the 18th century. The parish churches of Porreres, Campos and Sa Pobla also possess such "queens of the instruments", which now again sound just as resonant and full as they did hundreds of years ago.

Three men for five instruments: playing the flute and the drum at the same time demands utmost concentration.

Melons and Majorca rap
Villafranca

"... Then we'd rather feed them to the pigs!", shouted the farmer's wife from Villafranca indignantly after the wholesaler from Palma who had offered her a giveaway price for her melons. But her husband had already set up a set of scales and several cases of melons on the street: better to have occasional customers regularly buying small amounts than to bow to the yoke of the wholesalers with their price demands.

This defiant act was so successful that by the next morning he had already sold everything and his neighbors started to imitate him. That's the way it all started – at least, according to the legend in Villafranca. It did not take long for the main street to become a bazaar for fruit and vegetables. This all happened in the early 1930s, before the Spanish Civil War.

But one thing is for sure – many people traveling through Villafranca will find it well-nigh impossible to resist two urgent desires. The first is to stop, get out of the car, press a camera to one's face, and shoot away – the main street with all its elaborately draped stalls is just too picturesque, too beautiful. And the second is to listen to the concert given by the stall owners, who engage in loud verbal battles as they attempt to attract health-conscious customers with the shiniest apples, the juiciest grapes and the firmest lettuces.

As well as honeydew melons and watermelons, you can also buy tomatoes *de ramellet* in Villafranca. These are about three pounds of low-moisture tomatoes that have been grown without irrigation, then tied together on a string so that they can be easily hung up in a cool place. In this way, they keep their flavor and aroma for several months without becoming wrinkled or going bad in places.

Onions, cabbage, and garlic, the basic ingredients for every *sopa,* the Majorcan

In Villafranca, the bounty of the earth is displayed at the side of the street: melons and garlic, sweet peppers, called *ñoras,* and its spicy hot relatives, dried and hung up on strings.

soup, are also for sale. This soup consists of steamed vegetables – whatever happens to be in the garden – which are then poured, together with the cooking water, over thin, stale slices of Majorcan bread. Recently many pubs and restaurants have been including this traditional rustic meal in their menus again. Not that this simple stew is a culinary highlight; but it offers a home-grown alternative to burgers or schnitzel, imported dishes that have become all too common.

The most productive crops for small fields: grains and melons

In Villafranca, melons of all imaginable shapes and sizes are and always will be the main agricultural product. Once a year, they also give a welcome opportunity for a festival: the big melon festival *Sa Festa d'Es Meló* in autumn. This is a strange quirk of fate,

because Villafranca is situated in an area that is traditionally given over to cereal growing.

Melons, the sweet relatives of the cucumber and the pumpkin, began their triumphal rise in the early 20th century. At that time, several large estates were divided up into smaller plots, an action for which Joan March, the financial magnate and later patron of the arts, was partly responsible. This meant that more and more small farmers had smaller and smaller fields, and made less and less profit.

So they began increasing their profit margins by alternately planting vegetables and fruit instead of just grain crops. This

Left: Displays like these at the side of the road make it impossible simply to race past.

Below: Picking the peppers is backbreaking work.

meant that a farmer who did his sums right could have fields producing up to three harvests a year instead of just one. Melons were relatively undemanding and grew wonderfully well even in dry Villafranca. They also sold just as well as grain in the markets of Campos, Llucmajor and, later, Palma. The great demand made investments possible, such as a tractor to replace the traditional muscle power of the mule.

The farmers soon began using new agricultural methods, with the result that by the middle of the 20th century melons from Villafranca met the entire demand of the island. Tourists also came to hear of the quality of these fresh melons literally lying about on the street in Villafranca. Sales rose continually.

Following the motto: "If it works with melons, it will work with other crops as well", Villafranca's inhabitants have experimented with new produce, mostly the undemanding yet flavorful *de ramellet* tomatoes, without which a decent *pa amb oli* would be unimaginable.

Fields of almost ripe watermelons look like a group of balloons waiting for permission for takeoff. They have to be eaten soon after being harvested: once separated from the parent plant, they go bad quickly.

A gala performance for Sugar Baby
Sa Festa d'Es Meló

Since the time when that indignant farmer's wife from Villafranca started selling her melons right in the main street of the township in the 1930s, the colorful fruit and vegetable stalls have become an attraction for customers and tourists. The stalls with their golden, light or dark green, reticulated or velvety smooth melons now give the small town much of its character.

Sixty years later, the *meloners* decided to organize a melon festival, which has taken place every year since 1994. The climax of every *Festa d'Es Meló* is the *Concurs d'Es Meló*

– the melon competition. Here, quantity is more important than quality. The victor is the person who produces the heaviest melon. Each farmer drags along his largest green, yellow or striped produce and lays it next to the gigantic rival melons. Then the fruits, some weighing up to 33 pounds (15 kg), are placed on the scales accompanied by admiring and enthusiastic shouts from the onlookers, and the winners receive their prizes.

This is why "Sugar Baby" is never declared the winner, although it is the most frequently encountered melon in Spain and perhaps the one with the most charming proportions. It is round like a ball, and after 80 days maturation reaches a diameter of about 8 inches (20 cm). Bottle-green, shiny,

The rivals, "Sugar Baby" and "*Dulce de América*", lie in baskets before the competition.

and somewhat more ample than "Sugar Baby" is *Dulce de América*, the "sweetness from America". It is also called simply *Sa Rodona,* "the round one" – for obvious reasons. The most powerfully built melon, and therefore the main competition favorite, is the "Fairfax" with its long, yellowy-green stripes. It can sometimes reach a diameter of up to 20 inches (50 cm), and in the space of approximately 90 sunny Spanish days can attain a weight of 22 to 33 pounds (10–15 kg).

Although a distinction is made between only two main groups of melons, *síndria* and *meló* – watermelons and honeydew melons – there are innumerable varieties of this succu-

The fruits, as large as basketballs, are examined with expert eye.

Everyone waits in suspense for the infallible judgment of the digital scales.

lent fruit. There are long ones, round ones, plain and patterned ones, yellow and green ones; some are the size of a volleyball and others the size of a basketball. The farmers in Villafranca itself distinguish between three types of melon: the *Aiguerdanter* is the largest melon variety and tastes like *aiguerdiente,* fruit schnapps, when eaten at the right stage of maturity. The *Meló Eriçó,* or "hedgehog melon", is somewhat smaller than the *Aiguardanter,* and has lighter colored flesh and a yellowy green rind. The *Meló de Gra d'Arroç,* the "rice-grain melon", on the other hand, is a small, green melon with an unusually intensive flavor. No matter which of the three varieties you prefer, these round fruits have been big sellers for years. And both quality and price remain stable. Melons from Villafranca are on sale in all Majorcan markets, and they are one of the main Majorcan big sellers along with *ensaïmades* . And the unregistered trademark "from Villafranca" is already considered a guarantee of quality in itself, without there being any hard-won official stamp of approval.

Melons are in such great demand mainly because they contain 93 percent water, making them a unique and, above all, sweet thirst-quencher. And they are extremely beneficial for those people who have quenched their thirst with high-proof alcoholic drinks the evening before and have the feeling that their head is the size of *Sa*

Rodona, as they have a cleansing effect on the kidneys.

But real melon lovers – those who do not just eat it because of thirst or a hangover – know how important the right moment is for full enjoyment. For here, as with everything else, true delights are a matter of correct timing. It is important to catch the melons at exactly the right stage of maturity: if they are eaten too early, they are bitter; if they are consumed too late, they have a slightly fermented aftertaste.

The Spanish, being masters in savoir-vivre, have developed several philosophies concerning the expert evaluation of a melon's ripeness. Many tap the fruit with their fingers: if it sounds like a drum, it is a relatively sure sign that it is ripe and will provide pleasurable refreshment. Others apply pressure to the end opposite the stem; if the fruit gives way slightly, it is *en el seu punt* : at its peak.

Impressed spectators watch the presentation ceremony.

373

Modern minstrels
Folk music

Villafranca is also famous for an inedible commodity: Majorcan folk music. Right up into the 1980s, folk music was the business of folk groups that played at weddings and village festivals. Then Tomeu Penya from Villafranca succeeded in going beyond the island and gained a foothold on the Catalonian market. He made modern arrangements of traditional Majorcan folk music, combined modern and old instruments, included elements from the music of other cultures in the often monotonous music of his homeland, pepped up the songs with sometimes pointedly ambiguous, often critical lyrics on environmental issues – and was an immense success.

For, while drinking herbal liqueurs and *café* after a really good meal, Majorcans enjoy telling stories and singing songs. As the night wears on, these become more and more obscene, and tend to show an increasing lack of respect towards the authorities. For a true Majorcan, this is the most pleasurable thing there is. In earlier times, the person in the village who could put the wittiest and most explicit obscenities of all into verse enjoyed a very high standing. The modern minstrel Tomeu Penya has commercialized this tradition.

Tomeu Penya has successfully exported Majorcan folk music to the mainland – after combining it skillfully with rhythmic elements from other cultures and adding lyrics critical of society.

Actes religiosos i populars
Monti-Sion
near Porreres

The weather must have been good on 14 January 1954, when the inhabitants of Porreres began repairing the road from their township up to the Santuari de la Mare de Déu, the monastery of Monti-Sion. Full of good will, they began their project in the early morning, and in the course of that winter day achieved a record-breaking feat: the musclemen of Porreres actually managed to complete the work on the two miles (3 km) of winding road within a single day.

They did not even think of payment, despite the sweat running down their backs and foreheads: God would reward them. Their efforts were simply for the good of all, and it was a matter of honor to help. Since then, their reputation has been made: they are said to be extremely community-minded with a tendency to get themselves organized. The fact that they like to gather together every week in groups of people with similar interests naturally does nothing to detract from this. On the contrary: Porreres is considered the cradle of Majorcan organizations and societies.

Whether people in Porreres are in the choral society or the folk music ensemble, their interests tend to be cultural, if one disregards a few hunters and pigeon fanciers. This is probably the fault of the Franciscan friars who, as early as 1551, founded a school for rhetoric and grammar. Those wanting to become priests could learn Latin here, and the quality of instruction was apparently so high that the school soon had to be enlarged. By the middle of the 17th century, the reputation of this monastery school had spread well beyond the borders of Porreres. At that time, the school had an impressive 500 pupils – more than could be boasted by any educational institution in Palma, the capital. Even today, Porreres is considered a glowing example as far as education is concerned: the rate of illiteracy here is much lower than the 27 percent sometimes recorded in other rural areas of Majorca.

The hill of Monti-Sion, 712 feet (254 m) high, owes its name to the Virgin of Mount Zion, and the church belonging to the monastery is also dedicated to her. This small monastery church with its highly ornate portal is the loveliest for miles around, or at least on the Pla. Two aristocratic families, the Duzays and the Mesquidas, helped build the church, which is why their coats of arms can still be found inside. That of the Duzays is situated at the foot of a 15th century marble statue of the

The sunny cloister of the Monti-Sion monastery has five sides instead of the usual four.

376

Virgin of Mount Zion carved by a Majorcan stonemason; the Mesquidas only managed to get theirs placed in a side chapel.

The monastery was preceded in the 14th century by a hermitage dedicated to the eternal mystery of the appearance of Mary. In 1498, the accommodation obviously became too ascetic for the hermits, and they founded a new chapel, one decorated with Nostra Senyora de Monti-Sion, a Byzantine figure of the Virgin in wood. When the fame of the school of religion began to spread, however, a wooden Byzantine statue of the Virgin was no longer good enough, so it was exchanged for the marble one still found there today.

But even this could not prevent the usual fate of monasteries at the beginning of the 19th century. During the secularization process set in motion by the Liberals, the Santuari de Monti-Sion was abandoned and rapidly fell into disrepair. This situation continued until around the turn of the century, when reconstruction work began. Fortunately for tourism, however, this did not change the unspoiled nature of this place of pilgrimage.

As is only right and proper for a Majorcan *santuari,* the terrace-like forecourt has a fantastic view of nearby San Salvador and the Puig Santuari, and over the Pla to Campos, Felanitx, and Manacor. A set of

steps leads from here into the inner courtyard of the monastery. This courtyard is unique: the cloister with its solidly-built arcades of round arches is not square or even rectangular, but five-sided instead. The former monks' cells looking out onto it have now long been used as accommodation for pilgrims and tourists interested in art.

Standing on one of the sides of the courtyard in front of the small church, it is impossible not to be reminded of Mexican village churches as seen in American westerns. What one sees is a solid frontage with small windows, bells hanging out in the open, a façade higher than the roof ridge with two fake towers on either side, and an old well in front. The White Madonna, a strangely contradictory sculpture, dominates the interior. The marble figures of Virgin and child seem to be opposed to one another both in artistic execution and the message they convey. The Virgin seems gentle and maidenly, with only a halo marking her as being "blessed among women". Her garments are softly contoured, and her innocent, pensive expression makes her seem vulnerable while giving her a sort of sublime beauty. The infant Jesus, on the other hand, is crude and rough. It almost looks as if it were thrashing about in the arms of its tender mother, and makes such a heavy, solid impression that one expects it to fall at

any moment. This representation of Mary with her child is just like the Pla: delightful and gentle like the blossoming almond orchards, rustic and stark like the cracked, dry earth.

Once a year, the Monti-Sion is especially full. On the first Sunday after Easter, the *Diumenge del' Àngel* or Angels' Sunday, the people of Porreres are not the only ones to go up to the monastery: a seemingly endless procession winds its way around the curves of the road up into the Massís de Randa. On the way it traverses cool, shady pine forests and passes solitary Gothic columns, the last remnants of a group of 14 representing the seven joys and the seven sorrows.

Then the *actes religiosos i populars,* as the municipal administration of Porreres puts it, begin: groups in local costume and folk music ensembles make sure the mood is right – although the drinks served in the monastery bar probably help a little as well.

The fragrance of the Orient
Apricots

All of a sudden, everyone wanted apricots. At the end of the 19th century this sweet fruit, one that immediately puts Central Europeans in mind of the sunny south, experienced a veritable boom. The Majorcans themselves ate apricots fresh or dried, and exported them "to Europe" as jam or concentrate. Particularly the English, French, and Scandinavians were completely mad about them.

But apricots go back much further than that. In China, the apricot was known as early as the third century BC. In antiquity, this fragrant member of the rose family wandered across Europe, and continued its triumphal progress to Majorca, where it was introduced by the Arabs. The Arabs also gave it its name: they called it *al barkuk,* which the Majorcans changed to *albercoc;* the Spanish word for the fruit is *albaricoque.*

Into the 19th century, apricots were not precisely a common article. Apricots were grown without irrigation and almost entirely for personal use. This had a lot to do with the short harvest period and the fact that the fruit turns bad very quickly.

When the apricot boom finally began at the end of the 19th century, apricot production in Majorca prospered. Apricots were greatly in demand right into the 1970s. But then, other regions caught onto the idea of profiting from the apricot trade. Soon Majorcan apricots could no longer compete against their cheaper rivals from Morocco, Tunisia and Turkey. A sad business indeed: in the 1990s, the Majorcans had to destroy 50,000 tons of apricots a year because harvesting, packaging and transport had become too expensive.

The apricot was introduced to Majorca by the Moors at the end of the eighth century.

Fortunately, the Majorcans saw no reason to give up growing this versatile fruit. It still has an important place in Majorcan cuisine: in sweet desserts, stewed, as topping for the traditional *ensaïmades,* or as a final touch to hearty meat dishes. Or simply as "giant ears": very large dried apricots are sold in Majorca under the name of *orejones,* from orejón meaning "giant ear". These are cut open lengthwise in the middle to look like gigantic ears.

In June, the apricots land in the buckets of the harvesters.

Women halving and stoning the velvety fruit – a social event.

Crate after crate fills the room with sweet fragrance and glowing color.

The apricots are placed close together for transport so none can fall out.

The same sun that caused them to ripen now serves to dry them slowly.

The Majorcan sun ensures the apricots stay juicy and sweet even when dried.

East and west together on one plate: hearty beef entrecôtes with sweet apricots.

Entrecôte amb albercocs

Entrecôte with apricots (serves four)

Ingredients
4 beef entrecôtes
5 ¼ oz (150 g) bacon slices
1 lb 2 oz (500 g) ripe apricots
1 glass sweet white wine
1 tablespoon honey
salt and pepper

The interesting thing about this recipe is the apricot sauce, which can, of course, also be used as an accompaniment to other fried meat, veal cutlets, or lamb. It is important to be aware, however, that ripe apricots, which are essential for this recipe, have an intensity of flavor in Majorca that is not to be found in mainland European or imported fruits, except at the height of the apricot harvest.

Dab the thick beef entrecôtes dry using a dishcloth, sprinkle on salt and pepper, and fasten the slices of bacon to them using toothpicks. Heat some olive oil in a cast-iron pan, and sear the entrecôtes on both sides over high heat. Reduce the heat, and continue cooking them until the meat is a light pink inside.

Halve and stone the apricots. Place them in some water in a pot and bring to a boil. When the water has evaporated (after about 7–8 minutes), add the sweet white wine and the honey. Continue cooking until the mixture reaches a pulpy consistency. Put the mixture through a sieve. Serve the golden-brown beef entrecôtes and bacon slices on top of this apricot sauce. A cold, not too dry white wine is the ideal accompaniment.

Ensaïmada de luxe: halved apricots and sugar make these pastries into colorful summer tarts.

Sunlight in a jar: in the cold winter, apricot jam provides a touch of summer warmth.

Opposite: Stored solar energy: here apricots, not solar collectors, concentrate the power of the Majorcan sun.

A center for handicrafts
Porreres

Suddenly, on the left, a pottery jug shatters. On the right you can hear haggling, complaints, praise; people push their way past the stalls, there is the noise of angry grunting. From in front comes the clatter of copper kettles and cast-iron pans, zinc guttering and pewter goblets, from behind the sound of barking, mooing, and bleating: "Sa Fira" in Porreres. Once a year, at the end of October, the township holds this small fair at which local handicrafts are exhibited. For the town's inhabitants, it has long been more important than the traditional livestock market that still takes place next to it.

Otherwise, Porreres is not precisely at the hub of the world, or even of Majorca. Apart from the *Diumenge del' Àngel,* Angels' Sunday, the day one week after Easter when there is a pilgrimage to the monastery of Monti-Sion and the *Pancaritat* festival, life in this small town tends to take a leisurely course. Only on the 16 August, the *Dia de Sant Roc,* when the patron saint of the community is honored with a celebration, are the village streets given over to boisterous merrymaking. Religious ceremonies, parades, competitions and dancing ensure there is plenty to do and see for both the town's inhabitants and visitors.

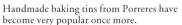
Handmade baking tins from Porreres have become very popular once more.

Every Tuesday there is a market in the Plaça d'Espanya. But the fact that this town was once of greater economic importance even than the royal seat of Sineu is now to be found only in history books. Only a few well-preserved manor houses with their typical broad driveways and the mighty parish church Nostra Senyora de Consolació still testify to the town's former glory.

But not everyone on the Pla is unhappy that the modern age has arrived. The town hall in Porreres houses a small but worthwhile museum of modern art with two Dalís. And, surprisingly enough, this small country town that seems to have been forgotten by time is an excellent example of how the fear of losing old values and customs can be turned into a virtue – and, above all, a lucrative business: by manufacturing skillfully crafted everyday objects using traditional methods, for example.

Once, selecting materials to make tools and utensils for everyday use was very simple: gutters were traditionally made of zinc, bells of copper, lanterns and household objects of iron or other metals. The small town of Porreres used to be a big manufacturer of such items, and it still is – or rather, has become so again.

Many antique shops have metal workshops connected to them where visitors both large and small can watch artisans at work and then buy the newly-made objects in the shop. Success is guaranteed, for these traditional products are becoming increasingly popular.

It used to be a different story. In the 1950s, traditional raw materials were forced

Oil cans, water jugs, and baking tins are skillfully made to look old.

Great care is taken finishing off a zinc gutter.

visit the workshops almost reverentially, admire the skills of the artisans, and are ready to pay good money for any freshly-made object that catches their fancy. It now pays again to produce such articles as zinc gutters, lanterns and other utensils made out of tin, fine pewter kitchenware in antique style, and traditional cowbells, *picarols,* which are made exactly as they used to be hundreds of years ago.

Nobody is worried if some of the products are not originally Majorcan. After all, shoes with soles made out of old car tires or canvas sell just as well as frying pans or baking tins. The fact that these shoes are sold all over southern Europe, for example in Crete and Portugal, is something the souvenir hunters do not notice anyway.

off the market when the newly invented synthetics overran Europe. Anyone with any pride had bowls, sieves, lemon squeezers, dustpans, airtight wrapping and brushes made of the new wonder material.

The return to the good old days

In the 1970s, plastic, once so highly prized, slowly but surely began to fall into disrepute. At first it was only for ideological reasons, because of its "artificiality": anything "natural" was now more in demand. Soon, however, medical grounds were also found: synthetic products contained additional substances both to increase their strength and hardness and to save material. These substances could be harmless ones like cork or sawdust, but asbestos was also often used. After the health risks posed by asbestos were proven, plastic products were no longer so popular.

As a result, traditional materials experienced a revival. Most plastic utensils were banished from the household, and there was a return to "natural" products. Several firms manufacturing such items in the "good old way" appeared on the market. Metals such as zinc, copper, and iron were suddenly in demand again. Particularly in central and northern Europe, products made of metal

became cult objects. People were ready to pay three or four times as much for them as for plastic ones.

The Majorcans, who since about 1950 have been overrun every year by a wave of foreign tourists, were worried that these crowds and the foreign influence they brought with them would cause a loss of identity, tradition, and local handicrafts. As far as handicrafts are concerned, however, exactly the opposite occurred. The foreign visitors had undergone a change of mentality. Whereas they once smiled pityingly at the old metal paella pan hanging above the oven, they now began to appreciate these simple utensils once more. A plain metal sieve was now the center of much admiration, and zinc guttering and the old iron stove in the middle of the house were also the objects of enthusiasm.

The inhabitants of the island recalled many of their old customs and began, as in Porreres, to work enthusiastically following old models and using original materials. This increasing recollection of Majorcan tradition has not only given impetus to the old workshops: it has also led to new ones being established, along with shops selling these products made using the working methods and manufacturing techniques of old.

Foreign tourists from northern Europe are the best customers for handicrafts. They

Traditional cowbells decorate entrances to houses instead of hanging around cows' necks.

Migjorn

settled on a permanent basis. The protected, often fjord-like bays in the south provided shelter, the extremely calm sea made for safe landing, and the surrounding area contained enough animals and plants to live off. The Phoenicians probably established their first Majorcan trading post on the tiny island of La Cobrera in 300 BC. But the Migjorn first made an indelible mark on history in 1349. Over 110 years after the Reconquista, Jaume III had been forced to look on more or less powerlessly as Pere IV of Aragón invaded the island and condemned him to exile in Roussillon. On 25 October 1349, Jaume tried to win back the lost island and the crown of an independent Majorca with an army weakened by the plague, but to no avail. Jaume III was killed in the battle and Majorca fell to the kingdom of Aragón.

Life without water

It is hard to say how much this directly affected the daily life of the peasants. The main key to their existence and survival in an area like this has always been the way they have adapted perfectly to their environment, no matter who has been the ruler. In a region where

Salt and sun, sand and stone
The Migjorn

When the sun is so high in the sky that your own shadow takes shelter under your feet, it has completed half of its daily journey: midday, *migjorn* in Majorcan. *Migjorn* also means the intersection between east and west: that is, the south. Majorca's "midday" does credit to its name. Here, this largest of the Balearic islands ceases to be an island of flowers, concentrating instead on fulfilling the promise of sun suggested by its name. Nowhere else on the island does it rain so little and so infrequently. The thirsty fields of the Migjorn receive only about a third of the average rainfall for the island, which is low enough anyway: only 176 US gallons per square yard (800 l per m²).

The Migjorn is situated between two elevations: the Puig de Randa (745 feet–501 m) near Llucmajor, and the Puig de Sant Salvador near Felanitx, which rises 777 feet (510 m) over the nearby sea. The rest of the Migjorn cowers before the glaring sun almost at sea level. It seems at first sight to be sleepy, withered up, abandoned in an endless siesta. But appearances can be deceptive. This dry, inhospitable area has a population of about 160 inhabitants per square mile (100 per km2), a figure higher than the Spanish average of 86 (80 per km2) and the Majorcan average of about 80 (75 per km2), Palma excepted.

Archeological evidence, such as that found in the prehistoric Talayotic settlement of Cabocorb Vell to the south-west of Campos, proves that the Migjorn was one of the first areas in Majorca to be

Previous double-page spread: In the south of the island, the mixed Mediterranean woodland provides cooling shade and prevents the dry, crumbly soil from being scattered by the winds.

Since 1596, this defense tower near the Colònia de Sant Jordi has kept watch to ensure that the Migjorn and its inhabitants are left in peace.

water is such a valuable resource, it is impossible to keep livestock, as this cannot subsist without large amounts of it. This does not mean, however, that agriculture has no chance at all here. Certain hardy species of flora and fauna actually thrive in this area. Near Felanitx in the north-eastern part of the Migjorn, for example, vines grow so well that they provide 90 percent of the white wine produced in Majorca. This is made possible by a combination of regular sunlight, chalky soil and at least some water from the Puig de Sant Salvador.

Apricot and almond trees have also shown themselves to be profitable sources of edible produce over the centuries, and both wild and cultivated varieties of olive tree as well as extremely undemanding plants like the prickly pear cactus have been winners in the Darwinian battle for survival of the fittest. Near Campos, the descendants of Frisian cows, here called *frisons* , provide milk for *piris* , the Majorcan variant of the square, tasty cheese speciality from the neighboring island of Menorca.

Hunger, plague, pirates
It is fairly obvious that agriculture under such climatic conditions does not make for an idyll. Water is and remains a problem: Today, machinery and fertilizers make work under the constantly blue skies a little easier, but even they cannot magically produce a lush, green and blossoming Garden of Eden.

Above: In the Migjorn, every fully-grown tree is an enormous achievement of nature. The views gained looking through them are breathtakingly lovely.

Below: Many a survival expert thrives here in the south.

In the 17th century, the church belonging to the Convent of Sant Bonaventura was renovated. It only received its new belltower in 1820. Majorcans associate Llucmajor above all with the loss of their freedom: in a battle just outside the city in 1349 against the occupying Aragonese, Jaume III lost his life in the attempt to win back his kingdom.

Chubby-cheeked and curious, this Baroque angel above the rose window looks over the roofs of Llucmajor.

In the 16th century, the rainfall was slight or non-existent for years, leaving people with no choice but to grind carob pods, normally used as animal fodder, into flour in the mills near Campos.

There were other afflictions besides hunger to act as constant and cruel companions of the mainly rural population of the Migjorn. Plagues, malaria, and ergotism, an illness caused by fungus-infected rye, found considerable numbers of victims among the undernourished peasants.

Other scourges arrived by sea. On St. Mark's Night in 1388, for example, Santanyí learnt the painful lesson that the Arab pirates would stop at nothing to sack entire cities and abduct their inhabitants, whom they later freed for ransom or sold as slaves. Santanyí's appearance still bears witness to the fact that only fortifications and strong walls made from the particularly fine, hard Marès stone found in the region offered some protection against the pirates right up to the beginning of the 18th century. Until they could feel secure, the people of this city, whose coat of arms contains the Lamb of God, had no time for decoration for its own sake. This was the reason why the city was built compactly for defense; only in the last 200 years has Mediterranean elegance started to play an architectural role.

The church of the apostle Andrew also became a fortress of faith and hope. It underwent alterations in the 18th century. Only the Chapel of the Rosary, whose vault is held together by the Lamb of God in the form of the keystone, remained in its original form. The fashion grew up of decorating ventilation openings in the houses with lovely rosettes, *estrelles mostrejades*, made out of the golden Marès stone from Santanyí. This would have been unimaginable at the time when the danger of a pirate attack was always hanging over the city. The pirates could have interpreted such luxuries as a sign that there was something worth plundering, and left their temporary domicile on the Illa Cabrera to go on another raid.

Today at Cala Pi, a lighthouse keeps one of the formerly 85 *talaias* from the 16th and 17th century company. These watchtowers surrounded the coasts of Majorca like a security cordon. They were within eyeshot of one another so they could give the red alert on the island using smoke and fire signals: pirates ahoy!

White gold and water cures

At least the coast served one good purpose, even if it scarcely brought any other blessings. But there was at least one more. As far back as Roman times, it was discovered that nature had provided a gold mine behind the long Playa d'Es Trenc with its fine sand: salt flats. During the long hot summers sea salt, the white gold of the sea, turned into a hard crust here on the flat alluvial land, and needed only to be carted away.

At the end of the 20th century, salt was still being mined over an area of 130 hectares. The technique used is one that simply improves

In rural areas of Majorca such as the Migjorn, the church is not only omnipresent in the form of buildings. Most nuns and monks still live in strict seclusion, however.

on the basic natural principle, filling the landscape with white mountains that are visible for great distances and cannot be viewed without sunglasses. Not far away, the Romans used to seek relief from skin disease, digestive problems, and circulatory disorders in Majorca's only thermal health resort, the Banys de Sant Joan. These slightly radioactive, sulfurous springs with their constant temperature of 101 F (38.5° C) were only equipped with a building to house them in 1516. Before that time, sick people mixed with pigs, cattle and all sorts of other unappetizing bathing companions in the brackish waters. Today, after much to-ing and fro-ing, both of the Sant Joan springs, Font Santa and Font Sa Bassa, are in private hands – with a hotel attached.

The coast of Migjorn became valuable in itself only in the 20th century. Because of the pirates, little fishing took place here. Only Porto Colom, the port for Felanitx, and Portopetro, Santanyí's gateway to the sea, have tiny harbors worth mentioning. Otherwise, the countryside must have looked uninhabited when viewed from the water. At the beginning of the 20th century, many farmers doubtless thought it an *innocentada*, an April Fool's joke, when they heard that people were going to the beach with picnic baskets just to sit and lie there or go swimming. For them, the sea only brought conquerors and pirates or, at the most, seaweed as fertilizer for their fields.

Idyllic bays

These strange visitors at the beach were the first sign that this evaluation was undergoing a great change. The growing tourist industry discovered bays ideal for its purposes on this unpopulated and undeveloped coastline. The one nearest to Palma, called Platja de Palma although it is partly in the municipality of Llucmajor, has managed to become a symbol for mass tourism within the space of a few years. The beach resort of S'Arenal at the south-eastern end of the bay is associated with package tourism, and has become particularly popular with German tourists. Such bargain basement tourism has also turned the 130 feet (40 m) wide sandy beach into an atrocity with blocks of cement masquerading as hotels: at least, that is how its critics see it. Fans of S'Arenal, on the other hand, maintain that ordinary people without much money and families with children find exactly what they are looking for there: a first-class beach with shallow, safe waters, and service that does not require them to put up with more foreign culture than is absolutely necessary.

Such experiences have at least made it possible to protect other beaches from suffering a similar fate. The most famous example in

Beginning the day in true Majorcan style in Café Colón in Llucmajor: *ensaïmada*, coffee, and newspaper.

the Migjorn is the beach of Es Trenc. In the 1980s this was to be transformed into a holiday paradise replete with a thirsty golf course. Vehement protests on the part of the inhabitants meant that even where building permission had already been given the plans were put on ice. These building licenses are still tucked away somewhere, and a parking lot and one or two ice-cream and sausage stands have found their way there already. But Es Trenc remains what is was: the largest almost untouched beach on Majorca.

Just the other side of the southerly cape Cap de ses Salines going east, however, instead of one long beach after another there is a row of romantic bays all the way to Cala Ratjada in the Llevant. The Cala d'or, Cala Mondragó and Cala Figuera have not been able to retain their original character like Es Trenc, but they have not suffered a mass invasion like S'Arenal.

And by winter they return to their sunny solitude. Then visitors of another sort come to the Migjorn in droves: perspiring, they pedal alongside the drystone walls across the warm plain. The remote but asphalted roads allow a less strenuous form of training than the Tramuntana, where the hardiest specimens fight against the mountains; and the Migjorn is also the home of one of the greats in this field, after all. In his home town of Felanitx, the six-time world champion in motor-paced racing, Guillem Timoner, provides the cyclists with spare parts and advice in his own shop.

Right: At the southern end of Majorca, desert winds from Africa can whip up the sea even in the morning. The rising sun turns it into a splendid symphony of blue-gray and red-orange.

Following double-page spread: Sun umbrellas on the beach at Ses Covetes wait to provide shade for visitors to the beach. Even at the height of the season, there are seldom problems with overcrowding.

In Cala Figuera, the sea pushes its way deep into the coast like a fjord.

He is not southern Majorca's only famous son. The contemporary artist Miquel Barceló first saw the light of day in Felanitx, as did the master builder of the Gothic style, Guillem Sagrera, who built the Llotja in Palma. And town legend has it that Felanitx is also the birthplace of no less a personage than Christopher Columbus, the "discoverer" of a new world. Which, for the people of the Migjorn, therefore starts here in the south, surrounded by salt and sun, sea and stone.

The struggle for freedom and a place in the sun
Llucmajor

The apricot trees that are so famous for the sweetness of their fruit probably already lined the roads to Llucmajor in the autumn of 1349, as Jaume III set out with 3,000 foot soldiers and 400 cavalry to wrest the kingdom of Majorca from the hands of his cousin Pere IV of Aragón and give it its freedom again. Pere IV had conquered Majorca in 1343 in a lightning attack to correct the historical error – from Aragón's point of view – of his great-grandfather Jaume I, who after his death caused his kingdom to be divided into two parts, Aragón and Majorca.

But Jaume III's troops, hastily gathered in Roussillon where he had taken refuge, were exhausted, and weakened by hunger and plague. They did not stand a chance against the soldiers of the usurper from the mainland. Jaume III was beheaded in the battle of Llucmajor on the 25 October 1349 by a soldier whose name has not come down to us in history books, in contrast to the place where Majorca lost its freedom for good. There are two monuments as reminders. A memorial cross in the Plaça de Sa Batalla on the south-eastern route into Llucmajor marks the site of defeat, a simple stone cross with the coat of arms of the kingdom of Majorca. In Llucmajor itself, a

On Sundays, the Plaça d'Espanya is filled with delights from the Majorcan countryside. Crunchy almonds and walnuts in sweet honey are difficult to obtain in shops, for example.

Right: A hairdresser in Llucmajor giving a young Majorcan a smart haircut.

Below: Old friends spend whole afternoons with a pack of Spanish playing cards, *cartes* .

group sculpture in stone shows Jaume III in a suit of mail dying on the ground while a soldier from his bodyguard holds up the banner of Majorca in the wind one last time. The remains of the last king of Majorca rested in the Sant Miquel church in Llucmajor until they were buried next to those of his grandfather Jaume II in the Palma cathedral in 1905.

The beach as battleground: S'Arenal – disgrace or delight

Llucmajor does not at all live in the past with memories of something that just was not to be. Extensive apricot plantations have

given the town one more claim to fame. And a third civic monument honors the members of a profession that was the second economic mainstay of the small town until well into the 20th century: the shoemakers, who today are sometimes found working for top French brand names. Some fine Art Nouveau houses in the Barcelona style also bear witness to the fact that the town was reasonably well-off.

At the time when these were built at the beginning of the 20th century, the place that 60 years later, along with Calvià, was to become the embodiment of mass tourism, was still an untouched beach enclosed by dunes and pine forests. S'Arenal belongs to Llucmajor and not to Palma, although today it runs into the outer suburbs of the capital without a break.

In 1861 it was a completely different story. This was the year the very first

connecting road to Llucmajor was built, the Camí de S'Algar, and 11 years later the first house was built in S'Arenal. Around 1900 a few summer vacationers built themselves a sort of beach refuge there, and the demand for farming land grew. This meant that small allotments, better streets and finally even a railroad connection came into being. In the 1920s, visitors to the beach – mostly Majorcans from nearby Palma – sunned themselves on the beach, separated according to sex. Part of the beach was even put aside for livestock. Only in the 1950s did the first small hotel extend beyond the dunes, giving the start signal for a development that to this day blemishes the reputation of the island as a tourist resort and awakes aggressive opposition.

Thirty years after the explosive expansion of tourism in Majorca, S'Arenal remains

At sunset, the beach of S'Arenal is completely empty. Behind the mountain ridge near Calvià, the next battery of sun umbrellas and beach chairs waits to go on duty the following morning.

controversial. For those wanting to learn from the mistakes of the past, S'Arenal stands for everything that should not have happened under any circumstances. To enjoy sand dunes and pine forests today, a long trip towards Cala Blava is necessary, a trip that takes you past miles of massive hotels, discos, restaurants, souvenir shops and supermarkets stocking mainland European products. The 130 feet (40 m) wide beach of S'Arenal no longer has the protection of the dunes and tree roots, and was washed into the sea during a winter storm in 1989. The nearly 400,000 tons of sand needed were replaced immediately, but now underwater dunes wander over the seabed, stifling some of the natural fauna. Artificial reefs made out of strong reinforced concrete have been built to provide a home for shellfish, fish and plants.

The beach, which is divided up into *balnearis* – spa baths – in the old-fashioned manner, has become an end in itself in the battle for a place in the sun. Each *balneario* has its own clientele; the former wooden booths have been replaced by flashier post-modern steel and aluminum pavilions. The most famous of them, *balneario 6,* has even featured in the German movie world as "Ballermann", and as a topic for sociologists researching mass phenomena. All rather strange, since this phenomenon has no cultural or intellectual pretensions, consisting only of skittle clubs, bachelor parties, and people escaping from the humdrum round of everyday life, ruining their livers by drinking one gallon bucket of sangría after the other, and then stumbling drunkenly back to their cheap hotel on the other side of the beach promenade in the afternoon amidst often hooligan-like behavior.

Majorcan culture of whatever kind has no business here. Hotels, shops and bars have adapted to the language and lifestyle of their customers, giving tourists the illusion that they are completely at home even though they are a couple of hours' flight away from their native land.

Give a dog a bad name…In *balneario 6*, the essence of mass tourism is seen in its most uninhibited form.

But seen under another light, the concept behind S'Arenal can be seen to be useful and essential. S'Arenal, with its extensive shallow waters, provides safe beach enjoyment for children, non-swimmers and elderly people. The high profits made at the end of the 20th century have been invested in generous improvements and renovations, like the new promenade, parks, and playgrounds. Even the notorious *balneario 6* has been given a new image, together with a security service and pot plants, and has become much tamer.

And not every visitor wants to go to *balneario 6*, say the fans of S'Arenal: such centers of mass tourism are essential for people who cannot afford to stay in a five-star hotel for two weeks in summer, for which they save up every spare cent in the other 50 weeks of the year. These guests want 14 days of beach and fun without culinary experiments. They do not need anything more ambitious in the way of culture than a simple, standardized Flamenco show in their hotel in the evening, and do not want to appear in their photo albums as golfing stars on the 13th hole, but instead covered with suntan lotion in their hard-won beach chair, gazing out to sea. They are not worried by the fact that there is one concrete hotel block after the other in the background, where nature intended a small paradise of sand dunes.

A few yards on, sun worshippers enjoy a completely normal day at the beach.

Smoke and flames pass on the message
Majorca's watchtowers

At Cala Pi, two buildings tower above the coastline, uniting new and old. One of them, a modern lighthouse, shows passing ships where land is; the other, a round, two-storied stone tower, was built in 1662 and has not been used for a long time. While it was in service, however, it had a task that was at least as important, although one directed inland as well: for many centuries, "Pirates ahoy!" was the message coming from such a *talaia*.

Once, the watchtower of Cala Pi had 84 companions along the Majorcan coast, each within eyeshot of the next. They began to be built at the end of the 16th century, a time when the Majorcans perceived the Arab pirates as being their greatest threat.

The people of Majorca had been the constant victims of raids since time immemorial – something that did not stop them going off on pillaging expeditions themselves – but the idea of a common defense only arose when a definite enemy emerged. This was too late for Llucmajor: in 1578 and 1579, Moorish buccaneers landed at Cala Pi and abducted some of the inhabitants, either to extort ransom money or to sell them into slavery and imprisonment.

The Barbarossa brothers, who murdered their way from being pirates to becoming Turkish governors, made life particularly difficult for Christians in the 16th century. Not even Charles V (1500–1558), the emperor of the Holy Roman Empire and Spanish king, was able to do anything about them: his attempt to bring them to justice in Algiers in 1541 failed.

That was when the pirate scourge really began. The Barbarossa brothers were to

From the 16th century on, a ring made up of 85 watchtowers like this one surrounded the island. They acted as an alarm system for the inhabitants, warning them of raids by North African and Turkish pirates.

control the western Mediterranean for many years: Majorca's cities were plundered, and Christian Europe moved swiftly to protect its coasts.

In Majorca, the inhabitants of coastal towns moved several miles inland, while those living in the important but unprotected ports were ready to flee at any time. Jacobo Paleazzo, the Italian master builder, was therefore given the commission around 1560 to construct a ring of watchtowers along the coast like that in his own country. As one can see by the date of construction of the tower at Cala Pi, however, it took another hundred years for the circle to be joined.

The *talaies* were manned day and night by two or three watchmen, who were paid for this duty by the village inhabitants. As soon as a pirate ship was sighted, the watchmen alarmed the neighboring towers using smoke signals during the day and fire at night. In this way, the central Torre del Angel, the Angels' Tower in Palma, received speedy news of the danger, and was able to send out defense troops. Until these armed riders arrived, the village people fought as best they could against the advancing plunderers, using stones just like their Talayotic ancestors.

The *talaies* protected the island until the end of the 19th century, when the ministry of defense made the towers over to the ministry of finance. Because the latter found no appropriate use for them, they were auctioned off. Since then, 30 of the towers have disappeared into thin air: they were probably knocked down so their stone could be reused. Most of the *talaies* still existing today have become lookouts for walkers and hikers, although some were able to celebrate a comeback as watchtowers in the 20th century to help in the pursuit of smugglers.

Towers that are within eyeshot of one another still exist only on the uninhabited peninsula of Ferrutx. Three of these, de Morei, Aubarca, and Jaumell, are situated far from any road, and even the Torre de la Mola, which has been restored to its original state by its new owner, can only be reached on foot.

If you are not keen on using shanks' pony, you can also get to some towers by car; for example, the Mirador de ses Animes, the "Lookout of the Souls", near Banyalbufar. It is situated 820 feet (250 m) above the sea and provides a view over the entire southern coastline. Its previous owner is responsible for its good state of preservation: Archduke Ludwig Salvator, filled with the desire to preserve anything Majorcan, had his *talaia* restored out of his own pocket.

When the pirate raids ceased, the *talaies* no longer had any useful function. Many were plundered for their stones or collapsed through lack of maintenance.

The devil's darling
Peppers

Em emporta un pebre : "it interests me (as much as) a pepper." Anyone who gets to hear this phrase in Majorca knows that the person they are talking to is not particularly interested in the topic under discussion. At first, a tourist cannot imagine what this could have to do with peppers. Except in September, when just a short look around is enough to understand the origin of this figure of speech.

This is when ripe peppers are harvested and threaded onto strings by the women. Then the Majorcans hang these carmine ribbons on the walls of their houses for a month to dry. Often, one sees entire façades with thousands of small, scarlet fruits. One pepper on its own is of absolutely no consequence.

Majorcan cuisine would be unimaginable without peppers. Used as a vegetable, it is an essential ingredient of the "summer salad", the *trempó,* a dish containing onions and tomatoes that is served in Majorca, for example, with squid as *sepia amb trempó,* or with a tart as *coca amb trempó.* It is also used in the *frit mallorquí,* a fried Majorcan dish that would be unthinkable without red and green peppers. Even cheese is pepped up with peppers: the *formatge sec,* a hard cheese that needs a whole year to mature, has olive oil and paprika rubbed into it to make it keep longer.

It is no coincidence that peppers are also called "Spanish peppers", because it was Columbus who collected the seeds of this member of the nightshade family in America. Today, it is familiar all over the world in many variations.

Devilish varieties

The *pimiento del piquillo de Lodosa,* which originated in Navarra in northern Spain, is the only variety of pepper with a protected designation of origin. *Piquillos* are small peppers, at the most 4 inches (10 cm) long, and are harvested only when red. They are first grilled over the coals of a wood fire before having their seeds and skins removed. Then the peppers can be put into cans or

Above: After the harvest in September, the ripe peppers are threaded onto strings. These colorful ribbons then decorate the walls of the houses for a month until they have dried completely.

jars. Any pieces of blackened skin remaining are considered to be a trademark of the best peppers in Spain.

The peppers grown by Majorcan farmers tend to be somewhat smaller than those from the mainland, but compensate for this with a more intensive flavor. The chalky soil and constant shortage of water on the island ensure that the fruits do not grow too large.

In Majorca, *pebres* are mostly grown in the region near Colonia de Sant Jordí. Normally, they are divided into two sorts: the *dolçes,* sweet peppers, and the *picants,* hot peppers. The *dolçes* are larger and resemble *morrones,* while the *picants* are smaller and, of course, hotter.

They are used to make *pebre vermell,* a condiment made of ground, dried peppers.

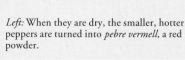

Left: When they are dry, the smaller, hotter peppers are turned into *pebre vermell,* a red powder.

After they have been hanging for about a month on the wall of a house, the peppers have been dried by the sun and shrunk owing to loss of moisture. The strings are taken down, and the stems removed. Then the peppers are dried in a wood oven at a constant, fairly low temperature. Following this, they are chopped into equal-sized pieces and put through huge mills until this flavorful powder is finally ready for use.

For example, in *sobrassada*, the way most black pigs in Majorca naturally end up. *Sobrassada* is the national sausage of the Balearic islands, and owes its red color to *pebre vermell*. Hot paprika also gives *cargols amb sobrassada*, snails with paprika sausage, the kick they need in addition to the *sobrassada*. And mild paprika is used as a spice in *arròs a la marinera*, rice soup with seafood.

Tumbet

Autumn vegetables (serves 4–6)

Ingredients
2lb 4oz (1 kg) ripe tomatoes (for the sauce)
8 cloves of garlic
4 ripe eggplants (aubergines)
2 firm, green zucchinis (courgettes)
4 sweet green peppers
8 medium-sized, waxy potatoes
olive oil
salt and pepper

Cut the tomatoes into pieces for the sauce. Fry four chopped up cloves of garlic slightly in some olive oil in a cast-iron pan. Add the tomatoes. Simmer over low heat.

Slice the eggplants and the zucchinis, cover with salt, and put aside for 30 minutes. Wash the peppers and cut them in half. Remove the seeds and white parts and cut the peppers up into pieces. Peel and slice the potatoes, then dry them in a dishtowel.

In a second pan, heat up some olive oil (about 3 fingers high), and deep-fry the slices of potato in it. Drain these and place them in a *greixonera* – a clay cooking pot – or a cast-iron pan. Deep-fry the eggplants and zucchini in the remaining oil and allow to drain. Place them in layers on top of the potatoes. Then deep-fry the peppers with the remaining cloves of garlic, crushed. Allow to drain, and lay on top of the pota-

toes, eggplants, and zucchini. It is important that as little olive oil as possible remains in or on the vegetables. As an added security, they can be placed on absorbent paper after being allowed to drain; this will remove the last oil remnants.

Sprinkle on salt and freshly ground pepper, then strain the tomato sauce through a sieve over the vegetables. Place the oven-proof pan in a pre-warmed oven at 360°F (170°C) for ten minutes. Serve hot or cold. This dish can even be heated up the next day. A good glass of red *vin ordinaire* goes well with this meal, for example one from Binessalem.

The ripe peppers have to be picked from the bush together with their stems. The stems are carefully removed only after the peppers have been dried.

No matter what shape they are, red peppers contain a lot of vitamin C. The Majorcan specialties *trempó* and *sobrassada* would be unimaginable without them.

Mild cheese and musty springs
Campos

Although Campos was founded a long time ago, the township has made little attempt to make itself *guapo*, pretty. The Sant Julià church, built in 1248, was renovated around 1879 in a rather merciless fashion, but fortunately mainly the exterior was affected. The beautiful coffered ceiling inside remained as it was, as did a unique painting by Bartolomé Esteban Murillo dating from around 1640: his *Santo Cristo de la Pacienca* tells, in melancholy colors that glow warmly even in the dim light of the church, of the humble patience with which Christ bore his sufferings.

Most people leave this rather characterless town again as soon as they have seen the painting by Murillo, and drive to the nearby beach of Es Trenc or the only thermal springs in Majorca, the Banys de Sant Joan. This means they not only miss out on the best *empanadas* in Majorca at the *pastisseria Ca'n Pomar* in the center of town; they also whiz past the large *fincas* on the edge of Campos. These manors built of Marès stone, which still look grand despite their obvious rusticity, offer the chance to try Majorcan cheese and buy it directly from the producer.

Above: Formerly, the cheese presses used to separate the cheese from the whey were made of wood. The whey was caught by the pail at the end on the right. These days it often flows from a shiny steel press directly to the pigsty.

Below: These cattle are called *frisons* after their Frisian ancestors.

For Campos is the dairy farming center of Majorca: large herds of dairy cattle stand around in the meadows grazing on grass and herbs or chewing the cud so as to be able to produce especially flavorful milk.

All-round talent: square piris cheese

It has to be admitted from the start that Piris cheese from Campos is a remote imitation of the famous Menorcan cheese with its D.O.C. label – but a fairly good one. One reason for this is that the dairy farmers meet up the second Sunday in May at the cattle market in Campos and learn about the latest developments in nutrition and methods of breeding and cross-breeding. The best *frison* dairy cow – *frisons*, widely distributed throughout Majorca, are the descendants of

Right: The salty sea air gives the creamy cheese a powerful flavor.

Above: While it is maturing, the piris cheese is regularly coated with oil to protect it from greedy flies.

imported Frisian cattle – is selected, and the best bull receives a prize ribbon for its services to breeding.

The curious thing about Majorcan (and for that matter Menorcan) cheese is its shape: it is square. This comes about because the curds are poured into a two foot square (60 cm²) cloth whose corners are then crossed over and tied. Once the farmers used to employ an enzyme derived from artichoke roots; today artificial enzymes in powder form are mostly used. The cheese is then placed in a powerful press that squeezes out any surplus whey – much to the joy of the farm pigs who get to slurp it all up.

After this the cheese is removed from the cloth and left to stand in brine for 24 hours.

It could now be eaten as mild, smooth unripened cheese. Most of it is intended to be sold as at least semi-ripened or even ripe, however, so it is coated with oil and paprika before ripening in the salty sea air for up to three months. This cheese does not taste quite as piquant as that made on the neighboring island, but exudes the same aroma of sun-ripened herbs and sea salt mixed with cream.

Taking the waters with cattle and pigs

If necessary, the nearby Sant Joan thermal springs can help in cases of overeating and general drowsiness from excessive cheese consumption. Even the Romans must have known that the two musty-smelling springs, Font Santa and Font Sa Bassa, were not only of great benefit in this case, but good for all sorts of skin ailments as well. In the Middle Ages, people attributed magical properties to these hot, bubbling, sulfurous waters. In the 14th century bathing here was in such demand that the island's government was asked to construct a bath house. Up till then, bathing out in the open was not always a pleasure. As one chronicle tells us: "…small worm-like creatures swam in the dirty water", and the bathers had to "compete for space with the cattle and pigs also refreshing themselves in the same water."

But it was 1516 before a simple bath house was built. Before this, the Church had to build a chapel, Sant Silvestre i Santa Coloma, to refute the springs' magical reputation. After the bath house had finally been constructed, the stream of people looking for a cure in the sulfurous, salty, slightly radioactive water increased further. This caused trouble, for the owner of the property, the Marqués de Palmer, did not agree with the thermal spring on his land being under the jurisdiction of the municipality of Campos. In the 19th century his descendants at last relented, allowing a small resort with a

Even the Romans probably knew the hot, sulfurous springs of Sant Joan. Nonetheless, a bath house was not built here until the 16th century – admittedly not so luxuriously tiled as the bathing rooms today here in Majorca's only thermal resort.

People looking for a cure used to have to bathe in Sant Joan alongside cattle and worms. Today marble baths and colorful tiles provide hygienic relaxation.

sewerage system, accommodation, and therapeutic facilities to be built. Since then little has changed, even though the baths have been in private hands again since 1909 and are now run like a spa hotel.

A dream beach that does not want to grow up

Uncomplicated bathing, albeit without any curative effect beyond the one a beautiful beach naturally has on body and soul: that is the motto in Es Trenc, one of the largest beaches in Majorca and with some of the finest sand. Perhaps the bunkers left over from the Spanish civil war are responsible for the fact that this idyllic beach is still peaceful even at the end of the 20th century. A few restaurants have found their way here, there are showers and sunshades, and in the former fishing village of Ses Covetes at the northern end of the beach there is a large parking lot. In Colonia Sant Jordí at the southern end, there is a row of small hotels and apartment houses leading to the only entrance to the beach. But none of this offends the eye as is the case in other places not far from here. To keep things this way, the ecological movement *GOB,* which could not prevent the huge parking lot near Ses Covetes, has managed to ensure that tourism in Sant Jordí remains in its infancy – if only just.

The beach near Ses Covetes is pleasantly quiet despite sunshade hire. At the end of the long bay, the fine sand merges into rocks washed smooth by the sea.

A Majorcan jigsaw puzzle
Drystone walling

It is a matter of contention whether the art of drystone walling is a legacy of the original Talayotic inhabitants, who piled up sacred monuments and watchtowers many feet high using huge square stone blocks without mortar, or whether it is another Moorish import. The Balearic Islands are not alone in employing this skillful form of stone recycling: similar techniques are to be seen in Brittany and the British Isles. But in all of these places the basic idea is a similar one: to turn a nuisance into something useful on the spot without having to use additional building materials of any sort.

Any stones lying about are a great problem for daily work in the fields. They break plowshares, animals and humans can injure joints if they fall on them, and they also block up drains. If they are made into walls, however, they separate one field from the other, protect soil, seeds, and crops from the wind, keep herds of cattle together, and make one steep piece of mountainous terrain into several flat areas.

The *tanques* or, more commonly, *marges,* are not by any means primitive piles of stones, even if the more rustic variety may sometimes look that way at first. On the contrary: if the wall-builder, the *marger,* has done his work properly, a wall will stand for an almost unlimited length of time. Once all

farmers mastered this ancient craft themselves, a multi-purpose skill, though it doesn't try to be beautiful: beauty is a byproduct, never an end in itself.

These days the skilled profession of "marger" has again become an official one. The drystone walling school in Sóller, the *Escola de margers de Majorca,* has even been teaching it since 1986. In two and a half years, the apprentices there learn what fathers used to show their sons: to pay attention to the nature of the stones.

For a good *marger* needs scarcely any equipment besides a basket, the *senalla,* a sledge for transport, the *carete,* an angle iron, called a *capserrat,* and a few feet of string. Muscle power, of course, and every so often

A piece of string just over three feet from the ground shows the *marger,* the wall builder, where the top of the wall is to be.

The cavity between the two sides of the wall is filled with detritus and soil. The *marger* chooses large stones for the last layer.

To achieve better stability, the stones used for the coping have to be tightly wedged in. A few blows with the hammer help the matter along.

The hard work has been rewarded. *Margers* maintain that no concrete wall can ever achieve the beauty and strength of a *marge.*

a hammer and chisel, but mostly an infallible feeling that comes from experience and patience – at least in the case of simple walls in the fields. At first he looks for large stones to form the base, the *asentament,* which is about three feet (90 cm) across. Then he piles up medium-sized stones on both sides to form two narrow walls that tilt towards one another towards the top, and fills the cavity with detritus. A layer of large stones only 32 inches (80 cm) across, the *filada de dalt,* covers the top of the wall.

So easy – but so difficult. Lifting up every stone to see if it fits, or cutting it till it does, would take much too long. Instead of this, the "marger" develops a perfect technique of three-dimensional thought. He can see just by looking at a stone on the ground where it will fit so that pressure and friction are exactly right and rainwater can run off without hindrance.

In a good wall, the stones in the middle layers, the *sostreig,* have their narrow side facing the outside. This means the wall needs more stones, but is much more stable. Stones that stick out, on the other hand, are not the mistakes of a beginner, but steps allowing people to climb over: after all, the walls can be up to five feet (1.5 m) high.

Advanced *margers* put hammer and chisel to purposeful and skillful use. When building house façades and walls that have to

Above: The most advanced form of drystone walling is called *marjat.* Here, the stones are cut exactly to shape and placed in patterns, sometimes simple ones, as shown, or very complicated ones. These walls can withstand great pressure and have proved their worth as retaining walls and house walls for centuries.

withstand great pressure, such as those under terraced gardens and streets, they place the stones so that seams and cavities are barely to be seen.

There is nothing that shows the warm, beautifully golden glow of the Marès stone to better advantage than these *marjades,* as these retaining walls are called. In modern times there have been attempts to replace this expensive, time-consuming technique with cheaper methods: concrete walls covered on the outside with rough stones. But these imitations are seldom worth it: they crumble inside and collapse. That does not happen easily with a true *marge,* if its *marger* has listened to his stones properly.

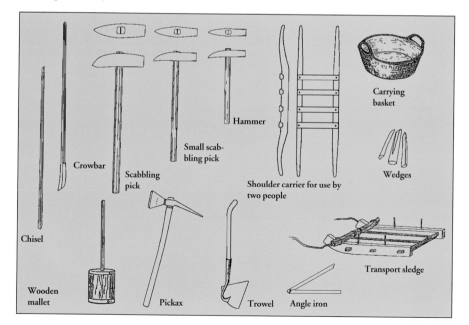

Left: Machinery has no place in drystone walling. The *marger* makes do with few tools and means of transport: various hammers, a crowbar, and a chisel are the most important pieces of equipment. The angle iron is often replaced by a simple plumb line. The trowel is not used to fill the cavity in the wall with mortar, but with soil and detritus.

The taste of the sea
Samphire

In the 15th and 16th centuries, always, crowds of women and children used to go along the Mediterranean beaches with baskets, always shortly before a ship went to sea on a long voyage. Here, they would carefully pluck huge numbers of leaves from a certain plant. Then they washed and pickled them so they would keep for several months when taken along as part of the sailors' provisions. In this way, they provided their husbands with vitamin C. It had been known for centuries that samphire, also called crest marine in English, prevents scurvy, and for this reason it was included in every sailor's kit.

After effective antiscorbutics were developed to combat this typical sailor's illness, samphire, with its yellow blossoms, became almost forgotten except in Mediterranean countries. At the end of the 20th century, however, homeopathists again discovered its health-giving properties. Since then, samphire powder can be found in good health food shops and on herbal stalls. A shame, as this otherwise flavorful plant loses its taste in powder form.

This member of the umbelliferae family is similar to wild fennel, which is why it is sometimes called sea fennel. It only grows near the shores of the Black Sea, the Canary Islands, the European Atlantic coast, and the Mediterranean. *Fonoll marí,* as the Majorcans call it, is often found together with other medicinal herbs, grasses, wild olive bushes, and the native maquis.

The plant has leathery, single or double pinnate, blue-green, succulent leaves that

For centuries, sailors' wives gathered samphire on the cliffs so their husbands would have a supply of vitamin C during sea voyages.

Left: After being soaked in vinegar for a month, samphire goes wonderfully well with paper-thin slices of raw ham. It is also used in other dishes as an original alternative to capers.

little bunch of blue sea lavender near the samphire to take home with you and dry as a holiday souvenir, while every so often enjoying a jar of pickled *fonoll marí.*

Below: What looks at first like normal grass is actually an aromatic ingredient in Majorcan cuisine.

can be up to three inches (7 cm) long. They are ready for harvesting in summer, when they are picked and pickled in mild wine vinegar. These slightly spicy leaves give many dishes added zest. When marinated, samphire goes well with typical rice dishes like *arròs brut* or *pa amb oli,* bread with olive oil and tomatoes. But *fonoll marí* is also much eaten as a pickle, rivaling the famous Majorcan capers in popularity. Samphire is also much easier to harvest than capers. Harvesting the prickly capers requires you to crawl around on the ground and be constantly careful not to get a hook-shaped thorn in your finger, while a search for samphire leaves can be combined with an edifying walk on the beach.

And on such a walk you will get to know other beach plants at home on Majorca's beaches, such as blue-blossomed sea holly, *Eryngium maritimum,* the pretty, lanceolate maritime crosswort, *Rubiaceae crucianella maritima,* and snowy-white cottonweed, *Diotis candidissima,* which looks as if it has just sprung out from a fairytale. And if you look carefully on the ground, you may find a

409

Water's curse and water's gold
Ses Salines

In summer, the air over the southernmost tip of Majorca seems to melt. The few wild and domestic plants that survive here do so with the utmost economy: small-eared cereal crops and trees with small leaves or needles try to make the most of what nature offers in the way of meager nourishment.

Thirsty yellows and browns dominate this part of the Migjorn from spring on. There is not much rain, and when there is, it has little effect on the cracked, hard ground. This area receives barely a third of the average rainfall for Majorca, which is about 176 US gallons per square yard (800 l per m²). This furnace reminds one more of the barren steppes of Greece or Judea than of the famous flowering island of Majorca.

But even in this dry, inhospitable region, nature has been generous with one special treasure: what at first looks like a barren, worthless lunar landscape running down from the west of the Sant Joan thermal springs to the Cap de ses Salines is actually a "goldmine".

Right: The sun needs from April to September to crystallize the salt from the seawater in the lagoons of Ses Salines. The glare from the mountains of salt becomes so bright that it hurts to look at them without eye protection. Once it has been cleaned and packaged in bags, the "white gold" of the sea makes its way into salt shakers and pantries.

Above: Only highly specialized creatures and plants have a chance in the salt fields.

In this region, Salines de Llevant, "white gold" is extracted from the sea: salt, a substance man cannot live without. As early as Roman and Phoenician times, people imitated the way nature produces salt here. Parts of the region lie below sea level and are flooded during the spring storms. In the course of the hot summer, the water evaporates from the salt lakes, leaving fine sea salt behind.

Since 1850, a industrial company has been producing salt here, but in basically the same manner as the Romans and the Phoenicians. In April seawater is let into a square pool 820 feet (250 m) across. About 335 acres (130 hectares) of such artificial salt lagoons are filled each spring. During the summer the sun evaporates the water, which is occasionally transferred to other pools to make the crystals finer and speed up the process. In September excavators transport the thick salt crust away. This is crushed and

piled up to form huge, blinding mountains until the salt is cleaned and packaged for use.

Survival artists in the salt biotope

Over the years, peculiar, highly-specialized flora and fauna have found a place to live at the edges of the salt pools. Only a few plants are able to live in the constant dampness of the salt flats. Those that can, so-called halophytes, form two groups: the chloride-tolerant plants are thick-skinned succulents like marsh samphire; and the sulfate halophytes, which include the feathery, somewhat ruffled-looking tamarisk and bush-like salt-wort, reduce their metabolism by the small surface area of their leaves.

That the pools lose their original whiteness and turn a reddish color is the work of a tiny organism, the halobacterium. It is the favorite food of the tiny salt crab, only a quarter of an inch (7 mm) long. This crab

The lighthouse at the Cap de Ses Salines has to make do with withered agaves as neighbors. At the southernmost tip of Majorca, 125 miles (200 km) from Africa, fresh water and rain are in short supply.

itself then becomes part of the menu for a variety of marsh birds like black-winged stilts, redshanks, and spoonbills. Around 170 species of bird live near the saltworks; even ospreys sometimes pay a visit to pick up a well-seasoned snack.

Cosmetic solutions for a saline water supply

Finding methods of separating water and salt has preoccupied Majorca since the 1990s in another way as well, albeit a less idyllic one. As Majorca has barely any springs of its own and depends on precipitation for drinking water, this is in short supply. Around seven million tourists who shower twice daily and want to dry themselves using freshly washed towels before setting off for the well-watered golf course do not help matters.

At the same time, the amount of rainfall in Majorca is constantly declining, from 233 US gallons per square mile (1170 l per m²) in 1991 to 103 US gallons per square mile (517 l per m²) in 1993, with no improvement in sight. Drinking water and water for other purposes are still not separated in Majorca, which means that a golf course receives the same water that a farmer does from his tap or well – if he gets any at all. Hosepipe bans have become usual in the inland in summer.

In the summer of 1993, tankers were even required to bring drinking water over from the mainland, while thousands of gallons of water were leaking out of ancient pipes or flowing directly into the sea because of a lack of them. As a result, salt is present in the ground water, where only small amounts are welcome, because the sea compensates for its deficit itself. Sometimes 0.16 oz (4.7g) of salt per 1.45 pints (1 l) have been measured, more than three times as much as the human organism can tolerate. The ground water is diluted with spring water from the Tramuntana to reduce its salt content to 0.05 oz (1.5 g) per 1.45 pints (1 l); but this is only a cosmetic solution, not the surgery that is required. Children, elderly people, and invalids have long been advised not to drink tap water.

For these reasons, a plant was established near Palma in 1995 that does more or less the same as the saltworks in the drought-ridden Migjorn: it breaks seawater down into its two main components, water and salt, although here the purpose is not to allow the water to evaporate in order to extract salt. This at least relieves some of the strain on the reservoir at Pont d'Inca, which also supplies Palma, but even that is only a drop in a very large ocean.

On the horizon lies the island of Cabrera, situated off the coast of the Migjorn. In the foreground, the afternoon sun bathes the rocks at the Cap de Ses Salines in a golden light.

Anything but an idyll
Farming life in Majorca

Until the last third of the 20th century, Majorcan farmers found the idea that people could want to spend two or three weeks on a farm of their own free volition almost absurd – let alone that they would be willing to pay for it. These visitors would call it a "farming holiday", and upon their return to their cold native country would give an enthusiastic account of life in the country: the animals, the smells, the noises, the simple, rustic food. This is one side of the coin: the modern side that can be marketed without revealing the other, negative aspect.

But the other side of life in the country is mainly a story of centuries of hunger and illness, of hard work for the enrichment of others, of the rigors of nature and the brute force of those who stole food from the plates even of the poor. People living in circumstances like these barely have a use for words like "holiday"; and if they do use the word, it will probably mean someone else's holiday, not their own.

At the end of the 20th century, 70 percent of Majorca was still devoted to agriculture, but only 11 out of 100 Majorcans were involved in farming, producing a mere

The vines cannot conceal the fact that a farmer's life was no pleasure even in the early days of photography.

two and a half percent of the gross national product. Before the arrival of tourism, the economy worked exactly the other way round: almost 90 percent of Majorcans lived directly or indirectly from agriculture.

If they could. During the Moorish occupation, the Majorcan peasants certainly did not live the high life, but they did have the right to be lord over their own piece of land. That changed drastically after the island was retaken by Christians in 1229. Scarcely were the Moors gone after the Reconquista, when the *repartiment* began: Jaume I divided half of the island up between the church and the Catalan nobles who had supported him. He declared the other half to be his personal property and appointed administrators to look after the farms, as did most of the Catalans who had received presents of land.

The simple peasants only had a chance to obtain land of their own if a large land-

The peasants harvested the grain under the burning sun without any help from machinery, and were grateful for the smallest yield: there had been too many famines on Majorca already.

owner decided to sell off parts of his property. Until then, they were at best supervisors or administrators, *missatges,* on a large estate, or at worst day laborers or tenant farmers, *roter,* on the most infertile land. Between these two extremes was an army of tenants without means or rights who had to share their hard-earned yields with the lord of the estate, the *senyor.*

Fate was especially cruel to the peasants from the 11th to the 14th century. One catastrophically bad harvest followed the other with merciless regularity, and a single good year in between could do little to alleviate hunger and misery. Having no rivers, Majorca was completely dependent on rainfall, particularly that which falls in April. This is because April is the month when the freshly sown fields have to produce the first shoots before the crippling heat of summer arrives. In the middle of the 14th century, when Majorca's peasants had already long learnt to bake bread from carob seed, there being no wheat or rye available, the Catalan governor set up the post of *botiguer.* This administrator was responsible for the storage, rationing, and distribution of the

From the cradle to the grave, a peasant's life on Majorca consisted of work, work, and more work. Anyone too old to work in the fields could still at least tend goats. Only in the 20th century did ideas like retirement make their way slowly into Majorca's rural areas.

meager harvests the farmers were able to bring to the barns.

But drought and the resulting famine were not the only scourges of the peasant population. Being an island and thus difficult to evacuate, Majorca provided the ideal breeding ground for all sorts of illnesses. There was scarcely any sewerage, wells on farms or in villages were a constant source of bacteria and viruses, and the cesspools in towns a playground for rats and flies. Not only did diseases have the best possible conditions: the peasants also had little resistance to them. Right into the 19th century the rural population lived mainly on broad beans, cabbage, olives, bread, oil, and dried apricots if they were lucky. Meat was served only on important holidays, if at all. "Typical" dishes like the *sopes mallorquines* are simply products of the cuisine of poverty with its use of leftovers, but they are no longer eaten three times a day.

When whole villages were not being carried off by the plague, malaria epidemics spread across the land. Chroniclers tell us

Large landowners often provided day laborers and their families with no better accommodation than primitive huts like this one.

that the swarms of death-bringing mosquitoes were so huge they stood like black clouds or columns in the air. It took until the 18th century for a doctor in Palma to make the connection between malaria and the fact that few people became ill where ovens were in use. After he had fires with sulfur placed strategically around his malaria-ridden native town of Artà, the epidemic immediately lost its virulence and subsided. But only tourists in the 20th century really put an end to the mosquito problem: massive complaints from these bringers of foreign currencies finally made the government do something about these biting pests.

If the peasants had to use rye in their bread they risked being afflicted by ergotism. Rye is especially prone to becoming infected with ergot, which causes high fever, cramps, diarrhea, vomiting, gangrene, and mental

There is barely any discernible difference between these two pictures. Just as in the engraving from the book on the Balearic Islands by Archduke Ludwig Salvator, mule and farmer were still an indispensable team in Majorca even in the 20th century.

disturbances. The already undernourished victims died quickly of exhaustion.

But even when the harvest had been good and there was no plague ravaging the island, one could not really speak of a peaceful life. From the 13th up to the 18th century, Arab pirates made Majorca one of their favorite destinations. They were sometimes more or less settled on the Isla Cabrera, and raided and plundered Majorca time and time again, particularly in the 15th and 16th centuries. The peasants often had to watch helplessly as any food they had stored was carried off by sea.

Today many people are of the opinion that the comparatively reserved character of the Majorcans is a legacy of these dark centuries. Oppressed and exploited by feudal lords, constantly in mortal danger because of lack of rain, bad water, and the diseases resulting from it, which neither medicine nor prayer could cure, and at the mercy of bloodthirsty plunderers, they had no reason to trust anyone. The only constants in life were the village community, the family, and misery itself. Every change, every intruder threatened to upset this structure. It was

thus difficult for a group like the *Societat Mallorquina Econòmica D'Amics del Pais,* the "Majorcan Economic Society of the Friends of the Country", founded in Palma in 1778, to introduce new ideas, new agricultural methods, and new products. For that was its aim: to replace a hopelessly outdated way of farming with modern agricultural methods.

But not even modern farming equipment and fertilizers have brought about as great a change for Majorcan farmers as has tourism. Surprisingly, it was the younger members of a family, who were traditionally at a disadvantage in the matter of inheritance, who at first benefited the most: whereas before they had had to put up with worthless properties at the sea, they were now the kings of the coasts.

The hotels and restaurants, bus companies, and souvenir shops needed so many workers that their children no longer had to follow the life prescribed by tradition: the oldest son on the farm, one daughter in a convent, one son a priest, another in the army. Now they became chambermaids and waiters, hoteliers and cooks, returned to their parents' village on the weekends, and perhaps sometimes felt as if they were taking a holiday on the farm.

Tools were manufactured on the farm itself. Mostly of wood, with a metal blade or shovelhead, they fullfilled their purpose.

This divining rod has possibly really shown the farmer one or two sources of water. This is good for his fields, as water, whether from the sky or the ground, has always been a problem for Majorcan farmers.

Pirate raids in the city of the golden stone
Santanyí

In the night of St. Mark's Day, 25 April 1388, the sky above Santanyí was a blazing red. Moorish pirates from the east had entered the coastal city, and sacked, stole, murdered, or abducted anything and anybody that came under their scimitars.

Shortly before this, the city fathers had discussed whether a defensive wall would be a better protection for the city – too late. As soon as the city, whose name is a shortened version of "Santi Annini", "Lamb of God", had recovered from the first and the worst attack in its history, it began to build a

Above: The name of the city, "Lamb of God", figures in one of the keystones of the Chapel of the Rosary.

monumental city wall along with a fortified city gate, the Porta Murdada, to which the defense tower Sa torre Vella was added in the 16th century. Houses, storerooms, and churches within the ring of defense were also fortified. Huge quantities of golden Santanyí Marès stone, known for its particular strength, were brought from nearby quarries, and the odd megalith from one of the many Talayotic sites in the area found its way into several house walls.

This did not make a great impression on the pirates. They continued to make raids on

Below: The courtyard of the presbytery of the church Sant Andreu Apostòl forms a peaceful oasis in the center of the city. It was built in the 16th century from the particularly hard, fine Marès stone from the quarries near Santanyí.

When alterations were made to Sant Andreu Apòstol in the 18th century, only a side chapel from the old fortified church of 1278 remained: the Capella del Roser, the "Chapel of the Rosary", with its Gothic cross vault.

The Catalan organ builder Jordi Bosch constructed this splendid instrument in the 18th century for a monastery in Palma. When the monastery was destroyed in 1837, the organ was saved and brought to Santanyí.

Santanyí right into the 18th century, although their attacks reached their zenith between the 14th and the 17th century. One of the most terrible things about their raids was that the pirates not only plundered, but took hostages as well, later demanding ransom for them. Many families lost their entire possessions by buying back their loved ones. News of this traveled as far as Central Europe, where Sebastian Münster wrote in his *Cosmographia* in 1544:

Its inhabitants suffer much at the hands of the Saracens from Africa / who constantly arrive in their ships / and carry away pris-

oners / assess their value / torment them / use them as slaves or sell them for money. For this reason, alms are gathered in the churches on holidays / to ransom the poor prisoners.

Not all the prisoners found their way back to Majorca. At first, they were mostly taken to Algiers and sold to slave dealers and ransom collectors. These then tried to force the kidnapee to tell them who in their family or circle of friends had money, and how much, to be able to set a ransom price. If ransom was not forthcoming, the hostages had to work as slaves in quarries or on

galleys. Women who had been abducted often ended up in harems.

In times of peace, walls may have holes in them

Only at the beginning of the 18th century did the pirate plague come to an end. For the first time, the citizens of Santanyí began constructing buildings that had nothing to do with defense or fortification. The precious Santanyí Marès stone had already been used in 1703 for the town hall in Palma, but even for ordinary people in Santanyí it was a matter of honor to employ it, if only for small decorative frills.

Typical examples of these are the *estrelles mostrejades,* star-shaped openings in walls that can be up to half a meter in diameter. They are always in walls adjoining rooms that need good ventilation, like storerooms, stairwells, bedrooms, and kitchens. At the beginning, these ventilation openings were very simple, but the stonemasons of Santanyí soon became very skilled in creating filigree patterns that are set into the wall like strange flowers or tangled up silk ribbons.

For the first time, the municipal and church coffers now contained money for other things besides fortifications and donations to the relatives of hostages. The medieval church Sant Andreu Apòstol was replaced by a new building as late as the 18th century, but the city fathers showed taste by allowing the Chapel of the Rosary from the old church to remain standing. This is fortunate, for the Capella del Roser, built in the 13th century and still in its original state, is decorated by particularly beautiful keystones upon which Palma's coat of arms and Santanyí's Lamb of God are clearly to be seen.

At the same time, Spain's then most famous organ builder, the Catalan Jordí Bosch, was hired by the Dominican monastery in Palma. When the monastery was destroyed in 1837 during a rebellion, the slightly damaged organ was taken to the Sant Andreu church in Santanyí. In the late 20th century, with help from Germany, it was restored to its former glory, both in the Late Baroque splendor of its appearance and the velvety beauty of its tone.

The bays near Santanyí cut their way into the coast like Norwegian fjords. Small beaches in the bays are attracting more and more swimmers and hobby sailors in pedal boats and sailing dinghies.

Over the heath to the gateway to the sea

Outside Santanyí, there is only flat, dry land extending for miles towards the fjord-like bays where the pirates once found safe, sheltered anchorage. Sheep and, above all, cattle patiently nibble away at any green they find on the barren ground, or look for shade under prickly pear cactuses, trees or beside a drystone wall. This expansive, light-flooded landscape – which is really a "skyscape" – only has one boundary: the sea, which reflects the deep blue and turquoise of the sky in well-known bays such as the elegant Cala d'Or and the lonely Cala Mondragó.

Even in such places as these masterpieces of natural composition, small villages here and there have managed to remain unnoticed by the rushing hurricane of mass tourism. Portopetro is one such tiny fishing village, which still takes cover away from the populous bays nearby as though it were enclosed in amber. Cala Figuera, Cala Santanyí, and Cala Llombart, on the other hand, are all overcrowded, at least in summer. But even they have treasures up their sleeves. A track leads from Cala Santanyí to the place where it joins the next bay. Here there is a view that makes time stand still for a moment: in the sea, there is a rock doing a cartwheel above the waves. This natural gateway is called Es Pontàs, although it is not clear where the gate leads: out to sea or in towards land. Today, with no more pirates wanting to come in, this is possibly an idle question.

A track leads up from Cala Santanyí to the natural gateway of Es Pontàs. Whether it is a gateway to the sea or the island is something everyone must decide for themselves.

Below: Just a few steps cut in the stone and flat places for sunbathing are enough to make a first-class open-air swimming pool.

Masts with a list
Llaüts

It cannot do what the boat in the Majorcan fairytale about the "ship that could travel on water and land" was capable of doing. A *llaüt* under full canvas looks at first sight as if the masts have only just survived a storm and urgently need to be set upright again in a shipyard: the masts, as a rule three of them, do not stand up vertically, but have a strong list towards the bow.

But they have to be like that. This sort of boat has been used in the Mediterranean for more than 1,000 years – some say since Phoenician times. In Sicily it rides through the waves under the name of *speronara* or *laoutella*, in Catalonia it answers to the name of *barca catalonia,* and all of them are descended, like the *llaüt,* from the *barca llatina*. *Llatina,* because the sail that catches the wind and causes the boat to move is called a lateen sail among experts. As opposed to those of large sailing ships, trawlers or catamarans, the masts of a *llaüt* are not vertical, but tilt forwards. Every mast bears a triangular sail whose longest side is attached to a yard. This yard, also called a lateen yard, is hoisted up like a crossbeam, while the opposite end of the sail remains fastened to the bow or stern of the boat.

Boats with lateen sails, like the *llaüt,* have cruised the Mediterranean for a thousand years. They are easy to tell apart from other types of boat because of their tilted mast.

This gives the impression that everything about the *llaüt* is crooked, especially when – something which rarely happens these days – all three sails have been hoisted and catch the wind in three different directions above the hull of the boat. But the fact that the *llaüt* is still being built and used would seem to indicate that all this has a purpose, even though every *llaüt* now has a motor and only puts up the *vela llatina* for additional power or in emergencies. A *llaüt* can be anything from 30 to 60 feet (10 to 20 m) long according to type, and is made of four sorts of wood: native holm oak for the keel, olive wood for the braces and struts, pine for the ribs and planks, and spruce for the deck. Only the spruce has to be imported from northern climes.

Today two types of *llaüt* are used: the small, maneuverable *llaüt senzill,* 30 feet (10 m) long and an excellent boat for coastal fishing. It once had three keels so it could be pulled on to land more easily. And the *llaüt coster,* 15 to 20 feet (5 to 7.5 m) longer, which remains reliably stable even in rough conditions on the open sea. The *llaüt coster* is also used for fishing with the *bou,* a trawl net that is taken between two *llaüts* and dragged along the seabed.

Reinstated–by popular demand

In former times a large *llaüt viatger,* a 60-foot (20m) long oceangoing ship, was used to transport merchandise from the Balearic Islands as far as the Netherlands and Great Britain. Steamers and, later, aircraft made its services redundant long ago. But redundant only for transport, not as far as sailing for pleasure is concerned. Every year around 300 *llaüts* are built on the island: not just small ones, but also the large, oceangoing ones with their often luxurious interiors. They are not used only by fishermen now, but also by hobby sailors in the sea around the Balearic Islands. *Llaüts* are fashionably in: the number of *llaüts* taking part in Majorcan ship processions constantly increases. This is despite the fact that the Spanish government almost put an end to them in 1993: they were not mentioned in the official shipping catalogue for Spain anymore. This would have

Four sorts of wood are used to build *llaüts:* holm oak, olive, pine, and spruce. Except for the spruce from central Europe, all the trees are to be found on the island.

meant that no more *llaüts* could have been built, as the permission to build them would not have been given. Only when the local shipbuilders protested indignantly was the necessary correction made.

These days the Majorcan shipyards only build the *llaüt senzill* and the *llaüt coster.* Every plank in these boats, which are used for fishing or in coastal waters, naturally has to fit perfectly.

Jaume Cifre, a *llaüt* builder from Porto Colom, knows every trick of the trade. After all, his boats are there to beautify the Mediterranean, not to sink in it.

Birthplace of celebrities
Felanitx

Felanitx is not easy to keep down. Even on the way from Santanyí, flourishing vineyards, *vinyes,* indicate the main product of this town of 14,000 inhabitants in the heart of the Migjorn: nine out of ten bottles of Majorcan white wine come from here. This was the case before the *Phylloxera* plague at the end of the 19th century, and is so again – or still – 100 years later.

This is because the wine-growers in Felanitx did not give up and re-plant their vineyards with almond trees as occurred elsewhere in Majorca. Instead, they obviously gave the matter deep consideration and decided to start at the beginning once more. As early as 1919 they established a wine-growing cooperative to take care of sales and distribution on a collective basis. Its headquarters has been used as a health center since the end of the 20th century, but this palatial building with its elements of Barcelona Art Nouveau style still speaks volumes about the importance of wine-growing in Felanitx.

At the time when the vine pest began attacking the vineyards, Felanitx had only just recovered from another disaster: on Palm Sunday 1844 a wall of the church of

In 1762 these imposing steps were built at the foot of the church of San Miquel.

San Miquel collapsed during the procession, burying more than 600 people beneath it. 414 of them could no longer be saved; there is only a plaque on a side wall of the church in their remembrance.

The partly Mannerist, partly Baroque appearance of San Miquel is deceptive: the church was founded in 1248, but like many other Majorcan churches it has been constantly altered and extended in the course of its existence. The broad steps in shimmering white leading up to the church, and the façade, for example, are fine examples of Baroque style. The portal, crowned and guarded by the archangel Michael, was carved during the Renaissance from best-quality Marès stone, as was the rose window that, together with windows at the side of the church, unfolds a veritable carpet of color in the interior.

Here in the church of San Miquel Felanitx is already introducing one of its most famous sons: the Sant Francesc chapel is the work of no less a person than Guillem Sagrera, the Majorcan master builder of the Gothic period who created the maritime stock exchange Sa Llotja in Palma and the Castilnuovo in Naples.

Two mountains, two fortresses
This is also one of the special things about Felanitx: it has produced more than its fair share of truly great men, considering the size of the city. In the case of Guillem Sagrera, there is another chance for an encounter across time: a path takes you up behind the

This impressive portal in classical style shows the way into the church under a coffered ceiling.

city past the picturesque backdrop of over 20 windmills without sails to the monastery of Sant Salvador, Majorca's second most important center of pilgrimage after Lluc, at 1640 feet (500 m). Majorcans have worshipped a statue of the Virgin here since the 16th century. Unusually, there are no known anecdotes about its provenance. The lord of the Santueri Castle founded the monastery in 1348. This fortress is situated opposite the monastery and within view of it, but there is no direct connecting route between the two. During one of the countless alterations Guillem Sagrera himself, or at least one of his pupils, made one of the very few Majorcan carvings in alabaster: a sculpture for the altar with scenes from Christ's passion and a Last Supper, so realistic it looks like a snapshot captured in the soft stone.

Below: This splendid house is not the home of aristocrats, but a wine co-operative.

The view both from the monastery and from Santueri Castle, which was once Moorish before being rebuilt by the Christians, seems to take you on a soaring flight over the south-west of Majorca. Santueri, like Alaró, was a thorn in the flesh of the Christian Reconquista. A Moorish refuge, it resisted a siege for a year. When Santueri fell, the inhabitants abandoned Felanitx as well, which stood empty for almost 100 years before Jaume II ordered its resettlement around 1300.

A professional cyclist, a rebel, an artist, and a seafarer

Some 657 years later, another great artist first saw the light of day in Felanitx, and was given the name of the patron saint of the city's main church: the painter and sculptor Miquel Barceló.

Left: This Art Nouveau house in the Carrer Nunó Sanç tries to outdo the sky in brightness.

Above: In Sant Salvador there are countless
pictures telling of help given by the Mother
of God.

That was already six years after the
professional cyclist Guillem Timoner from
Felanitx had won the title of world champion in motor-paced racing. Timoner, by
the way, dedicated his leader's jersey,
together with a poem of gratitude he wrote,
to the Virgin of Sant Salvador.

Joanot Colom's claim to fame is a slightly
less glorious one. He was the leader of the
workers' rebellion in the 16th century. But
this rebel from Felanitx is at least mentioned
in history books, even if not quite to the same
extent as his namesake, Cristòfol Colom:
Christopher Columbus. Any doubt that he
also came from here is not allowed in
Felanitx. The Museu de Colom tries to
support this theory, which has preoccupied

Left: In Santueri Castle, the Moors held out for a
year against the troops of Jaume I.

Felanitxians for generations, with all sorts of curious documents and other "proofs".

According to the local version of the story, Prince Carl of Viana (1421–1461) enjoyed the privilege during his imprisonment in Santueri Castle – which is documented – of being looked after by servants. One of them, a girl from Felanitx called Margalida Colom, looked after him particularly thoroughly. Carl, a crown prince of Aragón accused of treason, fell in love with her. The fruit of their love was baptized Christòfol Colom.

When Columbus had an audience with the Catholic monarchs Ferdinand II and Isabella I years later, he said he came from Genoa. It is said that the similarity between Columbus and Ferdinand II, who according to the "Felanitx theory" were nephew and uncle, struck contemporaries even back then. This theory claims to explain why the allegedly Genoese Columbus could scarcely speak Italian. Instead, he spoke Castilian, constantly mixing in Catalan words both in speech and writing.

The Genoa story also has a Majorcan variant, in Palma. According to this explanation, Columbus said truthfully that his birthplace was "Génova", but meant the village of the same name above Palma, something he did not explain further. The advocates of this version claim that Columbus was therefore a *xueta,* a descendant of converted Jews, which he of course had to conceal from the Catholic sovereigns. In the Majorcan Génova he would easily have found information for his planned circumnavigation of the world, as Arabian and Jewish astronomers and cartographers were working there right into the 16th century.

The one certain thing is that it was an Italian, Amerigo Vespucci, who gave his name to the two continents of the New World, much to Columbus' annoyance. Who knows: perhaps Columbus had intended to name the newly discovered country after his true place of birth. Then today we would possibly have the "United States of Majorca".

Pere IV of Aragón had the Sant Salvador monastery near Felanitx built in 1348 in gratitude for the end of the Black Death. Today's building dates from the 16th century, however.

Yoga on wheels
Cycling in Majorca

"...The same prayer came constantly from my heart, a prayer murmured very softly by my dry lips that were often bathed in tears of emotion ..." This is the way a cyclist performing at highest pitch feels. This poem can be read in several languages in the entrance of the Sant Salvador monastery in Felanitx. Its author: Guillem Timoner, born in Felanitx in 1926, who was champion in motorpacing – a track cycling discipline – six times between 1955 and 1965. In this sport, each athlete follows a motorcycle driving in front of him on a racetrack either for an hour or over a predetermined distance of 6.2 to 62 miles (10 to 100 km).

Timoner cycled his way to victory 1,172 times in his career as a professional cyclist. He was Spanish champion 24 times, and set off a cycling craze that has not stopped yet. Timoner was not only one of the first Spaniards to achieve the title of world champion: he also popularized a piece of sporting equipment that has often taken Spain to the top since then. The most famous example is Miguel Indurain from Navarra, born one year after Timoner retired from professional racing, the only cyclist in history to have won the Tour de France five times in a row, twice even together with the Giro d'Italia.

From January to May you are not unlikely to find the odd world-famous professional amongst the countless groups of cyclists. Indurain's successor, Abraham Olano, trains here, as do the German Jan Ullrich and the Swiss Alex Zülle. They peacefully share the streets with thousands of amateur cyclists and a few car drivers who want to explore the remote roads of the island without perspiration and leg power.

For that is the main reason Majorca provides conditions that are almost unique in Europe: it has an extensive network of asphalted roads that are barely used by cars. Majorcan also has outstanding climatic conditions: apart from the height of summer, Majorca has mild and reliably dry weather the whole year round. And as if that were not enough, the island offers all degrees of difficulty within a small area, from the flat terrain of the Pla to mountain tours for climbers in the Serra de Tramuntana. Hobby cyclists are particularly keen on the routes through the Migjorn and the Pla: they enthuse about becoming one with the landscape and the feeling of being part of a larger whole when they cycle past drystone walls and almond plantations, embraced by the fragrance of blossoming fruit trees and a sea breeze. Majorcan yoga on two wheels.

Even the tourist industry has discovered the cycling market and developed offers accordingly: the estimated 30,000 cyclists that come in the first months of the year can expect every comfort ranging from bike hire to transport to special sport diets. The cyclists even make it possible for many hoteliers to stay open all year round instead of shutting up shop from November to March as is usual.

In Felanitx, cyclists can rely on good service in the case of a breakdown: if he does not happen to be doing his daily 37 mile (60 km) ride, Guillem Timoner is ready to help in his cycling store with professional advice, spare parts, and the latest models.

From the sea to the mountains, Majorca provides cyclists with all degrees of difficulty – and plenty of places for a well-earned break.

Guillem Timoner was six-time champion in the cycling discipline of motorpacing. Today he prefers to ride along the beach with his granddaughter.

The mirror between the worlds
Miquel Barceló

Felanitx, in the foothills of the Serra de Llevant, remains nearly untouched by the noisy "fun culture" of the Badia de Palma to this day. This picturesque little town with its long tradition of handicrafts has an atmosphere reminiscent of the Majorca where the cultural influences of Europe, Africa, and Arabia all met, combining to form a national cultural identity.

This is where Miquel Barceló was born on 8 January 1957. Whether his family is related to the celebrated Antoni Barceló remains a matter for conjecture. Antoni Barceló, a seafarer who freed the island from raiding corsairs in the 18th century, already has a monument to him in the military harbor of Palma. Miquel Barceló is still on his way to earning one, but in a much less martial way and probably in a different place as well. Contradictions? Without them, there would be no explanation for Majorca.

Barceló grew up on an island that – because of its exposed position and almost constantly good weather – is inevitably conducive to a relaxed attitude to history, the present, and the future. A disposition

Setze Penjas is the name Barceló has given his frieze-like row of cadavers, executed in 1992 on paper using mixed media and then mounted on canvas – a "danse macabre of hanged creatures". Courtesy of the Gallery Bruno Bischofberger, Zurich.

The Majorcan painter and sculptor Miquel Barceló is shown here deeply involved in a drawing while he assimilates the impressions gained during a trip to the Dogon in Mali.

like this nurtures traditionalists in the best sense of the word. This means a life that contains simultaneous polarities. Majorca was always a place for pilgrimages made for all sorts of different reasons. First a refuge for organized piracy, then a political football for continental interests. First Islam, then Christianity. Mass tourism on the one hand, quiet retreat on the other.

Barceló personifies the island's ambivalence and makes it the subject of his works. He exposes points of friction caused by the geographical tension between Europe and Africa, and which question tradition in a new way. The basic themes of his artistic metamorphoses are emptiness as the absence of fullness, death as the absence of life, the desert, and saturnine melancholy. In 1976 he even placed carcasses in 15 wooden crates. The carcass became a symbol. In 1992 he painted animal carcasses across almost 30 feet (10 m) of paper. They hang out to dry like black washing against a background of Spanish yellow. The red stripe at the bottom shows symbols of "vanitas" and death. Two years later came "The Ball of the Hanged". Then there were the series of Polaroid photographs and carcasses in the refrigerator summing up his trips to Mali, the land of the Dogon. Barren desert impressions of Africa become expressive artworks for Europe.

Exhibitions in Bordeaux, New York, London, and Paris have displayed and acknowledged the Majorcan mirror between the worlds.

Barceló began to observe his surroundings closely early on, and collected what he saw and experienced, the events and impressions, thus storing up the dense complex of traditions making up his country. These are now at his disposal to connect up and transform in endless ways. What do plants and animals do? What does mankind do with them? What does light, color do? What do darkness and death do? Barceló reflects on these questions again and again during his walks along the *Cami del Dimoni* – the "demonic" path leading up the Calvary Mountain in Felanitx – and thinks of ways to use them creatively.

On a study trip to Paris, the then 17 year-old became acquainted with paintings by van Gogh, Klee, Wols, Dubuffet, and the "Art brut" style. Upon his return to Felanitx, deeply impressed by his museum visits, he began to find his own solutions. In Manacor he exhibited bizarre depictions of insects, beetles, worms, and other invertebrates alongside several "objets trouvés". A predilection for working with

carcasses (as bodies whose will has been destroyed once and for all) and their far-reaching death symbolism had already become apparent: flesh on the threshold to becoming carrion, a little too far gone to be able to serve as food… Barceló's art has internationalized Majorca's cryptic traditionalism and made the complexity of sometimes incompatible objects accessible for the viewer. But anyone wanting to understand this in its final consequences goes searching gnostically for a desert that could promise fulfillment.

This terracotta self-portrait of the artist was executed in 1995. The sculpture is very much influenced by the art of the Dogon people of Africa, who withdrew into wild territory in the bend of the Niger to escape the slave trade. In this remote location where they could no longer be manipulated, the Dogon developed impressive cosmological and creation theories. According to these, all planets in our solar system came from the placenta of the sun. This "placenta" theory of the cosmos is found on a small scale in nature here on earth as well. Skillful masks create communication between the universe and earth. Courtesy of Gallery Bruno Bischofberger, Zurich.

431

Llevant

The essence of Majorca
Llevant

For a proper *garriga*, take a layer of limestone rock prettily folded and shaped by wind, weather and rain and nicely built up into gentle hills; loosely scatter a few boulders over it; add mastic trees and broom, heather, a few wild or semi-wild olive trees, stone pines and Aleppo pines; lavender, rosemary and rock roses for aroma: a few gladioli, irises and wild orchids for a spot of color. Mix thoroughly, and you have your *garriga* or Mediterranean bush country. Examples to copy abound in the east of Majorca, named *llevant* like the morning dawn or sunrise.

Hills and mountains, cliffs and sandy beaches, dreamy coves and fertile fields make Llevant a kind of distilled essence of Majorca. Nowhere else on the island are all elements of this flowery and sunny island united so compactly. That is true not only in a geographical sense but in many others. And the *garriga* runs like a red – though more colorful – thread right through east Llevant as far as Cap Ferrutx in the north down to the dragon caves, the Coves del Drac, in the south. In the Coves, geologists and speleologist read the history of Majorca from the dripstones at a subterranean depth of 4,250 feet (1,300 m), while trippers enjoy a boat journey with music through the elaborately illuminated underworld of the island.

Right: A sweet name for a fortress: the Torre de Canyamel near Artà means "Sugar Cane Tower" No doubt approaching enemies did not find it so sweet.

Previous double-page spread: On the Ferrutx peninsula the tree line is under a thousand feet up. Behind the huge rock, the sea pounds the coast of Llevant.

Fortresses from three millennia

Historically, too, all the important Majorcan ages and events are easy to find in Llevant. Immediately behind the station in the town of Artà, it is only a step or two to the pre-history of the island and its inhabitants. Around 2000 BC, the first inhabitants of the island built houses and defensive walls out of giant stone slabs in the settlement of Ses Països, and also those strange towers that have given their name to the whole culture – the *talayots*, from the Arab word for tower, *talàia*. Along with the settlement of Capocorb Vell in the south of Majorca, Ses Països is the most important Talayot site on the island.

In the course of time, most other structures by these stone builders were used as quarries by invaders and rulers of the island. Prehistoric megaliths were even incorporated into the fabric of Palma cathedral. Little is known about the builders and their way of life, and that little comes from the stones, parallels in other megalithic cultures in Britain, Sardinia, the Near East, and descriptions by ancient travelers such as Timæus and Pliny. Although the original inhabitants did not write themselves, they are responsible for a word that is more inseparably associated with Majorca than the name of their culture. Their great skill in handling sling stones and the slings for them gave the name for the whole group of islands – the Balearics, from the Greek word *ballein*, to throw.

In and around Artà, the practiced eye will find all kinds of traces of Moorish culture. The lush blossoming gardens and fruit and vegetable plantations outside the fortified gates of the town were laid out by the Moors. One of the finest views from the old town of Artà looks down from the terrace of the parish church of Transfiguració del Senyor towards the plain. When the church was still a mosque, this was the place to wash hands and feet before prayer.

Above the parish church of Artà, the walls of the castle range up the castle hill, an elegant but massive warning to an outside world that in some centuries was all too ready to attack. Yet it was an unloved construction, because no-one wanted to live within the protective ring wall. Peasants and citizens fled here against raids, but withdrew along with the danger.

The same half-obstinate, half-admirable phenomenon happened in Capdepera: closer to the sea and thus to the pirates. From 1300 onwards the kings of Majorca constantly rebuilt and extended the Moorish fortifications, doubling the outer walls until they had produced Majorca's largest fortress which included a church. Yet not even an almost hopeless raid in the 14th century could persuade the

Just outside the gates of Artà are the remains of one of the few preserved Talayot settlements of Mallorca. Ses Païsses still contains foundation walls, alleys and outer defensive walls of the prehistoric village.

population to take up permanent residence within the walls. On that occasion, a wonder-working Madonna helped them out of the scrape with a miraculous mist, but not even she remained in the castle. The Mare de Déu de la Esperança, the Blessed Virgin of Hope, lives in the niche of honor in the town church of Sant Bartomeu. Similarly, the tourists who visit both castles for the sake of their splendid panoramic views, also do not stay the night.

Trees and sheep, horses and rabbits
The fact is, what they see from both castle hills is an irresistible invitation to further investigation. The hinterland of Llevant's coasts is a textbook example of the co-existence of man and nature. Where the *garriga* has had to yield to human hunger, man planted apricot, peach, carob, almond and olive trees. In between, tomato and lettuce beds and wheatfields promise salads to come and daily bread.

Draw wells and drystone walling irrigate and guard the plants, particularly from adventurous sheep and goats. A flock of sheep being rounded up by a sheepdog at the whistled instructions of the shepherd is still a normal sight, even if the life of shepherds has changed fundamentally. The shepherd used to be responsible for the flocks of the squire, the *senyor*, or the whole village. Now he owns them and their wool or milk himself. Days of shearing and swapping tales with colleagues have given way to high-speed shearing by machine. But sheep still get lost, as ever want their troughs or get stuck in the *garriga*, and machines can't help here – they need the *pastor*.

On the drystone walls, an occasional sign warns against flying shot: *coto privado de caza*, private game lands, it says. In many cases, this is just a gamekeeper's definition of the terrain, not that hunting necessarily takes place. But in Llevant, at Son Servera, the kings of Majorca always used to hunt when there were still stags, wild boars, pheasants and roedeer. Noble falcons plunged elegantly on their victims from on high, but that too is in the past. The 30,000 or so strong hunting fraternity of Majorca have to be content with rabbits and hares, partridges, thrushes and wild doves to pep up their Sunday menus.

The estates around Manacor are home to another island resident who is otherwise rarely in evidence: the horse. Traditionally, donkeys and mules do bleak, heavy work such as treading the water wheel or carrying burdens. Horses just pull carts – and how! At the beginning

Bleating and tinkling bells are a common acoustic backdrop in Llevant, thanks to large flocks of sheep.

of the 20th century, the fashion for organizing improvised horse races reached Majorca. Majorca's farmers discovered that their powerful black horses were particularly good at it, and began to hand-grade them for the trotting stud. Twice a year, Majorcan horses flit round the track at Manacor in competition for large prizes, frequently shaking off the sons and daughters of the wind from the mainland.

Pearls far from the coves

Laid waste by Vandals and Christians and stubbornly rebuilt, Manacor is at the same time home to one of Majorca's greatest export commodities and an example of the successful implanting of industry in a traditionally purely farming area. In 1902, a German inventor set up a factory here to produce something that had been a cracking success in the fashion houses and jewelers' stores of Europe, – artificial pearls. Unlike cultured pearls, patented Majorica pearls are created not in a shell but layer by layer in an oven. The heat of the oven melts a secret mixture of all kinds of solid matter from the sea into a dye-resistant, indestructible, and genuine-looking gleaming pearl which at first glance even experts cannot distinguish from the real thing from the bottom of the sea – nor can the skin of the wearer.

It is some way from Manacor to the sea. The shortest route is to Majorca's newest port, Portocristo. Founded in 1880, the latter served as a fishing port only briefly before devoting itself to the 20th century's boom industry – tourism. The sheltered harbor and beach in the fishhook-shaped fjord attracts yacht owners and sandcastle builders in equal number, and hardly any of them know that Majorca's fate in the Spanish Civil War was decided in Portocristo. In 1936, the Republicans launched a final attempt to win back the island from the Fascists, alas without success.

Towards the north-east, Llevant has further bays to offer, strung out on a chain like Majoricas. The famous ones are Cala Millor, Sa Coma and S'Illot, which have long developed from places for the cognoscenti to mass destinations. It is still worth looking for lonely coves with a strip of sand for the lilo, just to be there in the morning when the sun peeks over the horizon and a ray of light feels its way across the sea to go ashore in Llevant.

Above: A peaceful scene not far from the trotting course in Manacor. For generations, farmers in Llevant have bred horses for pleasure rather than utility.

Following double-page spread: There is room for everything in the bay of Alcúdia: long, long beaches, a cool breeze ruffling a peaceful sea, and here and there a *finca* or summer cottage.

Below: In S'Illot harbor, a bridge carries you dryshod over the inlet.

In the cloister of the former Dominican monastery, the bells that ring nowadays are those of telephones rather than compline and vespers. This is Manacor's administrative center.

Furniture and pearls in the shadow of the minaret
Manacor

A proud 275 feet (84 m) high, the tower of Manacor's main church Dolors de Nostra Senyora welcomes from afar. Where Our Lady's Sorrows have been contemplated since 1236, there once stood, until the Reconquest, one of the island's finest mosques in one of Moorish Majorca's most prosperous towns, where the nobility maintained town palaces and summer residences. They built this elegance on the ruins of the settlement which had presumably been occupied since Talayotic times and used as a trading center. In the mid-fifth century, the Vandals razed Romano-Byzantine Manacor, and 500 years passed before the town came

into its own again under the Moors, making it one of their most important cities.

The second destruction was handed out by the Christian conquerors, particularly to the great mosque, which as a symbol of the previous rulers could not be allowed to remain standing. At least they and their descendants replaced it with a worthy successor, including the record-high tower, whose very slenderness is reminiscent of a minaret.

Down to the 19th century, the Sorrows was expensively rebuilt, added to and extended, because the town prospered even after the Moors were driven out. A large rose

Right: Defiant walls outside, fragile miniatures inside. The 15th-century watch tower of the *palau* now houses a furniture museum.

Below: The city of pearls and furniture stretches quite a way over the plain under a blue Mediterranean sky.

window over the main altar bathes the choir and nave in a magical light, while masons have wrought miracles of stone in the two tall pulpits left and right of it.

The most unusual thing is the altarpiece itself, a crucifixion scene. A small staircase behind the figure enables the visitor to admire the embroidered gold silk robe and the genuine hair of beard and head close up. The little staircase is plastered with ex-votos: pictures, photos and other grateful testimonials of continual miracles by this figure of Christ.

The old 14th-century town palace directly opposite had to wait for the 20th century before it got a thorough beauty treatment.

On the other side of the old town, the administration of Majorca's second largest town has settled pragmatically into the former Dominican monastery. In the 19th century, the monks' cells were used to confine shameless delinquents, the monastery housing the prison among other things. The administration goes about its business without stopping the public visiting the old cloister, which reposes on 32 columns and with its loggia invites visitors to linger and dream awhile. The small church of Sant-Vicent-Ferrer belongs to the former monastery of Sant Domènech. It is named for the Valencian saint who preached here and whose rosary chapel is a bewitching sight.

Wealth from oil trees and pines

No-one would really expect anything like that in Manacor, which is known above all for its pearl factories: "hand on heart", as the name of the town says so elegantly and several coats of arms in the Dominican cloisters demonstrate. Nor indeed the Museu Arqueológic with Byzantine mosaics from one of Majorca's first Early Christian basilicas, or the former fortified tower called Torre dels Enagistes. One would tend to expect more the furniture museum in the Torre del Palau, which incidentally, with the Torre de Ses Puntes, represents the remains of fortifications against possible pirate raids.

Long before the invention of Manacor's greatest industrial success ever, the artificial

Who said it's only industry? In the center of Manacor, the sun lights up the 14th-century town palace beside the principal church of Dolors de Nostra Senyora.

From his airy eyrie, this prince of the Church gazes down on the hustle and bustle round the corners of the church square.

pearls, the town was already flourishing industrially. As Salvator reports, it was turning out large clay bricks, and furniture – originally from olive and pine wood, nowadays also from imported materials such as aluminum, plastics and Nordic woods. And even if the wood is not as old as the living originals of the life-size dinosaurs outside the "supermarket for olive wood products" on the Palma road leaving town, some of the wonderful workmanship of the olive grain is worth a look.

Even experts can't distinguish Majorica pearls from real pearls just like that. Invented by a German, these imitation pearls have been a worldwide sales success since 1897.

Second nature
Pearls from Manacor

Every day, thousands of curious sightseers come to the town by bus, lured here by a perfect illusion. Not even experts, they say, can distinguish a flawless artificial pearl from Manacor from a real one just like that. And although all three pearl factories in Manacor generously show visitors the pearls being made, the basic secret, the magic chemical formula underlying the process, is still closely guarded.

The success of these pearls goes back to 1897 in Barcelona, where a German, Friedrich Hugo Heusch, began to imitate nature in a small way. But just a few years later, by 1902, the demand from stores and jewelers in London, Berlin, Rome, and Paris was so great that he decided to open factories in Felanitx and Manacor in Majorca. From then on, there was no stopping the marketing triumph of the Majòrica brand name.

Up to 1948, the Heusch family and their 1,000 or more employees were protected from imitators by patents, but immediately after the monopoly ran out numerous other firms tried to muscle in.

Few managed to survive, though there are three factories in Manacor, because undercutting Majòrica on price and still keeping the same quality was like squaring the circle. And even the two rivals of Majòrica have to put up with their pearls being called majoricas worldwide.

Not helping things along but doing it better
Whereas the Japanese with their cultured pearls help the natural process along and implant a tiny particle in the culture shell so that the shellfish forms a mother-of-pearl coat round it, Majòrica pearls are produced on the same principle but by quite different means.

A tiny artificial core toughened by high pressure is first fixed into a special mounting. It is then dipped up to 30 times in a kind of mother-of-pearl paste, except that this does not consist of ground mother-of-pearl but all kinds of fauna particles from the sea such as fish scales and shell sand. Each layer is heated so strongly with gas burners that the individual molecules of the sea mixture cluster together into larger molecules, a process called polymerization.

This process not only guarantees perfect, compact fusion but also preserves the color as well. Black, and in recent fashions gray and gray-blue, pearls get their color from additives of colored minerals. Once all layers have been applied, the new pearls are carefully filed and polished.

Genuine for ever
They then feel like real pearls on the skin, cool but pleasant, and unlike cheap plastic pearls they warm to body temperature. Neither perspiration, make-up, perfume, heat nor cold affects them. Even if someone inadvertently treads on them, nothing terrible happens. The 30-fold hardening process has made their shape unalterable. In that, Majoricas have an advantage on natural pearls, because disasters can happen to the latter, as to anything natural. Ashes to ashes, dust to dust.

The almost-real pearls have two things in common with their natural colleagues: first, they are not cheap. Cheaper, of course, than what a pearl oyster produces only at a cost of its life, but still a tidy sum. This is not surprising given the lengthy process involved, much of it done by hand. And with a lifelong guarantee.

Second, you cannot give either pearls or Majoricas as a present, because it brings as many years of bad luck as the piece of jewelry has pearls. However, if someone comes along with a jewel case and beaming smile, don't panic. A token payment of one *duro* (5 pesetas) breaks the spell.

Fine layers of mother-of-pearl paste are fired on to a special core up to 30 times. The make-up of the preparation is kept a strict secret.

Unlike the natural versions, Majòricas are virtually indestructible. Perspiration and cosmetics do not affect them either.

It takes strict quality controls to separate the wheat from the chaff. Many a cheap imitator has already had to give up.

To make a piece of jewelry from individual gleaming pearls, they are hand-sewn on to a thread one by one.

A steady hand is needed to hit the tiny drilled holes spot on. As with strings of real pearls, Majòricas are tied individually.

The term "imitation pearls" is misleading, and not just optically. They are not cheap – but then they are not cheap copies.

From the farm to the race track
Horses on Majorca

Work? Pull the plow, haul sacks of corn, pump water in unending circuits round the winch of a *sínia*, a Moorish draw well? A Majorcan horse would snort in scorn at the idea. After all, what are donkeys and mules for?

Majorcan horses have nothing to do with all that . Maybe pull a cart, OK, but not even then for transport purposes. Majorcan horses are real runners.

Trotting enthusiasts gather twice a year along with bookies and breeders at Manacor's trotting course, waiting impatiently for the three-year-olds with their sulkies to streak past as fast as their hooves can carry them in the Gran Premio para Potros de Tres Años, or for the fully grown runners to scuff sand at the spectators round the curves in the Diada dels Reis.

Unlike classier meetings such as Ascot, everything here is very folksy. In between betting and shop talk there is always time for

Above: Horses on Majorca are not expected to work hard. That's what donkeys and mules are for.

Below: It was not aristocrats but farmers who began breeding horses in the early 20th century.

a glass among friends, and whole families wander around the stables and exercise tracks to wish their favorites luck.

Light sulkies instead of Sunday coaches

That's because breeding horses and trotting in Majorca have never been an upper-class sport but a hobby for anyone who had a stable with an empty loosebox in it – farmers. Since the mid-18th century, peasant farmers in central Europe have made a pastime out of organizing races for horses whose main work was to pull carts for practical reasons.

This mostly happened on improvised race tracks outside villages. In 1915, the habit crossed over into Majorca and quickly became a favorite pastime for which simple race tracks were set up in Sineu and Sa Pobla, Palma, Manacor and Felanitx. These small courses were modest facilities under 400 yards (250 m) long. Only later, in the 1920s, when trotting had conspicuously established itself – by then having little in common with the original race idea – were the two larger race courses in Palma and Manacor constructed.

By then, farmers had already begun to choose the real runners among their working horses – of lighter build than the average farm nag – and built them fast, lightweight race carts or sulkies.

Racing his cotton socks off: the trotting course of Manacor has been the center of this sport in Majorca since the mid-20th century.

They kept breeding books and set up boards of control. And discovered – as did the world beyond the island – that the improved specially bred Majorcan horse was very suitable for trotting races.

Elegance and strength on black feet

With a height of up to 16.3 hands (170 cm) Majorcan horses in general are very large, mostly black or dark brown, with a thickset but elegantly curved neck. They are both full of character and fascinating.

As *S'Arxiduc*, the Archduke Ludwig Salvator, had already noted, their manes are generally clipped to tuft length so that they "vividly recall the shapes of horses of antiq-uity". Both nimble and temperamental, they are not ridden much in Majorca. Majorcans keep Andalusian grays for this purpose.

However, on the last weekend of March when Palma has its city festival, Majorcans thunder in medieval racing tradition down Es Born avenue at full gallop against mainland horses, for bets. And many a jockey astride an Andalusian and wearing the colors of his commune sees only the fluttering tail of a Majorcan ahead of him.

Without a chat among experts, trotting would be only half as good. At the stadium in Manacor they can take a look at any horses that might be suitable for breeding. As a group of trotters goes past in their sulkies, the next lot get ready for the start.

Nature's chamber music
Coves del Drac

It is 1339: on the order of the Governor of Majorca, men are sent down into the blackness of the Coves del Drac, the Dragon Caves, whose phantasmagorically formed walls glow eerily in the light of torches they have brought with them. The men make sketches of their route and the shape of the cave, because their secret mission is to look for the treasure of the Knights Templar, which after the suppression of the Order – as powerful in Majorca as elsewhere – was deemed to have vanished and was presumed concealed in the cave. Unfortunatley, whether they found anything while on their mission is not noted in the document from 1339 which records their expedition and is now in the archives of the kingdom of Majorca.

The inhabitants of Majorca have known about the caves, located about half a mile from Portocristo, for around 3,000 years. Pre-historic finds in the immediate vicinity revealed not only half the equipment of a Talayot settlement but also the entrance to the cave. Even the name bears witness to general knowledge of the subterranean refuge system: the story was that pirates and Templars entrusted their treasures to the guardianship of a dragon.

But neither the original inhabitants of Majorca nor the pirates even ventured further in than about 200 yards – as far as the exit remained in sight. The Dragon Caves hit the headlines in 1878, when a group of Catalans disappeared inside for three days and were given up for lost. The explorers re-emerged still alive, to tell wonders of the interior, though without being able to determine how far they had gone.

Sensation at the third attempt

In 1880, a German speleologist called Will went in, drawing up a map, though again only of the front parts. But even that was considered a daring, exceptional deed, because no-one knew how far the needle of a compass is deflected from north underground.

It was only in 1896 that the Frenchman Edouard-Alfred Martel first studied and mapped the whole 1,420-yard (1300 m) cave system thoroughly, at the instigation of and with finance from Archduke Salvator. Martel found a huge, crystal-clear lake deep in the interior of the cave at a constant temperature of 68°F (20°C). *No hi ha esperança*, there is no hope any more, wrote the lost, desperate Catalans at this place on the cave wall in 1878. Named Llac Martel after its cartographer, the

The underground lake is connected to the sea and its water is therefore brackish.

lake is 193 yards long (177 m), 44 yards (40 m) wide and 30 feet (9 m) deep.

Overarching it is a natural dome 56 feet (17 m) high hollowed out by nature over millions of years as rain and oxygen removed the limestone. The whole cave is full of dripstones in the most bizarre shapes. These formations arise from, as it were, the opposite process to hollowing out a cave, as the chalk removed by the water re-solidifies. As the water does not drip in exactly the same spot for millions of years, strangely truffled shapes often develop with stalagmites growing up from the floor and stalactites hanging from the roof of the cave, both at a maximum speed of under 1 inches (2 cm) per annum.

The silence is lent color and sound

In the case of the Dragon Caves, a Majorcan, Joan Servera, realized soon after Martel's investigations that something could be done with the caves. In 1922, he paid a lot of money for the relatively unattractive site near Portocristo that included the natural entrance. Because according to the law of the time, as the co-founder of the tourist office well knew, the cave belonged to the person on whose land the entrance lay, however far it went underground.

Servera installed paths, stairs and seats and opened a new entrance in the Cala Murta. After a few private shows involving music and ballet in the caves, in 1935 he had the caves illuminated in color as if it were a fairy world. Lit-up orchestral boats had chugged over the lake since 1931, followed by two boatloads of visitors. Little has changed in the form of the presentation since then. Light effects and soft music turn this subterranean cathedral into a tourist spectacle. Its natural silence returns only at night.

Nature can manage to drip about an inch of dripstone a year. As the drop of water does not always land in the same place, the oddest shapes develop.

449

A Mediterranean fjord
Portocristo

For hoards of vacationers on land and amateur sailors on the water, Portocristo with its long, fjord-like natural harbor is tantamount to a perfect world of eternal leisure and its benefits. Fishing vessels scarcely wander in here. Where the long arm of sea has probed into the town center like a fish-hook, where once Moorish trading ships unloaded goods for Manacor, one of their most important towns, gentle ripples now rock sailboats and pedalos, yachts and motorboats at anchor, through leisurely days and nights.

An unscathed 17th-century *talàia* watches the proceedings as though all this modern activity did not concern it. Otherwise there is little in Portocristo that is old. A broad *passeig marítim* allows sunny strolls past cafés and restaurants, souvenir shops and chandlers, and were it not for the strangely uncoordinated war memorials standing around, one would conclude that the place had no more history than character.

Attempted liberation, with consequences

That is not quite the case. For Majorcans, Portocristo is permanently associated with an episode from the Spanish Civil War in August 1936, when Majorca had fallen to Franco's Fascists without a fight. The battleship *Jaume I* with 12,000 Republican solders under the command of Alberto Bayos entered the harbor. They succeeded in retaking Portocristo and about 6 miles (10 km) of the island for the Republic.

It lasted just three weeks, after which the Nationalists and the Italian air force struck back from Palma. The episode in Portocristo ended in a bloodbath, and the surviving Republicans took to flight. The memorials erected at Franco's behest have enriched the town neither historically nor aesthetically, any more than the mass graves of the fallen Republicans buried in haste on the shore.

International understanding beside the fishing boat. Tourists and natives alike find direct sales from the boat rewarding.

The harbor promenade in Portocristo is nowadays very popular. In 1936, this is where an attempt to drive the Fascists out of Majorca came to grief.

The consequence is that, over 60 years later, when the sand is bulldozed morning and evenings, again and again bones are turned up. Most visitors do not know that, of course, and are not informed about the macabre finds. For them, Portocristo is and remains a piece of Paradise. And a very well-organized one.

The sea reaches into the harbor of Portocristo like a fish-hook. This makes it all the more surprising that a larger settlement developed here only at the end of the 19th century.

The Sheepskin Madonna
Sant Llorenç ds Cardassar

How long animals and people have lived here is not recorded in the chronicles. Finds in the soil indicate that Sant Llorenç must probably have been occupied in late Roman times, and the name too, which was retained in Moorish times, suggests an early Christian settlement. The village (population 3,000) did not get its nickname until after the Reconquest, of course. Just when Jaume I and his troops were setting their feet on the island, a Madonna figure revealed itself in a field near Sant Llorenç having hidden in the undergrowth of thistles during the heathen rule. The miraculous find of the Mare de Déu dels Cards or Madonna of the Thistles, led to the prickly addition des Cardassar, "of the thistles" to the village name.

Despite the thistles, the Madonna figure was undamaged, and was immediately accorded a more pleasant and more appro-

The Bellver church was built in the early 13th century for the Madonna of the Thistles.

priate setting. She is now in a side chapel of the church of Santa Maria de Bellver in Sant Llorenç, which is documented from 1236, shortly after the Reconquest. The wooden figure, probably of the Romanesque period, looks peasant-like, as if the unknown sculptor had portrayed a girl from the village. Nothing has been touched up on the Mare de Déu Trobada, the Rediscovered Madonna. Her mantle falls around her in soft folds, and she holds the Child a little uncomfortably on one arm, and holds up a fruit in the other hand as if she had just picked it in a neighboring garden. Only a small group of angels on clouds at her feet sing joyfully and pray, to indicate that the nice peasant girl-next-door is in fact the Blessed among Women.

Unfastidious landscape minders and curious climbers

That the Sant Llorenç Madonna chose a patch of thistles as a resting place and hideout is no surprise. Though almonds, wheat, chick peas and beans were always cultivated in the fields around the village, in the more remote pastures in the foothills of the Serra de Llevant peasants and land-owners have also bred sheep and goats since the 14th century. And these animals are of course not only highly effective landscape minders as long as they do not graze where they can get at the crops, but also not in the least picky. Thistles that other four-legged vegetarians would have despised get chewed up with the same apparently disinterested dedication and patience as juicy grass and fine clover.

Until late in the 19th century, it was not unusual to keep flocks of up to 500 sheep. Nowadays, 100 sheep counts as a large flock as people increasingly fence their land and more and more land is built on or is used for tourism. Sheep and shepherds are accordingly allowed less freedom to roam freely through the landscape in great numbers, as used to be depicted romantically in art.

Now as then, the life of a shepherd has little of the contemplative character to offer that urban imaginations used to conjure up, – a little snooze under a tree while the dog kept the herd together. The reality is a lot of work for little pay. Ownership has changed:

The street door usually opens directly into the parlor.

previously a shepherd was signed up by a great landowner or the village community, and he shared the income with his employer. Nowadays he usually owns his own flock.

How often a shepherd gets to see other people depends on whether the flock grazes on the open pastures near the villages or has to look for forage in the mountains where agriculture is not carried on. In the former case, he lives quite normally in a village, in the latter he spends long periods with the flock far from his home fire and good company, as he has done for centuries.

Keeping the flock together, watching that the animals do not strip agricultural trees, tending injured animals, supporting lambs and mother ewes in their hour of need, looking for water – a shepherd's day has usually too few hours to do everything. Stone bothies and wooden huts provide shade and refuge for man and beasts on hot summer days. The few water troughs in areas where water is scarce, usually natural basins in the soft Marès stone called *cocós*, are often protected against evaporation in a way known to shepherds for generations – with a hunched circular structure of rubble, constructed without mortar and furnished with a low doorway.

Kitted out for summer and away they go

Before summer comes, the sheep are shorn so that they can stand the heat better and offer less accommodation for vermin. Modern machine shearing has robbed this event of some of its charm, because man and beast get through the process so quickly that the shepherds are seldom together days at a time to heap up the mounds of wool, sing round the camp fire in the evenings and tell stories. Likewise, almost everywhere chemistry has replaced the traditional method of protecting sheep against flies. They used to be treated with oil. But they are still marked with a blob of colored dye on the skin, to indicate ownership.

Sheep that are particularly enterprising are loosely tied together with a chain of rushes or simple rope by the front or rear legs. This prevents them going further than the dog can keep track of them, but the shepherd has also to watch that they do not get tangled in shrubs and bushes.

However, there is no remedy against the adventurousness of goats, and goatherds still allow them to roam freely in the mountains and collect them again in the evening.

Shepherds in Majorca

Ideas about a shepherd's life vary. There is the pastoral image of bucolic poetry, inspired by the traditional picture of the shepherd who, equipped with a full bread pouch and a flute, wanders from pasture to pasture with his flock. And there is shepherding as an occupation, an independent business operating over an area often no larger than 2–3 acres (10,000 m²) trading with thousands of sheep.

Somewhere between these two extremes lies the reality of the shepherd's life as it still exists in Majorca. It is neither a peaceful,

Shutters remain closed during the day as well, as a protection against heat and dust.

Shepherds used to work for an estate or a whole village, often roaming around the island for months. These days they mostly own their flocks and graze them only on a restricted area.

and then share part of the proceeds from the sales. It is a tiring and dangerous job for the herdsmen, who often risk the lives of valuable dogs and even their own lives in attempting to capture struggling and escaping goats.

The job is concluded with a boisterous meal late in the afternoon as twilight approaches, in a friendly atmosphere and with the feeling of a job tackled as a team. The goatherds tell jokes and stories, talk shop and agree to do the same the following year.

A similar important day for shepherds takes place in May, when the sheep have been shorn so they can endure the heat of the forthcoming summer. Shearers used to work in groups of ten or twelve, working with large, sharp shears, disencumbering hundreds of sheep in a single day.

The families of the shepherds used to help, and at the end of the day they would join in a festive meal with the shearers, with good wine. This would happen every year. Nowadays, the shearing is done by machine, so fewer people are needed than before, and even then the work of shearing is often taken over by Polish or Arab piece workers.

contemplative life nor a particularly profitable job. Chiefly, it is a completely different way of earning one's livelihood, and is often passed on from father to son: as an inheritance, tradition, vocation, custom or simply only a livelihood. Whichever, the life of the shepherd involves a lot of work, which has to be done in cold wet winters as well as the burning heat of summer and, even nowadays, also at night, out in the open.

Flocks are now much smaller, because the pasture land available has shrunk as a result of rural tourism and the construction of holiday cottages but above all because of the rapid spread of enclosure in the last decade. The customs and lifestyle of the shepherds remain nonetheless identical to that of a century ago, even though drastic changes have taken place. In almost every village on the island and around Palma there used to be independent shepherds with flocks of 100–200 sheep. These independent shepherds, who effectively looked after the whole village's flocks, have become perceptibly fewer. Shepherds are small businessmen, and the sheep belong to them.

Shepherds look after not only sheep but also goats. Goats were kept particularly in the mountainous and inaccessible regions of the Serra de Tramuntana. They lived (and still live) half wild, and are difficult to control. The large estates in the mountains are contiguous, and boundaries in rough terrain are not well-defined; it is thus impossible to check ownership, numbers and grazing movements of herds. In the plains of Majorca there are still individual small domesticated herds of goats which often provide milk for rural families.

It is a festive day for goatherds in the mountains when they drive together the widely dispersed animals of several owners

Time for a restful break was and is something shepherds usually get only in pictures.

454

A shepherd's life would be inconceivable without a well-trained sheepdog. During the months of roaming, the dog is also the shepherd's only company.

Below: Goats are particularly prone to wandering off and exploring areas where even sheepdogs cannot follow. When they are rounded up in autumn, there are always two or three missing that have set up new semi-domesticated families in the wild.

Vegetables with heart
Artichokes

Zeus, lord of the gods, hadn't bargained on getting the cold shoulder from Cynara, just like that. Especially not when he had set about wooing the long-haired beauty himself instead of sending Hermes in advance as he often did. The Thunderer was not used to that sort of treatment, and could not let it pass. So Cynara had to share the fate of many a stroppy mortal who had refused a god or goddess something – metamorphosis. Zeus changed the prickly lady into a thistle-like plant, the artichoke. For a long time she eked out an existence as a bush unheeded by man, a prickly weed with whom no-one could or wanted to do anything. But Cynara

was clearly good-hearted, and even if it took time for mortals to catch on and realize what a delicacy lay concealed in the tender heart of the flower with its shroud of leaves, they did in the end grasp the "point".

Globe artichokes (*Cynara scolymus*) were known in antiquity. It was the Arabs who introduced the purple flowering *al-harsuf* to the Balearics and taught the Majorcans how to cultivate and prepare the thorny plant, whose slightly nutty flavor so convinced them that they adopted the plant as an Arab loan-word *carxofa* in their language. It is not so common in their cuisine as other vegetables but is still universal, for example in

A prickly member of the thistle family with a soft heart. Only the most delicate inner leaves find their way into the preserving jar.

Carxofes a la parrila

Grilled artichokes

Ingredients
6 artichokes per person
olive oil
lemon juice
salt and pepper
Pa moreno or mixed-grain bread suitable for toasting

First remove outside leaves and cut off the artichokes almost flush at the bottom, leaving only $^1/_{10}$–$^2/_{10}$ of an inch (3–5 mm) of stalk, then cut in half vertically. Set out two slices of *pa moreno* per person. Let the wood fire burn down, then put the grill into the white heat. Place the dry artichoke hearts cut side down on the grill (about 7–9 minutes), then turn the artichokes. Carefully drizzle olive oil into the inner side of the artichokes, which now face upwards. After five minutes, season with salt, pepper and a little lemon juice.

Set out the toasted slices of bread on a plate. Pile up the artichokes on the bread in several layers with the cut side downwards. Cover with another plate. Press down slightly, then serve. Remove the slightly burnt outer leaves. The bottom part of the artichoke can be eaten whole.

The toasted bread can be flavored with garlic before being covered with the artichoke halves, according to taste. Chilled rosé wine, particularly from Binissalem, is a good accompaniment.

escaldum, the spicy poultry dish with chicken or turkey, or in *sopes mallorquines*.

Artichokes can develop eight successive flower heads for four or five years before their output gradually declines. They are harvested from December to May, but depending on the variety the plants can bear all year round. They have to be cut before they flower, because after that they are inedible. The slightly bitter taste in *carxofes* is due to cynarin, a bitter principle that has a detoxicating effect on the liver and gall bladder, strengthens the bladder and kidneys and alleviates rheumatic diseases.

There are several varieties, such as the *Violeta*, *Blanca de Tudela* and *Monquelina*, with the small, elongated and violet varieties being suitable for consumption raw. To be eaten raw, though, artichokes have to be quite young and very fresh, before the "hair" forms. Along with the cultivated *carxofa*, Majorca also has a smaller wild variety called *carxofa bordes*. *Alcauciles* come up in spring and autumn at the sides of fields and uncultivated gardens, and are noticeable for their deep blue shades that turn purple. Occasionally they are sold in weekly markets.

To prepare, separate the heart, cut it into fine leaves and cook until al dente. In the case of large round green heads, mainly the broad bottoms or chokes are used – hence the expression, after sitting together in good company for a while, that you are "broader than an artichoke." With another variety that requires somewhat more patience, the whole flower is cooked and the fleshy swellings at the lower end of the leaves are dunked in a dressing or melted butter.

Lighting a fire of olive and holm oak branches, patiently waiting for the logs to develop a glow, putting a large grill on top and barbecuing large quantities of *carxofes bordes* is still the obligatory prelude to a sumptuous feast in Majorca.

With larger artichokes, the part generally eaten is the bottom or choke from which the leaves grow.

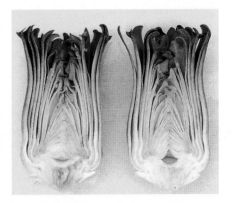

457

Hot tips and their consequences
S'Illot, Sa Coma, and Cala Millor

Once upon a time there were three magical beaches in Majorca. Turquoise and emerald waves lapped at the graceful semi-circular curves of their bays. Even in summer, the fine white sand refused to become red hot underfoot, and now and then a local family trooped along laden with a picnic basket, parasol and digging equipment for the children.

Then foreign vacationers began to leave the packed beaches in the south of the island to look round for alternative bathing sites in the north. The extensive bay of Alcúdia was soon discovered; only the hidden coves on the rocky west coast with their difficulty of access were briefly spared. Around then, tourist yearnings began to focus on the Son Servera area; the tiny fishing hamlet of S'Illot was torn from its twilight existence and thrust into the harsh light of mass tourism and its needs. Its name soon found its way into every guide bought by sun-starved northern Europeans as a "hot tip". Just as rapid was the onset of the reverse ABC of mass tourism: diggers, concrete, building sites, accommodation. The resultant hotels and apartment blocks were soon followed by souvenir shops and discotheques.

Right next door, in Sa Coma, an even longer, still finer sandy beach cuddled up to

Don't jump to conclusions – to the rear of this beach, diggers and concrete blocks have already made the dream "inhabitable".

the edge of the bay right out to Cap d'es Pinar, against the stage-like backdrop of the ruins of an old castle. Those who found, both visitors and investors, that too many people had already been tipped the secret of S'Illot, repaired here to seek the wide open space of a long, lonely, unspoiled beach ... and back home told their friends about the new hot tip of Majorcan sunshine.

A bay further north, the same fate overtook the elegant, extensive beach of S'Estanyol d'en Roig in Cala Millor, and with lots of lovely land available, the hot tip was built on extra-quickly, efficiently and

Somewhere between the concrete blocks the old town of Sa Coma is hidden. There will soon be hardly any fishermen left who remember the village as it was before tourism.

Visitors want for nothing in S'Illot, except perhaps the solitude that once distinguished the place. Hotels and restaurants abound.

Cala Millor is a popular destination for wintering visitors of every age from colder regions of Europe. There's long been no danger of being left alone any more.

extra-bedfully. Soon the new suncream and lilo mecca was blasphemously called S'Arenal de Son Servera in imitation of the hotel silos of the south coast. You took it as a sign of expectation or warning, depending on your stake in the boom. The new grid-designed estates created residential and holiday accommodation for long-stay vacationers and employees of the service industry. In the old harbor of Cala Millor

the few remaining fishermen were soon confronted with sightseers and shoppers asking prices and names of the catch in English or German.

Very close by, other visitors from distant lands – this time not from the north but the south – occupy a different temporary accommodation. In the Reserva Africana, accessible to anyone in their own car or one of the safari vehicles, elephants and giraffes, lions,

ostriches, antelopes and gnus adjust to a European climate and European faces before going on to their final destinations – zoos in northern Europe. There they will no doubt recognize some of the peering faces again, where the latter will be at home, of course.

A topsy-turvy world: since vacationers have taken over the beach and sea, fishing boats have been pulled up on dry land in S'Illot.

Falcons, traps, and nets in the Royal Forest
Son Servera

"In the year of Our Lord 1229 the knight Jaume Cervera received from the hand of His Majesty King Jaume I a village in the district of Llevant, the said village henceforth to bear his name as an expression of gratitude for his help in the glorious conquest of the island of Majorca." A document of this sort does not alas exist. Alas, because the dispute about the etymology and correct orthography of Son Servera might have been resolved long since. The village is documented since the 13th century, and in all probability was named for its owners, the noble Catalan family of Cervera.

But when in the 1990s the island government prescribed Balearic spellings for place names, a dispute broke out over the c and the s alternatives. The s-party "served" up the argument that the area was named in the 13th century for the abundance of service-trees (*serves* in Majorcan) in the area. The c-party insisted the first settlers of the village came from a Catalan place called Cervera, meaning the "place of many deer", which also applied to Son Servera. In the event, the service-trees won the day.

Our Lady of the Ruins

The 8,000 or so inhabitants of the etymologically challenged town work mostly in the nearby tourist bunkers of Cala Millor, Cala Bona, and Cala Morell. The commune of their fathers is a place to sleep and escape, but at least neither harsh rural life, nor bad harvests nor the death-dealing hand of the plague now occasion nightmares. They accept the almond and fig trees as a self-evident rural backdrop, just like the ruins behind Bar Nou. The latter were supposed to become a church, laid out on a grand scale in Neo-Gothic style round a foundation stone laid in 1906, as the walls of nave and choir still bear witness. The money ran out

It was to be a grand new church, the *església nova.* Unfortunately the flow of funds dried up in 1931, after 25 years.

even before the aisles could be started, let alone the roof. After 25 years of building the dream was over, and wild oleander and climbing roses have taken over where once rosaries were to be said – an ideal venue for an occasional *revetla* or folk show in summer, presenting dances and scenes from rural Majorcan life.

A distant relative of Artemis, the favorite deer of Empress Elizabeth ("Sissy") of Austria, Which visited Archduke Salvator in Majorca with its mistress towards the end of the 19th century.

Coto privado de caza

Another kind of art – that of the hunt – also came to an end in the woods and meadows around Son Servera, in its courtly, aristocratic form at least, because stags and wild boar, pheasants and roedeer were no longer there to be hunted. The noble brotherhood of falconers is also long extinct. The unused royal forests were broken into small parcels of land and sold to serfs and their descendants for farming purposes. The fact that even today most of them display signs saying *Coto privado de caza* does not necessarily mean the owner is running around in smart hunting togs looking for careless game animals. In

most cases, all it means is "my land begins here, and anyone entering without permission risks a lead pellet in the rump."

For the last few decades, only smaller species have needed to fear for their lives, i.e. rabbits, hares, partridges, thrushes and wild doves. Times such as when the king himself went stalking are long gone. In 1302, Jaume II paid 85 *llivres* to secure hunting areas in Llevant for his falcons, nets and arrows.

The end result, between Capdepera and Còlonia de Sant Pere, was the *Dvhesa de Farrutx* or royal forest. Where nowadays painter Miquel Barceló seeks inspiration in the natural surroundings of his island, royal game-

Hunting royal game was already virtually a thing of the past when this engraving was made in the 19th century. These fleet-footed hunting dogs went mainly after duck, rabbits, and partridges.

hunting with nets. It is mainly blackbirds and pigeons that remain permanent components of island cuisine, even though the very brutal hunting techniques involved do not meet with general approval. Rabbits and hares also find their way into the kitchen for succulent stews, though nowadays in the modern way with a round of shot still in them. If a falcon catches them, it does not come from the leather gauntlet on a nobleman's arm but of its own accord from the Majorcan sky, delivering its prey to a host of hungry chicks.

keeper Pedrolo was once commissioned to stock up the forest with game such as to guarantee His Majesty a capital stag bellowing in front of his nose whenever he had a mind to hunt. From 1312, the game business flourished, and within a short space of time inns were serving game on their menus.

The favorite hunting sport – particularly for small game, of course – was falcony. Falconers enjoyed high status in Majorca, as the 14th-century Castilian poet López de Ayala noted: "The tree falcons bred on the island of Majorca are the best." The falcons, whose beaks were clipped as young chicks so they could not fill their own stomachs with the prey, were trained for a year, learning to obey just one master, swooping from on high and always delivering the luckless prey to him.

But even by Jaume III's day hunting was in decline as a noble pastime. The political situation on the island was so delicate that no time remained for such ultimately useless activities. The game stocks developed with such effort suddenly became a problem, with too many stags eating too many precious peasant crops, and when nothing helped any more, Jaume III sold his forests. The new owners, peasants on small parcels of land, dispatched the deer indiscriminately and

without system to fill their plates until none were left any more.

Falcons from a free sky and shot for the long-eared infantry

Still popular is the ancient technique of battue with dogs, or in the case of fowl,

Wild boars have become rare in Majorca's mountains, but feral goats and mountain partridge (*Alectoris graeca*) are still hunted

plantations. Nowadays, the mini-palms, which grow to a height of three feet, cover fields by the acre, because the art of basket-making is still written large in Artà, despite all the plastic.

The technique is as simple as it is brilliant: they first chop the fan-shaped leaves of the palm off the stalks that hold nature's work of art together. Because they are so long and thin, the leaves' exposure to the sun is mostly of very short duration.

Once the leaves are dry and golden yellow, they are soaked in water until they are flexible enough to be able to adjust to even the trickiest loops. The soaking also has the practical effect of making it less likely that the weaver will cut his hands open from time to time on the sharp edges of the leaves while at work.

And so work starts: the fundamental techniques are those of weaving, regardless of whether it is a pannier for a donkey or a hanging basket to keep cheese from the cats and mice in the kitchen or store in the drying kiln. The leaves are woven at right angles into the firmer vertical leaves or stems forming a frame. When the leaves dry out a second time, they shrink slightly, which gives the weave greater stability and denseness.

Of course, if a palm is to carry out its future job of providing shade as a sunhat, or

Left: This basket maker is making the basic frame for a basket. Experience and skill were and still are required.

Below: Covered baskets, shopping bags, containers, Archduke Ludwig Salvator did his own inventory of Majorcan basket production.

Endurance test for palm leaves
Basket-making

The palm is a plant of rare utility. Large species such as date or coconut palms supply not only cool, prettily dappled shade but also very delicious fruits, while being very undemanding as far as thirst goes. Though smaller cousins of the palm family such as the dwarf palms native only to the Balearic Islands provide no fruit for dessert or heat-

proof oil, they do provide shade – it doesn't always have to fit a man underneath – and flexible, sturdy leaves of a useful size.

Whereas leaves of the large varieties are ideal for fanning or even as a rainproof covering for the roof, in the hands of a skillful weaver those of dwarf palms can be transformed into everything used to keep things together in the house and garden, on the beach and out shopping.

In the fields between Manacor and Artà, the dwarf palm already felt at home in an age when no-one thought of planting them in

if a smart shopping basket is to accompany its mistress to the market or a mat is to serve as a beach bed or wall hanging, more imagination and skill is required.

The use of dyed leaves allows pleasing and artistic patterns to be developed. They can either be woven into the basic weave or added as a quasi-sculptural second or third layer. Naturally, every weaver has his repertory of special tricks to achieve striking patterns in the palm leaves without resorting to color, i.e. mysterious forward and backward operations, ladders and retrogressions.

As almost always in peasant life, nothing is wasted here. The stalks and parts of the leaves discarded during weaving are split into their long, tough fibers.

Loosely tied, they make an excellent broom. Firmly intertwined, they make rather tough ropes and cords. With which

Above: Small palm trees, great effects. Basket products are still made from the leaves of dwarf palms.

Below: A few skilled hands later, these bases will get a woven body for carrying.

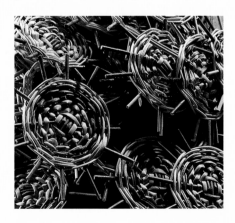

goats, donkeys, and sheep can be tethered, water buckets sunk in a well to bring up precious water, boats moored and even chair seats covered. Admittedly, standing rooted to the spot and providing shade is an easier service to provide.

Dancing under supervision
Artà

Artà is a bit of everything. From the hill at its center, all you need do to see the variety of Majorca is revolve: north-westwards is the sea, in the other directions mountains scored by fertile valleys; almond plantations, olive groves, cornfields and pine forests.

It is thus quite logical that Artà and its delightful, rich environment were settled very early on. The Talayot settlement of Ses Països on the way out of town is over 3,000 years old. Finds prove that all the important cultures that ever tried to make a home or money in Majorca – from the original inhabitants through Phoenicians, Greeks, Romans, Vandals, Moors and Christians – occupied the site at one time.

The first great heyday of Artà came when it was called Jartan or Gertan – the Arab word for "garden" – and a Moorish nobleman ruled the town. The Christians left nothing standing of his urbanizing efforts but they spared the wonderful gardens outside the town gates.

The present appearance of the town dates back to the centuries after the Christian Reconquest. Jaume I had a new fortress built on the foundation walls of the Moorish *almudaina* or castle. It was big and powerful enough to offer the population protection and warn arrogant attackers: not here! Ten years later, work was started also on the new parish church, naturally on the foundations of the mosque.

These two buildings, the castle with its extensive double ring of fortified walls and the parish church which stands directly below

Some 700 years after a new castle rose on the Moorish ruins, Jaume's plan to settle the town within the walls has still to be realized. The town has developed round and about the castle instead of seeking protection within.

the castle at the foot of the hill, are what first catch the eye from afar, and, once caught, the eye lingers. The parish church of the Transfiguració del Senyor in its present form dates mainly from the 16th century, but although surrounded by the Renaissance, it is a substantial work of Late Gothic design whose valley-side elevation looks over the town with a six-arch arcade. Inside a large rose window and stained glass windows to ceiling height illuminate the interior with the colors and stories of the most important saints. A very lavishly carved Majorcan wooden pulpit provides a transition into the choir and high altar with a scene of the

Transfiguration of Christ on Mount Tabor (hence the dedication).

Outside the church the Christians either overlooked or, thankfully, left behind part of the mosque. The former place of meditation and purification seems to float, light as a feather, halfway above the roofs of the town and offers incomparable views of the countryside.

From here a flight of 180 steps bordered by cypresses like a guard of honor leads up a *via crucis* towards the castle. The very first glance into the unbuilt-up interior of the defensive walls gives rise to the question who lived here. Just as in Capdepera, peasants and artisans could never bring themselves to locate their homes within the security of the castle walls. But just like there, they took refuge here if pirates and other envious people approached who were obviously not going to pass by rich, self-satisfied Artà without taking action.

A book of etiquette for castle life

With one exception that is still recorded in the annals of the town chronicles in Artà: at the beginning of the 15th century, Artà was so continuously exposed to serious attacks from corsairs that the mayor decided the whole population should move into the castle. With so many people assembled in a confined space, a few special regulations had to be issued, otherwise the *Artayencs* would

From time to time, the whole population of Artà had to take shelter within the medieval town walls. So that no discord should arise in a confined space, the town council devised special rules of behavior.

have finished each other off without needing pirate help.

So the mayor or *batlle* laid down the following rules for Sunday: no trading in cloth, slaves should have a day off, no-one could go fishing, be shaved or have their hair done, swear or write anything except wills and marriage cards. Women should not deck themselves with ribbons or pearls. In 1433, all weapons were banned (which led to immediate armed rioting).

By 1459, the population of Artà, crammed into the castle, had lost interest in their traditional pleasure of goose racing, and henceforth devoted themselves to a new one – dancing! Several people with impeccable moral credentials were immediately appointed supervisors and informers – it doesn't bear thinking about what can happen when exhilarated men and women touch on the wings of music!

The lovingly restored castle walls and buildings cannot tell us much about that, of course. The main attraction of the castle precincts is the view down to the sea and the distant hill landscape, where a defiant bulwark provides a military echo. The Torre de

At Christmas the town walls fill with heavenly hosts, when the whole castle serves as a backdrop for the colorful drama of the Nativity.

467

Canyamel, the Sugar Cane Tower, was built in the 14th century for a less sweet reason. It was a defensive tower to protect the adjacent *possessió* and was fully equipped with machicolations, battlements and safety ladders in readiness against all kinds of disaster.

From Artà's castle you have to tear yourself away from the view to visit the pilgrimage church of Sant Salvador. The present building dates from 1832. Architecturally it is no masterpiece, nor a disgrace either. Its predecessor burnt down in 1820 after a cholera epidemic carried off 1,000 people and the church suffered use as an infirmary.

The church is the proud possessor of a remarkable collection of paintings, including two that are reproduced in numerous books: *The Moorish wâlî surrendering Majorca to King Jaume I,* and *The Martyrdom of Ramón Llull.* The latter depicts the legendary stoning of the martyr by the "heathen" in North Africa.

Prehistory in the museum and walls of houses

Back in the town, at least two more pleasures await. One is the Museu Regional d'Artà. Laid out like a corner shop, it is stuffed full of quantities of collectors' bric-à-brac, with a few individual delights among them: pottery shards, coins and equipment left behind by Phoenicians, Romans and Greeks. And astonishing little warrior figures and household equipment from the neighboring Talayot settlement of Ses Païsses.

And then a lengthy stroll through the narrow, rather offputting back streets of the town, whose defensively constructed buildings are often windowless but always flower-bedecked. Don't be too brisk, or you'll miss seeing the massive doorways of the sturdy buildings and admiring the lavish coats of arms. If you look closely – in the right place of course – you will note many a piece plundered from the masonry of the nearby prehistoric settlement.

A complete general store within a square foot or two.

Artà's basketmakers often hang their wares out in the street. The palm leaves that make their raw material come from plantations outside the town.

The old town and its splendid town mansions beckon for prolonged strolls, but there are plenty of delightful cafés to break the pilgrimage.

The present
appearance of
the Gothic
parish church is
the result of
16th-century
Renaissance-
style alterations.

Back to the Stone Age
Ses Países and its Talayot Culture

Directly behind the former railway station of Artà it takes only a minute or two to pass through the monumental stone gateway made up of three giant individual stones and step back 3,000 years into the prehistoric settlement of Ses Païsses. Along with a similar site in Capocorb Vell near Llucmajor, Ses Païsses is the only settlement of the first Majorcans whose foundation walls still survive. (Things are quite different in neighboring Menorca, where there is scarcely a field that does not conceal prehistoric finds). In Majorca, it is probable that continual invasions and the subsequent plunderings of old settlements as quarries has almost extinguished the memory of the earliest civilization of the Balearics.

In Ses Païsses, people lived behind a double ring of walls made of stone blocks nearly seven feet (2 m) high. Within the walls, the outlines of houses are identifiable, which nestled in an irregular circle round a central building that was probably a shrine.

How people lived there, what they looked like and what their social system was are matters little is known about. Even the extensive finds on Menorca admit assumptions rather than conclusions, because Talayot culture left no written records, and the people that did write about it – mainly Greek and Roman travelers – did so at a historical and cultural remove.

The Greeks called the islands Gimnesias, because the inhabitants ran around as the Greeks were more used to seeing their athletes in the *gymnasion* – in other words, virtually naked. Virtually, because the primeval Majorcans did wear sheepskins. To writers of antiquity such as Timæus (fourth century BC) or Diodorus of Sicily, 300 years later, the partly Bronze Age, partly Neolithic Balearides must have seemed very primitive. On the other hand, buttons, brooches and pottery in the

Nature has reasserted its rights in the 3,000-year-old prehistoric settlement of Ses Païsses.

museums of Capocorb Vell, Deià, Manacor, Costitx and the Museu de Majorca in Palma indicate that they were capable of producing things that did not fall from trees. In battle, they used not only slings and goatskin shields but also copper and later iron arrowheads and spears. The bulls' heads of Costitx show that they were highly skillful bronze workers. Skeleton finds show that they knew enough medically to undertake skull surgery without killing the patient.

The culture of stones

Another skill that bestowed the name of *Balearides* on them and thus later the name of *Balearics* on the islands made them valued mercenaries in the Carthaginian and Roman armies. This was the use of the sling. The name came from the Greek verb *ballein*, to throw. The Balearides were so adept at this that they attacked Roman ships, forcing crews to seek shelter below deck. Only when Rome seriously undertook to conquer Majorca were its inhabitants forced to recognize that they were no match for the clockwork Roman military machine. They fled to their tumuli, as a Roman report notes. Balearic tumuli are called *talayots* by archeologists, a word derived from Arabic *atalaya* or watch tower. On the strength of this, Menorcan archeologist Joan Ramis adapted the term to cover the whole culture.

Above: Water supplies were collected in large, sub-surface cisterns.

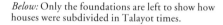

Below: Only the foundations are left to show how houses were subdivided in Talayot times.

Out of the caves and on to the hilltops

When the Romans arrived, the islands had long been occupied, in fact for more than 5,000 years. Presumably it was hunger in the sixth millennium BC that drove people from Provence out to sea in simple boats. On the Balearics they found caves hollowed out by the sea in the cliffs that offered them shelter, and a world of flora and fauna so rich that they could survive. They soon began to extend the caves, digging out rooms in the rock, painting the walls with natural pigments and fashioning strange small grave niches for their dead, whose legs and arms were broken before they were interred.

From the second millennium BC they built communal graves above ground looking like upturned ships, which are therefore called *navetes* (ship barrows). Around the same time they began to construct their peculiar towers on high ground, the talayots from which their culture takes its name.

The actual function of the talayots is unclear. Their situation on hilltops and usually with a view of the sea, sometimes free-standing, sometimes within a village, suggests that they were used as watchtowers and

471

defensive forts. Any other purposes (assembly rooms, stores, armories) are only conjecture; but all talayots have at least three rooms inside.

They were certainly not shrines, because they were always in the middle of the village and were always the same in design: an oval formed of upright stones accessible from two sides, whence a few steps led up to the *taula*, one of the strangest creations of this culture. Named after the word *tabla* meaning table, the *taules* consisted of stone blocks up to twelve feet high, which like a table top carried a second perfectly engineered stone block. The *taules*, which have only been found on Menorca, cannot have served as altar or sacrificial tables because they were too high; the puzzle is, where the "primitive" builders learned the engineering skills to construct such a thing.

In fact, it is their handling of megaliths which bears the greatest resemblance to other prehistoric sites, such as the Nuragh towers in Sardinia, the megalithic graves in northern Europe and stone circles such as Stonehenge in the British Isles, and also the fortifications of Mycenæ in Greece, with their imposing Lion Gate. What other features in common these cultures had is still a matter of scholarly speculation.

In villages of the Talayot culture such as Ses Païsses several families lived together as a kind of clan, no doubt headed by a chieftain or priest. According to Diodorus they were not very squeamish about their women and children, even if the former were uncommonly valuable to them: on the one hand an abducted woman was worth a ransom of up to four men, but on the other a bride at her wedding had to be available to every guest – a problem probably more for us than for her. Children learnt precision slinging by their parents placing their food out of reach in the branches of trees, forcing the children to shoot it down with stones.

The widespread legend about the original Balearides, that they must have been giants to move tons of stone, is contradicted by this survival-of-the-fittest diet.

Above: Skill with the sling made the original Majorcans valued mercenaries in the Carthaginian and Roman armies.

Right: Tower structures like this one were what gave the prehistoric Majorcan culture its name – *Talayot*, from *atalaya*, the Arab word for tower.

Bethlehem, Majorca
The Ermita de Betlem

Somewhere here in these hills the last fighting Moors must have gone into hiding against the invading *conquistadors*, hoping – in vain – to save Majorca for themselves. Westwards from Artà you pass through a picturesque, graphically named valley, Torrent de Cocones, Drinking Pool Falls, winding up to the pass and over the crest of the Serra d'Artà and down over the other side into the high valley. There you find Majorca's most recent hermitage, the Ermita de Betlem, named for Bethlehem because initially the hermits here shared the spartan surroundings of a stable, like their Lord at his birth.

The road to the hermitage traverses gentle hills, past a splendid country house belonging to the family that let five monks have a chunk of their estate around 1800 for them to realize their dream of contemplation and undisturbed meditation far from all hustle and bustle. The country house, Can Son Morey Vell, bestrides one of the undulating hills in the foothills of the Serra d'Artà.

Tiled walls decorate the former stables.

Near the hermitage of Betlem, your gaze seems to take wing and soar over the Bay of Alcúdia.

Renouncing the world attracts the world

But as so often happens, things turned out differently from expectations. Even without a miracle-working Madonna, crowds of pilgrims soon came to Betlem. That was the end of renouncing the world, but fortunately the pilgrims brought donations, so that the church could soon be enlarged. The figure of Christ and the noble gown had been paid for by the Capucins of Palma. Now the dome of the church could be furnished with a Coronation of the Virgin painted in vivid, radiant colors, and devout, well-to-do local people stumped up for further developments. A sundial and tiled pictures soon graced the whitewashed walls, and herbs and flowers sprang up in the monastery garden.

Above: Thanks to donations from pilgrims, the originally primitive accommodation of the monks in a stable were soon expanded into a proper monastery.

A handful of monks from the orders of St. Paul and St. Antony still run the small pilgrims' hostel and look after the plants. Only a few steps from the main complex there is more than a breath of the vision that led to the founding of the hermitage in the first place. Close by is a spring, the Font de l'Ermita, that beckons with stone benches and a small grotto. The visitor can take a break, not just from walking but from the world. The *mirador* or observation terrace seems to float over the bay of Alcúdia and the Victoria Peninsula, suspended between earth and sky.

Right: The interior of the Bethlehem church is still very plain. The altar picture shows – as one might expect – the birth of Christ,

From the magic castle to the bay of dreams
Capdepera and Cala Ratjada

If the Mother of God had not come to the rescue at the right moment there would now probably be only stumps like hollow molars left against the Llevant sky over Capdepera. In the 14th century, a particularly savage attack by pirates was about to hit the town and the inhabitants were in total despair because not even the castle appeared capable of protecting them from the murderous, plundering mob. So they resorted to the ultimate weapon. They fetched a small, frail, Madonna figure from the castle chapel and placed it on the battlements of a tower. Immediately the pirates were enveloped in a white sea fog. This so baffled the marauders that they promptly took to their heels and headed out to sea. This event is still remembered in folk songs as the *Miracle de Capdepera*, and the Madonna has been accorded the name *Esperança* or "hope", and given a place of honor in the church of Sant Bartomeu. The tower was renamed Torre de la Boaira, Fog Tower, and now serves as a gateway to the miraculously spared castle, which is the largest in Majorca and thanks to skillful restoration is splendidly preserved.

No-one wants to live on the miraculous site

Visible from afar on Recó Hill, the castle mounts guard over the town and surrounding area. Its battlements and towers gleam warm and golden in the evening

Not even with King Sanç I as a neighbor did the citizens of Capdepera want to move into the castle, which is the largest in Majorca. When pirates attacked, they took refuge within the walls. Once the danger was past, they went back to their houses at the foot of the castle, which over time developed into a separate closed town.

Above: Dried fish and preserved olives for sale in the market.

Right: The Moors previously fortified the hill so as to keep the surrounding area under watch.

sunshine. That its walls have nothing to protect but the Governor's House, a defensive tower and the afore-mentioned chapel has its reasons. The bailey has been more or less unoccupied since 1300. Long before that, the Moors had maintained a fortified site here, and it was one of the last to fall to the Christians. It was in the ruins of the Moorish castle that Jaume I received the Moorish embassy from Menorca, who surrendered their island without a fight. Jaume wanted the castle to be rebuilt and populated by peasants living in the area.

But the plan came to nothing. Neither Jaume II, who doubled the exterior walls, nor his successor Sanç I, who constructed a chapel within the castle perimeter and occasionally lived here himself, succeeded in getting the peasants to move into the castle. When pirates attacked, the locals sought refuge in the castle, but moved out again once the danger was past. What happened to the formerly scattered settlement around the castle can be seen from perambulating the castle walls: a busy, flourishing town with stepped alleys full of flowers and cactuses, ivy-clad walls and dreamy backyards.

Crayfish, cake, and contemporary art

Leaving town, the options are manifold: north to Cala Mesquida through a landscape full of wild olives and mastic trees in which nightingales, wrens and robins nest to the – still – almost undeveloped cove of Mesquida. Or eastwards to Cala Ratjada, another rewarding

itinerary, even though since the start of mass – mainly German – tourism the little fishing town has acquired more and estates to spread in the direction of Capdepera. But despite the largely summer-time invasion of bathers and omnipresent Black Forest gateau, German numberplates and German nameplates on houses, the heart of Cala Ratjada has succeeded in preserving the charm of an old port, and its status as Majorca's second-ranking fishing port after Palma.

That is mainly because the fishing grounds in the channel between Majorca and Menorca remain rich in commercially popular species, especially crayfish, which are sold for both domestic and restaurant consumption. Thus *llaüts* and motor yachts, trawlers and sailboats peacefully coexist within the fortified harbor, and in the cafés and restaurants around the harbor natives and foreign visitors alike face a stage-like panorama of boatbuilders and netmakers, freshly landed fish on the quayside and proud yacht owners polishing their brass. Polishing is of course not much use for the 21 rusty anchors strangely heaped up on the quay. The sculpture – by the French sculptor Arman – was a gift to the fishermen from the March Foundation.

Other works of modern sculpture await on a hill overlooking the harbor. Where there once stood a windowless and therefore "blind" tower (*torre cega*) dating from the 15th-century, Joan March erected a traditional-style country house which nowadays belongs to his son Bartomeu. In the 15 acres (60,000 m²) of park around it, which is planted only with Mediterranean flora, the March Foundation has erected 53 sculptures, mostly by Latin American and Spanish artists – including a Chillida – but also representing names such as Auguste Rodin, Max Bill and Henry Moore. On the way to the lighthouse at the Punta de Capdepera, where the headland thrusts cheekily eastwards as if it wanted to sniff at Menorca, the eye lights on one pine-framed image after another: Cap Vermell in the south, Cap de

Two generations of watch towers in proximity: the 16th-century *talaia* have had their day as protection against pirates. The other tower – the light-house – protects not the land against the ships but the ships against the land.

Freu in the north and, directly below the road, a succession of idyllic coves: Cala Moll and Cala Gat, where there are even modest ice and drinks stalls, Cala Agulla further on with its fine sandy beach and grassy dunes, and at the end Cala de la Font. They are no longer wholly unspoiled, but they are still so far from the main tourist routes that virtually everyone emits a profound sigh of delight at sky and sea.

Right: Cala Ratjada remains Majorca's second most important fishing port.

Below: It does not always have to be a sandy beach. Even surrounded by rocks, a day bathing on the north-east cape is decidedly agreeable.

479

Thunder and dories
Majorcan Fish

The good times for Majorcan fish are long past. They did not last long anyway. Only in the 16th century did Majorcans almost wean themselves from their fish diet because of the constant threat of pirates, concentrating for safety's sake on agriculture in the interior. But when peace returned to the seas, the pursuit of the denizens of the sea with nets and traps resumed immediately. The threat to the fish is still there. Already in the first light of dawn the fish must glimpse the shadow of a *llaüt*, the typical Balearic boat, gliding over the sandy sea floor and be warned of danger.

Of course, from a point of view of those in the boats on the water, there is an impor-

tant difference from the past: Majorca's fishermen no longer have a monopoly of supply to their own island, "thanks" to faster transport and improved refrigeration. Competition from the Atlantic coast of Spain is notably massive. More than three dozen species of seafood and six dozen species of fish, naming which is a challenge even for specialists, populate Galician coastal waters. In face of such a wealth of species Majorca cannot compete.

Even so, and even at the end of the 20th century, more than 1,300 Majorcans lived directly from fishing, setting out to sea every day. Though the fishing grounds no longer produce such large quantities of fish, they nonetheless offer an enormous variety of edible fish and crustaceans and shellfish. Majorca is particularly privileged because it is an island, and the different types of coast

Fishermen approach Majorca's steep cliffs at their own risk. If the fish is lucky, it is adjudged too small for lunch and is thrown back into the sea.

offer something for everyone. Many sea residents are permanent tenants.

In the south of the island there are, despite numerous ecological disasters, intact sea grounds which are feeding areas for all kinds of sea creatures. And on the sandy bottom of the shallow waters, in depths of up to 100 feet (30 m), the table is even more heavily laden. A uniquely Majorcan world of underwater plants extends in the clear waters of the island, finding ideal growth conditions in them and growing only here (endemic species, as they are termed). For many fish and shellfish it is an ideal residence. In such underwater oases fantastic spawning and living conditions coincide.

When the island was subject to continual danger from the pirates, Majorcans hardly ventured out to sea. Nowadays, the Mediterranean rocks them in a peaceful manner.

And further down, on the extensive, deeper sand banks and at the feet of the underwater cliffs things below are rather like at the hotel pool on the island: lovely shapes and gaudy colors stretch out on the coral reef.

Deep grounds with costly crustaceans

Even further down, at a depth of 1,300 feet (400 m) beneath the sea, crayfish and lobsters creep, especially in the north of the island, where the steep drop of the cliffs into the sea along the Tramuntana coast offers an excellent environment. These are privileged crustaceans, because they enjoy benefits other sea creatures do not have: from 1 September to 1 March they must not be disturbed by fishermen in the Balearics. If they nonetheless crawl into one of the baskets in the remaining time – nets cannot be used at such depths – each specimen under 7 inches (19 cm) long has the legal right to be thrown back into the sea. The problem of overfishing was known to fishermen over a century ago. Fishing with the *bou* (trawl net) was therefore restricted to six months.

The aristocrat of the crustaceans, the lobster, is thus caught from June to August in lobster baskets or with trawl nets dragged along the bottom. They react quickly by turning sour when this happens and have to be treated pretty carefully after being caught: stress reduces the quality, and makes the flavor go off.

How to outwit fabulous fish

At various depths around Majorca there are currents that flow the length of the Mediterranean and bring species of fish with them not actually native here, like swordfish, for example.

Tuna, happy to have escaped the mile-long nets of Portuguese fishermen beyond the Straits of Gibraltar and the Spanish Costa de Azahar, likewise lead a dangerous

In Ludwig Salvator's time, fishermen used basket buoys to mark where their traps were placed to catch lobsters and crawfish.

Two *llaüts* work together to drag a trawl net across the sea bottom.

life here. In the Balearics, they prefer to remove them from the water and life with a line or drag line with artificial bait, mainly along the fringes of the coastal shelf at depths of 500 to 650 feet (150–200m).

These fishing grounds are certainly among the most interesting, as this is where the largest dories, barbels, brace and perch are found. Happily, fishermen do not have it in for dolphins, which in Majorcan fairy tales, as in other Mediterranean stories, feature as friendly helpers of mankind.

In Majorca, a fisherman who does not know what species are to be found at what time in what place will be the laughing stock of all fish, setting to work with the wrong net, especially if he does not know the sea bottom properly and only finds bits of coral in his nets that have ruined the mesh.

Anyone who knows Majorca's waters well, catches fish in winter with nets that are drawn in twice a day. In summer, trawl nets

Above: Fishermen used to have to spend months at a time away from their families in simple huts on the shore. Nowadays it is only on a few minutes from the fishing boat to home – on a motorbike.

Left: Freshness is all. Only when the catch is embedded in ice does the fisherman exchange oils for shore dress.

are used in which larger fish, or sometimes even small, harmless sharks are caught.

At the end of the summer the whole of Majorca waits impatiently for the rare *raor*. This has a mind of its own and does nothing to help the fisherman. It digs in to the sea bed, and is therefore difficult to find. A special line has to be used. The relatively high effort involved makes it an expensive fish, but the expenditure is justified by the quality: the texture is very fine, and has an excellent flavor.

Catching the *raor* is problem enough, but in other cases thunder and lightning are required. Even if no normal seaman would set to sea in a storm, Majorcan fisherman do just that, waiting for the moment when Jupiter dispatches thunderbolts from the heavens to launch their *llaüts* into the billows. At least, they do so when they are after the *llampuga*, the legendary golden mackerel. If they are caught during a storm, golden mackerel are supposed to taste particularly delicious, perhaps, it is thought, because they release fear hormones when the waves whirl them round.

Traditionally a number of cork boxes or *capes* are used to catch *llampuga*. A heavy rock serves as an anchor and holds them in position. That is how it has been done for generations, as Ludwig Salvator noted at the end of the 19th century: "These fish are caught in the twilight or on moonlit nights, because that is when the *llampuga* seek the shade of the *capses*. The fisherman goes

round the *capses* in his *llaüt* one after the other pulling out the *llampugueras*, a kind of bag for shutting the *capses*. Once this is done, he gets closer to the *capses* in the sense that he pulls in the net and catches the fish, which are now unable to escape."

Below: A problem that as yet has no remedies: fine meshes that become gaping holes. The net has therefore to be checked every afternoon and repaired if necessary.

Above: The alarming appearance of the sea-devil or angler fish means many stores only serve it ready filleted.

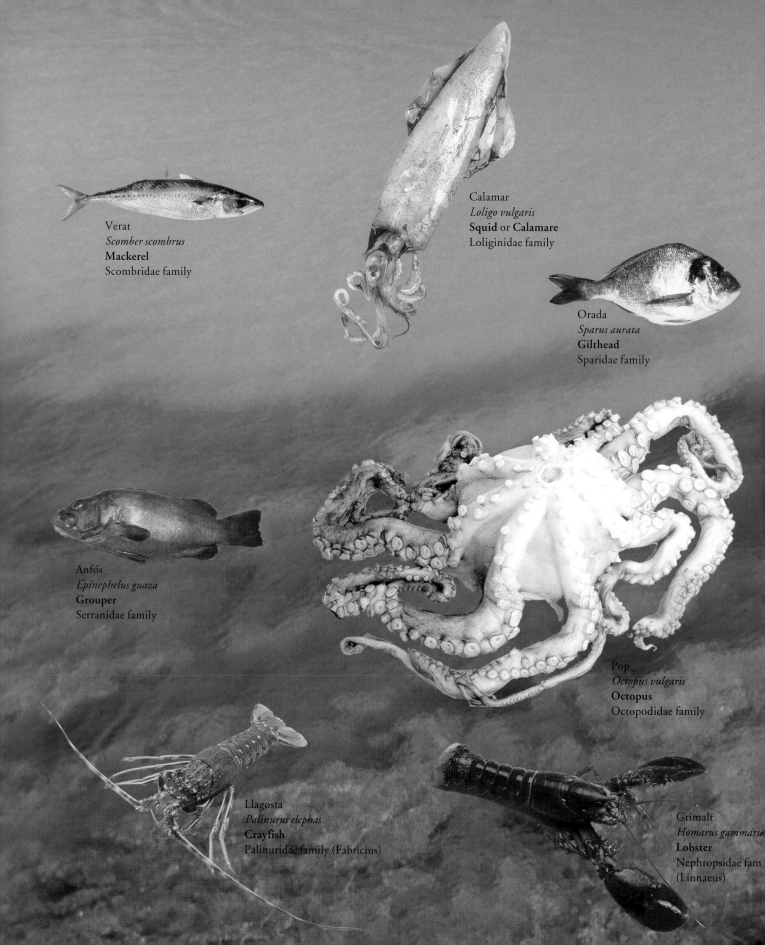

Verat
Scomber scombrus
Mackerel
Scombridae family

Calamar
Loligo vulgaris
Squid or **Calamare**
Loliginidae family

Orada
Sparus aurata
Gilthead
Sparidae family

Anfós
Epinephelus guaza
Grouper
Serranidae family

Pop
Octopus vulgaris
Octopus
Octopodidae family

Llagosta
Palinurus elephas
Crayfish
Palinuridae family (Fabricius)

Grimalt
Homarus gammarus
Lobster
Nephropsidae fam
(Linnaeus)

Llop
Dicentrarcus labrax
Sea bass
Serranidae family

Bis
Scomber japonicus colias
Spanish mackerel
Scombridae family

Déntol
Dentex dentex
Sea-bream
Sparidae family

Tonyina
Thunnus
Tuna
Thunnidae family

Rap
Lophius
Sea-devil or **Monkfish**
Lophiidae family

Petxinas
Callista chione
Venus
Veneridae family

Morena
Muraena helena
Moray eel
Muraenidae family

Appendix

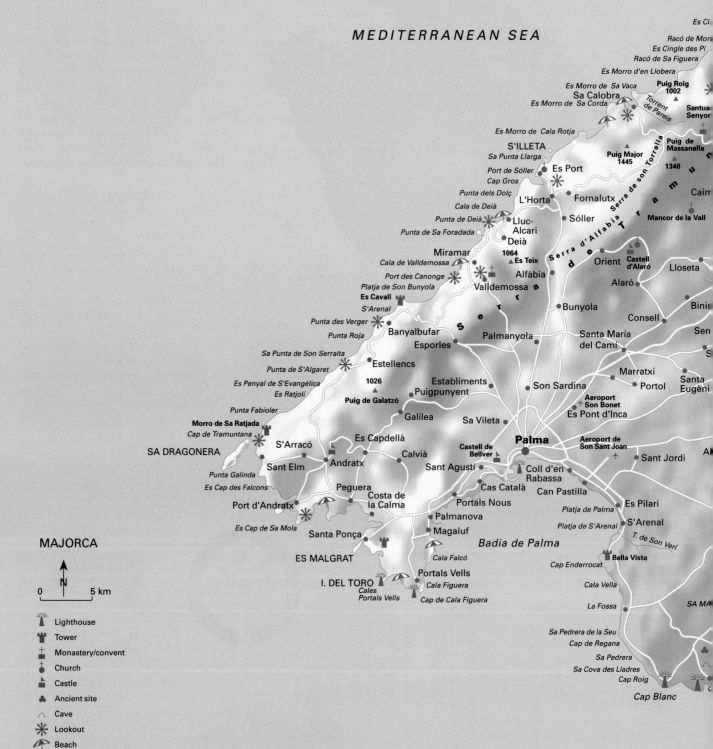

MAJORCA

N

0   5 km

※ Lighthouse
▲ Tower
† Monastery/convent
‡ Church
■ Castle
♣ Ancient site
∩ Cave
❋ Lookout
☂ Beach
✈ Airport

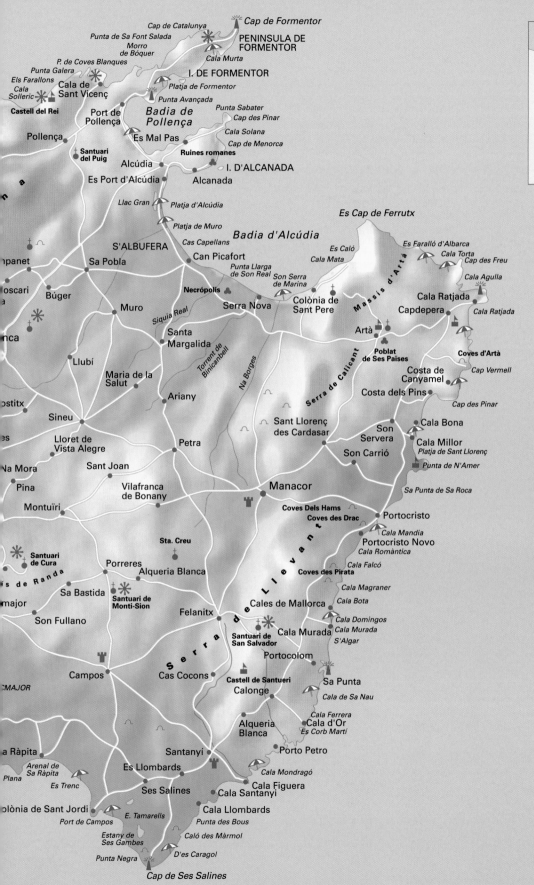

Cap de Catalunya
Punta de Sa Font Salada
Morro de Bóquer
P. de Coves Blanques
Punta Galera
Els Farallons
Cala Solleric
Cala de Sant Vicenç
Castell del Rei
Port de Pollença
Pollença
Santuari del Puig
Alcúdia
Es Port d'Alcúdia
Alcanada

Cap de Formentor
PENINSULA DE FORMENTOR
I. DE FORMENTOR
Platja de Formentor
Punta Avançada
Cala Murta
Badia de Pollença
Es Mal Pas
Punta Sabater
Cap des Pinar
Cala Solana
Cap de Menorca
Ruines romanes
I. D'ALCANADA
Alcanada

Llac Gran
Platja d'Alcúdia
Platja de Muro
Cas Capellans
S'ALBUFERA
Sa Pobla
Can Picafort
Punta Llarga de Son Real
Son Serra de Marina
Necrópolis
Serra Nova
Colònia de Sant Pere

Badia d'Alcúdia
Es Cap de Ferrutx
Es Caló
Cala Mata
Es Farralló d'Albarca
Cala Torta
Cap des Freu
Cala Agulla
Cala Ratjada
Capdepera
Cala Ratjada

Muro
Santa Margalida
Llubí
Maria de la Salut
Ariany
Búger
Sineu
Lloret de Vista Alegre
Sant Joan
Petra
Vilafranca de Bonany
Montuïri
Pina
Na Mora

Siquia Real
Torrent de Binicanbell
Na Borges
Serra de Calicant
Sant Llorenç des Cardasar
Manacor

Artà
Poblat de Ses Païses
Massis d'Artà
Coves d'Artà
Cap Vermell
Costa de Canyamel
Costa dels Pins
Cap des Pinar
Son Servera
Son Carrió
Cala Bona
Cala Millor
Platja de Sant Llorenç
Punta de N'Amer

Sta. Creu
Santuari de Cura
Porreres
Alqueria Blanca
Sa Bastida
Santuari de Monti-Sion
Felanitx
Cala Murada
Santuari de San Salvador
Cales de Mallorca
Portocolom

Serra de Llevant
Coves Dels Hams
Coves des Drac
Portocristo
Cala Mandia
Portocristo Novo
Cala Romàntica
Cala Falcó
Coves des Pirata
Cala Magraner
Cala Bota
Cala Domingos
Cala Murada
S'Algar
Sa Punta de Sa Roca

Montuïri
Son Fullano
Campos
Cas Cocons
Calonge
Alqueria Blanca
Santanyí
Es Llombards
Ses Salines
Cala Santanyí
lònia de Sant Jordi
Port de Campos
E. Tamarells

Castell de Santueri
Sa Punta
Cala de Sa Nau
Cala Ferrera
Cala d'Or
Es Corb Martí
Porto Petro
Cala Mondragó
Cala Figuera
Cala Llombards
Punta des Bous
Caló des Màrmol
D'es Caragol

a Ràpita
Arenal de Sa Ràpita
Es Trenc
Estany de Ses Gambes
Punta Negra
Cap de Ses Salines

Serra de Randa
Sa Bastida

Campanet
oscari
 nca
stitx
es
Na Mora
Pina
majar
MAJOR
Plana

FRANCE
CORSICA
SPAIN
BALEARIC ISLANDS
SPAIN
MINORCA
MAJORCA
IBIZA
FORMENTERA
ALGERIA

What language do Majorcans speak?
Catalan, Castilian, and Mallorquí

Not all Spaniards understand each other straight off, because Spain does not constitute a homogeneous language area. There are in fact four languages: Galician in the north-west, Basque in the Basque Country and northern Navarre, and Castilian in the center and the Canary Islands. Catalan is spoken in Catalonia, Valencia, and the Balearics.

More than six million people speak Catalan as their mother tongue. If the various dialects of Catalan, e.g. Valencian, Menorcan, Majorcan, and Ibizan, are included, the total rises to 11 million. The language and its dialects are thus the largest minority language in the Iberian Peninsula. It took Don Francesc de Borja Moll of Biniali 43 years to compile his dictionary of the three Catalan variants, Catalan, Valencian, and Balearic; but anyone who has learnt one or more Romance languages will find many words immediately familiar.

Many visitors believe that Majorcan and Menorcan are different languages with their own grammars, but they are in fact varieties of Catalan, which after decades of suppression by Franco now predominates in public life.

Loved, banished, and allowed back: Mallorquí

After the Reconquest of Majorca by Jaume I, Catalan and its dialect Mallorquí (Majorcan) replaced the previous official language, Arabic. In literature, it was first used by the missionary and philosopher Ramón Llull (1235–1315), who is considered the "Dante" of Catalan literature.

At the end of the 15th century, the crowns of Aragón and Castile were united through the marriage of, *los reyes católicos* the Catholic Kings, Ferdinand of Aragón and Isabella of Castile. The political supremacy of Castile meant that Castilian increasingly ousted Catalan in Aragón. However, this decline of the language was restricted to literature. The uncontested official, legal and popular language remained Catalan, as intact as the special political rights enjoyed by Aragón-Catalonia.

At the end of the War of the Spanish Succession (1701–1714) Catalonia lost its political independence, and the Bourbon kings embarked on a policy of reinforcing the Spanish centralized state as we know it. The Catalan national holiday, the Diada on 11 September, still recalls the fall of Barcelona and the loss of autonomy.

Castilian asserted itself as the received language of Spain, not because the population of all Spain wanted it but because it was laid down in law, even for Catalonia. In 1716, Spanish was made compulsory as the language of education. And in 1779, the authorities' fear of Catalan became so chronic that plays could not be performed in Catalan.

Catalan did not make a comeback until the early 20th century. This renaissance or *renaixença* saw the language promoted by dedicated Catalan institutions and itself become the subject of research. But the wings of Catalan speech were quickly clipped again, as always, once an insecure and therefore rigid centralized state was in power and could only maintain itself with effort and force. After the Spanish Civil War in 1939, the public use of Catalan was once again massively obstructed. Franco had his own bone to pick with the Catalans, because they and the Basques were the ones who resisted the Fascist troops the longest.

The consequences of the *decadència* of Catalan is still evident. The majority of the inhabitants of Majorca speak Castilian and use regional dialects among themselves, but many Majorcans find it normal to talk Castilian on official occasions. Some inhabitants of the island have an additional problem. They grew up under Franco's dictatorship, learnt only Castilian at school and therefore find it difficult to make themselves understood in Mallorquí.

Since the constitution of 1978, Castilian has become the official and state language of the whole country, while for all other languages reference is made to the statutes of autonomy. These provide for Catalan, Galego (Galician), and Euskara (Basque) to have the function of official regional languages. Squares and streets were thus rechristened with their original dialect names. Thus Andraix became Andratx once more, Bañalbufar changed to Banyalbufar and San Juan to Sant Joan. The *cuevas* were *coves* once more, the *puerto* the *port*.

Mallorquí, the language of Majorca, is a variant of Catalan. The differences in the written language are small, but things are quite different in the spoken language, which leaves many a Romance specialist doubting his linguistic skills. Majorcans have a weakness for [sh] and [ch]: **x** is spoken [sh], or [ch] after a **t**. Thus Felanitx is pronounced [felanich]. The letter **uig** get a similar treatment; thus *puig* sounds like German *putsch*, and **aitx** and **atx** are both [atch], as in [andratch].

Index of Mallorquí phrases in use

actes	acts	calamar	squid, calamary
agermanats	associations of artisans – guilds, for example - that joined forces against the establishment and their privileges; the word nowadays means "rebellion"	camaiot	spherical blood sausage, black pudding
		camí	road, path
		camilla	small table with a thick cover round which people gathered in winter
aguila	eagle	cap	head, cape
albercoc	apricot	capella	chapel
alcauciles	wild artichokes	caproig	redhead
allioli	Majorcan garlic cream (lit. "garlic and oil")	capsa	box for lobster fishing
		cargols amb sobrassada	snails with sausage spread
alou	feudal property tax payable in kind to landowner	carraques	rattle
		carrer	street
alqueria	estate, landed property	carretera	road, lane
ametlla	almond	cartoixa	Carthusian monastery
amitger	rent to landowner	carxofa	artichoke
amo	lord, owner	casa	house
angel	angel	cascabeles	bells
anguila	eel	cascall	opium poppy
anxoves	anchovies	cases dsa neu	snow houses for cooling
arenal	sandy beach	cassola	bowl, small pot
arròs a la marinera	sailor's rice / rice with seafood	castanyola	castanets
arxiduc	archduke	castell	castle
assentament	foundation	catedral	cathedral
avinguda	avenue	cava	cava, champagne-type wine
badia	bay	cega	blind
ball des cossiers	folk dance	celler	wine cellar
bandolers	bandits	Ciutat, La	the City (Majorcan term for Palma de Majorca)
barraca	hut, shack		
barri xinès	Chinese quarter	claustre	cloister
batle	mayor	cocó	drinking pool for livestock
batuda	olive oil production, including harvesting	coent	sharp
		confraries	fraternities
besada	kiss	confrares	brothers
biga	beam	conill amb ceba	rabbit with onion
blocs	blocks	conversos	(Christian) converts
boira	mist	copa de vi	a glass of wine
botella labrada	Majorcan musical instrument	cossier	dancers
botifarró	Majorcan blood sausage	costelletes de porc	pork chops with pomegranate sauce
bou	trawl net, bull	coturnix	quail
braser	(charcoal) brazier	amb salsa de magranes	
brossat	curd, fromage frais	cova	cave
bunyol	doughnut	cremadillo	Majorcan punch
ca'n	short for: the house of	crespells	star-shaped biscuit
cabàs	flat straw basket	creus de terme	wayside cross
cabell d'àngel	angel hair, pumpkin jam	dimonis boiets	small, good-natured demons
cafè amb llet	milk coffee	diumenge	Sunday
cala	cove	dolç	sweet

drac	dragon	greixonera	traditional Majorcan clay pot still used for cooking
dragons	lizards	grimalt	lobster
duro	five pesetas	guaret	fallow field
els Blavets	the Little Blues (choir boys from Lluc)	guàtlleres amb figues	quails with figs
		guàtlleres emborratxades	drunken quails
embassament	reservoir, artificial lake	guitarra	guitar
empanades	pasties, pies	herbes	herbs, herbal liqueur
emperador	swordfish	hivern	winter
en ls seu punt	be ripe, be *au point*	horta	vegetable garden
ensaïmada	Majorcan yeast dough bun	illa	island
entrecôte amb albercoc	entrecôte with apricots	innocentada	the Spanish equivalent of an April fool's trick, on the dia dels innocents (28th Dec.)
envinagrat	preserved in vinegar		
es	the (masc.)		
esclata-sang	type of mushroom	jonquillo	small fish
escorxador	butcher	jurats	jury, jurors
espardenyes	espadrilles	llagosta	crayfish
espinagada	spinach dish with eel	llaüt	felucca, two-mast coastal vessel
esportins	flat mats used in olive press	llaüt coster	coastal felucca
estiu	summer	llaüt senzill	simple felucca
fang	clay	llaüt viatger	traveling felucca
fava	broad bean	llengua amb tàperes	tongue with capers
fava pelada pagesa	peeled broad beans	lluç	hake
faixa	bodice, sash	marger	drystone waller
ferret	triangle	marges	drystone wall construction
ferrocarril	railway	maridet	"husband", warming pan
festa	festival, celebration	marjat	drystone walling (occupation)
festa des pa i des peix	bread and fish festival	matador	butcher
festa des sol que balla	festival of the dancing sun	matança	butchering
fideus amb cabra	noodles with goat meat	meló	honeydew melon
figa	fig	mestre	master craftsman
figuera	fig tree	mirador	view, lookout (place)
figuera de moro	prickly pear cactus	missatge	administrator
figues de moro	prickly pear fruit	molí	mill
finca	country property	mona de pasqua	Easter cakes
fira	fair, funfair	monestir	monastery
fira de sa perdiu	partridge festival	Moreneta	Black Madonna (lit.: little brown woman)
fira del fang	pottery festival		
flaviol	flute	moriscos	Muslim converts to Christianity
flor	flower	moros i cristians	Moors and Christians, also the name of a Majorcan festival
foguerons	bonfire		
fonoll marí	sea fennel, samphire		
font	spring, well	murter	mortar
fonteta	little spring	musclo	mussel
forn	bakery	navetes	ship barrow (Talayot burial site)
frisons	cows of Frisian origin	negre	black
frit de matança	pork offal dish	nispero	medlar
garriga	Mediterranean bush landscape	nevaters	men who used to bring snow from the hills
garrover	carob tree		
gató d'ametlles	almond cakes	nit	night
gelat	ice	nit de foc	fire night
gelera	fridge	obra	work
gent	people	oli d'oliva verge extra	extra virgin olive oil
granissat	fruit juice with crushed ice		

oliva	olive
olivera	olive tree
olleria	pottery
orellons	dried apricots (lit.: large ears)
ossos	musical instrument made of bones
pa amb oli	bread with oil
pa de figa	fig bread
pa moreno	(almost) unsalted Majorcan bread
pagès	peasant, farmer
palau	palace
panades	Easter pies
pancaritat	blessing of the bread
pandereta	small tambourine
pandero	tambourine
passeig	promenade
pastisseria	patisserie
pati	patio, inner courtyard
pebre	paprika, pepper
Perdix Rebhuhn	
petit	small
peus de cabra	acorn shells (*Lepadomorpha*)
pi de Sant Antoní	St Anthony's pine
picarol	cow bell
pixa de porc	pig penis
pla	plain
plaça	square (in town)
plaça monumental	large main square (in town)
platja	beach
porc negre	black pig
porcella negra	little black pig
possessió	landed estate
primavera	spring
profund	profound, deep
puig	mountain, peak
raconet	corner
raor	type of fish
rap	sea devil, monkfish
reclams	decoy birds
Reconquista	reconquest of Spain from the Moors
repartiment	distribution of land by Jaume I
robiols	pasties
rodó	round
rondàies	Majorcan fairy stories
rostolls	stubble field
roter	peasant with poor-quality land
sa	the (fem.)
sabater	shoemaker
santuari	sanctuary
semiseques	medium dry
senyor/a	(form of address) sir/madam
seques	dry
siquia	irrigation ditch
serra	sierra, mountain range
semana santa	Holy Week
síndria	water melon
sínia	draw wheel
siurells	Majorcan clay whistles
sitja	charcoal kiln
sobrassada	spicy Majorcan sausage spread
sofrit	tomato sauce for cooking
solera	well-trodden earth
sopes	Majorcan stew / the dried *pan moreno* used in a stew
sorbet de figues de moro	prickly pear sorbet
tabac	tobacco
talàia	coastal watch tower
talayot	prehistoric tower
tambor	drum
tàpera	caper
taperera	caper bush
tapiceries artesanals	carpet manufacture
taronja	orange
taula	table (in Talayot settlement)
tavernes	taverns
teatre	theater
tela de llengües	material named for tongue-shaped pattern
temps	weather, time
terra	earth
terreny	area, terrain
tomàtigues de ramellet	tomatoes hung on strings to dry
torn	mechanical winch in baptistry
torrent	torrent, fast-moving stream
tramutja	funnel
trempó	Majorcan salad
trullada	a complete milling sequence
valentes dones	brave women
vall	valley
victòria	victory
vila	settlement, "town"
vinyes	vineyard
xeremia	Majorcan bagpipes
ximbomba	Majorcan instrument
xocolateria	confectioner's
xueta	Jew converted to Christianity

Selected bibliography

Specialist books:

Abulafia, David: *Un emporio mediterráneo. El reino catalán de Majorca,*, Barcelona 1996.
idem: *A Mediterranean Emporium: the Catalan Kingdom of Majorca* (English version of above), Princeton 1994

Belgin, Tayfun (ed.): *Miró, Werke aus Majorca (Miró's works from Majorca, exhibition catalog from Museum am Ostwall, Dortmund, Germany, 14.8.- 14.11.99),*, Dortmund 1999

Bonner, Anthony (ed.): *Selected Works of Ramon Llull*, Princeton 1985

Borja Moll, Francesc: *Gramàtica històrica catalana*, Valencia 1991

Bota Totxo, Miquel: *Llegendes i tradicíons* Plama de Majorca, 1986

Bronisch, Alexander Pierre : *Reconquista und Heiliger Krieg*, Münster 1998

Cabot Llompart, Juan: *Palacios y casa señoriales de Majorca*, Palma de Majorca 1965

Catoir, Barbara: *Miró in Majorca*, New York 1995

Crichton, Tom: *Our Man in Majorca*, London 1963

Ferrer, Maria: *Majorca*, Cologne 1997

Font Obrador, Bartomeu: *Fray Junípero Serra, Doctor de gentiles*, Palma de Majorca 1998

Frade, Francisco Soriano: *Pequeña historia del turismo en los Baleares*, Palma de Majorca 1996

Frank, Herbert: *The Great Cathedrals*

Frontera, Guillem, Guillem Rosselló-Bordoy and Guillem Soler: *Palma*, Palma de Majorca 1988

Garrido, Carlos: *Majorca mágica*, Palma de Majorca 1988

Graves, William: *Bajo la sombra del olivo. La Majorca de Robert Graves*, Palma de Majorca 1997
idem: *Wild Olives - Life in Majorca with Robert Graves*, London 1996 (English version of above)

Hahn, Ulla and Rainer Pöschl (eds.): *Majorca*, Hamburg 1994

Headington, Christopher: *Chopin*, New York 1995

Hofstadter, Dan: *My Life* by George Sand, New York 1979 (English translation of autobiogrpahy)

Jordan, Ruth: *George Sand - A Biographical Portrait*, New York 1976

Kobylánska, Krystyna (ed.): *Frédéric Chopin. Briefe*, Frankfurt 1984

König, Angelika: *Majorca (Spanien)*, Cologne 1991

Llompart, Gabriel: *La Majorca tradicional en los exvotos*, Palma de Majorca 1988

Llompart Moragues, Gabriel, Maria Josep Mulet Gutiérrez and Andreu Ramis Puig-gors: *Majorca: Imatge fotogràfica i etnografia. L'arxiu de Josep Pons Frau*, Palma de Majorca 1992

Llull, Ramón (Raimundus Lullus): *Ars inventia veritatis*, Valencia 1515
idem: *Secreta secretorum*, Cologne 1592
idem: *Ars magna, generalis et ultima*, Frankfurt 1596
idem: *Llibre d'amice amat*, Zurich 1998

Maier, Henes and Gloria Keetman: *Mallorcas verborgene Reize. Auf den Spuren von George Sand und Frédéric Chopin*, Munich 1999

Mestre Campi, Jesús: *Atlas de la Reconquista. La frontera peninsular entre los siglos VIII y XV*, Barcelona 1998

Oliver, Tonina and Frank Schauhoff : *Zu Gast auf Majorca. Die schönsten Rezepte*, Cologne 1993

Radatz, Hans-Ingo: *Mallorquinisch Wort für Wort*, Bielefeld 1998

Salvator, Ludwig: *Die Balearen*, 2. vols, Würzburg/Leipzig 1897, reprint Palma de Majorca 1989
idem: *Bougie, die Perle Nordafrikas*, Prague 1899
idem: *Ramleh als Winteraufenthalt*, Leipzig 1900

Schwendinger, Helga: *Erzherzog Ludwig Salvator*, Munich 1991

Swift, Francis Darwin: *The Life and Times of James the First, the Conqueror, King of Aragon, Valencia and Majorca*, Oxford 1897

Tocabens, Joan and Jean-Pierre Lacombe Massot: *Les rois de Majorque/ Els reis de Majorca*, Canet 1995

Völger, Gisela: *Majorca*, Cologne 1996

West, Gordon: *Jogging Around Majorca*, London 1994

Wiggershaus, Renate (ed.): *George Sand*, Frankfurt 1987.

Belles lettres:

Bernhard, Thomas: *Beton*, Frankfurt 1982

Dario, Rubén: *Poesías completas*, Madrid 1967

Distler, Elvira: *Majorca*, Munich 1999

Graves, Robert: *Goodbye to All That*, London 1929
idem: *Collected poems*, London 1948
idem: *Collected short stories*, London 1966
idem: *Majorca Observed*
idem: *I, Claudius. From the autobiography of Tiberius Claudius, emperor of the Romans, born B.C. 10, murdered A.D. 54*, London 1935
idem: *Claudius the God and his wife Messalina*, London 1935

Masoliver, Juan (ed.): *The Origins of Desire: Modern Spanish Short Stories* (includes Majorcan authors Valentí Puig and Carme Riera)

Matute, Ana María *School of the Sun*, Columbia, (Novel set in the Balearics), New York 1989

Oehrlein, Sieglinde (ed.): *Majorca* (a literary portrait, in German), Frankfurt 1998

Rauter, E.A: *Majorca,*, Hamburg 1988

Sand, George: *Un hiver à Majorque*, Paris 1869
idem, translated Graves, Robert: *Winter in Majorca*, Chicago 1978
idem: *Le beau Laurence*, Paris 1870
idem: *Journal intime*, Paris 1926
idem: *Elle et lui*, Neuchâtel 1963

Seymour, Miranda *Robert Graves. Life on the Edge*, London 1995

Thelen, Albert Vigoleis: *Die Insel des zweiten Gesichts*, Munich 1999

Theroux, Paul: *The Pillars of Hercules*, London 1985

Villalonga, Llorenç: *Bearn o La casa de las muñecas*, 1956
idem: *The Doll's Room*, London 1956 (English version of above)

Index

Places

People

Majorca – Picture Credits

The publisher would like to thank all the museums, photolibraries and photographers for allowing reproduction and their friendly assistance. The publisher made every effort right up to going to press to discover all further owners of reproduction rights. People and institutions that may not have been contacted and are claiming copyright on illustrations used are asked to get in touch with the publisher.

All photos not listed separately are by **Günter Beer, Barcelona.**

© **Agustín, Carlos & Tánago, Belén:** 15 bottom right, 17 top right, 18 bottom left, 24 top left, 25 top left, 26 bottom right, 34 top and bottom, 35 top and bottom, 48 bottom right, 68 left, 96 top, 97 bottom left, 115 center right, 118 bottom right, 122 top and bottom, 123 top and bottom, 139 bottom right, 142, 145 bottom right, 146–149 top left, 153 top and bottom, 159 top, 160 top and bottom, 164 bottom and top, 165 all, 171 center right and bottom right, 179 bottom left, 184/185, 189 all, 258/259, 262, 264/265, 266 bottom right, 269, 270, 277 bottom row, 278 right and left, 279 top and bottom, 281 top and bottom left, 284/285, 294, 295 left, 297 top and bottom, 300, 301, 302, left (3), top right and center, 303 top, 306 bottom, 307 bottom, 308 top (2) and bottom left, 315 top, 316/317, 319 all, 320, 321 top, 324/325, 326 top and bottom, 327 top and bottom, 328 top and bottom, 329 top and bottom, 330 left, 331, 334 right and left, 335 top and bottom, 337, 341 bottom, 342, 344, 345 top and bottom, 346, 348, 350 bottom and top left and top right, center and bottom, 351 right, 352, 353 top, 364/365, 366, 367 top and bottom, 372, 373 all, 378, 379 left center and below, top right, center and bottom, 380 bottom left, 381, 383 bottom right, 386 bottom right, 389 bottom right, 390, 391 top, 408, 430 bottom, 436, 437 bottom, 447 top and bottom, 450, 451 top and bottom, 452 top right, 453–455 bottom, 456 top and bottom, 457 bottom right, 458, 459 all, 460/461, 465 top and bottom, 467 bottom left, 468 all, 470, 476 bottom right, 477 left and right, 481 top, 482 top and bottom.

© **AKG photo, Berlin:** 75 bottom, 88 bottom, 254 bottom, 255, 310, 311

© **Archivo Bestard, Pollença:** 33 bottom, 464 left

© **Bauer, Martin:** *Tempelritter, Mythos und Wahrheit*, Munich 1997: 256, 257

© **Bibliothèque Nationale, Paris:** 91 top

© **British Library, London:** 230 left

© **Diario de Majorca:** 280 top, 294 right

© **Fabrica de Sinfones, La Paduana:** 353 bottom

© **Ferrà, Miquel:** *Sollerics arreu del món, imatges d'ahir*, Palma de Majorca 1992: 59 top left, in Sollerics p. 74, 150 bottom right, in Sollerics p. 84

© **Fischer-Leidl, Astrid, Munich:** 490/491

© **Forment de Torisme:** 215

© **Galerie Bruno Bischofsberger:** 430/431 top, 431 bottom

© **Graves, William:** *Bajo la Somra del Olivo*, Palma de Majorca, 1997.: 69 bottom, the illustrated part in Bajo

© **Könemann Verlagsgesellschaft mbH:** photo: Pierre Parcé: 187 left

© **laif/Gernot Huber, Cologne:** 16, 130 bottom, 202 bottom, 204 bottom, 205 bottom, 213 top, 245, 246 top, 248, 251 bottom right, 479 bottom, 486/487

© **Llompart, Gabriel:** *La Majorca Tradicionals en los Exvotos*, presentación de Julio Caro Baroja, La Isla de la Calma 1988: 73, in Majorca p. 109

© *Malerische Studien:* Neuchâtel, undated: 222 bottom

© **Micer, Pollença:** 39

© **Moragues, Gabriel Llompart, Maria Jospe Mulet Gutiérrez, Andreu Ramis-Puig-gros:** *Majorca: Imatge Fotogràfica i etnografia, L'Arxiu de Josep Pons Frau*, Palma 1992: 304, in Imatge p. 238, 338, in Imatge p. 180, 349, in Imatge p. 102 and 112

© **Muntaner Darder, Andreu:** *Memoria gráfica de Majorca, La vida cotidiana (3):* 145 top, in Memoria correction sheet

© **Museo de Majorca, Palma:** 223 bottom

© **Oronoz, Madrid:** 449

© **Picture Press, Hamburg:** 448

© **Pomar, Marcos:** 260, 261

© **Rolli Arts, Essen:** 205 top, 222 bottom, 266 top, 312 bottom (from: Abulafia, David, *Un emporio mediterráneo, El reino catalán de Majorca,* Cambridge University Press, Barcelona 1966), 356 right, 357, 488–489

© **Salvator, Ludwig:** *Die Balearen, geschildert in Wort und Bild,* Palma de Majorca 1989, Vol. I: endpapers, frontispiece, in Balearics p. 479, 81 bottom, in Balearics p. 235, 143 top, in Balearics p. 344, 144, in Balearics p. 197, 155 top, in Balearics p. 189, 162 bottom, in Balearics p. 252, 181, in Balearics p. 185, 188, in Balearics p. 237, 214 bottom, in Balearics p. 432, 224, in Balearics p. 385, 367, in Balearics p. 201, 446, in Balearics p. 303, 454, in Balearics p. 295, 463 bottom, in Balearics p. 308, 463 top, in Balearics p. 314, 464 bottom, in Balearics p. 352, 481 bottom left, in Balearics p. 323, bottom right, p 319; Vol. II: in Balearics p. 94, 74, in Balearics p. 29, 342, in Balearics p. 342

© **SCALA, Antella (Florence):** 89

© **Soler, Guillem (ed.):** *Palma,* Inca, undated: 203 top, in Palma p. 88, 236, in Palma p. 119

© **Studio für Landkartentechnik, Norderstedt:** 206/207

© **Terrasa, Sebastian, Palma:** 25, 93, 106, 130 top, 138 top, 156, 157 bottom right, 181, 182 top, 183, 192/193, 291, 326, 340, 374, 375, 380 bottom left, 472

© **Tocabens, Joan, Jean-Pierre Lacombe Massot:** *Les rois de Majorque,* Perpignan 1995: 312 top, in Rois p. 67, 313 top, in Rois p. 75, 313 bottom, in Rois p. 17, 314, in Rois p.133

© 1999 Könemann Verlagsgesellschaft mbH
Bonner Strasse 126, D – 50968 Cologne

Publishing and Art Direction: Peter Feierabend
Project Management: Uta Edda Hammer
Assistant: Kerstin Ludolph
Layout: International Design UK Ltd., London
Cartography: Astrid Fischer-Leitl, Munich; Rolli Arts, Essen;
Studio für Landkartentechnik, Norderstedt
Production: Mark Voges
Reproductions: C.D.N. Pressing, Caselle di Sommacampacna

Original title: Mallorca, Kultur und Lebensfreude

© 2000 for this English edition:
Könemann Verlagsgesellschaft mbH
Bonner Strasse 126, D – 50968 Cologne

Translation from German: Paul Aston, Peter Barton, Ruth Chitty,
Timothy Jones, and Eileen Martin in association with Goodfellow
and Egan
Editing: Susan James in association with Goodfellow and Egan
Typesetting: Sheila Kirby in association with Goodfellow and Egan
Project Management: Jackie Dobbyne assisted by Karen Baldwin for
Goodfellow and Egan Publishing Management, Cambridge
Project Coordination: Alex Morkramer assisted by Paul Embleton
Production: Ursula Schümer
Printing and Binding: Neue Stalling, Oldenburg

Printed in Germany
ISBN 3-8290-2597-1

10 9 8 7 6 5 4 3 2 1